Mastering
Blender

Mastering
Blender

Tony Mullen

Wiley Publishing, Inc.

Acquisitions Editor: Mariann Barsolo
Development Editor: Kathryn Duggan
Technical Editor: Nathan Letwory
Production Editor: Rachel Gunn
Copy Editor: Sharon Wilkey
Production Manager: Tim Tate
Vice President and Executive Group Publisher: Richard Swadley
Vice President and Publisher: Neil Edde
Assistant Project Manager: Jenny Swisher
Associate Producer: Shawn Patrick
Quality Assurance: Angie Denny
Book Designer: Maureen Forys, Happenstance Type-O-Rama
Compositor: Jeff Lytle, Happenstance Type-O-Rama
Proofreader: Josh Chase, Word One New York
Indexer: Ted Laux
Project Coordinator, Cover: Lynsey Stanford
Cover Designer: Ryan Sneed
Cover Image: Soenke Maeter

Library of Congress Cataloging-in-Publication Data

Mullen, Tony, 1971-
  Mastering Blender / Tony Mullen.
    p. cm.
  ISBN 978-0-470-40741-7 (paper/cd-rom)
  1. Computer graphics. 2. Computer animation. 3. Three-dimensional display systems. 4. Blender (Computer file) I. Title.
  T385.M847 2009
  006.6'930285536--dc22
                      2009001899

10 9 8 7 6 5 4 3 2 1

Dear Reader,

Thank you for choosing *Mastering Blender*. This book is part of a family of premium-quality Sybex books, all of which are written by outstanding authors who combine practical experience with a gift for teaching.

Sybex was founded in 1976. More than thirty years later, we're still committed to producing consistently exceptional books. With each of our titles we're working hard to set a new standard for the industry. From the paper we print on, to the authors we work with, our goal is to bring you the best books available.

I hope you see all that reflected in these pages. I'd be very interested to hear your comments and get your feedback on how we're doing. Feel free to let me know what you think about this or any other Sybex book by sending me an email at nedde@wiley.com, or if you think you've found a technical error in this book, please visit http://sybex.custhelp.com. Customer feedback is critical to our efforts at Sybex.

Best regards,

Neil Edde
Vice President and Publisher
Sybex, an Imprint of Wiley

To Hana Marie Mullen, with love

Acknowledgments

As always, my thanks go first and foremost to Ton Roosendaal and all the Blender developers for all their hard work and dedication. You guys are doing important work and deserve the heartfelt gratitude of the entire community of Blender users. I am tempted to begin naming names, but I would not know where to stop. Please visit `http://wiki.blender.org/index.php/List_of_Contributors` for a complete list of the current developers and the specific work they have done. I would, however, like to single out Blender developer Nathan Letwory (jesterKing), who allowed me to benefit from his expertise as technical editor of this book.

Many other developers and users have helped me in researching and writing this book, and I'm very grateful for all the support I've received from the Blender community. I can't list all of the individuals at BlenderArtists.org whose artwork, comments, and tutorials have helped me to learn what I know about Blender, but I am particularly grateful for those who helped me as I ventured outside my comfort zone to write about the Blender Game Engine. Special thanks to BlenderArtists.org forum members Social, Mmph!, Blendenzo, and the other BGE gurus who were always eager to help me with my questions and investigations of this sometimes arcane functionality. I'm also very grateful to Dolf Veenvliet (macouno) and Campbell Barton (ideasman_42), who helped me enormously to deepen my knowledge of Blender's Python API.

Throughout this book, I have referred to websites, tutorials, support threads, and other resources created by members of the community, and I am very grateful to all of those who have shared their knowledge. Once again, many thanks to Bart Veldhuizen and the contributors to BlenderNation.com, and to Roel Spruit and all the moderators and administrators at BlenderArtists.org for their support and for the great service they provide the Blender community.

This book would not have been possible without the efforts of my editors and colleagues at Sybex/Wiley, and I'm very grateful to all of them. Thank you to Mariann Barsolo, Pete Gaughan, Kathryn Duggan, Rachel Gunn, Kelly Trent, and everyone else who had a hand in publishing and promoting the book.

I'm also very grateful to my colleagues and students at Tsuda College for their support and encouragement of my Blender-related work.

As always, I am grateful to my wife, Yuka, for her tireless support, and especially for looking after the baby while I was spending all those hours working on this book!

About the Author

Tony Mullen is a college lecturer, animator, independent filmmaker, and writer living in Tokyo. He has worked as a newspaper cartoonist, a graphic designer, a software developer, and a researcher in natural language processing, among other things.

Since discovering Blender, he has been involved in CG animation to the point of obsession, but he also maintains a keen interest in stop-motion techniques, notably as the lead animator and codirector of the award-winning 16mm film *Gustav Braüstache and the Auto-Debilitator* and other independent shorts. He is an active member of the Blender community and one of the original members of the Blender Foundation's Trainer Certification Review Board. He is the author of *Introducing Character Animation with Blender* (Sybex, 2007) and *Bounce, Tumble, and Splash!: Simulating the Physical World with Blender 3D* (Sybex, 2008), as well as numerous magazine articles and tutorials on Blender for the Japanese magazine *Mac People*.

Contents at a Glance

Contents

Introduction

Things have changed rapidly in the last few years for Blender and Blender users. The number of books and training DVDs available have gone from zero in-print English Blender books in 2006 and no DVDs to a growing plethora of books and training DVDs by major and minor publishers covering animation, architectural visualization, physics simulation, and general use. The Blender code itself has changed dramatically also. Although Blender has been under development since the early 1990s, the size of the code base has nearly doubled since 2005 thanks to increasing interest on the part of CG developers around the world who seek to contribute to a major graphics phenomenon. When the planned event system recode is complete, it will be possible for Blender development to progress even more rapidly.

All of this progress is driven by the ongoing explosion of the Blender user base. Blender is widely used by students, hobbyists, artists, scientists, and CG professionals, and its use by these groups and others is growing every day. As the world of 3D software applications has become increasingly consolidated, Blender has emerged as the major alternative for people who want a free, open, and independent 3D solution. The Blender community is active in its support for the software, and as it grows and gains momentum, so does every aspect of Blender—from the availability of professional support and training to the stability and functionality of the software itself.

This book is also a product of that expanding user base. Up until a few years ago, there were not enough intermediate or advanced Blender users to warrant a book like this. Those intrepid users who did gain a high degree of expertise did so by studying the code and release notes, participating in extensive forum and chat discussions, and putting in endless hours of experimenting with the software itself. My intention in writing this book is to provide today's intermediate and advanced users with the book those early pioneers might have wished for. This is not a book for beginners. This is a book for Blender users.

Who Should Read This Book

To get the most out of this book, you should already know how to get things done in Blender. You should know your way around a polygon mesh, and you should be able to set a keyframe and tweak an Ipo curve. In some areas, you may be pretty confident of your skills. Perhaps you are an expert modeler, or a master at texturing and materials. You might be able to create beautiful, photorealistic scenes and render them in eye-popping quality. Maybe you're a top-notch character animator.

If you're like the vast majority of Blender users, however, there's a lot you've been quietly ignoring about your application of choice. You may have long since stopped wondering about that obscure buttons panel that you never touch. You may have disregarded some new development and now feel left too far behind to bother trying to catch up on it. You may have been under the impression that some areas of functionality, such as scripting, were too dry and difficult to get into, or maybe you've simply never been clear on how they might be useful to you and what you want to accomplish. Hopefully, this book will be a step in the direction of changing that.

In short, this book is for Blender users who wish to deepen and expand their knowledge of the software. As the title suggests, this book is for people who want to master Blender. If there are areas of Blender that you've wondered about but never looked into deeply, if there is functionality you've toyed with but never truly mastered, then this book is for you.

What You Will Learn from This Book

This book is an attempt to cover functionality in Blender that has not been sufficiently dealt with in other books and to cover specific workflow topics that will help intermediate Blender users boost their productivity and improve the quality of their work. The functionality of Blender is so extensive that even with the available books and training materials, there remains a great deal that has not received the attention it deserves.

As such, the subject matter covered here is broad. The first part of the book is the most varied, with chapters on a wide variety of Blender 3D features. The second part of the book focuses on Python and scripting for Blender, and the third part of the book deals with the Blender Game Engine. The only background that is assumed is an intermediate or advanced level of standard Blender usage. No knowledge of Python or the game engine is required. By the end of the book, you will have an advanced skill set in both of these areas, as well as numerous new insights in other areas of Blender.

How to Use This Book

The chapters in Part I of this book are organized in a loosely logical order, but do not depend on each other in any significant way. As an intermediate or advanced Blender user, you should have no trouble reading them in whatever order you choose. Parts II and III are more strictly ordered. Both of these parts of the book are organized in such a way as to give complete introductions to the topics they cover. Part II first presents an introduction to Python itself, and then works through Blender Python scripting topics starting with the most generally applicable and finishing with the most specialized. The information follows in order, so you should skip only what you feel confident that you already know. Correspondingly, Part III begins simply by describing how to create assets for use in the game engine and ends with the relatively advanced topic of using Python in the game engine environment.

A Word about Software Versions

The version release scheduling of open source software is not constrained by co-marketing considerations, and it is inevitable (and wonderful) that development will continue at a brisk pace regardless of the publication schedules of books. Experienced Blender users know this, and they know that mastery of one version sows the seeds for mastery of the next version.

This book was written to be accurate to Blender version 2.48. The usual caveats apply: For the most predictable results, you should use the appropriate version of Blender to follow the tutorials in the book. I heartily encourage you to forge ahead into newer versions, armed with this book and the online release notes, in order to keep your knowledge as up-to-date as possible, and to cultivate the mindset of regarding Blender as a constantly developing thing. Even as you read this, new and exciting functionality is being added to Blender and released in official or unofficial versions that you will be eager to learn about.

My advice on keeping up with all the latest developments: Read fast!

The *Mastering* Series

The *Mastering* series from Sybex provides outstanding instruction for readers with intermediate and advanced skills, in the form of top-notch training and development for those already working in their field and clear, serious education for those aspiring to become pros. Every *Mastering* book features the following:

◆ The Sybex "by professionals for professionals" commitment. *Mastering* authors are themselves practitioners, with plenty of credentials in their areas of specialty.

◆ A practical perspective for a reader who already knows the basics—someone who needs solutions, not a primer.

◆ Real-World Scenarios, ranging from case studies to interviews, that show how the tool, technique, or knowledge presented is applied in actual practice.

◆ Skill-based instruction, with chapters organized around real tasks rather than abstract concepts or subjects.

◆ Self-review test "Master It" problems and questions, so you can be certain you're equipped to do the job right.

How This Book Is Organized

As mentioned previously, the book is organized into three parts. Part I includes Chapters 1 through 5. This part deals with general Blender topics, and each chapter within it covers a specific aspect of Blender functionality. Part II gives a complete overview of Python scripting in Blender, beginning with a basic introduction to Python itself, suitable for nonprogrammers. Part III gives a thorough introduction to the Blender Game Engine (BGE), including using Python in context of the BGE. In more detail, the chapters' contents are as follows:

Part I: Mastering Blender 3D

Chapter 1: Controlling Your Environment shows you a variety of ways you can customize your Blender environment and streamline your workflow. This chapter also gives you some early warning about changes to expect from upcoming Blender releases.

Chapter 2: Sculpting and Retopo Workflow takes an in-depth look at Blender's powerful sculpting tools and shows you how to use them in conjunction with the retopo and normal mapping functionality to obtain highly detailed sculpt effects while maintaining good model geometry and manageable polygon counts.

Chapter 3: Creating Realistic Images with UV Textures and Node-Based Materials shows you how to take your texturing skills to the next level, with tutorials on using GIMP in conjunction with Blender's multiple UV texturing functionality to create totally seamless photographic textures, and on using the material node system to combine materials for highly realistic effects.

Chapter 4: Video Compositing with Nodes shows you how Blender's powerful node-based compositing system can be used to pull a green screen matte and do color correction with live-action video, and how to use animated curves and hooks to create a simple rotoscoped garbage matte.

Chapter 5: Working with the Video Sequence Editor brings Part I to its logical conclusion, showing you how to put everything together in Blender's versatile Video Sequence Editor. You'll learn to edit sound and video, do sophisticated transitions and overlays, and bring the full power of the compositing system to bear in a fully integrated, nonlinear video-editing environment.

Part II: Mastering Blender Python

Chapter 6: Python for the Impatient provides a quick and painless introduction to the Python programming language itself. Assuming no programming experience at all, this chapter takes it from the top, giving you all the Python basics that you need to know to sink your teeth into the next few chapters.

Chapter 7: Python Scripting for Blender gets down to business with Blender-Python. You'll learn how to use Python to access 3D information, automate tasks, and build your own user interface for scripts. You'll gain familiarity with the Blender Python API and learn how to find the information you need to do what you need to do.

Chapter 8: The Many-Headed Snake: Other Uses of Python in Blender explores all the ways besides vanilla scripting that the power of Python can be brought to bear in Blender. You'll learn to write your own PyDrivers, design your own PyNodes, and define your own PyConstraints. You'll learn how to use script links to execute scripts on the fly, and how to use space handlers to create script interfaces that overlay the 3D viewport itself.

Part III: Mastering the Blender Game Engine

Chapter 9: Creating Assets for the Blender Game Engine walks you through the creation of a simple game world and a fully rigged character for a game. Among other things, you'll learn about texture baking and 3D texture painting, and how to set up armature actions for use in the game engine.

Chapter 10: Making Things Happen in the Game Engine gives an in-depth overview of a plethora of things you can do in the BGE: controlling characters and scenes with logic blocks, using properties and states to create complex interactions, creating dynamic text and in-game animated textures, and creating 3D sound effects.

Chapter 11: Python Power in the Blender Game Engine brings several threads together and takes it all a step further, showing you how to use Python to create more streamlined, organized, and powerful game logic than can be created with logic blocks alone. You'll learn how Python can enable you to create effects and logic that wouldn't be possible otherwise, with examples such as a simple teleportation machine and a login screen. You'll see how to handle multiple cameras and split-screen effects and to gain even more control over in-game sound.

To help ensure maximum clarity for the illustrations, there is a 24-page color insert full of images from the discussions and tutorials throughout the book. Also, an appendix is included that details the module and class hierarchies for the Blender-Python 2.48 API.

What's on the CD

This book comes with a CD that includes Blender 2.48 installers for Windows and Macintosh and a source tarball for users of Linux and other flavors of Unix. You will also find a variety of .blend files intended to support the text.

How to Contact the Author

If you run into trouble at any point in reading this book, or if you have any insights or tips you would like to share, the first place I recommend to turn for quick responses and knowledgeable feedback is to the community itself at www.blenderartists.org/forum, where I post regularly under the handle bugman_2000. You can also contact me directly at blender.characters@gmail.com.

Part I

Mastering Blender 3D

Chapter 1

Controlling Your Environment

Blender incorporates a dizzying amount of functionality in a single application, and learning to use all the tools as efficiently as possible is a daunting proposition. Even after the initial shock that every beginner feels upon seeing the buttons window, experienced users often still sense that there is a great deal of potential that they have not fully tapped into. Indeed, many Blender users use only a small fraction of its capabilities for controlling their work environments. These capabilities include options available in the User Preferences window and a variety of lesser-known techniques and workflow shortcuts. Furthermore, by gaining insight into the design principles behind the Blender interface, you can prepare for the ways that upcoming changes in the code base will help to enhance the power, flexibility, and accessibility of the interface in the future.

In this chapter, you will learn to

◆ Set the options available to you in the User Preferences window

◆ Use lesser-known methods for selecting, grouping, and organizing 3D elements to speed up your workflow

◆ Prepare for changes in the evolving Blender interface by understanding the principles behind its unique design

Getting Your Way with Blender

As I wrote in the introduction to this book, this is a book for people who want to push the envelope of their Blender abilities—people who know how to use Blender but want to know more. Likewise, this is a chapter for people who know Blender's interface and workflow, but want to know it better, to understand it more deeply, and to learn to use it faster and more efficiently—in short, to master it.

This chapter is intended to help you get beyond simply knowing how things are done in Blender and to truly explore the way *you* do things in Blender. In this chapter, you'll learn about the preferences you can set to take control of your own working environment. You'll learn about workflow tricks and techniques to give you more options for how to get from A to B in your Blender work. This chapter is intended to give you the knowledge and the confidence to start telling Blender how you want things done.

User Preferences

When you think about options and customization for any software, the first thing that usually comes to mind is the set of user preferences available. Like most applications, Blender has a variety of user preferences that you can adjust. The User Preferences window is the "hidden" third window in the default screen configuration shown in Figure 1.1. The bar across the top of the default screen may look similar to the menu bar that lines the top of many other applications, but in fact it is the header of the User Preferences window, which you can bring into view by left-clicking on the window border and dragging downward, as shown in Figure 1.2. Seven buttons are located along the bottom of the User Preferences area. Each of these buttons displays a different subcontext of User Preferences.

FIGURE 1.1
The default screen configuration

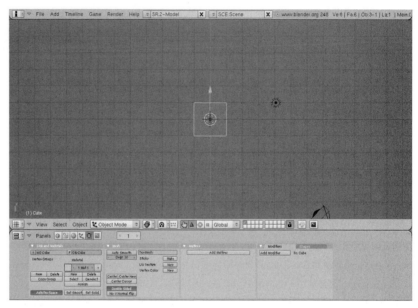

FIGURE 1.2
Dragging the User Preferences window into view

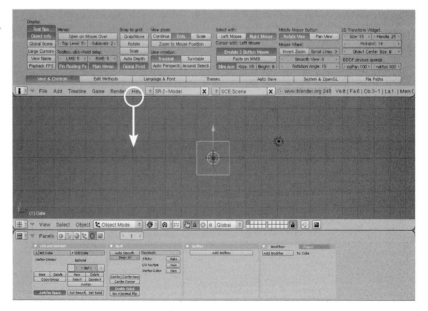

VIEW & CONTROLS

The first subcontext of the User Preferences buttons area is the View & Controls subcontext, shown in Figure 1.3.

FIGURE 1.3
The View &
Controls user
preferences

The Display options include six buttons that control how information is displayed throughout the interface or in the 3D viewport. Those buttons are as follows:

Tool Tips enables and disables the display of tooltips when the mouse is over interface elements.

Object Info displays the name of the active object in the lower-left corner of the 3D viewport.

Global Scene causes the active scene to hold constant over various screens. If this option is enabled and the scene is changed in any one screen, all the screens will change scenes. If this option is disabled, a screen will continue to display the scene it last displayed, even if the scene is changed in another screen.

Large Cursors enables alternate mouse cursors if they are installed in your system.

View Name displays the name of the view (Front, Back, Top, Bottom, Right, Left, Orthogonal, or Perspective) in the upper-left corner of the 3D viewport.

Playback FPS displays the number of frames per second in the upper-left corner of the 3D viewport when the animation is playing.

The next column of buttons and fields includes controls for Blender's menus, toolboxes, and panels. The options you have here are as follows:

Open On Mouse Over enables menus to open automatically when the mouse is held over them, without clicking. The numerical values for this option determine how long the mouse must be held over the main menu or submenus before the menus open.

Toolbox Click-Hold Delay values determine how quickly the toolbox opens when the right or left mouse button is clicked and held. For immediate toolbox access, the spacebar is used.

Pin Floating Panels causes floating panels such as the Transformations panel or other tool panels to be pinned to the spot in the viewport where they opened last. If this option is not activated, panels will appear at the spot where the mouse is.

Plain Menus causes the ordering of the menus to remain fixed, rather than reversing depending on whether the menu opens upwards or downwards.

The next column of buttons controls snap-to-grid and other 3D navigational controls. The buttons here are as follows:

Grab/Move causes snapping to the grid when objects are moved.

Rotate causes snapping to the grid when objects are rotated.

Scale causes snapping to the grid when objects are scaled.

Auto Depth causes the rotation and zoom of the 3D space to pivot around the point directly under the mouse. This option automatically calculates the depth of the nearest object under the mouse as the pivot point.

Global Pivot causes the selected pivot to be fixed over all 3D viewport windows. If this option is not selected, each 3D viewport can use a different pivot.

The next column of buttons controls the way the 3D space itself can be navigated and manipulated. The buttons here are as follows:

Continue causes the view zoom to continue forward or backward as long as the left mouse button is held down and the mouse is moved above or below the center of the viewport. The distance of the mouse from the horizontal center of the viewport determines the speed with which the zoom moves forward or backward.

Dolly causes the zoom to move forward when the mouse movement is downward and to move backward when the mouse movement is upward, by default.

Scale causes the zoom to move forward when the mouse is pulled away from the center point of the viewport and to move backward when the mouse is pushed toward the center point of the viewport.

Trackball causes the entire view to rotate freely in all directions, analogously to the motion of a trackball.

Turntable causes the entire view to rotate strictly around the three spatial axes, resulting in a more constrained rotation than the Trackball option.

Auto Perspective causes the view to enter Perspective view whenever it is rotated out of Front, Side, or Top views, and to enter Orthogonal view when it enters those views by means of hot keys on the number pad.

Around Selection causes the view to rotate around the median point between selected elements.

The next column of buttons controls the way you can use your mouse. There are also buttons to control the display of the mini axis in the 3D viewport. These buttons are as follows:

Left Mouse causes the left mouse button (LMB) to be used for selecting.

Right Mouse causes the right mouse button (RMB) to be used for selecting.

Emulate 3 Button Mouse enables Alt+RMB to emulate the behavior of the middle mouse button (MMB).

Paste On MMB causes the middle mouse button to paste from the clipboard in the text editor.

Mini Axis controls the display of the miniature axis in the lower-left corner of the 3D viewport.

The next column includes buttons and fields that control the behavior of the middle mouse button and view changes made with the number pad. These buttons include the following:

Rotate View causes the middle mouse button to rotate the 3D view. With this option selected, Shift+MMB pans the view.

Pan View causes the middle mouse button to pan the 3D view. With this option selected, Shift+MMB rotates the view.

Invert Zoom causes the view to zoom forward when the mouse is moved upward and to pull away when the mouse is moved downward across the 3D view (as opposed to the default behavior, which is the reverse of this).

Smooth View sets a time interval in milliseconds for an animated transition between number-pad views.

Rotation Angle sets the degree of rotation used by the 2, 4, 6, and 8 keys on the number pad to rotate the view incrementally.

Finally, the last column includes settings for the 3D Transform Widget and object center displays, and settings for six-degrees-of-freedom (6DoF) devices such as the SpaceNavigator. These values include the following:

Size, **Handle**, and **Hotspot** values control the overall size, the handle size, and the size of the clickable area (hot spot) of the 3D manipulator.

Object Center Size controls the display size of object centers.

ndPan and ndRot values control the speed with which the navigation responds to input from a 6DoF input device.

RECOMMENDATIONS FOR VIEW & CONTROLS SETTINGS

Of course, everybody has their own preferences, which is why options like the ones described in this section exist. Nevertheless, a few nondefault options are particularly worth experimenting with. The Around Selection option for view rotation makes navigating around selected vertices for modeling much easier, particularly when you are working on vertices that are not positioned in the middle of the screen.

The Smooth View value is a great way to visualize the change from one view to another. For example, if you are using Blender to give instruction to students or to create video tutorials, setting this option at 500 (half a second) makes it much easier for observers to maintain their bearings as you navigate the space.

For those who use the 3D Transform Widget, increasing the size of the hot spot can make it much easier to engage the widget.

People accustomed to other 3D packages often feel more comfortable using Turntable view rotation as opposed to Trackball. However, Trackball rotation offers greater flexibility, so it's worth getting used to. Likewise, the temptation to switch the selection button to the left mouse button (LMB) should be resisted, because it will lead to a variety of undesirable side effects. For one thing, the capability to use Alt+LMB as an alternate to the middle mouse button (MMB) is no longer available to you if you choose this option, making it out of the question for people with two-button mice.

EDIT METHODS

The Edit Methods user-preferences context is shown in Figure 1.4.

The options in this window are as follows:

Material Linked To controls whether materials are linked to an object itself or the object's mesh datablock by default.

Add New Objects options enable you to choose whether to switch to Edit mode automatically upon object creation, and whether newly created objects should be aligned to the view or should be placed at the 3D space origin with default orientation.

Transform: Drag Immediately enables you to select and move elements with one mouse button. If you right-click to select an object and drag immediately, this option will cause the object to follow the mouse until you release the right mouse button. With this option disabled, you must release the mouse button and click again to verify the transformation.

Undo options enable you to set the number of levels of Undo, the amount of memory devoted to Undo, and whether Global Undo is used. Global Undo requires more memory than regular Undo; however, regular Undo is limited in that you cannot undo edits made in Edit mode incrementally after leaving Edit mode and reentering Edit mode again. Global Undo enables you to do this.

Auto Keyframe options enable you to automatically set keyframes for selected sets of Ipo curves. With this option, keyframes are set in a frame anytime an Ipo's value is changed, making keyframing with the I key unnecessary.

Grease Pencil options enable you to determine specifically how mouse movements are used to draw lines with the Grease Pencil tools. The smaller the Euclidean and Manhattan distances, the less segmented the line will appear.

Duplicate With Object options enable you to select which datablocks will be duplicated when their owner objects are duplicated with Shift+D. Duplication involves a new, independent instantiation of the datablock being created. Datablocks that are not duplicated are shared between the two duplicated objects.

RECOMMENDATIONS FOR EDIT METHODS

Edit Methods options are a little less "personal" than the View & Controls options. The best options in this case are likely to depend on exactly the kind of work you do. If you typically find yourself going straight into modeling when you add a new object, you will save a step by setting the default to Switch To Edit Mode upon adding a new option. If you do a lot of animation and you are comfortable and confident working with Ipos, enabling Auto-Keying may speed up your workflow. For beginning animators, I think it's better to set your keyframes deliberately by hand until you are sure you have the hang of it. For Auto-Keying, the Needed option is useful to keep unnecessary keyframes from being set. For the Duplicate With Object settings, if you find that you rarely want a duplicated object to share an Ipo curve with the original object, you may want to select Ipo in addition to the currently set defaults.

FIGURE 1.4
The Edit Methods user preferences

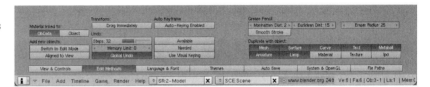

LANGUAGE & FONT

The Language & Font buttons context is shown in Figure 1.5. It is no secret that internationalization is an area of Blender that has been unfortunately neglected. One of the reasons for this is the difficulty of creating and incorporating language translation files for the software, which, like many things in Blender, must be done at a low level and compiled directly into the executable.

FIGURE 1.5
The Language & Font user preferences

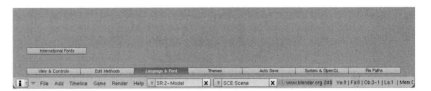

One thing you can do here is to adjust the size of the font that shows up on your buttons and menus. To do this, click International Fonts and select the size you want from the Font Size menu shown in Figure 1.6.

FIGURE 1.6
The Font Size drop-down menu

The Use Textured Fonts option may result in problems displaying the button labels with some hardware drivers. If you have problems seeing the button labels on your computer, deselect the Use Textured Fonts option, as shown in Figure 1.7.

FIGURE 1.7
Use Textured Fonts disabled

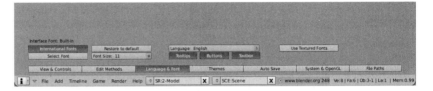

You can select international font systems if you have the necessary fonts installed. In Figure 1.8, you can see how Blender looks with Japanese selected as the language and a Japanese font selected. Nevertheless, this is of limited usefulness for several reasons. First, almost all documentation and learning material is written with the assumption that Blender is in English, and second, the translations are too incomplete to warrant any other assumption, as you can see in Figure 1.9.

FIGURE 1.8
Blender in
Japanese

FIGURE 1.9
The limits of internationalization

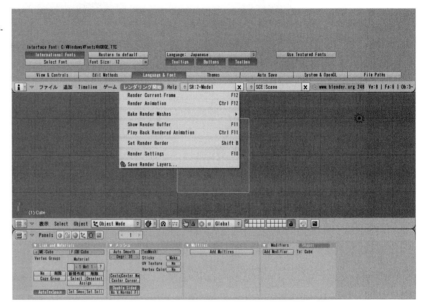

LANGUAGE AND FONT RECOMMENDATIONS

It would be very welcome if internationalization was made simpler, and perhaps this will become a possibility with the upcoming recode of the event system. For the time being, however, Blender's internationalization is superficial, incomplete, and largely outdated. The only real choice is to use Blender in English.

THEMES

The Themes context, shown in Figure 1.10, enables you to create and select themes with various options for the coloring and display of interface elements. You can select the theme you want to use from the drop-down menu. In order to add a new theme to the list, click the Add button. In addition to the default theme itself, another theme is included in the default distribution of Blender, the Rounded theme, shown in Figure 1.11. The theme used in this book is a variation based on the Rounded theme.

FIGURE 1.10
The Themes
user preferences

FIGURE 1.11
The Rounded
theme

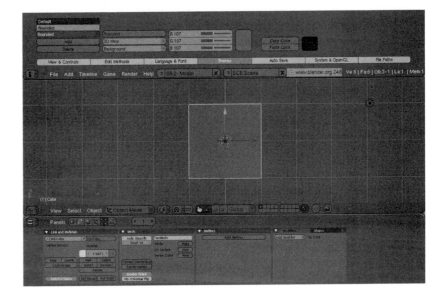

There are too many options to set in the Themes area to describe each one individually here, but they are mostly self-explanatory. You can change the color of almost every element in Blender, and in some cases such as drop-down menus and pop-up panels, you can change the alpha value as well.

If you have a properly formatted Blender icons file, you can also change the Blender icons, but it requires a small amount of preparation. To use alternate icon sets, you must create a new directory called icons in the .blender directory of your Blender installation. In Mac OS X and Linux, the location is slightly different. For these systems, you should create a .blender directory in your home directory (~/) and put the icons directory there. Then place the alternate icons files in the icons directory. These icons will appear in the drop-down menu that's displayed when you choose Icon File in the UI And Buttons user preferences list, as shown in Figure 1.12.

FIGURE 1.12
Icon File menu

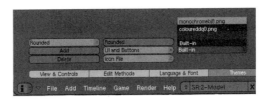

The icon file used throughout this book is shown in Figure 1.13 and repeated in color in this book's color insert. It was created by BlenderArtists.org user jendrzych, and the icon set itself can be found on that website at `http://blenderartists.org/forum/showthread.php?t=84971`. The file is also included on the CD that accompanies the book. Although this is not the official default icon set for version 2.48, it is a nicer-looking and widely used alternative. Furthermore, it has already been adopted as the official default icon set for Blender version 2.5, so getting accustomed to it is a small and painless way to prepare for the changes of that version.

In Figure 1.14 (also repeated in the book's color insert), you can see the default icons and the alternate icons as they appear in all the headers of the various window types in Blender. This should give you a good reference for which icons correspond to each other, in case you are using a different icon set from the one used in this book. Throughout the book, in cases where there might be some confusion, both default and alternate icons are shown in the appropriate contexts.

FIGURE 1.13
An alternate
icon set

FIGURE 1.14
Default and
alternate icon
sets in headers

Numerous Blender themes are available online for download. A quick Google search on *Blender themes* will give you the links for several good theme repositories. The themes may be downloadable in the form of a .blend file or in the form of a Python script. In the latter case, simply open the script in a Blender text editor window and execute it with Alt+P.

THEME RECOMMENDATIONS

Themes are a matter of taste; however, there's a reason why the two themes included in the default installation are largely gray and muted. Bright, lively colored themes can distract attention from what you are working on and can lead to eye strain. You should have enough contrast between elements to see them clearly, but large areas of white or very bright colors can quickly tire your eyes. Other theme options worth noting are those in the 3D View menu list. If you are planning to use Blender for instructing others or for making tutorials, you can change the size at which vertices and face dots are displayed.

AUTO SAVE

The Auto Save options context is shown in Figure 1.15. It enables you to set your preferences for how the autosave and backup features work. The Save Versions number enables you to select how many previously saved versions you want to keep backed up. In the past, you may have noticed the filename.blend1 files in the directory alongside filename.blend files. These are the default single-version backup files, and they represent the contents of the previously saved session. If you select a value greater than 1 (and apply it with Ctrl+U), the correspondingly numbered backup versions will appear in your directory.

FIGURE 1.15
The Auto Save
user preferences

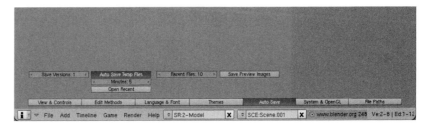

The Auto Save Temp Files option enables numbered, automatically saved files to be saved to your temporary directory (the default is /tmp, so ensure that this directory exists on your system or else change the directory to wherever you want the files saved). The Minutes value is how often these files are saved. The Open Recent button will open the most recently saved file.

The Recent Files field enables you to choose how many previously saved files are listed in the Open Recent menu entry in the File menu.

SYSTEM & OPENGL

The System & OpenGL user preferences context, shown in Figure 1.16, enables you to control a variety of display-related and miscellaneous values.

FIGURE 1.16
The System &
OpenGL user
preferences

There are three possible OpenGL lights that can be used to illuminate objects in the Solid Draw mode. By default, two of these lights are activated. The first is a key light from the left, and the second is a dimmer fill light from the right. A third light is also available, which by default is set to provide highlights from the lower right, as shown in Figure 1.17. You can enable or disable each of these lights, adjust their colors, or change their angles by clicking and dragging directly on the preview spheres for the lights.

FIGURE 1.17
3D view with
the default two
OpenGL lights
activated and the
same view with the
third solid OpenGL
light activated

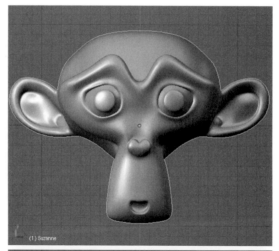

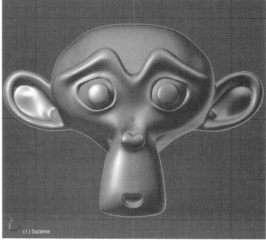

Returning to the System & OpenGL user preferences (Figure 1.16), the Enabled By Default button under Auto Run Python Scripts, when enabled, will allow Python scripts to be run automatically from within a `.blend` file. This is convenient in some cases, but it is not recommended if you're not sure of the source of your `.blend` files.

The Enable All Codecs button under Win Codecs appears on Windows machines. This option will enable the codecs you have installed on your system to be used for rendering in Blender. As the tooltip points out, this is not guaranteed to work in all cases, because support for some codecs remains experimental.

The Color Band button under Color Range For Weight Paint enables you to override the default blue-to-red coloring range for weight painting and to define your own range by using a color-band interface.

The Audio Mixing Buffer buttons enable you to select the amount of memory to devote to audio mixing.

The Emulate Numpad button enables you to use the number keys on the main keypad instead of the number keys on the number pad. This is particularly useful if you are working on a laptop that doesn't have a separate number pad.

The System & OpenGL buttons and fields in the rightmost two columns control a variety of specific values that you can adjust to improve your performance if you are having memory problems or you are experiencing slowdowns in your 3D viewport. Disabling Mipmaps or raising the Clip Alpha value can speed up the OpenGL drawing in your viewport at the expense of some image quality.

FILE PATHS

The last user preferences context is self-explanatory. The File Paths preferences, shown in Figure 1.18, enables you to define defaults for what the Blender file browser will open first when you import or save various types of assets. The default is //, which is Blender notation for the present working directory—that is, the directory you opened Blender from. For example, if you are opening Blender from the Windows Start menu, this will be your Blender installation directory. If you are opening from a file, this will be the directory that the file is in. The Relative Paths Default button causes the file paths to be read as relative to the present working directory.

FIGURE 1.18
The File Paths
user preferences

Other Options

Many other options are available throughout the Blender interface, and it is worthwhile to make a note of the ones that you often find yourself adjusting, and to use Ctrl+U to set them as you prefer them once and for all. The Occlude Background Geometry option in the 3D view header is a common option to activate. This makes unseen vertices and faces unselectable when not in Wireframe Draw mode, creating a sharper distinction between selection behavior in Wireframe and Solid Draw modes. If you usually rotate, grab, and scale using the R, G, and S keys, you may want to disable the manipulators, also in the 3D view header. Render settings such as the output format and compression quality are also common places where you might want to customize your defaults.

SAVING THE CHANGES

After you have set all the options the way you want them, don't forget to set the current setup as your default setup by using Ctrl+U. Remember, Ctrl+U saves the exact state of Blender at the moment you press it, so be sure you've put everything in place exactly the way you want to see it when you open Blender. Objects, materials, animations, and any other data in the .blend file will also be saved.

The resulting settings are stored in the .B.blend file in your .blender directory. To use these settings with another Blender installation, you can simply copy that file into the .blender directory of the Blender installation you want to use.

To save the current theme in the form of a Python script, go to the File menu and choose Export ➢ Save Current Theme. The resulting script can then be executed in another instance of Blender to import the theme.

Improving Your Workflow

Setting and saving your user preferences is the first step in optimizing your workflow. This section presents a variety of miscellaneous tips and tricks that you may find helpful for increasing your efficiency and improving your experience working with Blender.

View Hot Keys and Properties

The 3D viewport has a number of hot keys and properties associated with it that enable you to view your work. You are no doubt familiar with the most commonly used number pad shortcuts for Front view (number pad 1), Side view (number pad 3), and Top view (number pad 7). Pressing these keys with Ctrl will show you the reverse view; Ctrl+number pad 1 yields the rear view of the object, and so on. Number pad 5 toggles Orthogonal and Perspective view; and 2, 4, 6, and 8 rotate the 3D space by the amount determined in the Rotation Angle field in the View & Controls user preferences window.

The decimal (.) key on the number pad centers the selected object in the 3D viewport. Related keys on the main keypad include the C key, which shifts the view so that the 3D cursor is centered; the Home key, which displays and centers the median point of all the objects in the scene; and the Shift+C key combination, which does the same thing as the Home key with the addition of placing the 3D cursor at the zero point of the 3D space.

The slash key (/) on the number pad changes the display to show only the selected object. Pressing the same key again toggles back into full scene display mode. On the main keypad, the Alt+B key combination enables you to select even smaller portions of the 3D view for display. Pressing Alt+B and dragging the box to select an area results in clipping the display of everything outside of that box selection, as shown in Figure 1.19. The resulting displayed selection can be viewed from all angles.

The View Properties panel, shown in Figure 1.20, can be accessed via the View menu in the header of the 3D viewport. Here you can control the display and qualities of the background grid; the X, Y, and Z axes; and the relationship lines (dotted lines between parents and their child objects). You can toggle the drawing of textures in Solid Draw mode with the Solid Tex button, and toggle between displaying all object centers or only the selected object's center. You can toggle the drawing of an outline around the selected object. You can change the angle of the view lens, adjust the point past which the view is clipped, and place the 3D cursor by entering coordinates by hand.

FIGURE 1.19
Clipping the
view with Alt+B

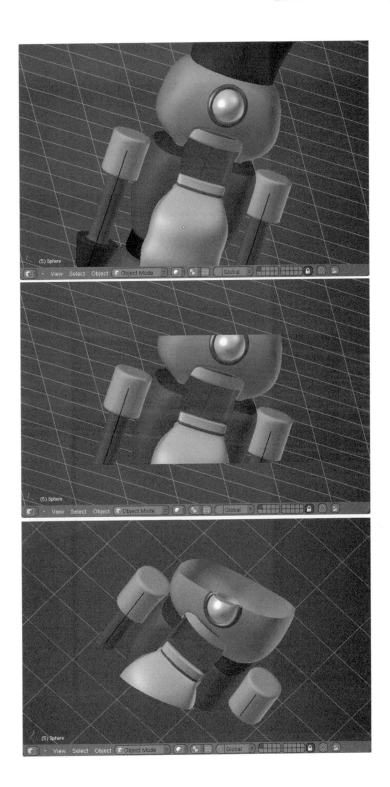

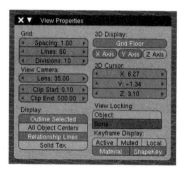

View Locking enables you to enter an object name (and in the case of an armature, a bone name) and force the view to follow the movement of that object, holding the object in the center of the view. This can be useful when you're animating detail on moving objects, such as when you're animating the movement of fingers on a moving hand.

Grouping and Selection

Objects can be grouped by selecting the object and choosing a group from the Add To Group drop-down menu in the Object And Links panel of the Object buttons area. Objects that share a group can be appended into other .blend files in one step by appending the group. When lamps are grouped, it is possible to restrict a material's lighting to lamps from the group by entering the group name in the GR field in the material's Shaders tab.

Groups are one of many criteria by which you can select objects. You can select variously grouped objects by selecting a single object and pressing Shift+G to open the menu shown in Figure 1.21. You can select other objects based on their relationship with the first selected object.

You can also select objects based on linked data, by pressing Shift+L to open the menu shown in Figure 1.22 and selecting the linked datablock upon which to base the selection.

Using the Select menu in the 3D viewport in Object mode, you can directly select objects by type or by layer. It is also possible to select a random collection of objects and to inverse the current selection.

FIGURE 1.21
The Select
Grouped menu

FIGURE 1.22
The Select
Linked menu

BOX, CIRCLE, AND LASSO SELECTION

Pressing the B key once initiates the Box selection state, where you can drag your mouse to select whatever falls within the rectangular area you define. Holding down the Alt key while doing this will deselect whatever falls within that area. Pressing the B key twice will enable the Circle selection state, where you can drag your mouse to select all that falls within a circular area following the mouse. Likewise, holding down the Alt key while doing this will deselect the elements.

Holding down the Ctrl key while dragging the left mouse button introduces the Lasso selection state, which enables you to define the area to be selected by moving your mouse around the area directly. This is a very fast selection method.

EDIT MODE SELECTION

Numerous little-known selection methods are available for meshes in Edit mode. The first option you have is whether to select by vertex, edge, or face. This is chosen by using the viewport header buttons shown in Figure 1.23 (both default and alternate icon sets). Vertex, Edge, and Face selection modes correspond with the buttons from left to right (the rightmost button occludes hidden geometry). You can choose more than one mode simultaneously by holding down the Shift key when you click these buttons.

FIGURE 1.23
Buttons for
choosing the
selection mode

Selecting Edges, Loops, and Rings

Many selection options are available independently of the specific selection mode you are in. Selection options that deal specifically with edges can be found by pressing Ctrl+E in Edit mode. The Region To Loop selection option in that menu enables you to choose the edge outline (strictly speaking, *loop* here is a misnomer) of any selected region of faces, as shown in Figure 1.24 (this image is repeated for visual clarity in the color insert of this book). The reverse, selecting a region of faces based on a selected closed edge border around the region, is possible with the Loop To Region menu entry.

Other very useful selection options include loop and ring selection using Alt+RMB and Ctrl+Alt+RMB. By holding down the Alt key and right-clicking on a single edge in Edit mode, you can select the entire edge loop that the edge belongs to. By using Ctrl+Alt+RMB, you select the perpendicular ring of faces that includes the edge you clicked on, as shown in Figure 1.25. In Edge selection mode, the behavior is similar, except that the edge ring selected with Ctrl+Alt+RMB does not include faces, as shown in Figure 1.26. In Face selection mode, there is no difference between the selections. Both hot keys select the same ring of faces, as shown in Figure 1.27. These figures are also included in the color insert of this book for visual clarity.

FIGURE 1.24
Choosing a loop
from an area

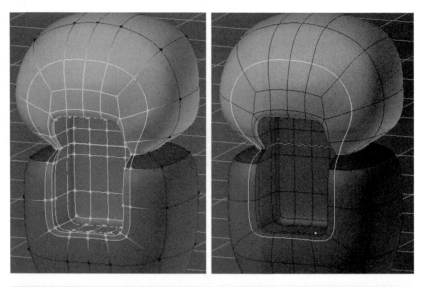

FIGURE 1.25
Edge loop and ring
selection in Vertex
selection mode

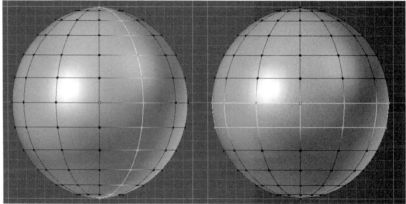

FIGURE 1.26
Edge loop and ring
selection in Edge
selection mode

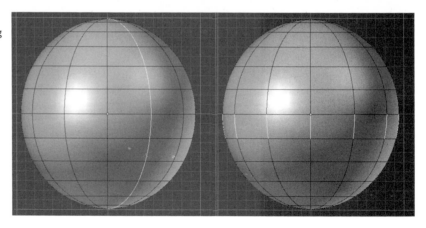

FIGURE 1.27
Loop selection
in Face
selection mode

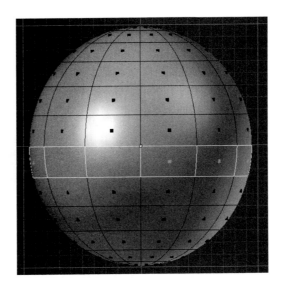

Another useful selection tool, Select Vertex Path, can be found in the Specials menu by pressing the W key over the 3D viewport. With exactly two vertices selected, this option will select the shortest edge path between the two vertices.

Selecting Similar Elements

The Shift+G menu enables you to select all similar elements to the currently selected element, based on a variety of possible criteria.

In Vertex selection mode, Shift+G enables you to select other vertices that share the same vertex normal direction as the currently selected vertices, vertices that are members of shared vertex groups with the currently selected vertices, or vertices that are used by the same number of faces.

In Edge selection mode, the Shift+G menu enables you to select edges that are the same length, run in the same direction, or have the same number of face users as the selected edges. You can also select edges based on whether they are part of a seam or crease, or based on their sharpness value. This is an excellent method for quickly selecting all seams on an object: Simply select on a seam edge, and then use this selection method to select them all.

In Face selection mode, you can select faces that share the same area, share a material, share an image, have common normal directions, or are coplanar, meaning that the faces share their normal directions and are located on a single imaginary plane in the 3D space. Finally, the Perimeter option enables you to select regions of faces that have the same size perimeter or outline as the originally selected region.

Object Manipulation

The most commonly used and taught methods of translating, rotating, and scaling 3D elements are the hot keys G, R, and S. These are the easiest to control, but using other methods can increase the speed and efficiency of your workflow in some cases. Most people are aware of the existence of mouse gestures and the 3D manipulator, because both are enabled by default (mouse gestures in particular can be a real nuisance to beginners who activate them inadvertently), but fewer people understand the correct way to use them.

Mouse gestures are a way of triggering the translation, scale, or rotation state, which are analogous to pressing the G, S, or R key, respectively. This is done by holding the left mouse button and dragging the mouse in one of the three patterns shown in Figure 1.28.

Almost as important as knowing how to use mouse gestures correctly is knowing when they are being activated by accident and what to do when that happens (click the right mouse button to cancel out of the transform). Mouse gestures can be particularly useful with pen tablets. The easiest gesture to use, by far, is the translate gesture. If you spend much time using a pen tablet, it is likely that you will soon quit using the G key altogether, even without thinking about it. The rotate and scale gestures are trickier. To be honest, although they are referred to as "mouse" gestures, I personally find it nearly impossible to consistently produce distinct rotation and scale gestures when working with a mouse. The important quality that distinguishes the rotate gesture is the smoothness of the curve. If your curve is choppy or angular, the gesture is likely to be interpreted as the scale gesture. It is much easier to do this correctly with a pen tablet, although it still requires a bit of practice.

It may come as a bit of a surprise, but the 3D manipulator widgets, shown in Figure 1.29 (and repeated in the color insert of this book), also require a little bit of practice to get a feel for using them properly. These can be enabled individually or all at once using the manipulator buttons on the 3D viewport header (to select more than one, hold down the Shift key while choosing, just as in other contexts).

The easiest way to use the manipulator widgets is to left-click on the colored manipulator hot spots (the arrows for translation, curves for rotation, and cube-shaped tips for scale) and drag. The transformations are shown in Figure 1.30 and repeated in the color insert of this book. The transformation is finalized when you release the left mouse button. To abort the transformation, either press the Esc key or click the right mouse button *before releasing the left mouse button.*

Another way to use the manipulators is to left-click once quickly on the appropriate hot spot. It's important that you do not begin to drag the mouse until after you have clicked. After you click, you will enter the appropriate transformation state, and the object's behavior will be identical to what it would have been if you had pressed G, R, or S. Right-clicking will cancel out of the transformation, and left-clicking will finalize the transformation.

The colored hot spots are not the only way to transform the object. Each manipulator has a thin, orange circle associated with it. Clicking on this will enter the corresponding unconstrained transform state: For translation and rotation, the transformation will be carried out with respect to the plane of the viewport; and for scaling, the object will be scaled along all axes.

FIGURE 1.28
Mouse gestures
for (top to bottom)
translation, scale,
and rotation

FIGURE 1.29
Translate, rotate,
and scale manipu-
lator widgets

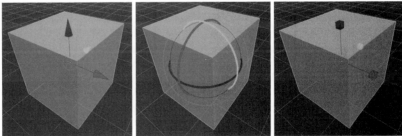

FIGURE 1.30
Translating,
rotating, and
scaling with
manipulator
widgets

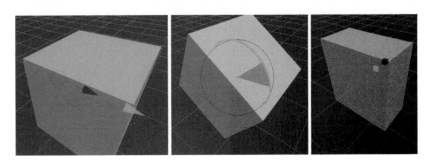

Finally, you can scale or translate along two axes by holding down the Shift key and clicking on the hot spot of the third axis. This is analogous to the way axes are constrained by hot key. Thus, to scale along the X and Y axis as shown in Figure 1.31, hold down Shift and click on the Z axis manipulator hot spot.

FIGURE 1.31
Scaling along the X and Y axis

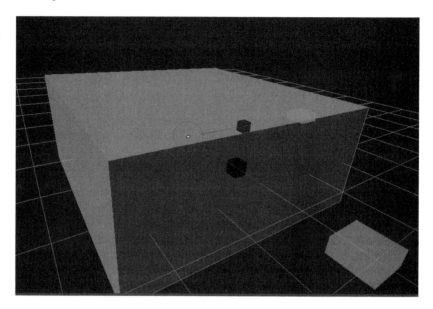

Keeping Up with the Blender Interface

As an open source application, Blender evolves at a more rapid pace and in a more organic way than many proprietary applications that you might be accustomed to. Releases are not timed to maximize profits or to coincide with other merchandising. Rather, they come when the developers decide that the recent developments are significant enough and stable enough to warrant the extra effort required for an official release. When this happens, resources are diverted from new functionality, and the user community and development team focus on intensive beta testing and bug fixing in preparation for the release.

By this point, many users are already familiar with the new functionality, because the code has been open and freely available all along. Several websites, such as www.graphicall.org, have regularly updated builds of Blender that are as easy to install as the official releases (although not necessarily as stable). It is no problem to install multiple versions of Blender side by side, so there is never a problem experimenting with Blender's bleeding-edge functionality. The BlenderArtists.org forum is always buzzing with discussions of all the latest features, and you're sure to find somebody to help you with even the most exotic new features.

Getting familiar with these resources is part and parcel of mastering Blender. Most readers of this book have probably already dipped into experimental, developmental Blender builds when a particularly attractive feature was introduced.

The Coming Changes

Anyone who has participated in recent online discussions about Blender has probably heard about the deep changes afoot for the upcoming Blender version 2.5, in particular as they relate to the interface. Indeed, this release has taken on an almost mythological status in some circles, and opinions (some better informed than others) have been flying thick and fast. There is excited hope that all the things that many people find annoying or counterintuitive about the Blender interface will be fixed, as well as apprehension that many idiosyncrasies that Blender users have come to love may be discarded.

Although this book is written to correspond to Blender 2.48, it is nonetheless worthwhile, in keeping with the thinking of Blender as a constantly evolving piece of software, to get a clearer idea of what direction the evolution of its interface is likely to take in the next few releases.

The 2.5 Event Recode

Blender began its life as an in-house animation tool for a commercial studio. It was developed in C by the same people who used it, a small group who knew the code inside and out and worked very closely together. Unfortunately, although the choice of C as an implementation language helped to ensure that Blender would be a fast and lean executable, the way that the development proceeded meant that many design decisions about even relatively superficial things came to be hard-coded at a low level and difficult or impossible to alter later in a simple way. This lack of modularity has been a common source of frustration to coders who are new to Blender. For years, it was accepted as a fact of life and worked around, but over time the problem became compounded by code written in an ad hoc way.

This is about to change. As I write this, the Blender Foundation's resources have been entirely devoted to a long-postponed, ground-up recode of the Blender event-handling system. The event system manages the way in which keyboard, mouse, and other input/output (I/O) events are dealt with, and as such, it is a crucial point of interaction between the interface and the functionality. Until the recode, much of the event handling happened directly in the code implementing the functionality itself. In order to change a single hot key, for example, it might be necessary to do considerable digging into the code of the associated functionality. To add such an apparently straightforward and often-requested feature as customizable hot keys, then, was a much thornier problem than many people realized.

It was possible to put off the recode for so long in part because individual requests and features that the current code makes difficult were often fairly superficial. Customizable hot keys, for example, are a common request of users seeking to switch over from some other 3D application. But there are arguments on both sides to be made about the actual importance or wisdom of depending heavily on nonstandard hot key configurations. Combined with the intractability of implementing configurable hot keys on the old Blender codebase, this was enough to ensure that such requests went for years without being acted on. Now, with the event-system recode underway, Blender users can look forward to not only many new interface features and customizability options, but more important, a new ease with which future adaptations and modifications can be made.

DNA AND RNA

Blender uses a unique internal format called *DNA* to store and reference 3D assets. The name is an analogy to the biological term, with the implication that DNA is a highly compact encoding of all the information necessary to re-create the contents of what Blender users know as a .blend file: scenes, objects, and all associated datablocks. DNA is a binary format, which makes it very fast to load and save. For example, the same data represented in XML may be several orders of magnitude slower to load and save, particularly in the case of large files with many scene elements. This is the main reason why .blend files are so flexible, and can be used to store large and complex scenes and even collections of scenes.

RNA is a current development that comprises an important behind-the-scenes component of the 2.5 changes. It is also loosely analogous to the biological meaning of the term. RNA will serve as a wrapper or low-level interface for accessing and setting values in DNA. In practice, RNA will be used to automatically generate interface elements and the Python API, making it easier to keep them up-to-date and consistent. The enhanced access that RNA enables will also have the effect of finally realizing the long-held dream of having *everything* in Blender capable of being animated!

The Evolution of the Interface

With the focus of development being on the task of implementing the new event system and porting the existing Blender functionality over to this new foundation, it is an ideal time for a review of the interface itself. In preparation for the coming interface paradigm shift, William Reynish delivered a presentation at the Blender Foundation's 2008 annual conference in Amsterdam, outlining the latest thinking on the direction that Blender's interface should take. A 25-page white paper containing a revised version of Reynish's proposals is available from the official Blender website at http://download.blender.org/documentation/bc2008/ evolution_of_blenders_ui.pdf.

Reynish's paper is an excellent overview of the thinking behind the Blender interface—past, present, and future—and a good read for anybody who would like to better understand why the interface is the way it is and how it is likely to evolve. The paper describes Blender's interface strengths, its weaknesses as of the official 2.48 release, and a number of design goals for the 2.5 release.

STRENGTHS

Reynish outlines four main principles that have informed Blender's interface. These are long-standing, deliberate design decisions that have made Blender extraordinarily fast to work with for experienced users. These principles are as follows:

The workflow should be as nonmodal as possible.   Modality in software means that certain functions work in certain modes and not in others. Although Blender does make use of explicit modes for editing and object manipulation, the overall interface is comparatively nonmodal in its behavior. Users have the option of having almost all of Blender's functionality laid out simultaneously before them, for immediate access at any time.

The window organization should be nonoverlapping.   For regular users of Blender, this is one of the main strengths of the interface. With functionality as complex as Blender's, overlapping windows could very quickly become a nightmare of digging around to find buried windows on the desktop. This never happens with Blender, because its windows are tidily organized in a nonoverlapping way. Users can quickly switch between Screen settings to access other nonoverlapping desktop configurations.

It should use fast, efficient, and consistent hot keys and interface conventions that are minimally dependent on their context.   Hot keys, menu entries, and other interface elements should be as consistent as possible across various points in the workflow. In Blender, this is accomplished in part by having similar or intuitively analogous functionality from different modes (such as the select, rotate, or grab functionality in Object mode and Edit mode) grouped logically to appropriate hot keys.

The various tools should be highly integrated with each other.   Blender has a wide variety of tools under its hood, ranging from mesh modeling and sculpting, to video editing and compositing, to scripting, game creation, and physical simulation. One of Blender's great strengths is the way all of these various tools are so tightly integrated that the transition from one to the next is nearly seamless. For individuals and small groups, this is a significant time-saver over a less-integrated pipeline that requires numerous export and import steps.

Weaknesses

Although Blender has done a good job of adhering to the preceding well-founded principles, some areas of Blender's interface as of 2.48 have been weak. The chaotic layout of the button areas is one key point that Reynish brings up, citing a variety of examples of highly arbitrary button placements, situations where the button type (radio, action, or toggle) is unclear, and cases where clutter is brought about by the need to maintain consistently square button tab shapes for ease of vertical and horizontal layout.

Another area that Reynish's paper homes in on is the difficulty of dealing with multiple objects simultaneously in certain specific ways. The example he gives is one of adding the Wire extra draw type to a large number of objects. This can be done using Ctrl+C to copy settings from one object to the others, but not everything can be copied in this way, and as Reynish points out, this is a distracting extra step.

Finally, Reynish's paper discusses the topic of customizability. Blender's interface is notorious for its lack of customizable key bindings. However, although customizability is a popular request among new users, Reynish concludes that it is a comparatively low priority when measured next to the importance of a good, solid set of defaults. Reynish argues that customizability in itself is an overrated solution—it is sometimes perceived that a poor interface can be improved by the user if the interface allows sufficient customizability, but this is not in fact the case. Nevertheless, there are a number of reasons why customizability in key bindings and input options is regarded as desirable. Some users may wish to preserve muscle-memory habits acquired from other software. More important, customizable hot keys enable the user to have more freedom in accessing custom-made scripts or other nonstandard functionality.

GOALS AND SUGGESTIONS

Reynish's paper outlines some key interface goals and some practical suggestions for attaining these goals. He argues that the interface should be nonmodal, nonlinear, logical, fast, flexible, innovative, and simple.

The practical suggestions are far-reaching. One of the most profound is Reynish's recommendation for the total removal of the buttons area window as it is currently implemented. Instead, it would be replaced by a Properties Editor that would enable logical, organized access to all the properties of any selected object or group of objects. Settings for all Blender datablocks would be accessible in this area.

Reynish further advocates a reworking of tool workflow. Rather than the highly modal workflow of tools such as the loop cut or the addition of objects to the scene, in which settings must be decided upon before finalizing the tool action, the recommendation is made to increase the interactivity of tools, enabling settings to be adjusted after the tool has been used.

Further recommendations include enhanced context sensitivity to rid the interface of unnecessary clutter when it is not needed, improved consistency in button and interface widget graphics so that distinct interface component types such as radio buttons and action buttons have a distinct and intuitively recognizable look, improved feedback for when the user is required to wait for something, and a preference for vertical layouts for buttons and fields for reasons of visual clarity and efficient screen real-estate usage.

WHAT TO EXPECT

Reynish's suggestions will not necessarily be implemented exactly as described in the report. Furthermore, the timeline for when they will be implemented is not set in stone. The 2.5 event recode will set the groundwork for making the evolution of the interface possible. Whether the most significant interface changes will be incorporated in that release or subsequently introduced remains to be seen.

Users can expect a more flexible workflow and more sensible and consistent organization of interface elements. There will likely be a preference for vertical panel configurations, rather than the horizontal panel configuration that has been the default for Blender's buttons area in the past. Eventually, users can expect the buttons area to be radically reworked or phased out entirely. Overall, the coming interface developments should go a long way to address many of the pet peeves that plague both new and experienced users of Blender, and help to make Blender an even more powerful and enjoyable tool to work with. As always, you should bring yourself up to speed with new developments for each release by studying the official release notes, which you can link to from the official downloads page at www.blender.org. You can learn more about the focus of the changes to come in 2.5 at http://wiki.blender.org/index.php/BlenderDev/Blender2.5/Focus.

THE DEVELOPING WORLD

As development on each Blender release intensifies, the #blendercoders IRC channel and the various development-related mailing lists are filled with developers communicating their ideas and intentions with each other. The 2.5 event recode and the huge task of porting existing Blender functionality over to the new base requires a high degree of organization and coordination, as does every release.

The smooth progress of Blender's development is all the more remarkable considering what a truly global project Blender is. According to the open source software resource Ohloh.net, Blender's regular committing developers are spread all over the globe—in Europe, North America, South America, Oceania, and Africa. If you count script contributions and recent coding that has not made it into the official trunk, the area is even wider, with recent code contributions beginning to come from Asia as well.

Some of the stories of Blender development around the world serve as inspiring reminders of the power of open source software. The work of Raúl Fernández Hernández (farsthary) on true volumetrics for Blender is an excellent example. As a student living in Cuba, Raúl has had limited access to many of the resources that people in other parts of the world take for granted. Nevertheless, he identified a glaring need in Blender for true volumetric simulations and took advantage of the open code to study for himself how to implement his ideas in Blender. Although he lacked regular access to an Internet connection and was unable to access the Subversion code repository directly, participate in chats, or take part in regular communication with developers, he nevertheless succeeded in creating an impressive foundation for true volumetrics. He reported about his work sporadically in his blog, `http://farsthary.wordpress.com/`, including some amazing renders and animations of convincing flame and smoke effects. Although initially carried out with very little interaction with others, Raúl's work quickly began to get attention from the Blender user and developer community. After hurricane Gustav devastated his town, leaving him without electricity for a week, the community rallied to assist him, and two core Blender developers, Matt Ebb and Daniel Genrich, became more actively involved in helping him recode the volumetric simulation to be more consistent with existing Blender code. The project is progressing very nicely, as you can see from Raúl's blog, and the exciting new volumetric features will surely be a welcome addition to an upcoming official release.

The Bottom Line

Set the options available to you in the User Preferences window.   A wide variety of often-overlooked options are available in the User Preferences window, including settings for View & Controls, Edit Methods, and Themes, among others.

> **Master It**   Create your own preferred default starting state and save it so that it will be active every time you start Blender.

Use lesser-known methods for selecting, grouping, and organizing 3D elements to speed up your workflow. There are numerous ways to select and group objects and 3D elements that can considerably increase your speed and efficiency when working.

Master It Use the selection methods described in this chapter to make the face selections as shown in the following graphic.

You should be able to make this selection using a single (modified) mouse click followed by a single hot key combination. There are several ways to do this.

Prepare for changes in the evolving Blender interface by understanding the principles behind its unique design. Blender is constantly evolving. It is in your interest to stay informed about developments, in particular at a time when the 2.5 release is promising big developments in usability.

Master It Inform yourself about the status of the 2.5 event recode and GUI update.

Chapter 2

Sculpting and Retopo Workflow

The method of modeling known as 3D sculpting has recently become increasingly popular as a way to create highly realistic, detailed models. In 3D sculpting, the 3D object is handled in a way that is closely analogous to actual clay. Blender has a powerful set of sculpting features that include multiresolution mesh modeling and a variety of tools that enable highly detailed direct manipulations of meshes. More than this, Blender offers the ability to use these detailed sculpted models as the basis of new models with corrected geometry. By means of Blender's *remake topology* (*retopo*) and normal map-baking features, you can create low-poly models with correct edge loop geometry that exhibit the same fine detail as your sculpted models.

In this chapter, you will learn to

◆ Get the most out of Blender's sculpting functionality

◆ Use retopo to convert a sculpted form into a polygon model with correct edge loop geometry

◆ Use normal map baking to capture finely sculpted detail for use on a low-poly model

Sculpting with Blender

3D sculpting is a method of manipulating the shape of 3D objects in a direct and intuitive way that is loosely analogous to the way a sculptor works with clay in the real world. It is an excellent way to model detailed organic forms, and many artists find it to be a much more natural way to model than the direct manipulation of vertices and polygons used in more traditional 3D mesh modeling. For this reason, 3D sculpting is rapidly growing in popularity in the professional computer graphics (CG) modeling world.

Among the modeling options available in Blender is a powerful set of features that enable you to perform 3D sculpting on Mesh objects. Although Blender's sculpting functionality lacks some of the versatility of the highest-end commercial sculpting systems, it is more than adequate for many sculpting tasks. In addition to the obvious advantage of being a free and open source, Blender's sculpting functionality also has the advantage of being seamlessly integrated with Blender's other modeling, texturing, and animation tools, making for a very smooth workflow.

Multiresolution Modeling

The cornerstone of the sculpting functionality in Blender is the ability to handle multiresolution mesh modeling. Multiresolution (or *multires*) meshes are meshes for which information is stored at more than one level of subdivision. At each level of subdivision, actual vertex data is maintained, so each multires level represents a mesh of the same overall shape as the other levels, but with a different density of vertices.

In Figure 2.1, you can see the default at multires levels 1 through 8. The figure shows the object in Edit mode so you can see the vertices. In fact, multires meshes are generally not dealt with in Edit mode for two reasons. The first reason is that some Edit mode functionality is disabled for multires meshes. Editing that fundamentally alters the topology or changes the number of vertices is not possible to carry out with multires active on a mesh. The other reason is simply that entering Edit mode on meshes with a very large number of vertices will slow or potentially crash your computer.

FIGURE 2.1
Multires levels

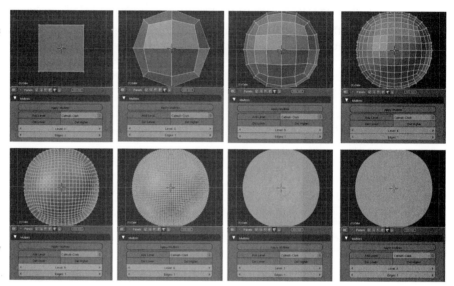

The intended way to model with multires meshes is to use the sculpting tools in Sculpt mode. You can switch up and down between multires levels as you work, so it is possible to edit details at a high multires level and still make broader edits at a lower multires level. Edits made at each multires level will be interpolated appropriately for the other multires levels.

HARDWARE REQUIREMENTS

Multires meshes and sculpting are areas in which the speed of your processor and the RAM you have available on your computer will come into play. A fast, recent workstation will have no problem sculpting very fine detail at a sufficiently high multires level, but an older computer or a midrange laptop may well become sluggish at lower multires levels. You will need to experiment with your own machine to see what vertex count it is able to handle easily in Sculpt mode.

In addition to a good computer, the other piece of hardware I recommend highly for the purposes of sculpting is a pen tablet input device. A pen tablet monitor is ideal for the most intuitive and appealing sculpting interface, but even an inexpensive USB pen tablet device is much better than a mouse for sculpting. Although the common analogy compares 3D sculpting to working with clay, the actual physical process is much more similar to painting or drawing, and as such, it is something that most people are more comfortable doing with a pen device.

SCULPTING TOOLS

When you enter Sculpt mode, several new tabs appear in the Edit buttons area. The Sculpt tab, shown in Figure 2.2, contains the main sculpting tool set.

The tools accessible in this tab are as follows:

Draw is a commonly used tool. By default, the Draw tool creates an indentation away from a raised area in the direction of the 3D view. With a texture active in the Texture panel, the Draw tool is used to draw the texture onto the surface of the mesh.

Smooth is a crucial tool for incrementally refining your mesh, as well as correcting mistakes and rough spots. The Smooth tool makes the distances and angles between vertices more uniform, effectively smoothing out inconsistencies and removing jagged areas. The Smooth tool also eliminates sculpted detail, so it should be used judiciously.

Pinch is a necessary tool for doing detail work, in particular for creating creases or sharp ridges. The Pinch tool pulls vertices toward the center of the tool's active area, causing the shape of the mesh to tighten around the line along which the Pinch tool is moved.

Inflate is similar to the untextured use of the Draw tool, except that the additive or subtractive change is along the normals of the mesh itself, rather than in relation to the 3D viewport. Consequently, the Inflate tool can be used to cause the shape of the mesh to swell or to deflate or shrink the mesh along its normals.

Grab is a simple and useful tool. The Grab tool enables the user to manually move portions of the mesh in the Grab tool's area of influence. Usually this tool is used to nudge portions of the mesh into shape or to shift their location slightly.

Layer acts as the equivalent of slapping a new layer of clay onto the shape, or, in its subtractive form, of scooping a layer of clay from the surface.

Flatten pushes vertices toward a plane perpendicular to the view, causing the mesh to become flat in the tool's area of influence.

FIGURE 2.2
The Sculpt tab

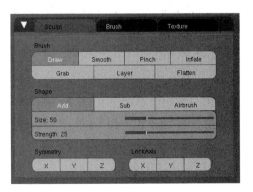

The Brush tab is shown in Figure 2.3. This tab enables you to control the shape of the brush used in the Draw tool. The dots in the panel's grid represent the curved shape of the indentation or protrusion of the Draw tool. As you can see in Figure 2.4, if these dots are arranged from upper left to lower right in a convex shape, the brush's effect is of a rounded, abrupt protrusion. The Anchored option changes the behavior of the brush with respect to the movement of the pen or mouse device. With Anchored active, the point that you begin "drawing" acts as the center of the brush's influence, and the point to which you move the pen or mouse is treated as the perimeter of the brush's influence. The result of an Anchored brush with a concave curve is shown in Figure 2.5. The arrow in that figure represents the movement of the pen or mouse device from the center of the brush's influence to its radius.

The Texture tab, shown in Figure 2.6, is where the texture that will be applied by the Draw tool is dealt with. You can load a texture here and control how that texture will be mapped to the object. The Rake option causes the texture's angle to change according to the direction of the motion of the pen or mouse device.

FIGURE 2.3
The Brush tab

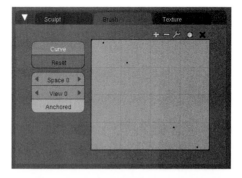

FIGURE 2.4
A convex-curved brush

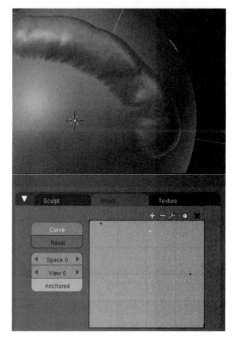

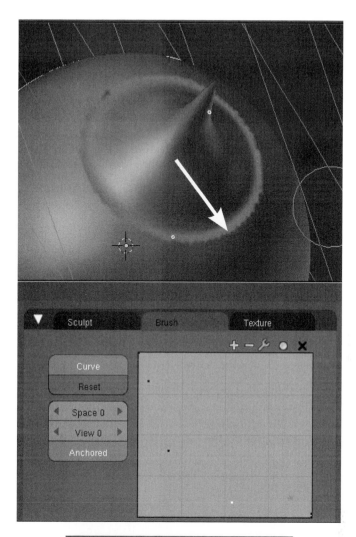

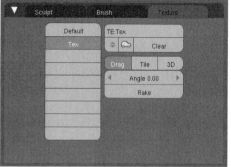

In the next section, you'll look at an in-depth example of the practical use of the primary sculpting tool set.

Sculpting a Baby's Head

The Sculpt tool is excellent for creating rough textures and uneven bumps and ridges, and for this reason, one often sees sculpted examples of demons, monsters, and old people. Unfortunately, such examples tend to leave the impression that the Sculpt tool is good *only* for this kind of modeling. To demonstrate that sculpting can also be effective for smooth organic modeling, I have gone in the other direction and used a photograph of a baby as the basis of this example.

PREPARING TO SCULPT

Before you begin the actual sculpting process, you need to prepare your mesh and reference images. To do this, follow these steps:

1. Split your modeling work area in two. In the window on the left, press 1 on the number pad to enter Front view. In the window on the right, press 3 on the number pad to enter Side view. Open the reference picture in each window by choosing View ➤ Background Image to access the Background Image panel. Click Use Background Image and then click Load, and then load the image from wherever you have it saved. You can find the image on the CD that accompanies this book in the file baby.jpg. To center the images correctly, adjust the X Offset value in the Background Image panel, as shown in Figure 2.7. In the left window, the front view of the baby's face should be centered. In the right window, the side view of the head should be centered, as shown in Figure 2.8.

2. Enter Edit mode and select all the vertices by pressing the A key. Press the W key to bring up the Specials menu and select Subdivide Smooth two times. Scale the resulting subdivided mesh to approximately match the size of the head, as shown in Figure 2.9.

FIGURE 2.7
Adjusting the X offset of the background image

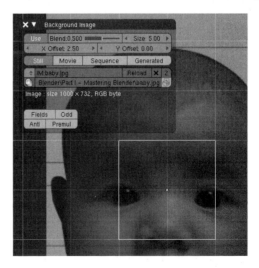

FIGURE 2.8
The reference image in front and side views

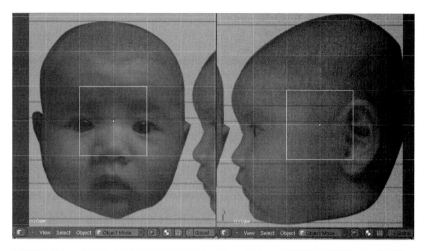

FIGURE 2.9
The subdivided cube

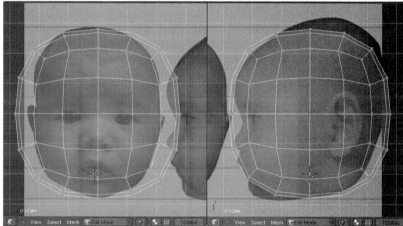

3. It is helpful to sketch out a rough shape before beginning to sculpt. Scale the whole mesh along the X axis to fit the size of the face in Front view. In Side view, select vertices in Transparent View mode to ensure that both right and left vertices are selected, and push them around to sketch out the shape of the head, as shown in Figure 2.10. The resulting mesh should look similar to Figure 2.11.

4. Now it is time to activate multires. Multires is a crucial function for sculpting because it enables Blender to store mesh information for a single mesh at multiple levels of subdivision. With multires activated, you can switch quickly between different levels of detail and add new levels of subdivision as they become necessary. To activate multires, click the Add Multires button in the Multires tab of the Edit buttons area, shown in Figure 2.12. Click the Add Level button twice to create multires levels up to level 3, as shown in Figure 2.13. In Object mode, click Set Smooth in the Links And Materials tab to make the object render smoothly in the viewport.

FIGURE 2.10
Rough editing the shape of the head

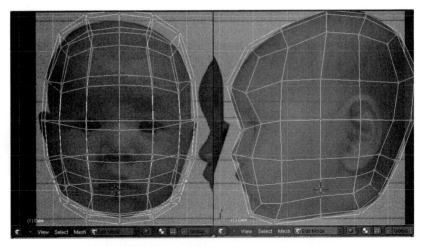

FIGURE 2.11
The base mesh for the head

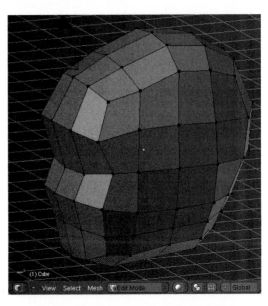

FIGURE 2.12
The Multires tab

5. You are now ready to begin sculpting. Optionally, you may wish to turn off the background grid and viewport axis lines. Do this by choosing View ➢ View Properties and disabling them in the View Properties panel, as shown in Figure 2.14. It is a good idea to keep an orthogonal front and side viewport visible with a Wireframe Mesh view so that you can see how your sculpt edits are affecting the overall shape of the mesh. Also, open

a UV/Image editor window with your reference picture in it, so that you can refer to it directly as you work. Finally, enter Sculpt mode and bring up the Sculpt buttons tab in a buttons window to have quick access to the sculpting tools. A recommended window layout is shown in Figure 2.15.

FIGURE 2.13
Multires level 3

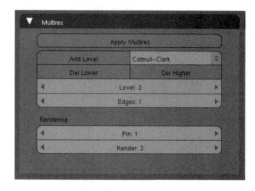

FIGURE 2.14
Adjusting view properties

FIGURE 2.15
Prepared to sculpt

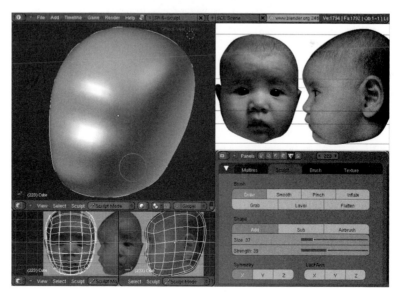

THE SCULPTING PROCESS

Sculpting, like painting a picture, is a gradual process that does not lend itself to rigid step-by-step instruction. This section describes the process in a roughly chronological order, but you should consider this section to be a collection of guidelines, techniques, and suggestions that will help you to get a clearer idea of how to progress rather than a strict series of instructions to follow. Take special note of the figures shown, in particular such values as brush size and strength at the various points in the sculpting process.

Roughing Out the Shapes

The Draw brush is used to push or pull the mesh surface directly toward or away from the viewport view axis. This is a good brush to start with for roughing out the basic shapes of your sculpture. To begin, set your brush to values like those shown in Figure 2.16. The brush is set to subtractive, with a Size value of 62 and a Strength value of 25. X symmetry is activated. X-axis symmetrical editing is similar in its effect to mirroring in Edit mode. In fact, the model is not perfectly symmetrical. Later, you will deactivate symmetrical editing and refine the whole sculpture.

FIGURE 2.16

Settings for a rough subtractive Draw brush

With the Draw brush settings as just described, begin to define the indented areas around the chin and the nose, as shown in Figure 2.17 and Figure 2.18. You may find that different brush sizes and strengths are necessary to get the shapes right. This is normal. You will adjust your brush settings often as you progress. The important thing at this point is to maintain fairly broad strokes and to keep the brush strength weak enough that you maintain control. Note also that the brush size remains constant regardless of the size of the sculpture in the view. After you begin adjusting the view of your own sculpture, the size settings you need will change. To get a sense of the brush sizes used throughout this example, pay attention to the circle representing the brush in the figures.

After you have things roughed out as well as you can at multires level 3, it is time to add another multires level and continue with the roughing. In the Multires panel, click the Add Level button and add a fourth multires level. This will enable you to sculpt in greater detail. Using the Draw brush in both additive (Add) and subtractive (Sub) modes, continue to rough out the face until it looks something like Figure 2.19. Use the additive brush to build the shape of the lips and nose, and the subtractive brush to continue to shape the indentations of the chin, around the nose, and around the eyes.

FIGURE 2.17
Roughing out the
shape of the chin

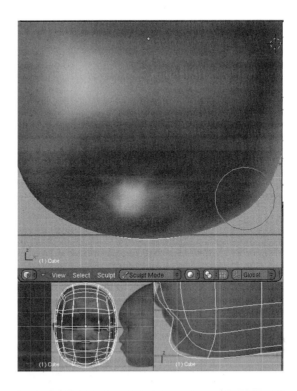

FIGURE 2.18
Roughing out
the area around
the nose

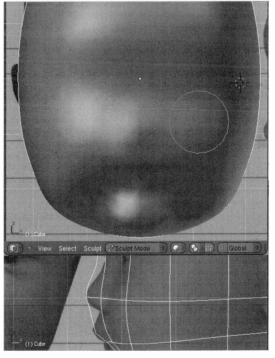

FIGURE 2.19
Additive and
subtractive Draw
brush at
multires level 4

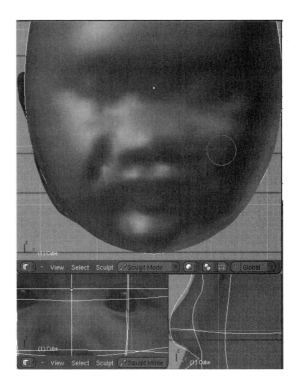

Incremental Refinement

The process of sculpting is a process of incremental refinement, and a key element of this is the Smooth brush. The Smooth brush may sometimes seem counterintuitive, because it can remove or minimize sculpt edits you have made with other brushes. Nevertheless, for the best possible results, you should use the Smooth brush frequently. Sculpt what you want, smooth it over, sculpt again, smooth again, and sculpt again until the result looks its best.

When you have gone over your rough sculpt with a light pass of smoothing (no more than 25 weight), add another multires level to bring the levels up to 5.

Another tool for incremental refinement is the Grab tool. Use this tool to push areas of the mesh in the direction of the mouse movements. Depending on the brush size you use, this can be a very powerful tool both for adjusting large areas of the mesh and for making refinements to details. In Figure 2.20, you can see the Grab tool used to refine the shape of the baby's lips. Note that the arrows should be understood as rough representations of the direction the tool is moving. The length of the arrows is an exaggeration. The actual tool motions for making these adjustments are much more subtle; just a gentle nudge is often enough.

The Layer tool is used to add a new layer of sculptable material on the surface of the object. The additive Layer tool can be thought of as analogous to slapping clay onto the surface of the object. In fact, however, this is slightly inaccurate. Like other sculpt tools, this tool does not alter any underlying geometry; it merely moves existing vertices, so the shape of the object is altered as though clay had been added. The subtractive Layer tool does the opposite. It creates an indentation of a fixed depth as though "clay" had been scooped out with a flat tool. The subtractive Layer tool can be very useful for marking out general indented shapes such as the eye area, as shown in Figure 2.21. Continue to smooth frequently.

FIGURE 2.20
The Grab tool

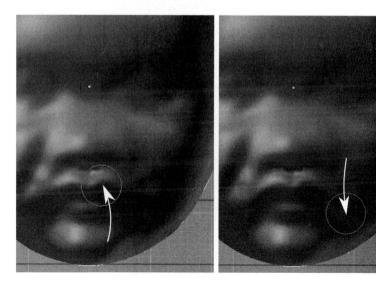

Using the Grease Pencil Tool for Reference Sketching

As you begin to indicate the shape of things like eyes, a problem becomes apparent. Although you have a photographic reference in the Image editor to work from by hand, it is not really straightforward to trace directly from the background image. You can sculpt in Wireframe view by entering Object mode, switching to Wireframe, and reentering Sculpt mode. The density of the wireframe depends on the Edges value in the Multires buttons tab. However, this is not ideal. Sculpting in wireframe is much less intuitive than sculpting with a solid object. When sculpting, it is important to be looking at a shaded surface to get a full sense of the way the surface's shape is changing.

FIGURE 2.21
Using the subtractive Layer tool to indicate the eye area

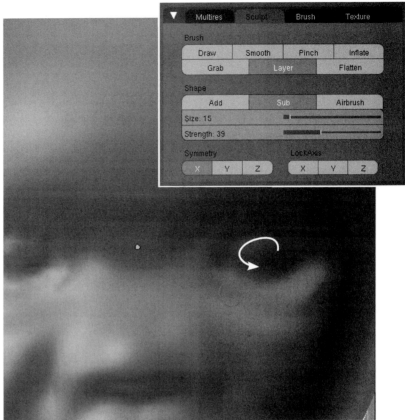

The simple solution to this dilemma is to use Blender's Grease Pencil feature. The Grease Pencil is a general-purpose tool that enables you to write annotations directly on the 3D view. You can set these annotations to remain with respect to the 3D viewport window or to be fixed in their position in 3D space, in which case you can dolly, zoom, or pan around them just like ordinary 3D objects. Grease Pencil is an invaluable tool for animators and people working in collaborative environments, and it is also useful for sculpting.

To use the Grease Pencil tool to set up reference sketches, follow these steps:

1. Enter Object mode. In Side view, place the 3D cursor directly in front of the sculpted face object by clicking the left mouse button (LMB), as shown in Figure 2.22. When you use the Grease Pencil tool to sketch in 3D, the 3D cursor defines the invisible plane upon which the Grease Pencil writes. In this case, the Grease Pencil writing should be in front of the object, so that is where the 3D cursor should be set.

2. Press the Z key to toggle the view to wireframe. Select Grease Pencil from the View menu in the 3D Viewport header, as shown in Figure 2.23. The Grease Pencil panel appears over

the 3D Viewport, as shown in Figure 2.24. Click Use Grease Pencil and select the Sketch In 3D option. Click Draw Mode to begin drawing with the Grease Pencil tool.

FIGURE 2.22
Place the 3D cursor in front of the sculpted face object.

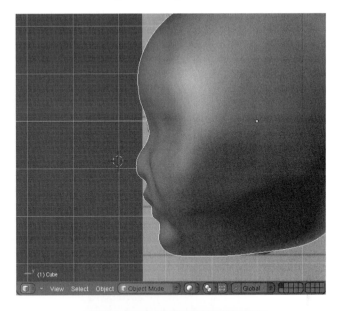

FIGURE 2.23
Selecting Grease Pencil from the View menu

3. Begin drawing with the Grease Pencil. The idea here is to sketch out the location of things to use for references, such as the eye outline shown in Figure 2.25. When you begin drawing, a new Grease Pencil layer is created automatically. You can also create separate Grease Pencil layers by clicking Add New Layer. Each layer can be deleted independently of the others and has its own property settings including color, opacity, and thickness of the lines, and whether the Grease Pencil will be treated as onionskin annotations over multiple frames.

4. Continue to sketch out the eyes, nose, and mouth, as shown in Figure 2.26. Give a hint of the main topological reference points of the face. Do the same thing in Side view, as shown in Figure 2.27. Remember to place your 3D cursor correctly to control where the Grease Pencil annotations appear in space. When you are satisfied with the reference

annotations for both Front and Side view, turn the Grease Pencil opacity down so that the annotations are less obtrusive. You should wind up with a set of annotations that look something like the ones shown in Figure 2.28.

FIGURE 2.24
The Grease
Pencil panel

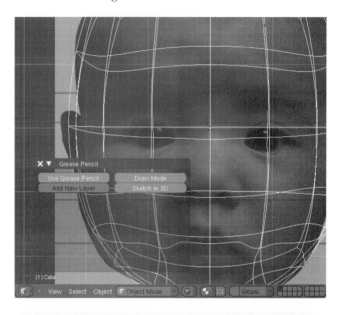

FIGURE 2.25
Sketching the
eye outline with
Grease Pencil

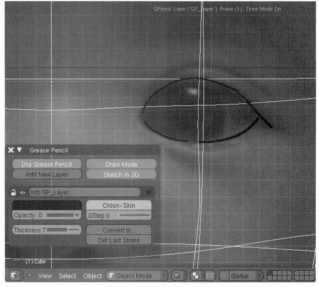

5. You can now continue your modeling with reference to the annotations. In Figure 2.29, you can see how the Grab tool is used to pull the mesh around the cheek area, toward the Grease Pencil annotation that indicates where the cheek should be.

GREASE PENCIL AND FRAME CHANGES

A primary use of the Grease Pencil tool is for animators to make annotations directly on their animations. For this reason, the tool is sensitive to the frame on which the annotations are made. Annotations on a given layer persist through frames until the next frame on which an annotation has been written. For example, if you draw a square while in frame 1 on the Timeline, the square will persist through all subsequent frames. However, if you move forward to frame 10 on the Timeline and draw a circle on the same Grease Pencil layer, the square will disappear on that frame and be replaced by the new annotation with the circle. After that, frames 1 through 9 will display the original square annotation, and frames from 10 on will display the circle annotation. If you want to further annotate the square itself, you must make the annotations in the same frame where the original square was drawn, namely frame 1. Onionskin enables you to see multiple frames' worth of annotations at the same time, as though through semitransparent onionskin overlays. When making reference sketches for sculpting, Onionskin should be disabled and you should make all your Grease Pencil annotations while on frame 1 on the Timeline.

FIGURE 2.26
Reference sketches
in Front view

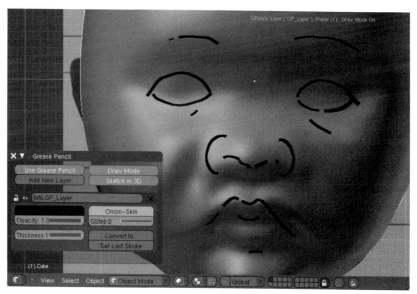

FIGURE 2.27
Reference sketches
in Side view

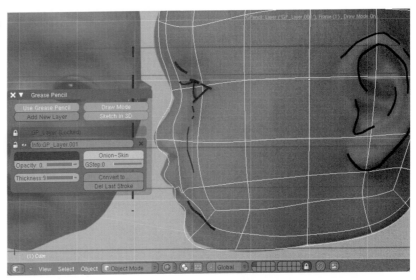

FIGURE 2.28
Front and side
sketches viewed
in 3D

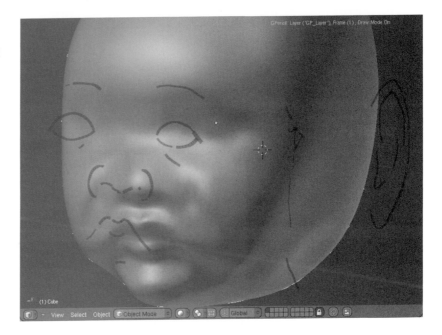

FIGURE 2.29
Filling out the cheek with the Grab tool

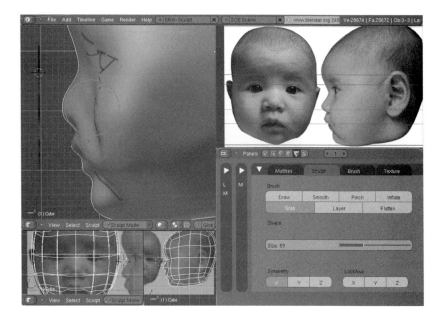

Adding Eyeballs

The simplest way to deal with eyeballs is to use ordinary mesh spheres. Add a mesh sphere in Object mode by pressing the spacebar and choosing Add ➤ Mesh ➤ UV Sphere. Add a UV sphere with 12 segments and 12 rings. Set the sphere in place as an eyeball and adjust its size and position from Side view with reference to your Grease Pencil annotations, as shown in Figure 2.30. Use the Grab tool to adjust the mesh around the eye, as shown in Figure 2.31.

FIGURE 2.30
Eyeball from the side

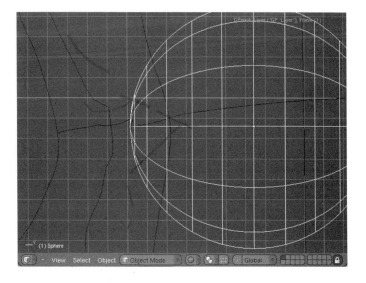

Adding the second eyeball is simply a matter of using Shift+D to duplicate the first eyeball, and then pressing the X key to constrain its translation to the X axis. Position the two eyes as shown in Figure 2.32.

FIGURE 2.31
Using the Grab tool to adjust the mesh around the eye

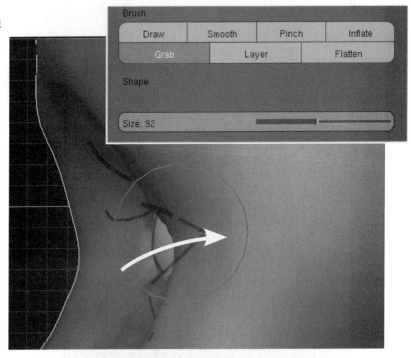

FIGURE 2.32
Two eyes

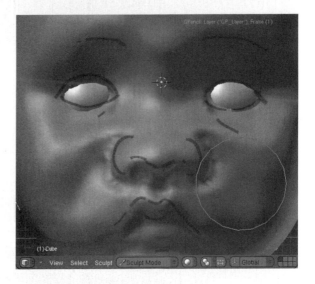

Use Draw mode, Inflate mode, and Grab mode to get the area around the eye to match the Grease Pencil annotations from all angles and to expose the correct amount of eyeball. At this point, you should have X-axis symmetry turned off, and you should be paying attention to the asymmetries of the face.

It is often helpful to set the eyeball object to display only in wireframe, as shown in Figure 2.33, particularly when refining the details of the edge of the eyelids. Do this by selecting Wire Drawtype on the Draw tab in the Object buttons area.

FIGURE 2.33
The eyeball in wireframe

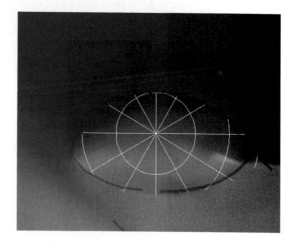

Refining the Nose, Mouth, and Eyes

As mentioned previously, good digital sculpting is a repeated process of rough modeling, smoothing, and refinement. The nose areas, mouth, and eyes all involve the same kind of incremental approach. From this point on, the multires level that you use will depend on what specific level of detail you are trying to refine. Obviously, the higher the multires level, the finer the detail you will be able to work with, but after a certain point, your hardware will limit how easily you can work with high resolutions. You will have to experiment with what your computer is capable of. Also remember that the multires level itself is not what determines the slowdown, but rather the number of vertices. If you have already subdivided a mesh before adding multires, then the number of vertices will obviously be higher at each progressive multires level. The highest multires level used in the example in this section is level 7.

In Figure 2.34, you can see how the subtractive Draw tool is used to roughly etch out the indentation around the edge of the nose. Again, after making the rough sculpt, go over the area with the Smooth tool as shown in Figure 2.35.

The Pinch tool is an important tool for creating creases and sharp edges. The Pinch tool pulls the mesh toward its center. When run along a bulge, the Pinch tool will create an edge; when run along the length of an indentation, it will pinch the indentation into the form of a crease. Use the Pinch tool as shown in Figure 2.36 to define the crease around the nose.

A similar approach should be taken with the mouth. Figure 2.37 shows the Inflate tool being used to add volume to the lips and the ridges under the nose. The Inflate tool is similar to the Draw tool except that instead of pulling the mesh toward or away from the view, it inflates or deflates the mesh along the mesh normals. The differences can be subtle, but they make Inflate a better tool for adding volume in cases like this. After the lips are smoothed with the Smooth tool, the Pinch tool is used to define both the ridges along the edge of the lips and the crease between the top and bottom lips, as shown in Figure 2.38. Note that both of these are done with the Pinch tool in additive mode. Subtractive mode for the Pinch tool pushes the mesh away from the tool's center and is not as frequently used as the additive mode.

The same basic methodology is used to model the eyelids. In Figure 2.39, you can see the process of adding ridges with the Draw tool, smoothing them with the Smooth tool, and then defining the crease with the Pinch tool.

FIGURE 2.34

Rough indentations around the nose

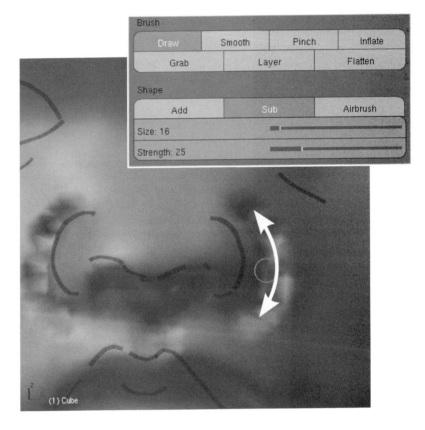

FIGURE 2.35
Smoothing the
edges of the nose

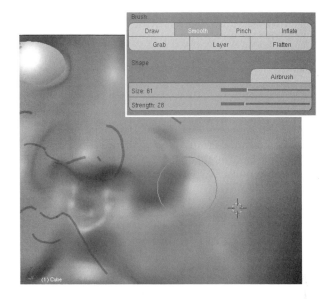

FIGURE 2.36
Defining the crease
with the Pinch tool

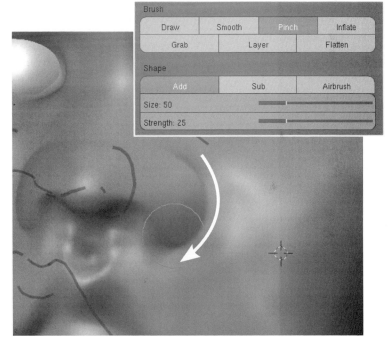

FIGURE 2.37
Adding shape to
the lips with the
Inflate tool

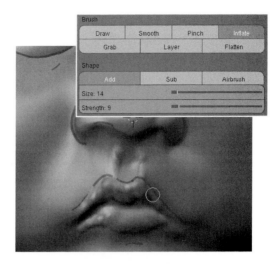

FIGURE 2.38
Adding definition
with the Pinch tool

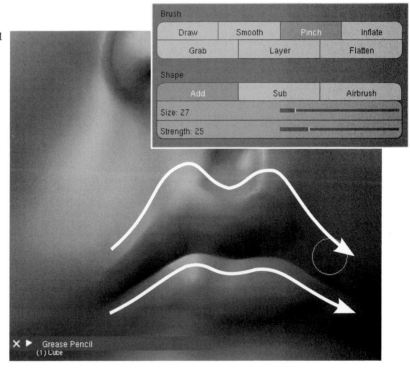

FIGURE 2.39
Adding the crease
above the eye

Modeling Ears

To model ears, first make sure that your tools have X-axis symmetry activated, so you don't have to model them twice. Begin the process by sketching out the shape of the ear with the additive Layer tool. This will start to raise the surface of the mesh in the shape of the ear to give you some material to work with, as shown in Figure 2.40. Follow the guidelines you drew with the Grease Pencil.

The shape of the ear is further sculpted using the additive Draw tool for the areas that protrude and the subtractive Draw tool for the recesses, as shown in Figure 2.41. Note that the front-view image used in this example is slightly foreshortened. The ears should protrude slightly more than they appear to in the photograph.

FIGURE 2.40
Beginning the ear
with the Layer tool

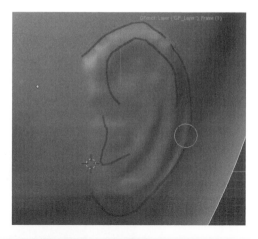

FIGURE 2.41
Adding shape with
additive and sub-
tractive Draw tools

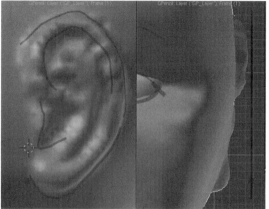

FIGURE 2.42
Adding more detail
with the Layer and
Draw tools

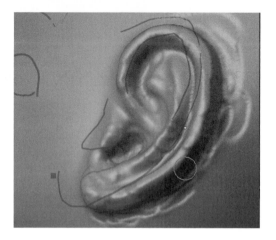

Use a light pass of the Smooth tool continually to keep the mesh tensions as balanced as possible. After you've coaxed the shape of the ear fully out of the side of the head, use whatever tools you need to get the shape right. The sculpting in Figure 2.42 used both additive and subtractive Layer and Draw tools as well as the Grab tool.

As you model, vertices become bunched up and the surface becomes rough. Regular use of the Smooth tool is necessary to keep the mesh looking good. In Figure 2.43, you can see how the ear looks when it has been freshly smoothed. Some detail is always lost when you smooth, so you will need to go back over the mesh with another pass of sculpting to get it back.

FIGURE 2.43
The smoothed ear

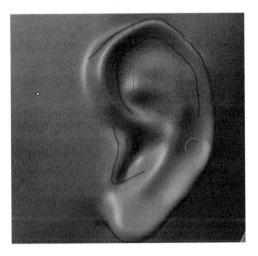

For an intricate object like a human ear, paying close attention to a photographic reference is invaluable. Finalize the details of the ear as shown in Figure 2.44. Edges and creases are created using the Pinch tool, and the overall shape can be easily adjusted using the Grab tool set to a brush about half the size of the ear itself or slightly more.

The final sculpted object, with a clay material added, should look something like the one shown in Figure 2.45. You can find the sculpted object (and the clay material used) on the CD that accompanies this book, in the file baby.blend.

FIGURE 2.44
Further refinement

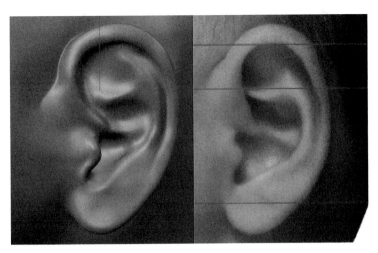

Forging Out on Your Own

Like playing the tuba or juggling zucchinis, digital sculpting is something that you can't really learn just by reading about it. This section has presented an overview of Blender sculpting techniques in action. These are the techniques you will need to master in order to get the most out of this powerful tool. Don't expect too much of your first attempt at sculpting. You will improve by leaps and bounds with just a little bit of practice. Stick with it, and very soon you will find that sculpting in Blender comes as naturally as drawing a picture.

 Real World Scenario

BLENDER SCULPTING TOOLS AND THE GOOGLE SUMMER OF CODE

The integration of multiresolution modeling and sculpting tools into Blender is thanks in large part to Google's annual Summer of Code program, which the Blender Foundation takes part in regularly. The Summer of Code program is intended in part to encourage student programmers to contribute to open source projects by providing them with stipends to carry out development on accepted proposals over the course of a summer. For each of the past four years, the program has sponsored hundreds of students from dozens of countries to develop code for over a hundred different open source software projects. The sculpting and multiresolution functionality in Blender was implemented under the auspices of the 2006 Summer of Code grant by Nicholas Bishop, who had previously been known for his creation of the open source sculpting application SharpConstruct. His mentor for that project was Jean-Luc Peurière.

Google and Nicholas's involvement with Blender's sculpting functionality didn't end with the 2006 Summer of Code either. Nicholas was back again in 2008 with another accepted proposal, this time for editable topology for multiresolution models. When this has been fully implemented, it will be possible to not just sculpt the models and push their vertices around, but to add, delete, subdivide, and extrude the mesh as well, all while keeping the multiresolution levels and sculpted details intact! Keep your eye on upcoming Blender releases for these exciting new features, courtesy of the Google Summer of Code.

FIGURE 2.45
The finished
sculpture

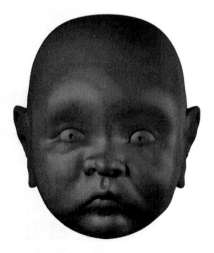

Using the Retopo Tool

At the end of the sculpting process, you will have a detailed sculpture. There's a problem, though. The detailed sculpture, at its highest multires level, is composed of a very large number of vertices. If you enter Edit mode with the object selected, you will see that the mesh is nearly solidly packed with vertices. (Be warned: Entering Edit mode on a high-resolution mesh may bring your system to its knees!) If you reduce the multires level, the sculpt detail also disappears. What's more, the fundamental geometry has not changed since the first time you subdivided the default cube. There's nothing resembling edge loops or the kind of shape-based topology that polygon models require for good deformation and animation. In short, there's not a lot you can do with the sculpted mesh as it is.

The solution to this problem is to use Blender's remake topology (retopo) feature. Retopo enables you to create a completely new mesh topology whose shape is identical to the sculpted mesh.

To use retopo to create a mesh of the baby's head with good geometry and a lower polygon count, follow these steps:

1. In Object mode, select the completed sculpted object, press Shift+S, and then choose Cursor To Selection to snap the 3D cursor to the object's center, as shown in Figure 2.46. Press the spacebar and choose Add ➢ Mesh ➢ Cube to add a cube object to the scene, as shown in Figure 2.47. By default in Blender 2.48, new objects are added in Edit mode with all vertices selected. If this is not the case with your settings, enter Edit mode, select all vertices with the A key, and then press the X key to delete them all.

FIGURE 2.46
Snapping the cursor to the sculpted object

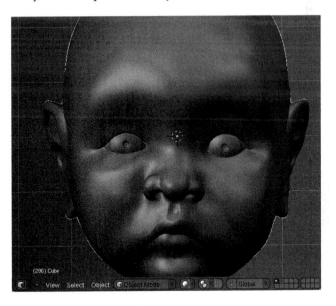

2. Activate retopo by clicking the Retopo button in the Mesh panel of the Edit buttons area, as shown in Figure 2.48. There are a couple of options associated with retopo. Retopo All will snap any selected vertices to the mesh below, all at once. The Paint option will enable you to draw on the 3D view in a way analogous to the way you did with the Grease

Pencil, and the lines you draw will be automatically converted to geometry. This is useful for quickly drawing large segments of geometry at once. In this example, you'll proceed in a more poly-by-poly way, so leave Paint unselected.

FIGURE 2.47
Adding a cube

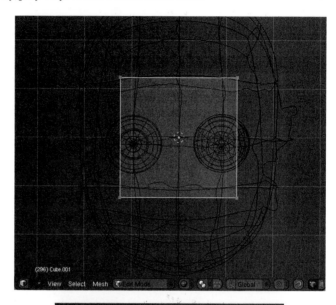

FIGURE 2.48
Activating retopo

3. Retopo works by evaluating the contents of the Z buffer and snapping vertices to the mesh below, along the view axis. For this reason, it is best to work with your view directly facing the portion of the mesh you are editing. Begin with the viewport in Orthogonal view (the 5 key on the number pad toggles between Orthogonal and Perspective views) and facing directly at the face of the model. Add a vertex to the cheek of the model by holding down the Ctrl key and clicking the LMB. The resulting vertex will appear as shown in Figure 2.49. If you rotate around your 3D space now, you will see that the vertex is placed on the surface of the baby's cheek.

FIGURE 2.49
Adding a single
vertex with
Ctrl+LMB

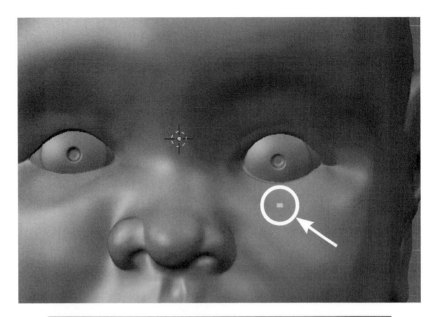

FIGURE 2.50
Extruding vertices
around the eyes

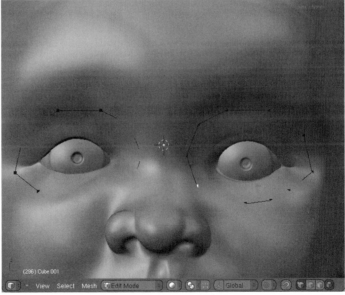

4. Add a Mirror modifier. Although the actual mesh is not perfectly symmetrical, it will be
   helpful to have the basic geometry mirrored as you go. Later, you will make the nonsym-
   metrical adjustments. With the Mirror modifier applied, begin extruding vertices from
   the original vertex you placed, using either the E key to extrude or Ctrl+LMB. Extrude
   around the eyes as shown in Figure 2.50.

5. You may notice at this point that some of the edges and vertices are concealed under the surface of the sculpted mesh. To see what you're working on, set the Draw Extra value to X-ray on the Draw tab of the Object buttons area, as shown in Figure 2.51. The mesh will then become completely visible. Extrude edges to create faces as shown in Figure 2.52.

6. This book assumes that you know the fundamentals of mesh modeling. If you are feeling uncertain about the basic mesh modeling tools, please refer to my book *Introducing Character Animation with Blender* (Sybex, 2007), which includes extensive in-depth modeling tutorials that cover both box modeling and poly-by-poly extrusion modeling of the kind used in this example. Assuming that you have basic mesh-modeling skills, it should be straightforward to mimic the topology you see in Figure 2.53. Model the eyes as shown in Figure 2.54. The geometry of the nose is shown in Figure 2.55. Extend the model around the back of the head as shown in Figure 2.56. Finally, model the ear as shown in Figure 2.57.

FIGURE 2.51
The Draw Extra
X-ray option

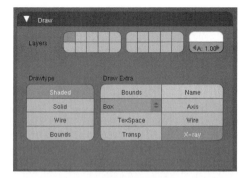

FIGURE 2.52
Creating faces
by extrusion

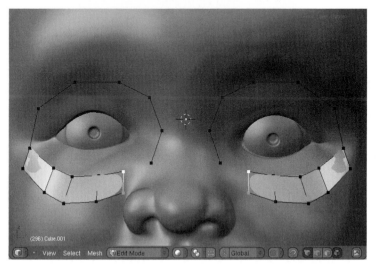

FIGURE 2.53
Geometry around
the eyes, nose,
and mouth

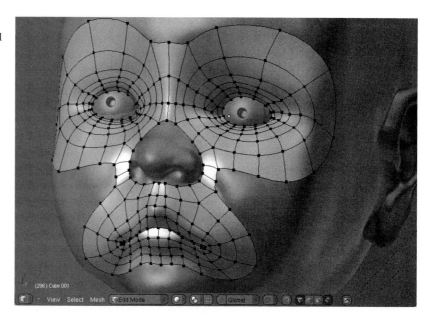

FIGURE 2.54
Eye geometry

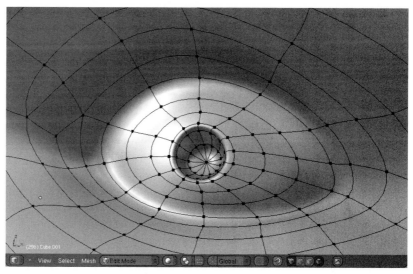

7. The full mirrored mesh should look something like the one shown in Figure 2.58. Apply the Mirror modifier by clicking the corresponding Apply button on the Modifier panel. The retopo snapping will not happen automatically on the mirrored half of the model, but if you begin pushing vertices around, you'll find that they will snap to the surface of the sculpted object, just as the first half did. Tweak each vertex lightly on the applied mirrored portion of the mesh, until the retopo model more accurately captures the asymmetries of the sculpted model.

FIGURE 2.55
A closer look at
the nose

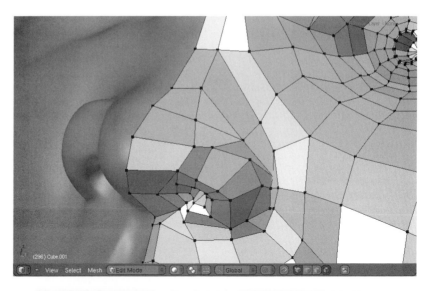

FIGURE 2.56
The topology of
the head

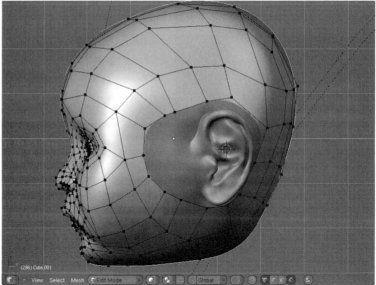

8. You may have noticed at this point that the retopo mesh appears smaller than the original mesh. That's because it is, in a way. Retopo works by sticking the vertices of the new mesh to the surface of the sculpted mesh. But the vertices of a subsurfaced mesh like the one in the example here do not represent the actual surface of the mesh as it is rendered. Rather, they represent the *modeling cage*—that is, the tension points that hold the subsurfaced surface in place. As you can see in Figure 2.59, if these modeling cage verts are flush

with the surface of the target mesh, the subdivided surface will be smaller. This effect diminishes with the density of the mesh. If you want the shape to be more accurate, add some extra geometry in the areas that need it.

FIGURE 2.57
The ear

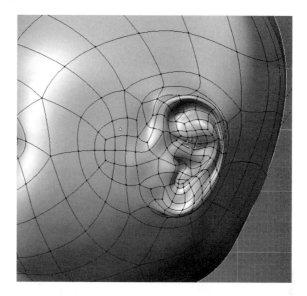

FIGURE 2.58
The mirrored mesh

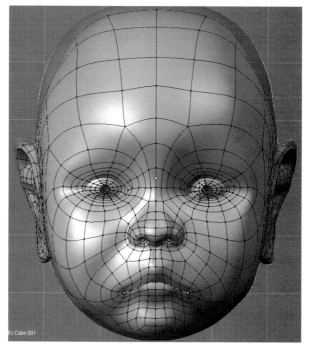

9. The finished retopo-modeled mesh should look something like the one shown in Figure 2.60 with a clay material applied. When you are finished using retopo, disable it to reduce the likelihood of problems when zooming later.

Notice that the asymmetry of the original is represented, but the finer details such as the slight wrinkling of the forehead and dimpling under the lower lip are not found in the new model. In the next section, you'll see how to deal with this.

POTENTIAL RETOPO PROBLEMS

Retopo relies on calculations of the Z buffer in the 3D viewport. A number of problems can occur if the tool becomes "confused" about the relative Z position of things. One problem can arise during retopo editing if you zoom the viewport scene by holding Ctrl and the middle mouse button while vertices are selected. If you do this, the selected vertices can get pulled out of position. Simply pressing Ctrl+Z will undo the damage, but it is still best to avoid zooming the 3D view with vertices selected when retopo is activated. Other problems are less predictable. The Z buffer error shown here is an example.

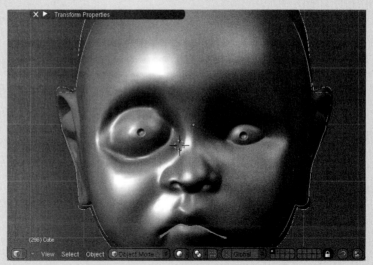

If you begin to realize that your retopo mesh is not taking the correct shape of the sculpted target mesh, disable retopo, move the vertices away from the sculpted mesh, and then enable retopo again and place the vertices back where they belong. Clearing the retopo should get things sorted out and get you back on track.

FIGURE 2.59
The retopo
mesh cage

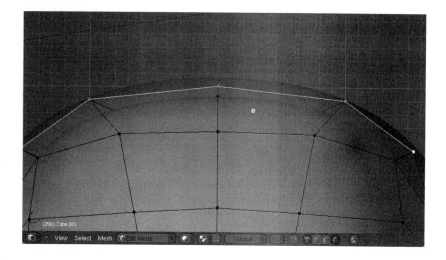

FIGURE 2.60
The finished
retopo mesh

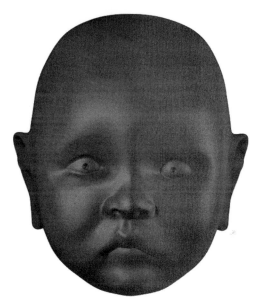

Normal Map Baking

You now know how to create a lower-poly, nicely topological mesh with the same shape as a high-resolution sculpted mesh. But there's an obvious drawback. Without the high-resolution, finely subdivided mesh, a lot of the detail you sculpted is lost. It would seem that this process would at least partially defeat the whole point of sculpting in the first place. Fortunately, this is not the case. Using Blender's *normal map-baking* functionality enables you to capture these details and represent them as two-dimensional textures mapped to the surface of your retopo mesh.

To do this, follow these steps:

1. In order to UV-map a texture to a shape like the head in the example, it is necessary to UV-unwrap the head. This requires marking seams. Blender has a convenient tool for marking seams. In the Mesh Tools More panel of the Edit buttons area, you will find the Edge Alt-Select Mode drop-down menu. By default, holding down the Alt key while clicking the right mouse button (RMB) on an edge of a mesh selects edge loops. By changing the Edge Alt-Select Mode in this menu to Tag Edges (Seam) as shown in Figure 2.61, you can change this functionality to make Alt+RMB automatically add seams to edges. Each time you press Alt+RMB on an edge, the shortest path between that edge and the previously marked seam will be marked as a seam.

2. Mark the seams on the head as shown in Figure 2.62. This will result in relatively undistorted unwrapping into three islands: one for the face, and one for each ear.

FIGURE 2.61
The Edge Alt-Select
Mode menu

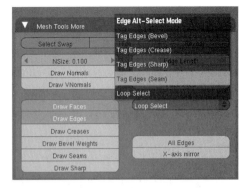

FIGURE 2.62
Marking seams

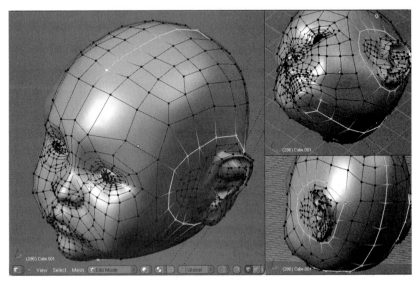

3. Open a UV/Image editor window. In the Image menu in the header of the UV/Image editor window, select New. In the New Image dialog box, set the Width and Height values to **1024** and select UV Test Grid, as shown in Figure 2.63. Click OK to create the test grid image in the window.

FIGURE 2.63
Creating a
new image

4. In the 3D view, select all the vertices of the mesh by pressing the A key, and then add a new UV texture by clicking New next to UV Texture on the Mesh buttons panel, as shown in Figure 2.64. Put your mouse over the UV/Image editor window and press the E key to unwrap the mesh. The resulting UV unwrapping should look similar to what's shown in Figure 2.65. Switch the Draw mode to Textured with the menu in the 3D viewport window header to see how the texture maps onto the surface of the mesh, as shown in Figure 2.66 (a color print of this image can be found in the color insert of this book).

FIGURE 2.64
Adding a UV texture to the mesh

FIGURE 2.65
The unwrapped
mesh

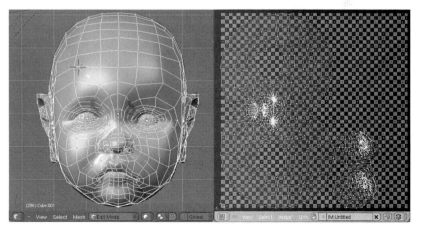

5. This step is where the magic happens. Tab into Object mode, select the original sculpted mesh, and then hold down the Shift key and select the new retopoed mesh. Go to the Bake tab in the Render buttons area, as shown in Figure 2.67. Click the Normals button on the right side of the tab. Select Tangent from the drop-down menu on the left side of the tab, and click Selected To Active to bake the Normals from the selected object (the sculpted mesh) to the active object (the retopoed mesh). Click Bake. Before your eyes, a normal map will be rendered to the UV test grid image you created previously, as shown in Figure 2.68. (This image is also included in full color in the color insert of this book.) Save this image to an actual image file by choosing Save from the Image menu in the header.

FIGURE 2.66
The mesh with
UV texture

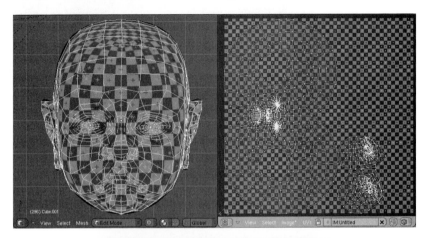

FIGURE 2.67
The Bake tab

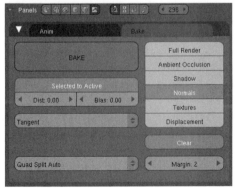

6. You now have a normal map texture to apply to the material on the retopoed mesh. Create an Image texture on the material, load the normal map in the Image tab of the Texture buttons, and select Normal Map and Tangent on the Map Image tab, as shown in Figure 2.69. The texture should be set to UV on the Map Input tab of the Material buttons and to Nor on the Map To tab, with a Nor value of 1.00, as shown in Figure 2.70.

FIGURE 2.68
The baked
normal map

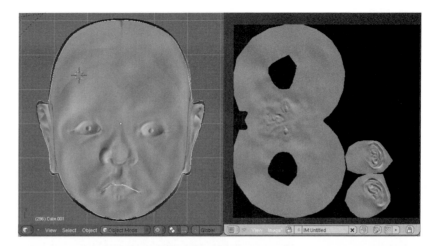

FIGURE 2.69
The texture set-
tings for the nor-
mal map

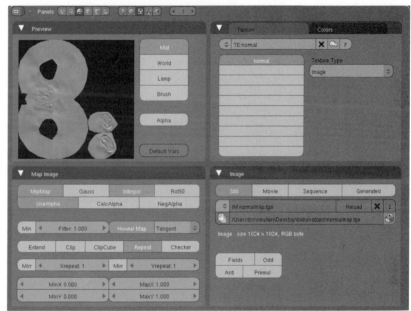

7. Render the image to see the results. As you will see, the normal map creates the illusion of detail on the surface of the lower-poly mesh. In the final render, the retopoed eyeballs have also been replaced by the original spheres. You can see all three renders side by side in Figure 2.71, which is repeated in the color insert of this book.

FIGURE 2.70
The material mapping settings for the normal map

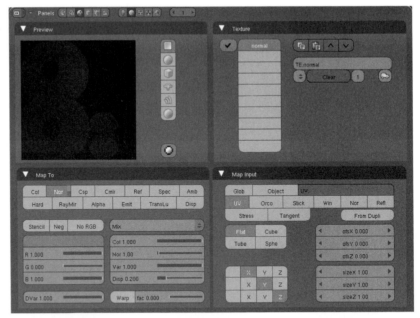

FIGURE 2.71
From left to right: high-resolution sculpt, retopoed lower-poly mesh, and retopoed mesh with normal mapping

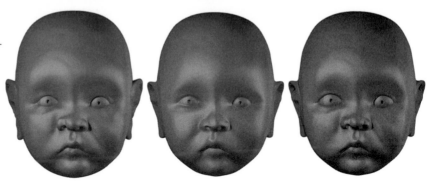

SAVE YOUR BAKED IMAGES!

It bears repeating that you must save baked images (such as normal maps) as image files, or risk losing them when you close and reopen Blender. The same goes for images that are painted within Blender by using the Texture Paint feature. Simply packing external data into the .blend file alone will *not* persist the images, because they do not exist as external data until they have been saved as such!

You now have one more powerful tool at your disposal for mesh modeling. As you've seen throughout this chapter, materials and textures are crucially linked to the modeling process. In the next chapter, you will learn much more about working with materials and textures to get exactly the effects you are after.

The Bottom Line

Get the most out of Blender's sculpting functionality.   Blender's multires modeling and sculpting features provide a powerful and versatile set of tools for 3D sculpting.

Master It   Nothing is more important than practice for improving your skills at sculpting. Following the guidelines in this chapter, create at least three more sculptures of human heads. Try sculpting old people, women, and men. Try working from orthogonal references as described in this chapter and also try freehand from informal photographs. When you're comfortable with heads, experiment with working on full-body sculptures. Note your impressions on the differences between the various subject matters and how they are sculpted.

Use retopo to convert a sculpted form into a polygon model with correct edge loop geometry. Blender's retopo feature enables you to create a new model whose shape is identical to another object, making it possible to recast a very high polygon sculpted object into a lower-polygon model with elegant edge loop geometry that can be easily deformed, animated, and rendered.

Master It   Select the model you are most happy with from the previous exercise and use retopo to create a lower-poly model of the same shape. Pay attention to edge loop geometry and keep the density of the mesh as low as you can while representing the underlying shape as accurately as possible.

Use normal map baking to capture finely sculpted detail for use on a low-poly model.   In order to represent the detail of a very high poly sculpted object, Blender enables you to bake the surface normal information of the sculpted object onto a 2D texture called a normal map, which is then used as a UV texture on the lower-poly model, yielding the illusion of a highly detailed surface.

Master It   Follow the steps described in this chapter to bake a normal map from your sculpted object to the retopoed model you created in the previous exercise.

Chapter 3

Creating Realistic Images with UV Textures and Node-Based Materials

The sculpting and retopo tools described in Chapter 2, "Sculpting and Retopo Workflow," enable you to represent a high degree of detail in your mesh models. However, modeling alone can attain only a certain degree of realism. Representing the surface properties of objects and the way the light behaves when it strikes them is vitally important to creating realistic images in Blender. To do this well, you must understand how to create textures and materials that look convincing. Furthermore, you have to master a few crucial tricks of 2D image manipulation when using the most powerful texture-creation tools. Blender has several powerful features that enable you to quickly and easily create seamless UV textures, and to combine them in convincing, realistic materials, but for the 2D images themselves, you will turn to another open source application: GIMP.

In this chapter, you will learn to

◆ Use Blender's texture-mapping functionality effectively

◆ Mix textures to create almost any surface effect

◆ Make the most of the Blender material system to create complex materials and shaders

Creating UV Textures with Blender and GIMP

Anyone who tries to create even simple images with any degree of realism in Blender will quickly realize the limitations of materials on their own. Blender's material and shader system enables you to have a great deal of control over the innate properties of a material such as specularity, reflectivity, transparency, and even subsurface scattering properties. Nevertheless, the uniformity of an untextured material is immediately recognizable. Real objects in the real world are not perfectly even in their color, shininess, or other properties—they have bumps, scratches, pores, indentations, and a host of other imperfections that testify to their physical interaction with the world around them. In Blender, such qualities of the surfaces of objects are represented by textures. Learning to create textures and have them interact with each other in the context of materials is a crucial aspect of learning to create truly convincing models and images.

Textures and Texture Mapping

All textures are represented as 2D patterns that influence the material of the surface of a mesh. Broadly speaking, there are two kinds of textures used in Blender: *procedural textures* and *image-based textures*. These two types of patterns have different effects and are used in very different ways.

In the case of procedural textures, the patterns are determined by a mathematical formula or algorithm. Working with procedural textures involves manipulating the parameters to the formula and adjusting how the resulting pattern will affect the material. In many cases, the formula for the procedural texture's pattern in fact results in a three-dimensional pattern, and that pattern's cross-section at the plane where it intersects the mesh surface is treated as its 2D manifestation. Blender's Clouds texture is a good example of this. Mapping a procedural texture to an object is a matter of determining the orientation of the pattern with respect to the mesh and with respect to the 3D space as a whole. Procedural textures, in general, are easy to work with, but they are also limited in the kinds of patterns and variations they allow.

Image-based textures use a 2D image such as a photograph, a hand-drawn image, or an image generated in some other way. In the case of images, a *mapping* is a correspondence between 2D points on the image and points on the 2D surface of the textured mesh. There are several set ways to map a rectangular image to a 3D surface. In Blender, the built-in mappings are a plane, a cube, a tube, and a sphere, as shown in Figure 3.1. Note that the image texture and the mesh are the same in all four cases. The only difference is the mapping—that is to say, the way that the 2D coordinates of the texture are translated onto the 2D coordinates of the surface of the mesh.

FIGURE 3.1
Plane, cube, tube, and sphere texture mappings

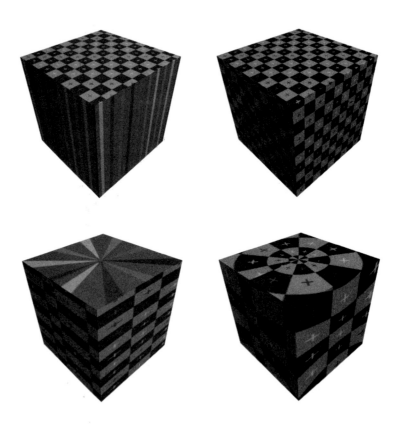

These built-in mappings are very useful for appropriate tasks. For example, a rectangular image of the surface of the earth can easily be mapped onto a sphere by using Blender's sphere mapping. Nevertheless, it should be obvious that these set mappings have their own limitations. For shapes that are not easily analogous to simple planes, cubes, tubes, or spheres, these mappings do not offer sufficient control over where the texture is applied to the mesh.

UV Mapping

For the kind of texturing you see in Figure 3.2 (a color version of this image is included in the book's color insert), it is necessary to have complete control over where every texture is applied to every part of the mesh. For this, a special kind of texture mapping exists, called UV mapping.

FIGURE 3.2
A UV-textured model (background skymap by M@dcow from BlenderArtists.org)

UV mapping derives its name from the 2D coordinate system describing the surface of the mesh. In traditional 2D environments, coordinates are described in terms of X and Y. However, in a 3D environment, X, Y, and Z are used to describe the 3D space. Another set of coordinates is required to describe the surface of the mesh, so the letters U and V are used. Logically, the third dimension in this coordinate system, W, would extend along the vertex normals of the mesh; however, this coordinate name is not used in Blender.

The idea behind UV mapping is to create the mapping between the 2D UV surface of the mesh and the 2D image by hand, albeit with a number of powerful tools at your disposal. Indeed, Blender's UV-mapping tools are among the best in the industry. The process at its simplest involves three steps: unwrapping the mesh, creating the texture, and applying the texture to the mesh. The unwrapping step is the key to the mapping, and requires that the mesh be correctly prepared in advance with seams to indicate where cuts will be made in order to flatten the surface with minimal distortion. The process of creating the texture is typically done outside of Blender, in a 2D image-manipulation application such as GIMP. In this chapter, you will follow the steps to do all of these things, but with an added twist that will involve using Blender's powerful texture-baking features to reprocess the images and remove all visible seams left from the initial mapping process.

Texturing a Locomotive Smokestack

In the next few sections, you'll focus on texturing a specific object, the smokestack from the locomotive model shown highlighted in Figure 3.3. The locomotive model itself is made up of several 3D objects, and the unadorned smokestack shown in Figure 3.4 can be found on its own in the file smokestack_no_mats.blend on the CD that accompanies this book.

FIGURE 3.3
The smokestack object

FIGURE 3.4
The smokestack with no materials

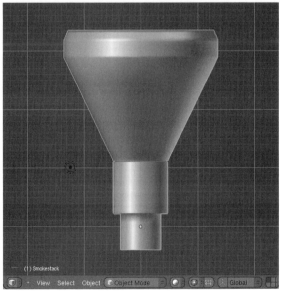

To complete the following tutorial for creating a basic UV texture, you will use both Blender and GIMP. An installation of GIMP is included on the CD that accompanies this book, or you can download it from www.gimp.org/downloads or from http://gimp.lisanet.de/Website/Download.html for Mac OS X installations. After you have installed the software, open the smokestack.blend file and follow these steps:

1. To create a flat UV mapping, you need to define places on the 3D mesh where the geometry will be "cut," as you saw in Chapter 2 when unwrapping the baby's head mesh. This is done by adding seams. As you learned in Chapter 2, there are several options for the Alt+Select mode found in the Mesh Tools More panel, including an option for automatically laying down seams between selected edges. However, in this case, the selected edges are much simpler, and it will be quickest just to use the default Loop selection to select the edge loops and add seams manually. To select an edge loop, hold down the Alt key while right-clicking on an edge in that edge loop. With the edge loop selected, press Ctrl+E and choose Mark Seam from the menu. In Figure 3.5, you can see seven edge loops that have been marked as seams. Six of the edge loops are circular loops following the circumference of the pipe, and the seventh edge loop is crosswise to the other six, cutting the pipe vertically. (If you have difficulty seeing the selections in this figure, refer to the color insert in this book, where the image is reproduced in color.)

FIGURE 3.5
Creating seams on the smokestack

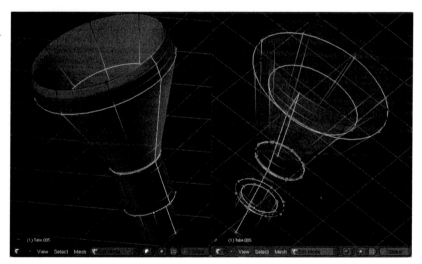

2. In the Mesh panel of the Edit buttons area, create a new UV texture as shown in Figure 3.6. Open a UV/Image editor window and create a new image by pressing Alt+N. In the dialog box that appears, enter **2048** as both the Width and Height values, and select UV Test Grid. In the 3D window, press the A key to select all vertices of the mesh, and then in the UV/Image editor, press the E key to unwrap the mesh as shown in Figure 3.7. Unwrap the mesh, and arrange the pieces of the mesh by selecting them with the L key and then moving them with the G key or rotating them with the R key so that they are laid out something along the lines of what's shown in Figure 3.8 (a color version of this image is included in the book's color insert).

FIGURE 3.6
Adding a UV
texture

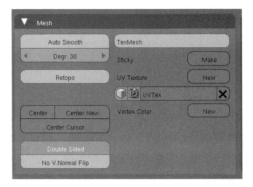

FIGURE 3.7
Preparing to
unwrap

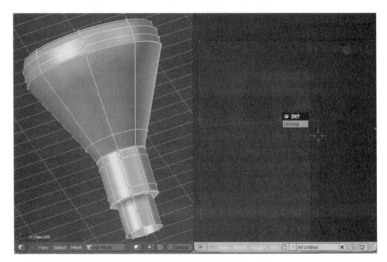

FIGURE 3.8
The unwrapped
mesh

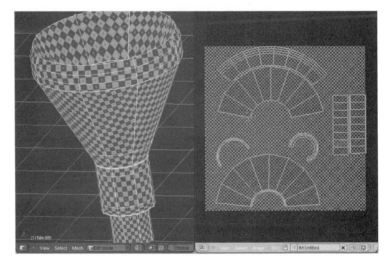

3. Save the face layout by going to the UV menu in the UV/Image editor window header and choosing Scripts ➤ Save UV Face Layout, as shown in Figure 3.9. In the dialog box, set the Size value to **2048** and the Wire value to **2**, as shown in Figure 3.10.

FIGURE 3.9

Saving the UV
face layout

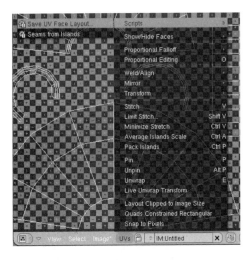

FIGURE 3.10

Parameters for
saving the UV
face layout

4. Now it is time to turn to GIMP for the task of creating the actual 2D texture. In GIMP, open the face layout Targa (.tga) file that you just exported, as shown in Figure 3.11. You will be working heavily with GIMP's layer functionality, so it is important to have the layers document in view. Display this by choosing Dockable Dialogs ➤ Layers from the Windows menu, as shown in Figure 3.12.

WHY GIMP?

Blender's UV/Image editor has some limited 2D painting functionality, as you will see in Chapter 9, "Creating Assets for the Blender Game Engine." However, it lacks many crucial features necessary to make top-quality realistic textures. Being able to work with 2D layers as well as control fades and transparency while manipulating photographs is crucial to constructing good UV textures. For this reason, GIMP is a natural complement to Blender and an indispensable tool in any open source 3D content creation toolkit.

5. To create realistic, photo-based textures, you must start with raw photographic materials. Numerous resources are available on the Web for free or as inexpensive stock textures. One of my favorites websites for this is www.deviantart.com, where you can find a truly dizzying variety of high-quality textures, most of which are released freely for most uses. The two textures used in this tutorial are from that website. The first is Wojciech Sadlej's metallic texture shown in Figure 3.13, which is also included on the CD that accompanies this book in the file metal_texture.jpg. This texture and other excellent textures like it can be downloaded from Wojciech's deviantART page at http://wojtar-stock.deviantart.com. The second texture, shown in Figure 3.14, is by deviantART-user Dazzle—it provides further weathering but is not crucial for following the main points of the tutorial. This texture can be downloaded at Dazzle's deviantART page at http://dazzle-textures.deviantart.com.

FIGURE 3.11
Opening the UV
face layout in GIMP

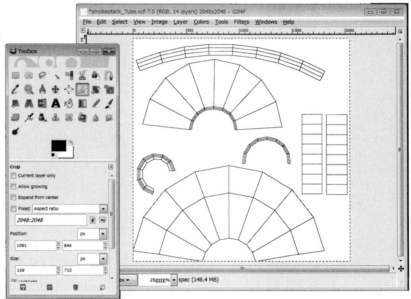

FIGURE 3.12
Accessing layers
in GIMP

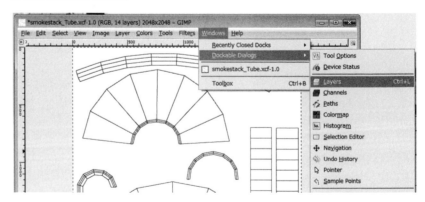

FIGURE 3.13
Metallic texture

FIGURE 3.14
A grimy, discolored
metal texture

6. Open the file `metal_texture.jpg` in GIMP. Press Ctrl+A to select the entire image and then press Ctrl+C to copy it. Return to the UV face layout file and paste the selection into the face layout file by pressing Ctrl+V. The result is shown in Figure 3.15. As you can see from the Layers window in this figure, the pasted layer is now treated as a *floating selection*. You must fix it to its own layer by clicking the New Layer button highlighted in Figure 3.16. Remember to do this each time you paste a selection into the window. You can now select this texture with Alt+S, or with any of the selection tools in the toolbox, but be sure that you are operating on the appropriate layer when you do so. For right now, select the metallic texture with Alt+S, and rotate and scale it by using the Rotate and Scale tools in the toolbox ( ), as shown in Figure 3.17. Also, reduce the opacity of the texture layer so that the UV face layout layer is visible.

FIGURE 3.15
Pasting the metal texture into the face layout file

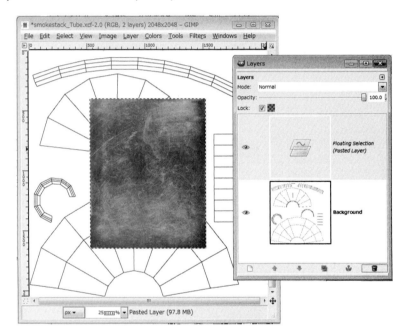

FIGURE 3.16
Creating a new layer to fix the pasted selection to

FIGURE 3.17
Arranging the
new layer

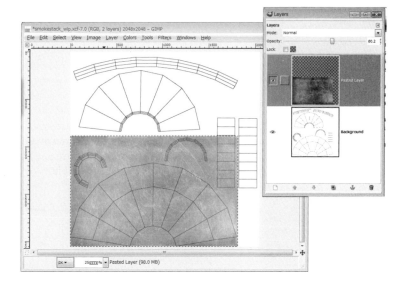

7. Select the Rectangle Select tool in the toolbox, as shown in Figure 3.18, and set it to Feather Edges with a radius of 50 pixels. This will enable you to copy selected areas with smooth, faded edges so that they can be pasted seamlessly. With the texture layer active, select a rectangular area as shown in Figure 3.19 and copy it with Ctrl+C. Paste with Ctrl+V. Once again, this will create a floating selection, as shown in Figure 3.20. Click the New Layer button again to fix this new selection to its own layer. Move the selection to cover the two rectangular portions of the UV face layout, as shown in Figure 3.21. Repeat this step to create another layer of texture to cover the upper portion of the face layout, as shown in Figure 3.22. Note that the opacity of all layers is reduced temporarily, so that the face layout is visible. Before exporting the texture, you will bring the opacity back up to 100 percent.

FIGURE 3.18
Setting the Rect-
angle Select tool to
feather edges
50 pixels

FIGURE 3.19
Selecting a rectangular section of the metal texture

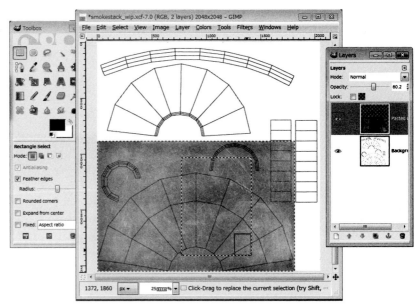

FIGURE 3.20
Pasting the selection

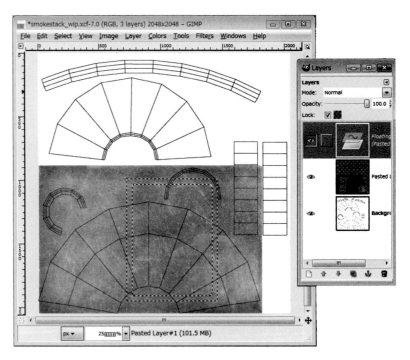

FIGURE 3.21
The pasted selection on its own layer

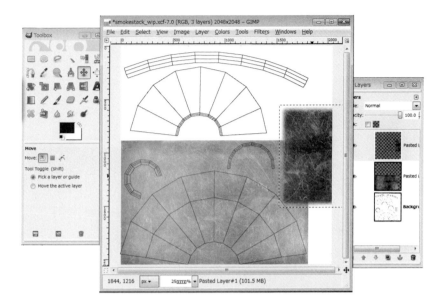

FIGURE 3.22
A basic metallic texture

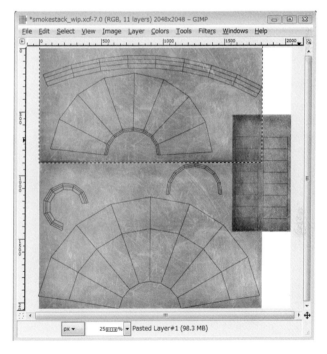

8. To add some grime and discoloration, open the grime texture in GIMP. Use the Lasso selection tool with Feather Edges set to 50, and then drag the mouse to select an uneven shape as shown in Figure 3.23. Press Ctrl+C to copy this selection. Return to the face layout and texture file you were working on and paste the selection with Ctrl+V. As in

the previous steps, add a new layer, and then rotate and scale the new texture layer as shown in Figure 3.24. Do this several times with differently shaped segments of grime, as shown in Figure 3.25. Note also that the layer's mode can be changed for different effects. In most cases, Normal mode will give the results you want, but Soft Light will also give appealing, subtle discoloration. Experiment with other modes for different effects.

FIGURE 3.23
Selecting an area of grime

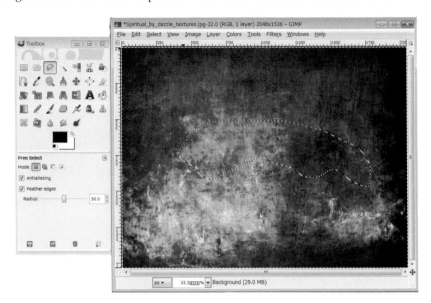

FIGURE 3.24
Pasting the copy of the grime texture selection

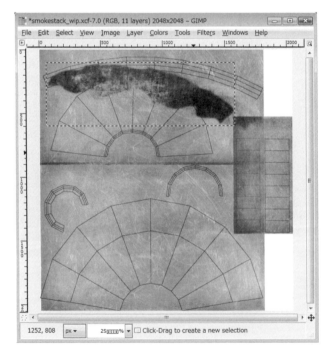

FIGURE 3.25
Adding more grime

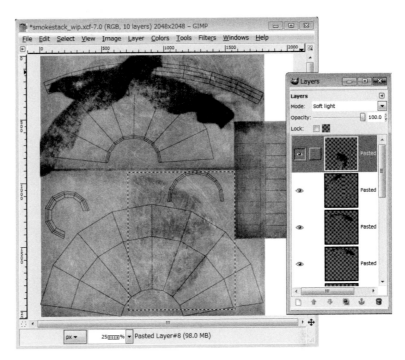

9. After you are satisfied with your texture, turn the opacity of all layers up to 100 percent, and make sure all the necessary layers are set to be visible by using the small eye icon to the left of each layer's thumbnail. From the Layer menu, select New From Visible to create a new single-composite layer from all currently visible layers, as shown in Figure 3.26. Rename this new layer **color** in the field to the right of the thumbnail, and set all the other layers above it to be invisible by clicking the eye icons, as shown in Figure 3.27. Go to the File menu and choose Save As. Give the file the name smokestack_color.png. Appending .png to the filename tells GIMP to merge the layers to export to a single image file. Note that the resultant PNG file will not have layer information. If you want to be able to go back later and work with the GIMP layers, you will need to save this file separately as an .xcf file.

10. You're finished with GIMP for the time being. Return to Blender. In the UV/Image editor, open the file smokestack_color.png and map it to the smokestack object, as shown in Figure 3.28. Finally, create a material for the smokestack. Call the material **BaseColor** and set it to Shadeless. Apply smokestack_color.png as a UV-mapped image texture. The full settings for this material are shown in Figure 3.29.

This is the end of the first stage in creating the finished material, but you're not quite there yet. The material you've created here is not the final material you will use to render the image, but rather a sort of interim material that will be used to create the final seamless textures, as you will see in the next section.

FIGURE 3.26
Creating a
composite layer

FIGURE 3.26
Creating a
composite layer

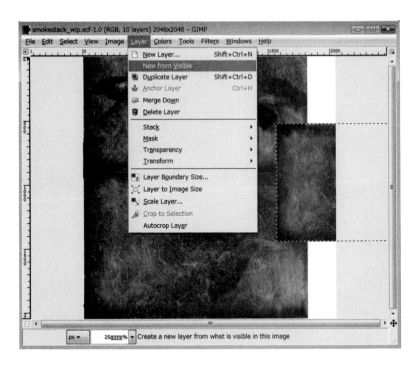

FIGURE 3.27
The color texture

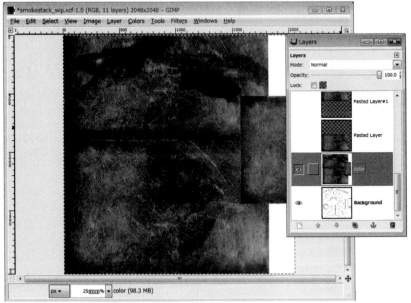

FIGURE 3.28
The texture
mapped to the
smokestack

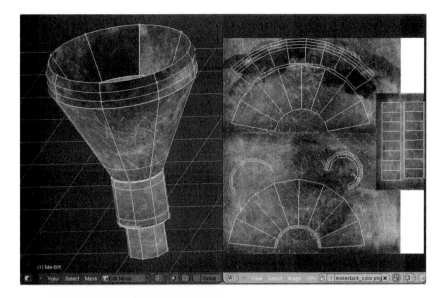

FIGURE 3.29
Creating a shade-
less material
with the color
UV texture

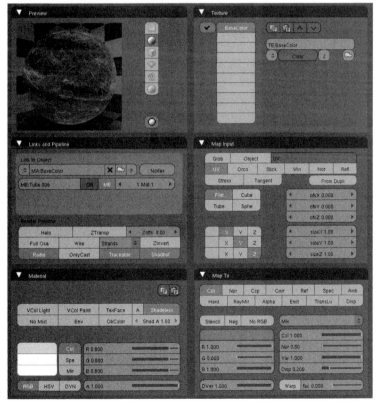

Smoothing the Seams with Texture Baking

The 2D-to-3D mapping shown in Figure 3.30 looks pretty good, but there are some obvious problems. The biggest problem is the visibility of seams, where the 2D texture meets itself and does not match. In this section, you will see how to eliminate such seams. Astute readers might point out that actual sheet-metal smokestacks are generally not composed of seamless whole surfaces. In fact, this is true, and in many cases, seams can and should be hidden by matching them with real-world seams or hiding them out of view. However, real-world seams do not always match up perfectly with the best places to cut your meshes for UV mapping, so it is best to understand how to create seamless textures when necessary. In this example, ironic as it may be, I ignore the existence of real-world sheet-metal seams, and concentrate on explaining the methodology of creating seamless textures.

FIGURE 3.30
Unsightly seams

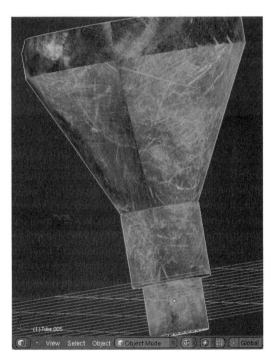

To eliminate the seams in this texture, follow these steps:

1. The trick to eliminating seams is to retexture the object by using a different UV unwrapping pattern, so that the areas previously showing UV unwrapping seams can be doctored in GIMP. For this, it is necessary to reseam the model and unwrap again. However, before doing this, it is a good idea to make a record of the seam patterns you used for the first unwrapping, in case it becomes necessary to revisit that unwrapping for some reason. First, select all the seams in the object by entering Edge select mode, selecting a single-seamed edge, and then pressing Shift+G or selecting the Similar To Selection option in the Select menu of the 3D viewport header, as shown in Figure 3.31. When you do this, the Select Similar Edges menu will open, as shown in Figure 3.32. Select the Seam option, which will

select all seams. Create a new vertex group by clicking New under Vertex Groups in the Links And Materials tab, and then click Assign to assign the selected vertices to that group. Give the vertex group a meaningful name such as **Seams1**, as shown in Figure 3.33.

FIGURE 3.31
The Select menu

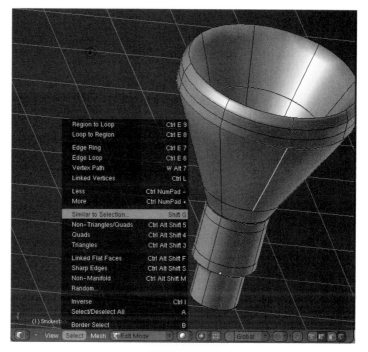

FIGURE 3.32
Selecting all seams

FIGURE 3.33
The Seams1
vertex group

2. Using the Alt+right-click loop-selection method, select only the seams shown in Figure 3.34. To do this quickly, clear any current selection with the A key and then select the vertices by using the Select button from the Vertex Groups panel for the vertex group you defined previously. Press Ctrl+E and select Clear Seams. Then select the edge loops shown in Figure 3.35, press Ctrl+E, and select Mark Seams. (Color versions of these images are included in the book's color insert.)

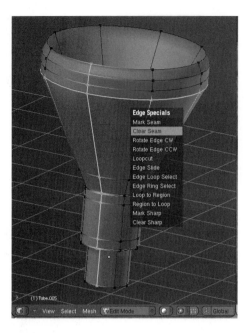

FIGURE 3.34
Clearing the
old seams

FIGURE 3.35
Marking new
seams

3. In the Mesh panel of the Edit buttons area, add a new UV texture as shown in Figure 3.36. Do not delete the previous UV texture. The new UV texture will automatically have the leftmost icon selected, indicating that it is now the active UV texture. The previous UV texture will still have the Render icon selected, indicating that it is the texture that will be rendered. In the UV/Image editor, once again create a new UV Test Grid image pattern with Width and Height values of 2048. Use the A key in the 3D viewport to select the entire mesh and unwrap it in the UV/Image editor, as shown in Figure 3.37. As you can see, the face layout pattern is similar to but still different from the previous one.

4. Now comes the interesting part. In the normal mapping section of Chapter 2, you baked the normals from one object to a UV texture on a second object. The baking step here is analogous, except that instead of normals, you will bake the previously UV-mapped texture, and instead of baking from one object to another, you will bake from one UV texture to another on the same object. Do this now by going into the Render buttons area, setting the Bake value to Textures, and clicking the Bake button, as shown in Figure 3.38. The resulting new texture image is shown in Figure 3.39 (a color version of this image is included in the book's color insert). Save this as a PNG file called `seams-color.png` by selecting Save As from the Image menu in the header.

FIGURE 3.36
Adding a new UV
texture

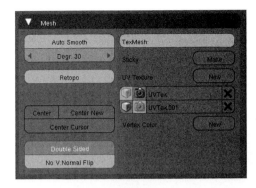

FIGURE 3.37
The new
unwrapping

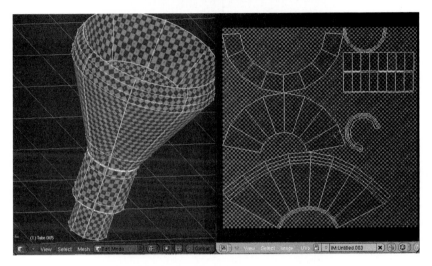

FIGURE 3.38
Baking the texture

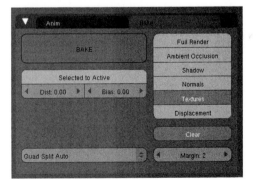

FIGURE 3.39
The newly
baked texture

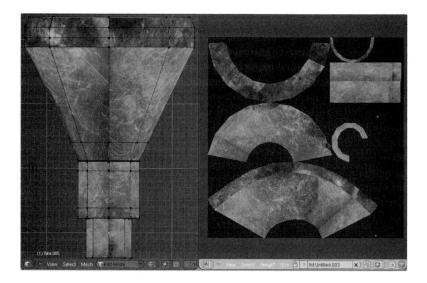

5. Open `seams-color.png` in GIMP. As you can see, the visible seams in the image are now separated from the edges of the UV mapping, so it is possible to doctor them directly. To do this, use the Lasso selection tool to select an area of the image that does not have a seam in it, as shown in Figure 3.40. Make sure the Lasso tool has Feather Edges set to 50 pixels before making the selection. After making the selection, press Ctrl+C and Ctrl+V to copy and paste the selection, and then press the New Layer button on the Layers window as you did previously to give the selection its own layer. Use the Move tool to move the selection over the visible seam, as shown in Figure 3.41. Use the Rotate tool to fit the selection to the new place as shown in Figure 3.42. Do the same thing for all other spots in the texture where there are visible seams. Be careful not to modify places near the edge of the new UV layout, where modifications would create new visible seams! When you finish, you should have a completely seamless texture like the one shown in Figure 3.43. Save the visible layer as `no-seams-color.png` by using Save As from the File menu.

6. Duplicate the layer by clicking the Duplicate Layer button shown in Figure 3.44. Rename the new layer **no-seam-bump**. This layer will become the bump map texture for the metal material. From the Tools menu, choose Color Tools ➢ Desaturate, as shown in Figure 3.45. Then desaturate the image based on Lightness by clicking OK in the Desaturate dialog box shown in Figure 3.46. From the Colors menu, select Invert to reverse the white and black values. Then select Brightness-Contrast and adjust the brightness and contrast as shown in Figure 3.47. Save the visible layer as `no-seams-bump.png` by using Save As from the File menu. The resulting texture file should look like the one shown in Figure 3.48. Remember to save the GIMP file separately as an `.xcf` file if you want to be able to go back and work with individual layers.

FIGURE 3.40
Selecting an area
of the texture

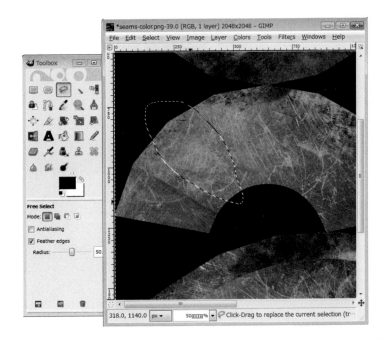

FIGURE 3.41
Moving the
selection to con-
ceal the seam

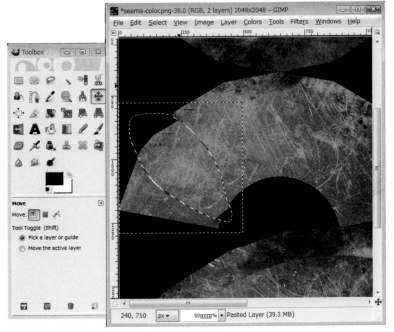

FIGURE 3.42
Rotating the selection into place

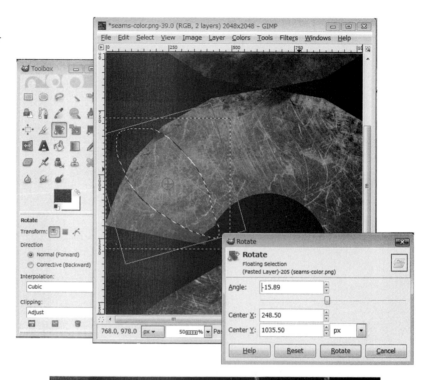

FIGURE 3.43
The final
color texture

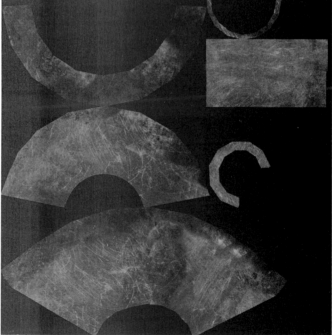

FIGURE 3.44
Duplicating the
layer

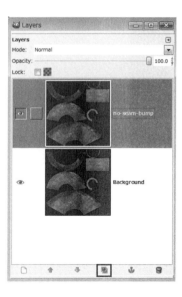

FIGURE 3.45
Desaturating the
bump layer

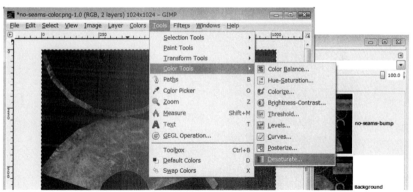

FIGURE 3.46
Desaturate
dialog box

FIGURE 3.47
Adjusting brightness and contrast

FIGURE 3.48
The final
bump texture

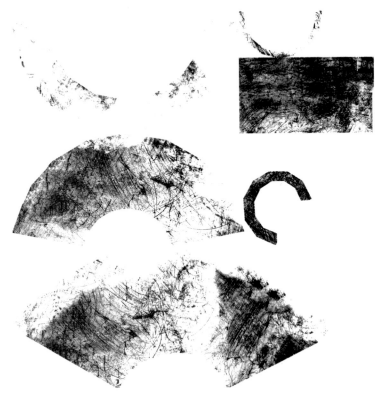

7. You now have the final texture. Return to Blender and load it into the UV/Image editor. As you can see in Figure 3.49, the seams have been eliminated. (A color version of this image is included in the book's color insert.)

FIGURE 3.49
The seamless texture applied to the model

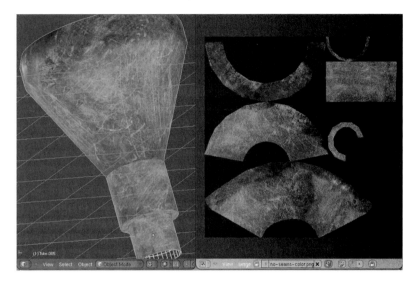

Now you have created the seamless color and bump UV textures that will be the basis of the final material. At this point, you can delete both the old UV texture and the previous BaseColor material. The next section tells you how to construct the new material by using the Blender material nodes system.

Achieving Realism with Material Nodes

Textures are an important first step to creating materials. The textures you have created so far will determine the base color of the metal smokestack as well as the pattern of scratches and pocks as represented by the seamless bump map you created from the color texture. Another important aspect of materials are the shader parameters that determine how light behaves when it strikes the surface of the material. Specularity, hardness, reflectivity, and other real-world qualities depend on these parameters for their representation in Blender.

In the example of the smokestack, it would be nice to represent the accumulation of soot on the upper portion of the smokestack with a blackening-in color and with a diminishing of specularity, because soot-covered metal is less shiny than relatively clean metal. There are various ways to do this. In this section, you will see how to do it by combining several materials with different specularities into a single node-based material.

To create the material, follow these steps:

1. If you haven't already, delete the BaseColor material you created previously by selecting its Material index panel in the Links And Materials tab of the Edit buttons area and clicking Delete. Then create a new material in the Links And Materials tab by clicking New. Open a Nodes editor window, and click Use Nodes to create a new node material, as shown in Figure 3.50. From the Material drop-down menu, select Add New, as shown in Figure 3.51. Name the new material **nospec**, as shown in Figure 3.52.

FIGURE 3.50
Making a
node material

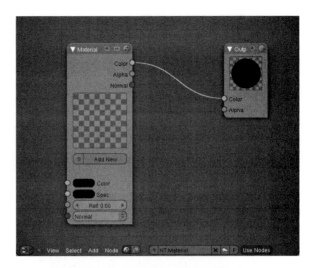

FIGURE 3.51
Adding a
new material

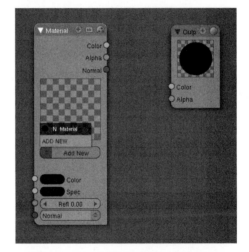

FIGURE 3.52
The nospec mate-
rial node

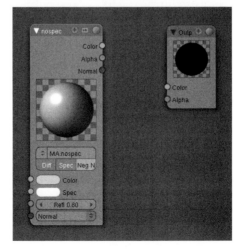

2. Turn now to the Material buttons to specify the values for the nospec material. The relevant values are shown in Figure 3.53. The specularity (Spec) value is set low, to 0.07, and hardness (Hard) is at 108. The shaders used are Lambert and CookTorr. Create three textures: Color, Bump, and Dark. The Color and Bump textures are both image textures, using the UV image textures you created previously, with UV mappings. Select UV in the Map Input tab.

FIGURE 3.53

The nospec material

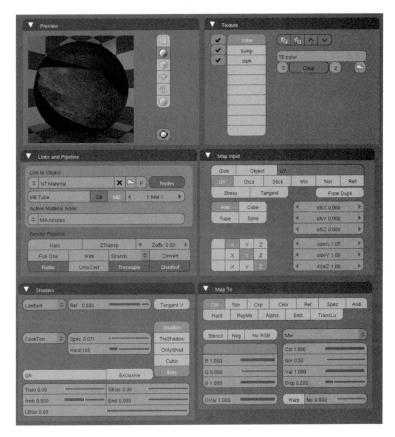

3. Set the Color texture to map to Col in the Map To panel. Select the Bump texture, and set it to map to Nor with a Nor value of 1.

4. The Dark texture represents the blackening from soot. Unlike the other two textures, this texture is a blend texture rather than an image texture. The texture's parameters are shown in Figure 3.54, and its mapping values are shown in Figure 3.55. As you can see, the mapping is Orco, and the mapping coordinates are all Z.

FIGURE 3.54
The Dark texture

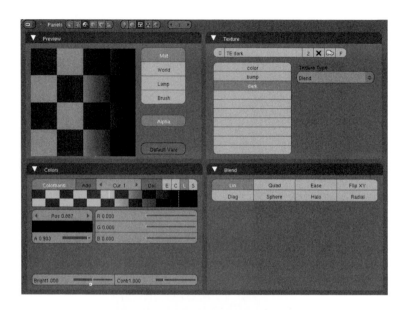

FIGURE 3.55
The Dark texture
mapping

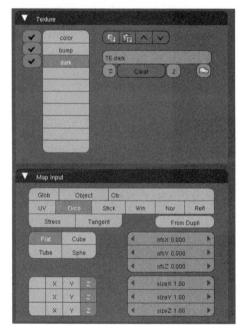

5. Return to the Nodes editor. Select the nospec material node, and then press Shift+D to copy the node, as shown in Figure 3.56. In the new copy, click the number 2 next to the Material name to unlink the node from nospec and create a new material. Rename this new material **spec**, as shown in Figure 3.57. The new material is the same as nospec in every respect except its specularity and hardness (Spec and Hard) values on the Shaders tab, as shown in Figure 3.58. Change these for the new material.

FIGURE 3.56
Duplicating
the nospec
material node

FIGURE 3.56
Duplicating
the nospec
material node

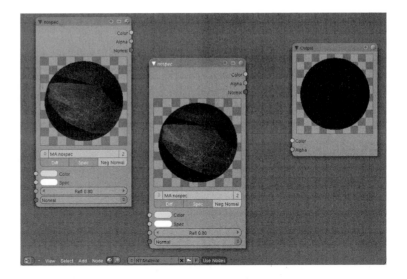

FIGURE 3.57
Creating a
new material
called spec

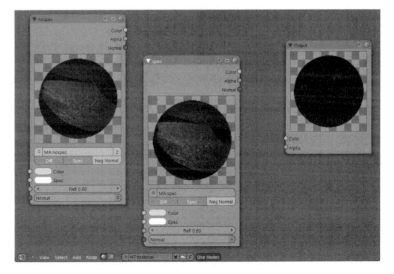

FIGURE 3.58
Shader values for
the spec material

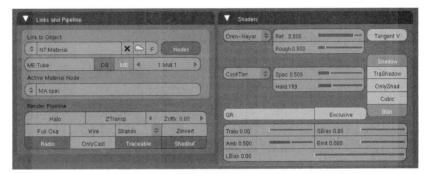

6. Return to the Nodes editor. Press the spacebar and add a new Material node. Once again, choose Add New from the Material drop-down menu and create a new material. Name this material **blend**. The parameters for the blend material are shown in Figure 3.59. This material is shadeless, so shader values have no effect. It has a single Orco-mapped blend texture on it. The blend texture is called blend, and its values are shown in Figure 3.60.

7. The blend material node is used to determine the values for mixing the spec and nospec material nodes. Add a Mix node by pressing the spacebar and choosing Add ➤ Color➤ Mix. Make the following connections, as shown in Figure 3.61:

◆ Connect the Color output socket from the blend material node to the Fac (factor) input socket in the Mix node.

◆ Connect the Color output sockets from nospec and spec, respectively, to the Color1 and Color2 input sockets in the Mix node.

◆ Connect the Color output socket of the Mix node to the Color input socket of the Output node.

FIGURE 3.59
The blend material

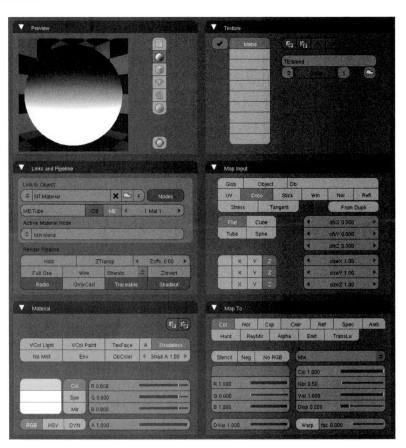

FIGURE 3.60
The blend texture

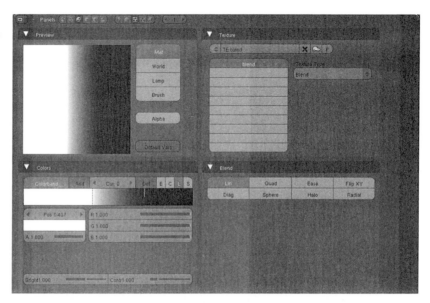

FIGURE 3.61
Putting the materials together with a Mix node

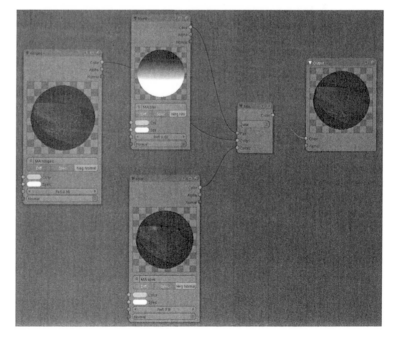

8. Render the finished product. The result should look something like the render in Figure 3.62, with the lower portion of the smokestack showing a worn metallic shininess and the upper portion sooty and dull.

FIGURE 3.62
The finished
smokestack

You've now seen how to create realistic textures by using Blender and GIMP, and how to incorporate them into a convincing node-based material. In the upcoming chapters, you will learn more about using Blender's nodes system for compositing images and sequences together.

Real World Scenario

Cog's Journey

Many Blender users learned much of what they know about Blender materials directly or indirectly from tutorials by Colin Litster, a long-time pillar of the Blender community best known by the nickname Cog—which also happens to be the working title of his ambitious, ongoing, independent, CG-animated film project. For several years, Colin has documented his progress on the project with tutorials and demo animations, as he has continued to explore the capabilities of Blender and push the boundaries of what can be accomplished with its tools.

The Cog project website has been a consistent source of some of the best free tutorials and learning materials on the Web, and many current Blender experts learned the basics from Colin's work. Colin has taught workshops at several official Blender Foundation conferences and contributed a chapter to *The Essential Blender: Guide to 3D Creation with the Open Source Suite Blender* by Roland Hess (the Blender Foundation/No Starch Press, 2007). A thorough exploration of all that is offered at the Cog Project website is a must for anyone who wants to get the most out of Blender's materials, textures, and nodes system.

Colin used a rich combination of UV-mapped image textures, procedural textures, and node-based materials to create the house in the graphic shown here, which will serve as one of the numerous settings for his film. (The full-color image is included in this book's color insert.)

The Bottom Line

Use Blender's texture-mapping functionality effectively.   Blender has a powerful set of UV-mapping tools that rank among the best in the industry. Using these tools enables you to place 2D textures exactly as you want them on the surface of a 3D model.

Master It   Find the file `engine.blend` on the CD that accompanies this book. Create seams, unwrap the mesh, and export a UV face-layout file for use in GIMP. Apply a UV test grid image to the mesh.

Mix textures to create almost any surface effect.   By using Blender's UV texture and texture-baking features, particularly in combination with a powerful image-manipulation application such as GIMP, you can create a wide variety of seamless texture effects.

Master It   Using the `metal_texture.jpg` file included on the CD, or other textures that you find online or create yourself, use the methods described in this chapter to create seamless color and bump map textures for the `engine.blend` model.

Make the most of the Blender material system to create complex materials and shaders. Creating textures is only the first part of making convincing materials. Mapping them correctly to the material and setting their parameters correctly are crucial to getting realistic material effects.

Master It   Combine the two textures you created in the previous exercise in a single material with both color and bump qualities. Set the shader properties in a way that creates a convincing metallic look.

Chapter 4

Video Compositing with Nodes

Blender's versatile and powerful nodes system enables you to access and manipulate a huge variety of compositional elements to combine rendered images in exactly the way you want to. You can use nodes to composite still images or video sequences that can later be edited in Blender's nonlinear Video Sequence Editor (VSE), which you will learn about in Chapter 5, "Working with the Video Sequence Editor." Here, you will look at an in-depth example of one of the most common tasks in live-action video compositing: the task of green screen compositing. After you see how this is done, you will have a basic understanding of the ways in which any kind of image can be composited with any other.

In this chapter, you will learn to

◆ Use the Blender composite node system to pull a green screen matte

◆ Use curves and hooks to do simple rotoscoped garbage matting

◆ Manipulate the video's color channels to reduce color spill

Pulling a Green Screen Matte with Nodes

A big part of video compositing is the task of extracting elements from their original surroundings so as to be able to composite them freely into different visual environments. There are several ways to do this, depending on what kind of source material you have to work with. Typically, the process involves the creation of a *matte*, which is a special image used to suppress parts of the original image and allow other parts of the image to show through.

The Blender composite node system enables you to take multiple images, videos, renders, or other 2D information sources as input, and then perform a wide variety of operations on them to combine them in an endless number of ways. The operations are performed in a nonlinear way and represented as nodes on a graph that can be edited directly. In this section, you will see how this system can be used to perform the common task of pulling a green screen matte from a live video. After you understand how to do this, many other uses of the composite node system should become clear.

Working with Green Screen Video

When you know in advance that you will need to composite a character or object into a different background scene, the typical approach is to shoot the foreground action against a colored background screen that can be easily eliminated by compositing techniques such as those described in this section. The most common type of colored screen currently used is a *green screen*.

Shooting green screen video obviously requires that you have access to a green screen. Most multimedia production studios, including those of many universities and technical colleges, have all you need to take green screen footage. It is also not especially difficult to build your own green screen equipment. You can find instructions on the Web for doing this.

For the tutorials in this chapter, you can find a brief clip of green screen video in the form of a sequence of JPEG images in the greenscreen subdirectory on the accompanying CD. The clip is from footage shot by Norman England for his film *The iDol* (www.theidol-movie.com) and features a character walking toward the camera, as shown in Figure 4.1 (also repeated in color in the color insert of this book). There are a couple of challenges that this particular clip presents for the compositor, and you'll see what those are and how they can be solved in Blender over the course of this chapter.

MORE ON CODECS

It is important for you to be aware of codecs if you plan to shoot and edit or composite video. Not all video codecs can be decoded by open source software, and professional-grade-equipment makers often assume that you will be using specific proprietary tools to work with your video. The footage included on the CD was originally shot on a Panasonic VariCam high-definition (HD) video camera. This camera records video by using the DVCProHD codec. Proprietary decoding software for this codec is available for Mac and Windows, but I am not aware of any open source options for working with this codec.

It is always a good idea to know what codec you will be working with before you shoot, and the restrictions are even tighter if you are working in an open source or Linux-based pipeline. Do your research before spending money and time on equipment rental and shooting.

Working with Composite Nodes

Creating, or *pulling*, a green screen matte is not at all difficult, but it requires that you familiarize yourself with Blender's composite node system.

A few general points about composite nodes are in order before you begin. The node network, sometimes called a *noodle*, is made up of nodes of several distinct types. Depending on the node type and its specific properties, each node has at least one input socket or one output socket and may have multiple input and/or output sockets. Input sockets are on the left side of the nodes, and output sockets are on the right side of the nodes. Nodes are connected to each other by curved lines that extend from an output socket of one node to an input socket of the other node.

To connect two nodes, hold down the left mouse button while you move the mouse from an output socket of one node to the input socket of another node, where you want the connection to be established. To break a connection, hold down the left mouse button while moving your mouse in a cutting motion across one of the connecting lines between nodes.

To set up the nodes for pulling the green screen matte, follow these steps:

1. Open a Node editor window in your Blender workspace, as shown in Figure 4.2. In the header, select the Composite Nodes button and click Use Nodes, as shown in Figure 4.3. The default composite node setup will appear with a single Render Layers input node on the left and a Composite output node on the right, as shown in Figure 4.4. The composite output node shows you what the final render will be when the Do Composite option is selected in the Anim tab of the Render buttons.

FIGURE 4.1
A video shot
against a
green screen

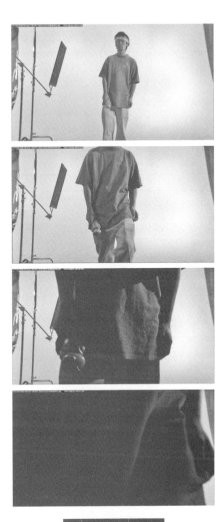

FIGURE 4.2
Selecting the Node
Editor window

FIGURE 4.3
Selecting the Composite Nodes button and Use Nodes

FIGURE 4.4
Default composite node setup

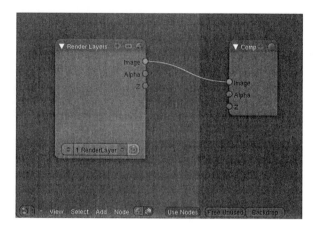

2. At this point, you don't yet need a Render Layers input node, so click that node and delete it with the X key. Instead, you will use the original green screen video as the main input here. Images and video can both be imported into the node system by using an Image node. Add that by pressing the spacebar and choosing Add ➢ Input ➢ Image, as shown in Figure 4.5. In the file browser window, navigate to the directory where you have copied the green screen image sequence from the CD. Select all images by pressing the A key, as shown in Figure 4.6, and then click the Select Image button. The resulting node setup will look Figure 4.7. Click the button with the little car icon on it in the lower-right corner of the Image node to ensure that the image is automatically refreshed when you change frames. Try advancing 10 frames by pressing the up arrow key to make sure that the image updates.

FIGURE 4.5
Adding an Image input node

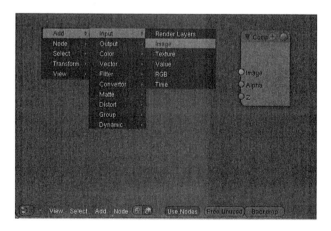

FIGURE 4.6
Selecting an image sequence

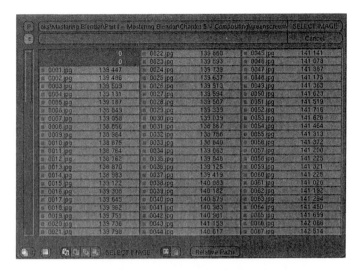

FIGURE 4.7
The loaded image

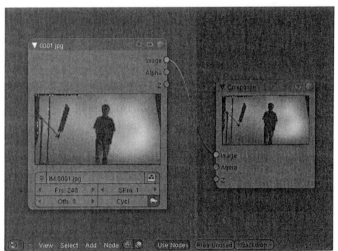

3. It's important to be able to see what you are working with. The Composite node represents the final rendered output, and there should be only one of these connected to the node graph. However, you can have as many Viewer output nodes connected to the graph as you want, and whichever one you select at any moment will display immediately in the UV/Image editor window when Viewer Node is selected from the drop-down menu. You can see this in Figure 4.8. The Viewer node is added by pressing the spacebar and choosing Add ➢ Output ➢ Viewer from the menu.

FIGURE 4.8
A Viewer node shown in the UV/Image editor window

4. The first thing you will use multiple Viewer nodes for is to take a close look at the individual color channels of the image. This is very helpful to get a sense of the actual values that you are working with, and can help to clarify how green screen matte pulling works. To do this, first press the spacebar and choose Add ➤ Converter ➤ Separate RGBA, as shown in Figure 4.9. The new Converter node has a single Image input socket and four output sockets representing the red, green, blue, and alpha (RGBA) channels. Add three new Viewer nodes (you can do this by copying the first one you added, by pressing Shift+D) and connect them to the three color channels, as shown in Figure 4.10 (reproduced in color in the color insert of the book). As you'd expect, the highest-contrast channel is the green channel, which has a high-intensity background thanks to the green screen. The red channel, on the other hand, is much more uniformly distributed. The process of pulling a green screen matte depends on this difference in intensity ranges between the green and red channels.

FIGURE 4.9
Adding a separate RGBA node

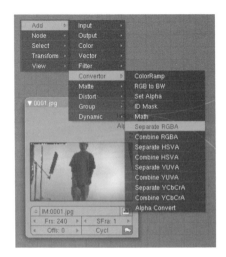

FIGURE 4.10
Viewing the
individual
color channels

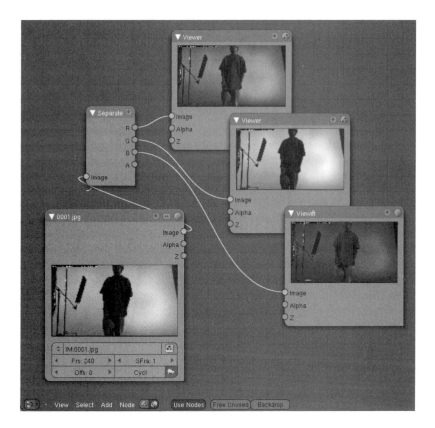

5. Now you can use the difference in channel intensities to pull the matte itself. Blender's node system includes specific nodes for creating mattes in fewer steps, but in order to understand exactly what is happening, it is good to do it yourself by hand. Also, walking through the process will make the subsequent garbage-matting step easier to understand. The idea here is to subtract the red channel of the image from the green channel by using a Subtract node. Add this node by pressing the spacebar and choosing Add ➤ Color ➤ Mix from the menu and then choosing Subtract from the drop-down menu on the node. Because there is proportionately less red in the background, this step results in darkening the foreground considerably more than the background, as you can see in Figure 4.11. This correctly separates the foreground from the background. Next add a ColorRamp node by pressing the spacebar and choosing Add ➤ Converter ➤ ColorRamp. Use this as shown in Figure 4.12 to invert the light and dark areas and to push the contrast to solid black and white. By adjusting the location of the value change along the length of the ColorRamp, you can adjust where along the grayscale range the black/white split occurs. This has the effect of enlarging or shrinking the black and white areas in the image. The resulting green screen matte should look something like the one shown in Figure 4.13.

FIGURE 4.11
Subtracting the red channel from the green channel

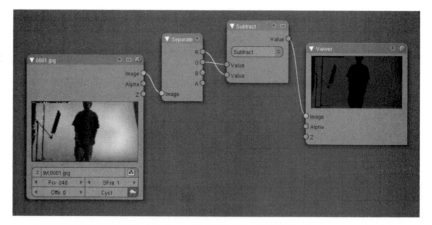

FIGURE 4.12
Inverting and pushing the contrast with a ColorRamp node

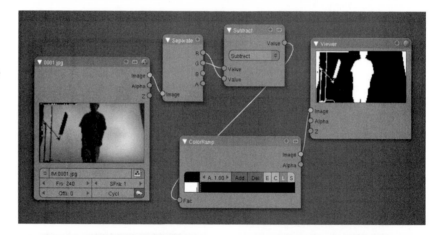

FIGURE 4.13
The basic green screen matte

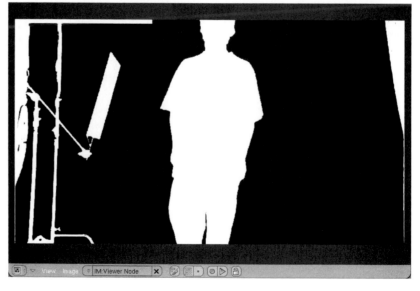

QUIRKS OF THE NODE SYSTEM

A presumably well-intentioned but slightly annoying quirk of the Blender node system is its behavior of second-guessing the user when a node connection is disrupted by a new connection made to the same socket. If you place a connection in an input socket where there is already an incoming connection, the previous connection will jump down to the nearest open input socket in the receiving node. This is almost never what you want, and requires you to make an extra mouse movement to sever the newly created connection. Frequently a connection that was entering an Image socket gets bumped down to the Alpha socket, suddenly causing the alpha value of the receiving node to go funny. Being aware of this quirk will enable you to cut the offending connection immediately, rather than wasting time and energy trying to figure out what has gone wrong. Hopefully, this behavior will be eliminated or made optional in upcoming releases.

Garbage Matting

The green screen matte you pulled in the previous section is a pretty good start, but it is immediately clear that it will not be sufficient to distinguish the character from the background. The problem is that the green screen does not perfectly cover the entire background. There are pieces of hardware and other nongreen areas that have been marked as white in the matte. The solution to this is a process called (for obvious reasons) *garbage matting.*

In the simplest cases, garbage matting may just be a matter of covering areas of the matte with blocks of black. However, our example has some added complications. The main problem is that the character is approaching the camera. As he comes closer to the camera, his silhouette interacts directly with the debris in the background, as you can see in Figure 4.14. This results in a green screen matte like the one shown in Figure 4.15, where there is no automatic, color-based way to distinguish between the foreground figure and the background garbage. Not only does the background need to be matted out, but it needs to be done in a way that distinguishes the correct outline of the foreground figure as it moves.

FIGURE 4.14
A complication for garbage matting

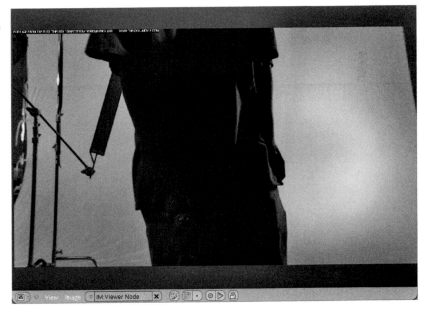

FIGURE 4.15
The problematic
green screen matte

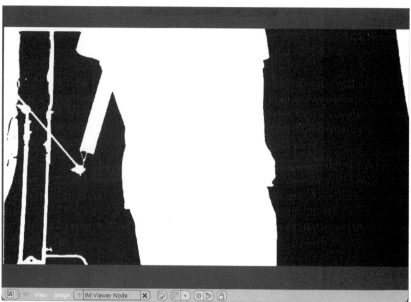

This problem can be fixed by using a curve and hooks to create a simple animated garbage matte. The solution is a simple form of *rotoscoping*, which involves creating images by hand on a frame-by-frame or nearly frame-by-frame basis. The approach shown here is useful for simple cases like this example. For more-complex cases, it would become very labor-intensive.

To set up the animated garbage matte, follow these steps:

1. As mentioned previously, the garbage matte will be created by using curves and hooks. These are 3D objects, so the garbage matte itself will be in the form of a 3D render. First, open a 3D viewport in Blender and enter Camera view by pressing 0 on the number pad. In the Format tab of the Render buttons, set the output dimensions to HD, as shown in Figure 4.16. This is to ensure that the dimensions of the rendered matte are the same as the dimensions of the green screen footage.

FIGURE 4.16
Setting the
correct dimensions
for the camera

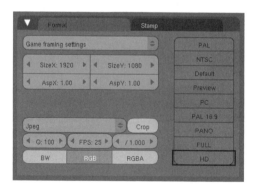

2. To see the video from the Camera view, you must import the video as a background image sequence. From the View menu in the header, open the Background Image dialog box. Click Use Background Image, and then click Load to load the image sequence. In the file browser, navigate to the greenscreen directory, select the first image (0001.jpg), and then click Select Image and import the image. In the Background Image dialog box, click the Sequence radio button and the Auto Refresh button and type **240** into the Frames field, as shown in Figure 4.17. When you have done this, the image will appear in the Camera view, as shown in Figure 4.18.

FIGURE 4.17
Importing the background image sequence

FIGURE 4.18
The 3D camera view with background image

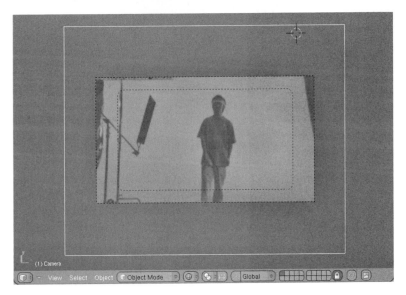

3. Make sure that your 3D cursor is located a reasonable distance in front of the camera, because this determines where new objects will be added. Also, make sure that Aligned To View is selected for the Add New Objects setting in the Edit Methods context of your user preferences. While in the Camera view, add a Bezier circle as shown in Figure 4.19 by pressing the spacebar and choosing Add ➤ Curve ➤ Bezier Circle. The resulting circle should look similar to the one shown in Figure 4.20 (a color version is found in the color insert of the book). If the size of your circle in the Camera view is somewhat different from what is shown in the figure, don't worry. You will be rescaling the curve shortly anyway. Just make sure that the curve is far enough away from the camera that you can see and work with the whole curve easily.

FIGURE 4.19
Adding a Bezier
circle

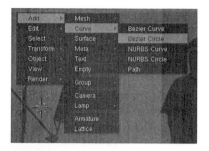

FIGURE 4.20
The Bezier circle

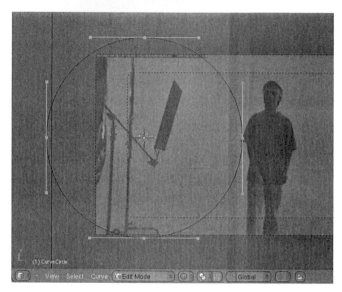

4. Select all the control points of the curve and press the V key to snap the control points into Vector mode. This will force each control-point handle to point at the adjacent one, causing the curve to take the shape of a square, as in Figure 4.21. Rotate the curve 45 degrees, as shown in Figure 4.22. Scale the curve along the local X and Y axes by pressing the S key followed by double X and double Y, respectively, to get the shape shown in Figure 4.23.

5. Press the Z key to see the curve in Solid Draw mode, as shown in Figure 4.24. This will be the garbage matte, and will eventually be used to black out the unwanted areas of the green screen matte, but first it will be rendered as white. To make this happen, you need to give it a suitable material. Add a material to the curve in the usual way. Set the material to be completely white and then activate the Shadeless option, as shown in Figure 4.25.

FIGURE 4.21
Snapping the
control points
to angles with
the V key

FIGURE 4.22
Rotating the
curve 45 degrees

FIGURE 4.23
The curve scaled
along the local X
and Y axes

FIGURE 4.24
The curve in Solid
Draw mode

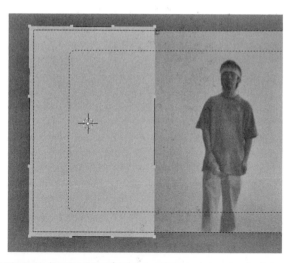

FIGURE 4.25
Adding a shadeless
white material

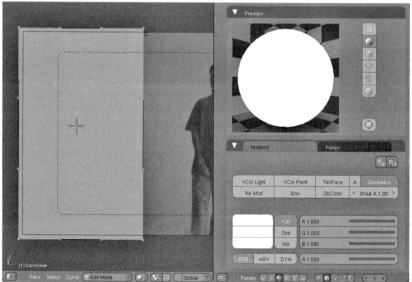

6. Finally, you need to rig the curve with hooks so that it can be animated. Select the inside (right-hand) edge of the curve by pressing the B key and using the Box select tool, and then subdivide by pressing the W key and choosing Subdivide. Subdivide the edge three times, so that it ends up as shown in Figure 4.26 (reproduced in color in the color insert of the book). The idea is to attach an empty hook at each control point. First select the control point in the upper-right corner. Make sure to select the actual control point itself so that both handles are also selected, rather than just selecting a single handle. Press

Ctrl+H and select Add, New Empty to create a new empty as a hook to the curve, as in Figure 4.27. Do the same with the control points down the inside edge of the curve. In each case, make sure that you have selected the central control point so that the entire Bezier triplet is selected, as shown in Figure 4.28 (repeated in the color insert in this book). Add hooks to all the control points along that edge and to the lower-right corner. Depending on where your 3D cursor was when you began the process, you may find that the empties are an awkward size. You can scale them now to the size you want. First select Individual Centers from the Pivot Point drop-down menu in the 3D viewport head. Then select one empty, press Shift+G, choose to select Objects Of Same Type, and scale the empties as you like. This may affect the shape of the curve slightly, as you can see in Figure 4.29, but this is fine. You will be keyframing these empties to the exact spot they are required anyway.

FIGURE 4.26
Subdividing the inside edge three times

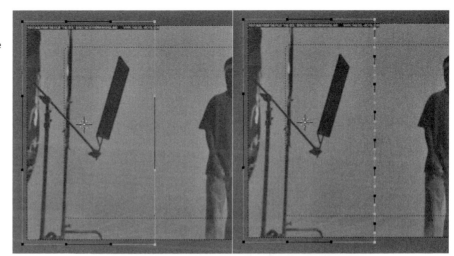

FIGURE 4.27
Adding a hook to the corner

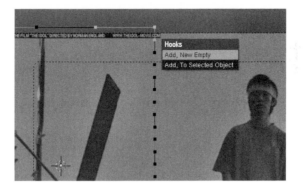

FIGURE 4.28
Adding a
second hook to a
control point

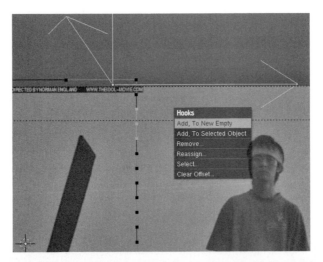

FIGURE 4.29
A full set of
hooks, scaled
down slightly

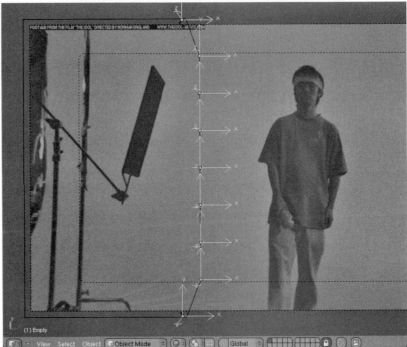

Animating the Garbage Matte

Now that you've set up the curve and hooks, you can animate the garbage matte to cover the
necessary background throughout the entire clip. To do that, follow these steps:

1. Begin in frame 1. Position the empties so that the matte covers everything in the background. If your matte is more or less the same as the one shown in the example, this

will require moving only one empty, so the burn-in in the upper-left corner is covered, as shown in Figure 4.30. Press Shift+G and choose Objects Of Same Type, as shown in Figure 4.31, to select all empties. Keyframe all the empties by pressing the I key and choosing LocRotScale, as shown in Figure 4.32.

FIGURE 4.30
Placing the hook to cover the burn-in

FIGURE 4.31
Selecting hooks by type

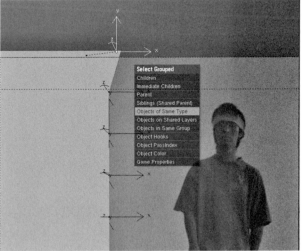

FIGURE 4.32
Keyframing
the hooks

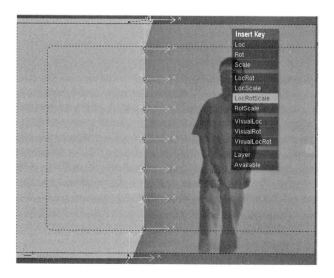

2. Use the up arrow key on your keyboard to advance 10 frames at a time. Advance to a frame shortly before the foreground and the background garbage overlap with each other. In this case, frame 150 is a good place. Position your empties again in a way that covers up the background garbage but stays well out of the way of the foreground, as shown in Figure 4.33. Continue to advance 10 frames at a time. Each time you advance, adjust the positions of the empties so that the matte covers the background and follows the contours of the foreground figure in places where background garbage and the figure intersect, as shown in Figure 4.34. It's not necessary for the matte to follow the entire contour of the figure—it's only necessary to distinguish in those places where the background garbage overlaps with the figure. You can also rotate and scale the empties for more control over the shape of the matte. When the figure has filled the screen, your matte should be keyed completely out of the Camera view, as shown in Figure 4.35.

FIGURE 4.33
Shaping the matte

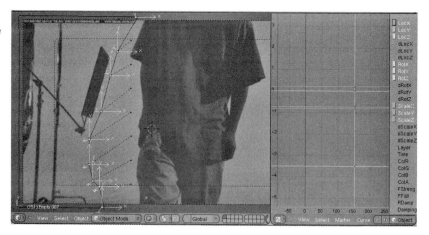

FIGURE 4.34
Masking the area
around the edge of
the figure

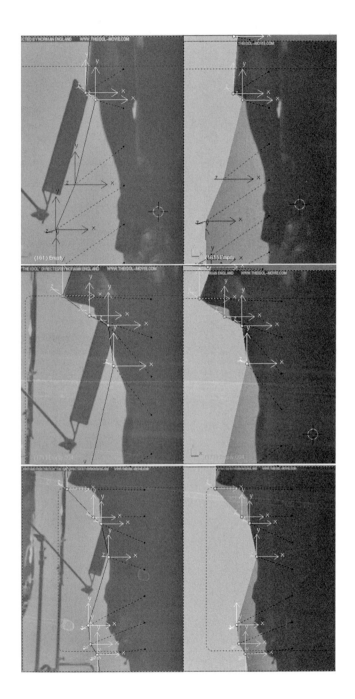

FIGURE 4.34
Continued

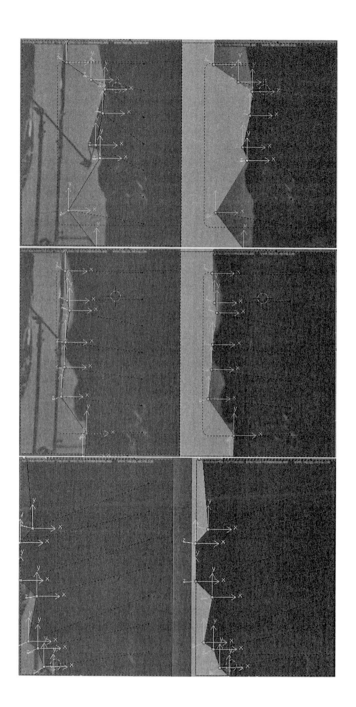

FIGURE 4.35
Keyframing
the matte out of
the frame

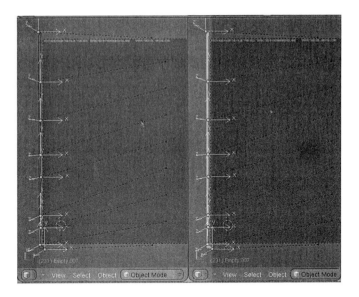

3. A small bit of garbage on the right side of the frame is also in need of matting. Setting up the matte to do this is basically the same process as the left-side matte, but on a smaller and simpler scale. Setting up this matte is presented as an exercise at the end of this chapter. After you have set the necessary keyframes at 10-frame intervals starting at frame 1, go back and start at frame 5 and advance through the sequence again at 10-frame intervals, adjusting any places where the matte pulls away from where it should be. When you have finished doing this, go through the entire sequence frame by frame to make any further adjustments and add whatever further keyframes are necessary. The final matte should look something like the one shown in Figure 4.36.

Using Render Layers and Nodes

As you saw, the garbage matte is created in the 3D space. It can be rendered simply by deselecting Do Composite in the Render buttons and rendering in the ordinary way. For compositing purposes, the World values will only get in the way, so delete them by going to the World buttons subcontext and clicking the X button next to the World field, as shown in Figure 4.37.

To incorporate 3D space renders into the node network, Render Layers input nodes are used. Render layers enable you to organize your rendered scene in such a way that different parts of the same scene can be used as separate input nodes in the compositor. Whatever information you want to be included in a single node should be organized into a distinct render layer. Objects are divided among render layers by their placement on ordinary 3D viewport layers.

In this example, the garbage matte is on layer 1 in the 3D viewport. By default, the first render layer is set to include objects on all 3D viewport layers, but in this case, it needs to hold only objects from layer 1. Later, you will be using other layers to hold objects that will be rendered separately. So go to the Render Layers tab in the Render buttons and click the Layer 1 button so that render layer 1 will render only objects on 3D viewport layer 1, as shown in Figure 4.38.

FIGURE 4.36
The complete animated garbage matte

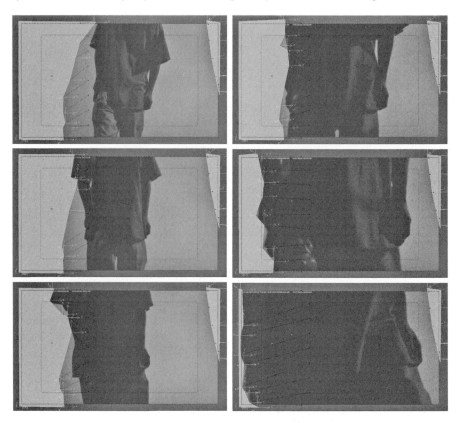

FIGURE 4.37
Deleting the World

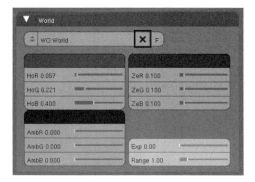

In the node editor window, add a Render Layers node by pressing the spacebar and choosing Add ➤ Input ➤ Render Layers, as shown in Figure 4.39. By default, this node will represent render layer 1.

FIGURE 4.38
Setting up render layers

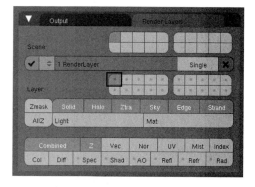

FIGURE 4.39
Adding a Render Layers node

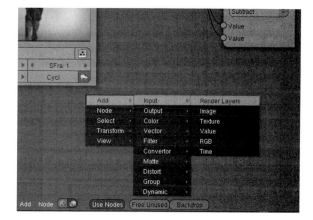

As you recall, the matte you created was solid white. With the World deleted, the rendered background will be solid black. This is the reverse of what the composited matte should be. To add an Invert node, press the spacebar and choose Add ➤ Color ➤ Invert. Connect the Render Layers node to this node, and add a Viewer node to see what the output looks like. In Figure 4.40, you can see both the green screen and garbage mattes side by side. The solution now is simple. If these two mattes are multiplied together, only the areas where both mattes are white (that is, have 1 values) will be white. All other areas will be multiplied by zero, and so will turn out black. Add a Multiplication node by pressing the spacebar and choosing Add ➤ Color ➤ Mix, and then selecting Multiply from the drop-down menu on the node. Connect both mattes to this node's input sockets, and connect the output socket of this node to the Composite node, as shown in Figure 4.41. The resulting rendered matte should look like Figure 4.42.

FIGURE 4.40
Green screen and
garbage mattes

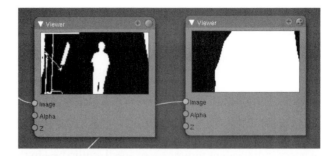

FIGURE 4.41
The node setup
so far

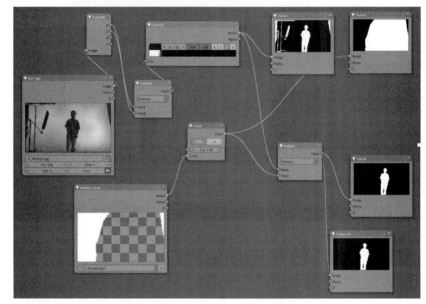

FIGURE 4.42
The intersection
(product) of
both mattes

Garbage Matting the Figure

Unfortunately, there's still a small problem with the matte. It turns out that one of the main props of this movie, which our character happens to be holding in his hand in this scene, is a bright green toy alien doll. Although the lighting in the foreground makes the doll's values much darker than the green screen, there are a few frames in which the lighting brings out the green and causes blemishes on the matte, as shown in Figure 4.43. Normally, the choice of the color screen should be made to be as far from the foreground colors as possible. In this case, knowing that a key foreground object was bright green, it might have been better to use an orange screen as a backdrop. However, choosing a different screen for each shot is a luxury that not every independent filmmaker or small studio has. In this case, it is easy enough to fix the situation in Blender.

FIGURE 4.43

A green screen matte with dark spots

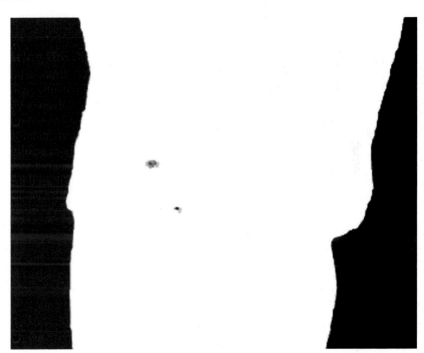

The solution for this problem is also considered garbage matting, except this time, you'll do the exact opposite of what you did earlier. Instead of creating a black matte to multiply with the green screen matte, you will create a white patch that will be added to the green screen matte to eliminate black spots. To set this up, follow these steps:

1. In the 3D viewport, in Camera view, add a new Bezier circle on layer 2, as shown in Figure 4.44. Position the object to cover the green toy. This matte will be used in a separate Render Layers node from the first matte, so it is important that this object be on layer 2, rather than layer 1 where the garbage matte was created. Add four control-point hooks as shown in Figure 4.45, in the same way you added the hooks for the garbage matte.

FIGURE 4.44
Adding a new
Bezier circle
on layer 2

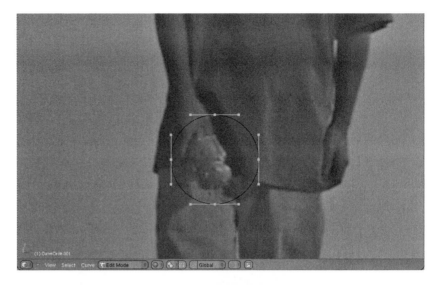

FIGURE 4.45
Adding control-
point hooks

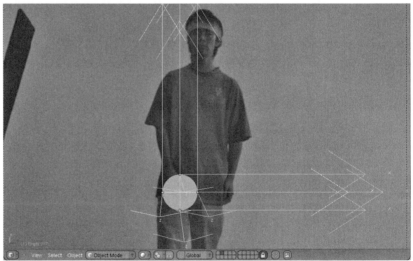

2. In the same way that you keyed the positions of the hooks for the garbage matte, go through the video in increments of 10 frames and key the hooks of this circle so that the object is covering the green toy at all times, but not extending beyond the contour of the character's silhouette. Do this until about frame 170, when the lighting on the doll becomes sufficiently dark that it will no longer be a problem for the green screen matte.

3. In Object mode, select all four empties and the Bezier circle itself. Key the layer value by pressing the I key and choosing Layer, as shown in Figure 4.46. Advance one frame. Press the M key and select the third button from the left, as shown in Figure 4.47. Click OK to send the five selected objects to layer 3. Key the layer value for the objects again. When you render or composite with layer 3 set to be invisible, this will cause the matte to simply disappear at frame 171, when it is no longer needed.

FIGURE 4.46
Keying the
layer value

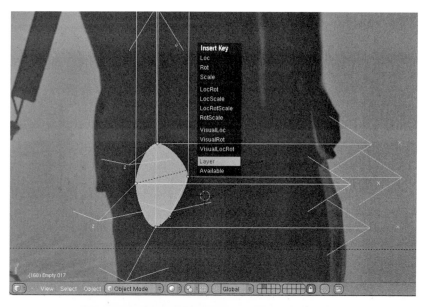

FIGURE 4.46
Keying the
layer value

FIGURE 4.47
Changing layers

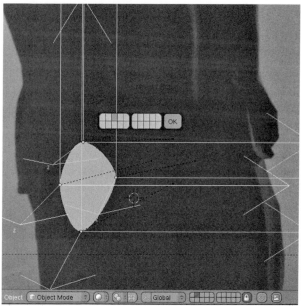

4. Now return to the Render Layers tab in the Render buttons area. From the drop-down menu, select Add New, as shown in Figure 4.48. This will create a new render layer, render layer 2. This render layer should contain the new matte you just created on layer 2 in the 3D view. Make this happen by selecting the second button from the left in the Layer buttons that correspond to this render layer, as shown in Figure 4.49.

FIGURE 4.48
Adding a new render layer

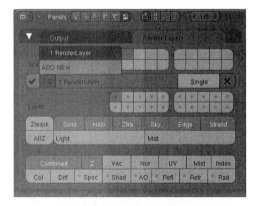

FIGURE 4.49
Render layer 2

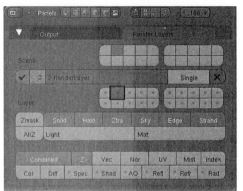

5. In the nodes editor, add a new Render Layers input node. From the drop-down menu on the node, select Render Layer 2. Add the output of this node to the output of the Multiply node you created previously by using a new Add node, as shown in Figure 4.50. Remember, in order to render both mattes, both 3D viewport layers must be set to be visible, as shown in Figure 4.51. Being on separate layers that are assigned to distinct render layers will keep the mattes separate. The final, cleaned-up matte will look like Figure 4.52.

Working with Node Groups

Large numbers of nodes can quickly become unwieldy. To help take care of this, you can bundle collections of nodes into single Node Group nodes. The nodes setup you just created is a good example, because although it is made up of multiple nodes, it functions as a logical unit to create the final green screen matte.

To create a node group out of this set of nodes, select the nodes as shown in Figure 4.53 (the Viewer nodes have been removed) and press Ctrl+G to create the Node Group node shown in Figure 4.54. You can make individual nodes even more compact by clicking the triangle in the upper-left corner of each node to minimize them. Ungroup grouped nodes by pressing Alt+G.

FIGURE 4.50
The node setup
with render layer 2

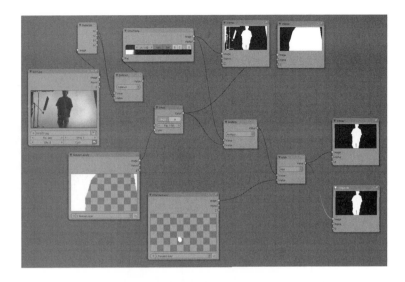

FIGURE 4.51
3D viewport
with layers 1 and
2 visible

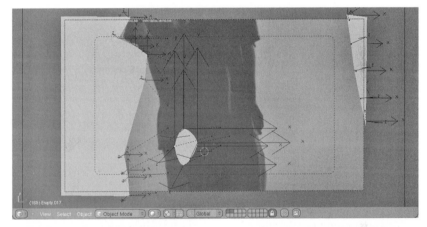

FIGURE 4.52
The cleaned-
up matte

FIGURE 4.53
Selecting the
matte nodes

FIGURE 4.53
Selecting the
matte nodes

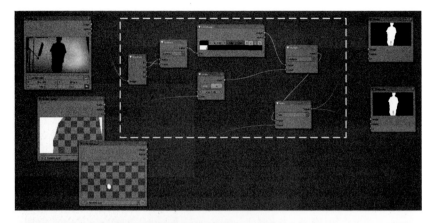

FIGURE 4.54
Creating a
node group

Using Alpha Overlays and Premultiplication

You now have a nice green screen matte with a solid black background and a solid white foreground in the shape of the character. This matte will be used to set the alpha value of the foreground image so that the white areas (the character) are fully opaque (alpha 1) and the background areas are fully transparent (alpha 0). The way to do this is to use a Set Alpha node, which you can add by pressing the spacebar and choosing Add ➢ Converter ➢ Set Alpha, as shown in Figure 4.55. Connect the original image to the Image socket and connect the matte to the Alpha socket.

To test the effect, add a solid color input as a background by pressing the spacebar and choosing Add ➢ Input ➢ RGB, and then adding an AlphaOver node with Add ➢ Color ➢ AlphaOver and connecting them all, as shown in Figure 4.56 (reproduced in the color insert of the book).

FIGURE 4.55
Adding a Set
Alpha node

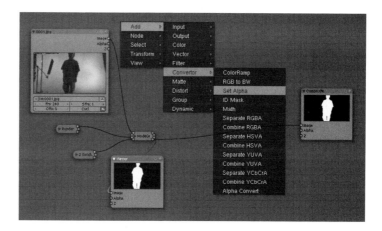

Premultiplication controls the ordering in which multiple overlaid alpha values are calculated. Premultiplication values that are incorrectly set can cause unwanted artifacts or halo effects. In this example, there are problems with the unconverted premultiplication values that result in some white streaky artifacts on the colored background and around the edge of the figure. These are fixed by the use of the Convert Premul option. You can see the difference between the two rendered outputs in Figure 4.57 (reproduced in the color insert of the book).

 Real World Scenario

BLENDER AND THE MILO MOTION CONTROL

Working with high-end professional camera equipment can provide exciting opportunities to exploit Blender's video-compositing tools to the fullest. For his sci-fi short film *minDrones*, Luca Bonavita made extensive use of the Academy Award–winning Mark Roberts Motion Control Milo camera guidance rig. The Milo enables cinematographers to program complex camera setups and moves, which can subsequently be repeated with a high level of precision, generating multiple shots of different scenes with exactly matching camera movements. In addition to enabling multiple live-action shots to be easily composited together, the camera movement information from the Milo can be entered into Blender's 3D space by means of a Python script, enabling the Blender 3D camera to exactly replicate the setups and movements of the original shot. Built-in motion-tracking and camera-placement features are in the works for future versions of Blender, but nothing beats the Milo when it comes to precision and power in controlling and matching camera motion.

Blender Artist Riccardo Covino presented this exciting work with Blender and the Milo motion control system at the 2006 Blender Conference, complete with some truly eye-popping visual effects from the movie. You can see the presentation online at www.blender.org/features-gallery/feature-videos/?video=imaging and download a PDF report of the work from http://download.blender.org/documentation/bc2006/blenderandmilo.pdf.

Covino returned to the Blender Conference in 2008 to present his impressive recent live-action/CG Blender compositing work for the Italian independent film *Un Mare da Favola* (*A Fabulous Sea*). The video of that presentation is also well worth checking out at http://river-valley.tv/conferences/blender_conference_2008/.

FIGURE 4.56
Node setup with a colored background and an AlphaOver node

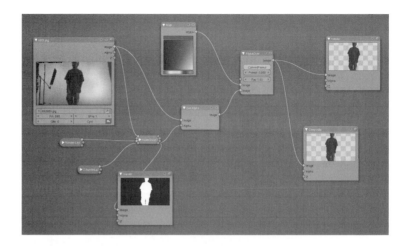

FIGURE 4.57
Without and with the Convert Premul option set

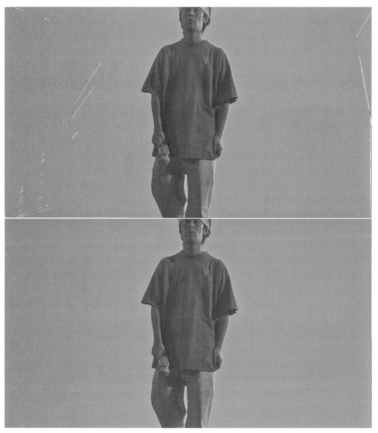

Spill Correction and Cleaning Up

Checking the alpha overlaid foreground image over a colored background is also a good way to highlight the problem of color *spill* that often occurs when doing this kind of compositing. Because the subject is being shot originally against an expansive, bright green background, there is a green tint to the reflected light from the background as well as background light that shows through transparent or semitransparent areas of the subject such as hair. You can clearly see the undesirable green spill in Figure 4.58, which is repeated in the color insert of the book.

FIGURE 4.58
Green spill

The solution to this problem is to adjust the color channels directly and to bring down the level of green in the image overall.

Tweaking Color Channels

To tweak the individual R, G, B, and A channels of an image directly, use a Separate RGBA Converter node described previously to split up the values, and then use another Converter node, Combine RGBA, to put the values back together as a completed color image.

In this case, you need to bring down the overall green level. However, there is a danger to bringing the level too low. Remember, the character is holding a green object. Adjusting the green channel affects the color of green things disproportionately, so an adjustment that might not make the image as a whole look unnatural may easily alter the color of the doll so that it no longer looks green. There must remain enough energy in the green channel that this object still looks green.

There's no single right answer to how to do this, but a simple solution is to average the energy levels of all three channels and to use this average as the green channel. This significantly reduces the strength of the green channel, but ensures that the green channel remains stronger than the other two channels in places that are predominantly green to begin with. This can be done by using two additive nodes and a Divide node, as shown in Figure 4.59. Collecting those nodes in a single node group and connecting the red and blue channels straight through yields the node setup shown in Figure 4.60. The difference between the image before and after adjusting the green channel can be seen in Figure 4.61, also repeated in the color insert of the book. Note that the doll is still green in the adjusted image.

FIGURE 4.59
Calculating a new green channel

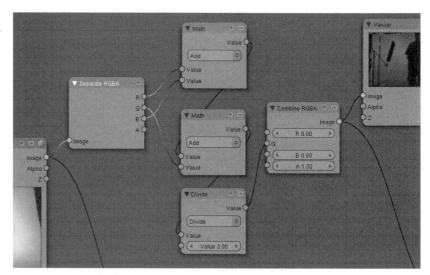

FIGURE 4.60
Red and blue channels connected

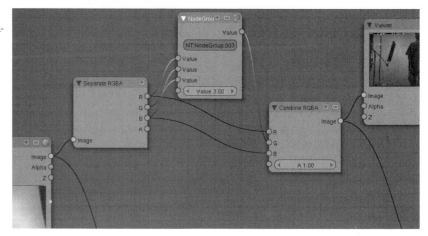

FIGURE 4.61
Renders with origi-
nal and adjusted
green channels

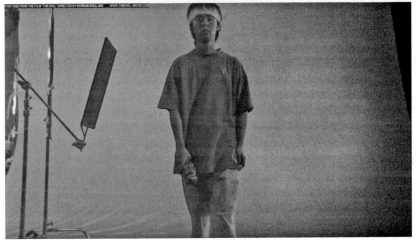

Finishing Off the Matte

There are a number of areas where a matte can be fine-tuned. You can add a Blur node from the Add menu under Add ➤ Filter ➤ Blur. Blur nodes can be used to soften the edge of the matte. Another filter node, Dilate/Erode, can be used to expand or shrink the white area of the matte, which can be useful for tightening, or *choking*, the matte around the subject. Blurring can be used on the matte itself before using the matte to set the alpha value of the foreground image, or later in the composite. The full node setup, including a slight blur effect and a slight erosion of the matte, can be seen in Figure 4.62 (the temporary color background has been deleted). This setup results in the output shown in Figure 4.63, seen here in the UV/Image editor window with the Alpha Value button (highlighted) set to visible. This image is repeated in color in the book's color insert.

FIGURE 4.62
Full node setup

FIGURE 4.62
Full node setup

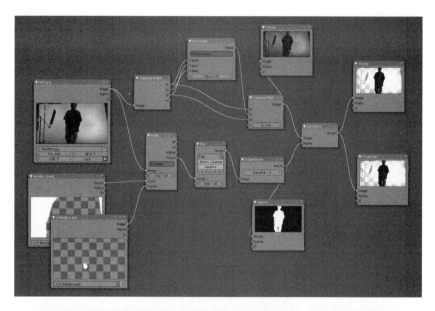

FIGURE 4.63
Image viewer with
the alpha channel
set to visible

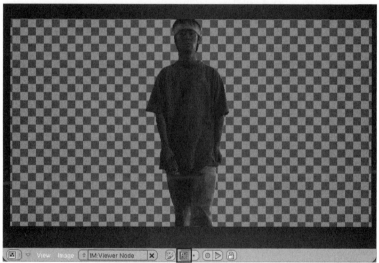

There are a couple of things you can do with this composited video. You can use it as the foreground to a more involved scene in the compositor, by introducing a background, as shown in Figure 4.64 (and repeated in color in the book's color insert). Doing this is left as an exercise for you in the "The Bottom Line" section of this chapter. The image file is a sky map created by BlenderArtists.org member M@dcow and freely available at http://blenderartists.org/forum. You'll find the sky_twighlight.jpg file on the CD that accompanies this book.

When you have composited the foreground image into a specific background, you can then do some further color adjustments. In Figure 4.65 (and repeated in color in the book's color insert), you can see the results of using a slightly purple screen over only the most brightly lit highlights of the foreground image. If you experiment with the nodes presented in this chapter, you should be able to work out how to do this. The actual node setup is included as an exercise in the "The Bottom Line" section at the end of this chapter.

FIGURE 4.64
Composited video with a background image

FIGURE 4.65
Composited video with a background image

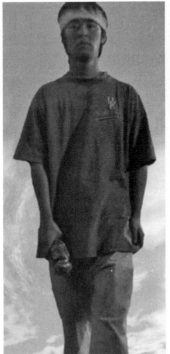

Another thing you can do is to export the video and use it as an alpha overlay in the Sequence editor. You will see how to do this in Chapter 5. If you render the image to an output and plan to use the alpha values, make sure that you render to a format that can represent alpha values, such as PNG (.png) or Targa (.tga). Also make sure that you have selected RGBA output in the Format tab of the Render buttons area, rather than the default RGB, which does not encode alpha information.

Muting Nodes

As you've worked with slightly larger node networks, you may have noticed that changing values, reconnecting nodes, or making other adjustments or modifications can take a while because of the need for Blender to recalculate the effects of all the nodes each time a change is made. You can mitigate this problem by muting selected nodes when you don't need them. You can mute and unmute nodes by pressing the M button over the node. Muted nodes' names appear in square brackets on the top of the node, and a red curved line is drawn across the face of a selected muted node.

Learning More about Compositing

This chapter has barely scratched the surface of what you can do with the Blender node system in terms of video compositing. There is a great deal more to learn about Blender's compositing functionality, but it is even more important to study the fundamentals of how 2D images are composited with each other. Coupled with what you have learned here about working with nodes, a thorough grounding in compositing will give you all the knowledge you need to get exactly the effects you are after. For this information, there is no better place to look than Ron Brinkmann's *The Art and Science of Digital Compositing, Second Edition: Techniques for Visual Effects, Animation and Motion Graphics* (Morgan Kaufmann, 2008). This is truly the bible of compositing, and is a must for anybody serious about understanding what they are doing and why in compositing. There is also an excellent website full of information about the book and about compositing at www.digitalcompositing.com. I highly recommend checking it out as you continue to deepen your skills in compositing with Blender.

The Bottom Line

Blender's composite node system is a flexible and powerful way to combine multiple original-image and video sources to achieve a wide variety of effects. One of the many things that the system enables is the creation of green screen mattes, which can be used to separate a foreground figure from its background in order to composite it into other scenes.

Use the Blender composite node system to pull a green screen matte. When you know in advance that you will be compositing a character or object into a scene, a common technique is to shoot the original video of the foreground figure against a colored background screen. This makes it possible to eliminate the background quickly and easily by using color channels in the node compositor.

Master It Using a nodes setup based on the example in this chapter, add a background image from an image file to create a fully composited image such as the one shown in Figure 4.64. You can use the sky_map.jpg file included on the CD.

Use curves and hooks to do simple rotoscoped garbage matting. Background clutter in the original footage can cause imperfections in the matte. To block these out, garbage matting is used. In cases when the garbage matte must interact with the silhouette of the foreground figure, some hand-keying or rotoscoping may be necessary.

> **Master It** Using a 3D curve animated with hooks, add a second garbage matte to the video example used in this chapter to cover the debris in the background of the right side of the frame.

Manipulate the video's color channels to reduce color spill. Anytime you composite footage shot under one set of lighting conditions with footage shot under another set of lighting conditions, color mismatches can occur. This is particularly the case when a green screen is used, which can cause a green cast or spill in the original footage. To eliminate this, it is possible to work directly with the color channels to adjust the mix of red, green, and blue energy in the image to better match the background.

> **Master It** In the composited image you made in the first "Master It" exercise of this chapter, create a slightly purple screen that affects only the most brightly lit highlights of the foreground figure to attain results similar to those in Figure 4.65.

Chapter 5

Working with the Video Sequence Editor

Blender is primarily known as a 3D modeling and animation application, but as you have seen throughout this book, in truth it is much more than just that. In addition to all of its other functionality, Blender also quietly holds the distinction of being the only cross-platform open source video-editing application worth its salt.

Although Blender is not gunning to replace high-end professional video-editing and compositing suites anytime soon in large studio pipelines, the Blender Video Sequence Editor (VSE) and the corresponding composite node system that you read about in Chapter 4, "Video Compositing with Nodes," are more than adequate for many common video-editing and compositing tasks. When the Blender VSE tools are used together, they're much more powerful than the majority of inexpensive consumer-grade video-editing tools. This chapter shows you how to use the VSE to put your animations, video, sound, and composited scenes together into a coherent whole.

In this chapter, you will learn to

♦ Import, edit, and render video with the Blender VSE

♦ Create transitions, overlays, and effects for your videos

♦ Incorporate content directly from 3D or composited scenes into your videos

Working with the Video Sequence Editor

The Blender VSE was originally created to meet the needs of 3D animators who needed a way to edit individual animated sequences together to create a completed whole. Previously, there had been no viable open source alternative for this kind of work. As the development has progressed, the VSE has begun to come into its own as a viable alternative for many video-editing tasks. Among its advantages is a simple, easy-to-use interface that is fully integrated and consistent with other Blender environments, so it is especially intuitive to use for people who are accustomed to Blender's hot keys and workflow.

Another very nice quality of the VSE is the ease with which it works with a wide variety of formats and codecs. Because it is not married to any specific proprietary format, it is equally comfortable with .avi files, .mov files, and most other video or image formats, provided you have the appropriate third-party codecs installed. Even high-end proprietary codecs can be easily used by Blender, enabling you to work with professional video formats. This flexibility makes Blender a terrific tool for file-format conversion. No other software makes it easier to output a video as a sequence of stills, or vice versa.

But this is not all there is to the VSE. The VSE is also a fully functional, nonlinear video editor capable of handling multiple video and audio channels and compositing them, both with and without the full backing of the Blender node system. A variety of built-in effects are included in the default installation of the VSE, and it can be expanded even further with external plug-ins, as you will see in this chapter. In addition to all this, the VSE has several powerful visualization tools built in that enable you to see detailed information about the color and luminance distributions of your video for precise adjustments and balancing.

Like all functionality in Blender, the VSE is accessed through a specific Video Sequence Editor window type, as shown in Figure 5.1. As always, you can set up your Blender workspace in whatever way you like. The built-in Sequence screen configuration can be accessed via the drop-down menu shown in Figure 5.2. The default Sequence screen configuration is shown in Figure 5.3. Even if you don't use this configuration exactly as is, it is a good basis from which to set up your own custom configuration.

FIGURE 5.1
Selecting the VSE
window type

FIGURE 5.2
Selecting the
Sequence screen
configuration

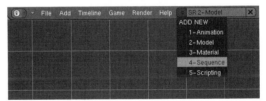

The windows in this configuration are as follows:

◆ The upper-left window is an Ipo curve editor window set to display Sequence curves. This is used to control the Fac values (strength) of animatable sequence effects.

◆ The upper-right window is a VSE window set to Image Preview display mode. The header of this window is hidden in this screen configuration by default. To view the header, move the mouse over the window itself and then over the edge of the window where the header should be, and right-click. Select the Add Header option to display the header. The header drop-down menu shown in Figure 5.4 is where the Image Preview display mode is selected.

◆ The middle window that extends the width of the workspace is a VSE set to Sequence display mode. This is where the video and audio strips are displayed in their corresponding channels, and where you will be doing most of the actual video-editing work. In general, when this chapter refers to a *VSE window* or a *Sequence editor window,* it means the VSE window is set to Sequence display mode, as shown in Figure 5.3. If the chapter refers to other display modes, such as the Image Preview display mode, it will specify the display mode explicitly.

◆ The window below the VSE window is the Timeline, which should be very familiar to any Blender user.

◆ The window at the bottom of the workspace is the familiar Buttons window.

FIGURE 5.3
The default Sequence screen configuration

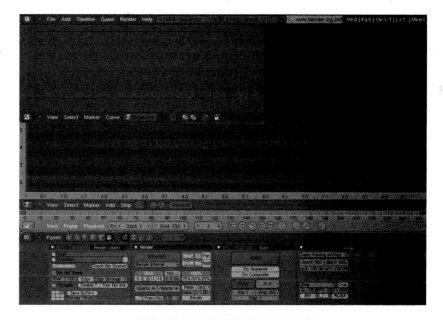

FIGURE 5.4
The VSE window with Image Preview selected

Importing Video and Image Sequences

After you have set up your video-editing environment, the first step in working with the VSE is to import a video or image sequence to work with. Do this by moving the mouse over the VSE window and pressing the spacebar to bring up the menu shown in Figure 5.5. As you can see from the menu, there are several choices of strip types you can add. For importing new video or image sequences, you can choose the Image Sequence option, the Movie option, or the Movie + Audio option.

VIDEOS ON THE CD

There are two short video clips included on the CD that accompanies this book. You should use them to follow along with the descriptions in this chapter. They are both found in the video_clips subdirectory of the CD. The first, end_zone_clip.avi, is an excerpt from *End Zone*, a film directed by Rob Cunningham (www.dualactionpictures.com). It is a black-and-white movie with sound. The frame rate for this clip is 24fps. The second clip, idol_clip.mov, is a composite of green screen footage from Norman England's film *The iDol* (www.theidol-movie.com) and a sky map created by BlenderArtists.org user M@dcow.

FIGURE 5.5

The Add Sequence Strip menu

If you choose to add an image sequence, a file browser will open and you can navigate to the directory where your images are and select them all with the A key, as shown in Figure 5.6. Image sequences rendered by Blender are automatically numbered, and the numbering is read by the VSE, so ordering is also automatic. Image sequences not created by Blender will also be ordered automatically if they are numbered. Numbering should include leading zeros and be the last part of the filename before the dot.

If you add only a single image, Blender will automatically create a 50-frame sequence from the image.

FIGURE 5.6

Selecting an image sequence in the file browser

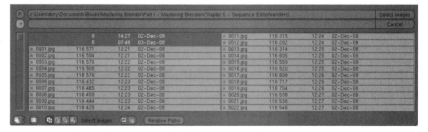

FILE SELECTION IN THE FILE BROWSER

Selecting files in the file browser has its quirks. There are two ways to select single files. Either left-click the filename so that it appears in the field at the top of the file browser and then click Select Images, or right-click the filename so that it is highlighted and then click Select Images. Either method works the same.

To select multiple images, you must right-click on the image names to highlight them. You can drag the mouse while holding the right mouse button to drag-select filenames. Right-clicking more than once (or dragging over already selected files) will deselect the files. Unfortunately, there is no good way to select a range of files based only on the first and last files in the range. This means that large sets of files in a directory can be difficult to select distinctly from other large sets of files in the same directory. The easiest way to deal with this is to make sure that each individual image sequence has a directory all to itself. In this case, you can simply select all images with the A key.

The process is exactly the same for importing a movie, which can be in any movie format for which you have an installed codec. Either left-clicking or right-clicking on the filename and then clicking Select Movie will work. You can add multiple movie files by right-clicking on multiple movie filenames and highlighting them, and then clicking Select Movie, as shown in Figure 5.7. In this case, the two movies will be added on the same channel, one directly after the other, as shown in Figure 5.8.

FIGURE 5.7
Selecting multiple movies

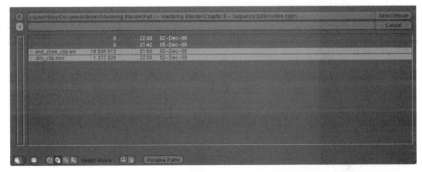

FIGURE 5.8
Multiple movies added to the VSE at the same time

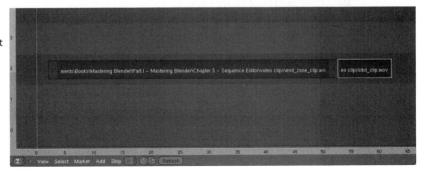

The Movie + Audio option imports video and audio channels simultaneously.

Different kinds of sequence strips are color coded. The colors for the basic input sequences are as follows:

◆ Gray strips are repeated still frames.

◆ Blue strips are movies.

◆ Purple strips are image sequences.

◆ Aqua strips are sound.

◆ Green strips are Blender scenes.

Each type of effect strip also has a distinct color, to make each easier to distinguish when the different types occur together in the editing area.

MORE ON CODECS

The Xvid codec was used for the sample .avi file on the CD that accompanies this book. Xvid is a very good open source codec for creating small but relatively high-quality videos for personal use. You can download the codec at www.xvid.org if you don't already have it installed on your system. The .mov file was encoded as a QuickTime MPEG-4 file. For playing back both videos outside of Blender, VLC is among the best no-frills video players available. Installing VLC automatically installs a variety of useful codecs onto your system. You can download the latest VLC player at www.videolan.org.

Setting Frame Rates

The *frame rate* of a video is the number of frames that make up a second of normal-speed play. The frame rate is expressed in frames per second (fps). The most commonly used frame rates are as follows:

◆ 24fps is typical for 16mm and 35mm film.

◆ 25fps is often used with the PAL television encoding system, the encoding system used in Europe, much of Africa, and elsewhere in the world.

◆ 30fps is often used for high-definition TV.

◆ 29.97fps (30 × 1000 ÷ 1001) is typically used with NTSC encoding, which is used in North America, parts of Asia, and some other countries.

Digital video files can come in any of these or other frame rates.

When you add a video to the Blender VSE, Blender calculates the video frame rate based on the frame rate value you have set in the Format panel of the Render buttons, shown in Figure 5.9. After you have imported the video, the time spanned by that video strip is fixed. If you change the frame rate and re-render, the number of frames that make up the video will be altered to adjust for the difference.

FIGURE 5.9
The frame
rate fields

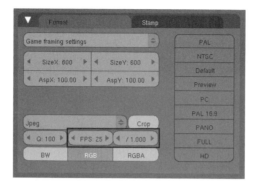

This is important because it means that you must have the frame rate set correctly when you first import a video. Figure 5.10 shows the results of importing a Movie + Audio file at 25fps when the original video was encoded at 29.97fps. As you can see, the video and audio channels do not match. You cannot fix this from within the VSE. You must delete the strips and add them again with the correct frame rate. In this case, the correct frame rate should be entered in the frame rate field like this: ◀ FPS: 30 ▶ ◀ / 1.001 ▶ . This is a more accurate way to represent the 29.97fps frame rate, which is actually a 30fps frame rate counted with a *drop frame*.

FIGURE 5.10
A mismatched
video and audio
strip added
with the wrong
frame rate

If you are dealing with a file that you did not create yourself, you may not know what frame rate it was encoded at. You may need to import it more than once to find out which frame rate gives accurate results. You should first try the common frame rates listed previously.

Use the T key to toggle the VSE to display frames or seconds along its X axis.

DROP FRAMES

The 29.97 drop-frame frame rate is a historical relic of analog television encoding. The original motivation for dropping the frame was to make up for the extra time taken by color transmission while maintaining the 30fps frame rate of previously used black-and-white televisions. In spite of what the term might seem to imply, no actual video frames are dropped; the dropped frame refers only to the way the frames are counted. Frame dropping has no effect on the quality or content of the video.

Working with Sequence Strips

After you have added a video, you can drag it, extend it, or edit it in a variety of ways.

BASIC SEQUENCE STRIP OPERATIONS

When you add a video or audio strip (or both at once), the strip will be fully selected and will follow your mouse until you left-click on the spot where you want to place the strip. The strip will still be selected until it has been deselected or until another strip or strip end is selected.

There are three places where a strip can be selected. You can select the entire strip by right-clicking on the middle of the strip. With the strip selected in this way, you can move the strip around the VSE editing area by pressing the G key and moving the strip with your mouse. By right- or left-clicking on the arrows at the far-right or far-left ends of the strips, you select only those ends, as shown in Figure 5.11. You can then move the ends independently by using the G key, either truncating the sequence or extending the sequence strip. If you extend the strip beyond the length of the original video clip, the extended portion will be composed entirely of frames showing the last frame (if the strip is extended to the right) or the first frame (if the strip is extended to the left). The extended portion will be colored gray, representing a duplicated still frame, as shown in Figure 5.12. All three of these possible selections can also be made by pressing the B key and using a box selection method. If the middle of a strip falls within the box area, the whole strip will be selected. If only one end of the strip is within the box area, only that end will be selected.

When moving the full strip around the editing area, you can constrain the movement to a single channel by pressing the G key first and then the X key. Likewise, you can press the G key first and then the Y key to constrain the movement to "vertical" movement from one channel to the other, without allowing the strip to slide along the channels. These are analogous to the X-axis and Y-axis constraint hot keys in the 3D space, except that they operate on the 2D axes of the VSE editing area.

You can snap a sequence strip to the current frame, represented by the vertical green bar, by pressing Shift+S.

FIGURE 5.11
An unselected sequence strip, a selected sequence strip, a sequence strip with only its left end selected, and a sequence strip with only its right end selected

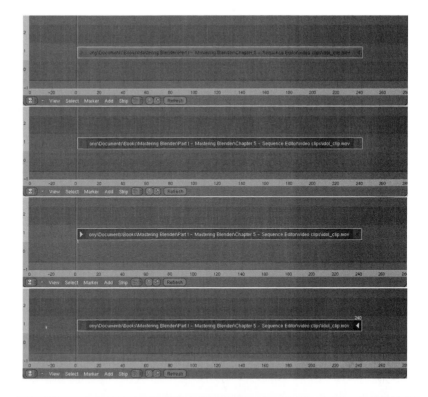

FIGURE 5.12
A sequence strip extended beyond the length of the original clip to the right

THE FILTER PANEL

Other important operations on video strips can be carried out in the Filter panel of the Sequence buttons subcontext. In this panel, you can flip the image along the X or Y axis, reverse the video in time, set a *strobe* value so that only every *n*th frame is displayed, and set several other parameters related to the video strip.

CHANNELS

Sequence strips in the VSE occupy numbered horizontal slots called *channels*. Channels are numbered from zero, with zero at the bottom and the channel numbers increasing upward.

Although it appears empty, the 0 channel implicitly contains the final composited sequence, and so you cannot place sequences to be edited in this channel. The VSE Image Preview display mode enables you to select which channel to display, as shown in Figure 5.13. Note that when no compositing is involved, the highest-numbered (topmost) channel is given precedence. For this reason, on frames where both sequence strips are present in the figure, the strip in channel 2 is displayed when the Chan value is set to 0 in the Image Preview header.

FIGURE 5.13
Displaying the contents of channels 2, 1, and 0

CUTTING AND COPYING

There are two main ways to cut a strip. The K key cuts the strip destructively at the current frame. This type of cut is *destructive* in the sense that both of the resulting cut parts are incomplete, exactly as if you cut actual video or film. Shift+K, on the other hand, cuts the strip nondestructively, in that both of the resulting cut portions are not incomplete; they are merely truncated to the point where the cut was made. You can see the difference between destructive and nondestructive cuts, performed simultaneously on audio and video strips, in Figure 5.14. Note that in the nondestructive case, a representation of the continued clip can be seen extending from each cut part to the point where the truncated clip actually extends. (A color version of this figure is included in the book's color insert.) Figure 5.15 shows a nondestructively cut video strip with the two parts separated. You can see the continuations of the strips clearly here. Extending the strip by moving the strip end will reveal the original clip.

Strips can be duplicated with Shift+D and deleted with the X key.

FIGURE 5.14
Audio and video strips cut destructively and nondestructively

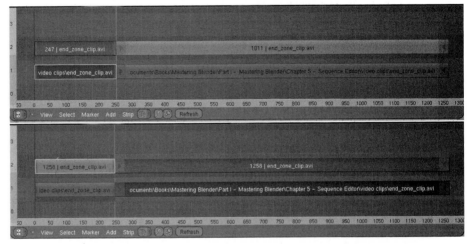

FIGURE 5.15
A closer look at a video strip cut nondestructively

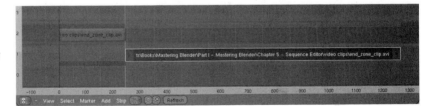

Editing Sound

Sound strips can be added in two ways. The Sound (HD) option in the Add menu plays the sound directly from the hard disk without loading it into RAM. This option enables you to import a variety of different types of sound files, including MP3s and the soundtracks of video files. If you add Movie + Audio, the HD option is the only choice. The Sound (RAM) option can be used only with .wav files. When you use the RAM option for importing sound, the sequence strip displays the audio waveform, as shown in Figure 5.16. An advantage of this method is that you can pack the sound file into the .blend file by using the External Data ➢ Pack Into .blend File option in the File menu. When the sound data is packed into the file, it is no longer dependent on the external copy of the file.

FIGURE 5.16
The same sound
file imported with
the RAM option
(top) and the HD
option (bottom)

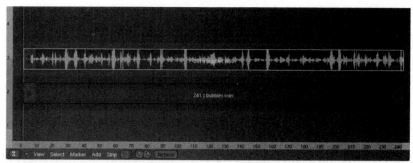

The Sequencer panel in the Sound Block buttons subcontext, shown in Figure 5.17, gives you access to several important functions. The Sync button synchronizes the playback of 3D animation with sound in real time, but is not especially pertinent to the VSE. The Scrub option, however, is very useful in the VSE. It enables you to drag the current frame up and down the Timeline with your mouse, and hear the corresponding audio in real time. The buttons at the bottom of the panel enable you to control the volume of the final mix, mute it, or export a .wav file of the complete audio mix by using the Mixdown button.

The Filter panel in the Sequence buttons subcontext shown in Figure 5.18 contains a numerical field for controlling the Gain (volume) of the currently active audio strip, and another field for controlling the left-right stereo panning of the sound. A 0.0 value in this field represents an even stereo sound, 1.0 causes the sound to come from the right speaker, and –1.0 sends the sound to the left speaker. The Pan value cannot be animated directly, but the volume of individual audio strips can be. To animate a stereo pan, it is necessary to use multiple audio strips with different pan values and to fade their volumes into each other.

FIGURE 5.17
The Sequencer
panel in the
Sound Block buttons subcontext

FIGURE 5.18
The Filter panel

Controlling the volume of an audio sequence strip can be done by adding a Sequence Ipo curve in the Ipo curve editor window, as shown in Figure 5.19. If there is no curve in the Ipo curve editor, Ctrl+LMB (left mouse button) will add a curve. If there is a curve already, Ctrl+LMB will add points to that curve. By default, a Sequence Ipo curve is 100 frames long in the Ipo curve editor, and this length corresponds to the full length of the sequence strip, regardless of how long the sequence strip actually is. You can force the Ipo to use the same frame-numbering system as the actual sequence by selecting IPO Frame Locked in the Edit panel of the Sequence buttons subcontext, as shown in Figure 5.20.

In Figure 5.21, you can see the same Ipo and audio sequence as in Figure 5.19, but the frame counting is different. In 5.19, the indicator at frame 95 in the Ipo curve editor window corresponds with an indicator 95 percent of the way through the sequence, at about frame 234 in the VSE window. With the Ipo frames locked to the sequence as in Figure 5.21, frame 95 in the Ipo editor window corresponds directly to frame 95 in the VSE window. The green current frame indicators in the sequence area are difficult to see in grayscale, so Figures 5.19 and 5.21 are repeated in the color insert of this book.

FIGURE 5.19
The Fac Ipo curve controlling the volume of an audio strip

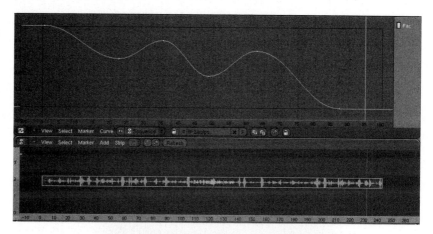

FIGURE 5.20
Forcing the Ipo frames to conform to actual sequence frames

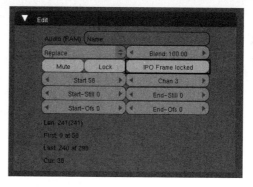

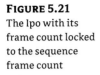

FIGURE 5.21
The Ipo with its frame count locked to the sequence frame count

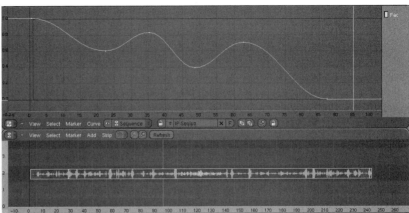

AUDACITY

Audacity is a powerful audio editor and an indispensible part of any open source multimedia tool kit. You can use it to edit or adjust audio waveforms in a multitude of ways and to convert audio files from one to another. It's extremely versatile and surprisingly easy to use. You can download Audacity for all major platforms at http://audacity.sourceforge.net.

Using Markers

You can add, delete, and edit markers to the VSE. To add a marker to the current frame, press Ctrl+Alt+M. To select a marker, right-click on the marker; and to select multiple markers, use Shift+RMB (right mouse button). To deselect a marker, use Shift+RMB. To toggle between all markers and no markers selected, use Ctrl+A. To delete a marker, press Shift+X. To move selected markers, press Ctrl+G.

Accessing Other VSE Display Modes

The most-used display modes for the VSE are the Sequence display mode and the Image Preview display mode. Three other display modes are available: Histogram, Chroma Vectorscope, and Luma Waveform.

HISTOGRAM

The Histogram view enables you to see the correspondence between color channels and luminance levels. Low to high luminance levels are represented from the left side of the graph to the right side, and the number of pixels of each color at each luminance level is indicated by the height of the corresponding vertical bar. For example, a long red bar near the right of the graph indicates that the image has a large number of red pixels with high luminance. Figure 5.22 shows histograms for three frames from a video. As you can see, the contours of the histogram change as the luminance levels change (reproduced in the color insert of the book).

FIGURE 5.22
Histograms for
three frames
from a video

CHROMA VECTORSCOPE

The Chroma Vectorscope enables you to see the distribution of colors and saturation in your image. The points around the colored hexagon indicate the color, and the distance from the red dot in the center indicates saturation. Each pixel in the image is represented by a point in the graph. Points near the colored hexagon are the most-saturated pixels. The highly saturated colors in the character's hair in Figure 5.23 can be seen in a Chroma Vectorscope representation with many points distributed near the edges of the graph (also reproduced in the color insert of the book).

LUMA WAVEFORM

The Luma Waveform visualizes a separate curve representing the luminance (brightness) of each row of pixels in the image. As you can see in Figure 5.24, the middle of the image, where the figure blocks out the background light, is represented by steep drops in the luminance of all rows of pixels. By clicking the CS (color separation) button in the header, you can also see the Luma Waveforms of each of the three color channels, as shown in Figure 5.25, which is also reproduced in the color insert of the book.

FIGURE 5.23
Chroma Vector-scope display mode

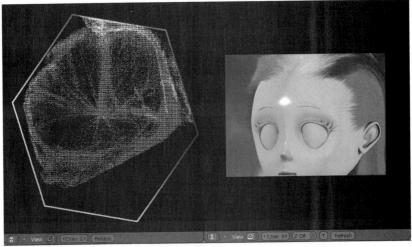

FIGURE 5.24
Luma Waveform display mode

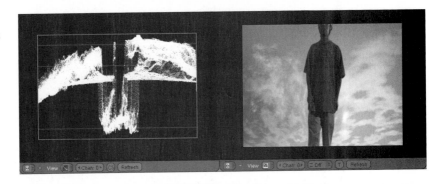

FIGURE 5.25
Luma Waveform display mode with color separation

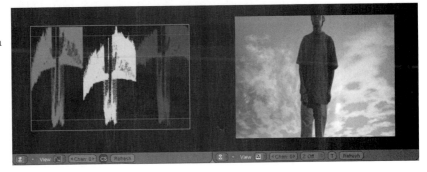

Adding Transitions and Compositing in the VSE

You can do much more than just cut and paste strips. You can combine and transfer between strips in a variety of ways.

Alpha Overlays

One of the most important compositing features of the VSE is the ability to use alpha overlays. When an alpha overlay is used, the alpha value of the overlaid strip is used to determine the visibility of the strip under it. The alpha values of the overlaid strip range from 0 (transparent) to 1 (completely opaque).

To use an alpha overlay, select two strips in the VSE. The last selected strip is the active strip. With the two strips selected, press the spacebar and select one of the three alpha overlay options from the Add Strip menu. The three options are as follows:

Alpha Over places the active strip over the other selected strip. With this option, the overall transparency of the overlaid strip can be animated with the Fac Ipo.

Alpha Under places the active strip under the other selected strip. With this option, the overall transparency of the *bottommost* strip of the two can be animated with the Fac Ipo.

Alpha Over Drop places the active strip over the other selected strip. However, unlike Alpha Over, the overall transparency of the *bottommost* of the two strips is animated with the Fac Ipo.

Having these three options for alpha overlays gives you a great deal of flexibility in how you combine strips. Alpha overlays do not depend on the ordering of the channels that the input strips occupy, but only on the order in which the strips were selected.

In Figure 5.26, you can see the results of overlaying a PNG image sequence with an alpha zero background over a movie clip. The Image Preview windows along the right of the figure show the contents of VSE channels 3, 2, and 1. The large Image Preview window above the VSE strips shows the final composited image in VSE channel 0. The PNG file used here was created using the node setup from Chapter 4 and can be found in the video_clips subdirectory on the CD.

FIGURE 5.26
An alpha overlay

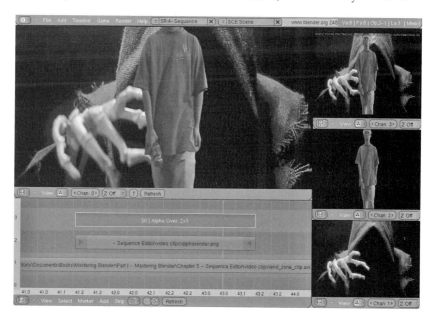

Alpha overlaying directly in the VSE does not offer all of the control that compositing in the nodes compositor gives you. However, it is a quick and easy way to do basic compositing, and in many cases, it may be all you need.

Fades and Transitions

Transitioning from one strip to the next is done in a similar way to alpha overlays: by creating a new strip for the transition type you want. A commonly used transition is the *cross fade*, which fades gradually from one sequence to the next.

To create a cross fade, first select the sequence that is being transitioned from, and then hold down the Shift key to select the sequence that is being transitioned to (that is, the order of selection should be the same as the chronological ordering of the sequences, for an ordinary cross fade). Press the spacebar and add a Cross sequence from the Add Sequence menu. The Cross strip will extend over the length of the overlapping portions of the two original sequences, as shown in Figure 5.27. The transition will occur over the course of the Cross strip. In the Image Preview windows along the right of Figure 5.27, you can see previews of VSE channels 3, 2, and 1. The main Image Preview window above the sequence strip editor shows the fully composited image from channel 0.

FIGURE 5.27
A Cross transition

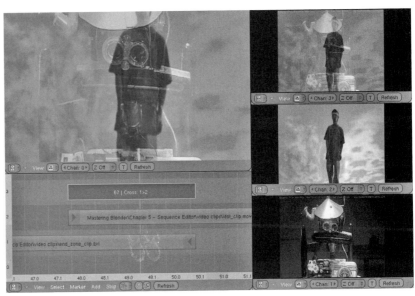

Gamma Cross behaves like Cross, except that it also performs gamma correction on the output image, which can result in improved color and luminance balance.

Wipes are another way to transition from one sequence to another. Wipe strips are added in exactly the same way that Cross strips are added, as shown in Figure 5.28.

Wipes enable somewhat more complex transitions than fades. You can choose the type of wipe you want to use from the Effect panel in the Sequence buttons subcontext, as shown in Figure 5.29.

You can also set a level of blurring to soften the line where the two sequences meet, and the angle of the wipe, where appropriate. The four types of wipes are as follows:

Single wipe transitions with a straight wiping movement across the screen from one sequence to the next.

Double wipe mirrors the movement of the single wipe to create two borders between the transitioning sequences.

Iris wipe creates an expanding (or contracting) circle in which the new sequence appears in place of the previous sequence.

Clock wipe transitions to the new sequence with a radial motion like that of the hands of a clock.

Figure 5.30 shows each of these wipe types with a blur value of 0.20.

FIGURE 5.28
A Wipe strip

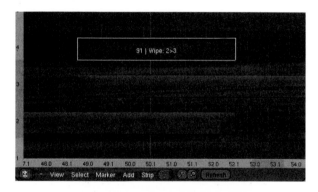

FIGURE 5.29
Setting options for
the wipe

FIGURE 5.30
Single wipe,
double wipe,
iris wipe, and
clock wipe

FIGURE 5.30
Continued

Fading to Black

A cross fade can be used to fade to black or another solid color. Add a color strip by pressing the spacebar and selecting Color Generator from the Add Sequence Strip menu. The strip is 50 percent gray by default. Change the color of the strip in the Effect panel of the Sequence buttons subcontext. Click on the color field to open a color picker, as shown in Figure 5.31, and choose the color you want to fade to. Add a Cross strip as shown in Figure 5.32 to fade from the video sequence to the color strip.

FIGURE 5.31
Picking the color of
the color strip

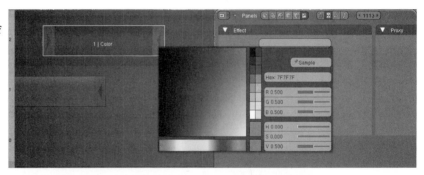

FIGURE 5.32
Using a Cross strip
to fade to black

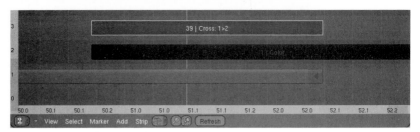

Transform

You can transform the dimensions, offset, and rotation of the video and animate the transformations with an Ipo curve by means of a Transform strip. Select the video strip you want to transform and add a Transform strip to it from the Add Sequence Strip menu. The transformation itself is controlled in the Effect panel of the Sequence buttons subcontext, as shown in Figure 5.33. Each possible transformation has a Start value and an End value. The Start value represents the value applied when the Fac Ipo for the strip is at 0, and the End value represents the value when the Fac Ipo for the strip is at 1, as you can see in Figure 5.34, where the values from Figure 5.33 are shown animated with an Ipo curve.

FIGURE 5.33
A Transform strip
and settings

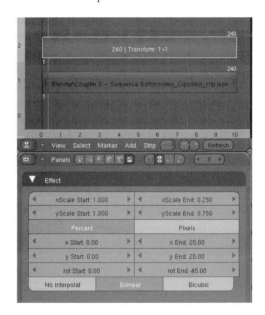

FIGURE 5.34
Transforms
driven by an
Ipo curve

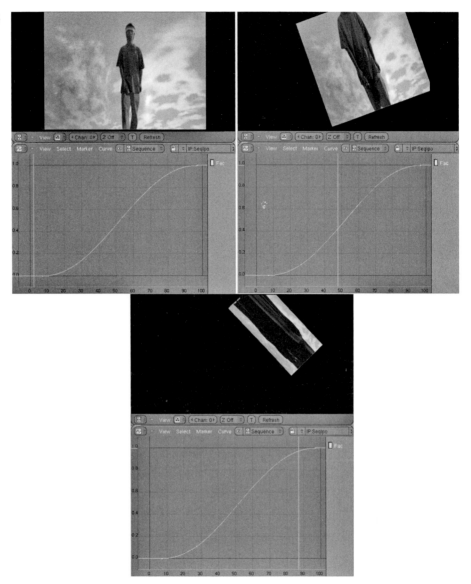

As in the case of sound strips, the default frame count for the Ipo is 100, which is divided along the length of the strip. In order force the Ipo to use the same frame counts as the sequence strip, select the IPO Frame Locked option in the Edit panel in the Sequence buttons subcontext.

You can control the speed of the video with a Speed Control strip. When using a Speed strip, you can opt for the Fac Ipo to control either the frame (with a value of 1 representing the end of the sequence and a value of 0 representing the beginning of the sequence) or the velocity (speed) of the video. This is controlled in the Effect panel of the Sequence buttons subcontext.

As in other cases, the Fac Ipo for a speed strip can also be locked to the sequence frames by using the IPO Frame Locked option in the Edit panel.

Other Effects

In addition to alpha overlay, there are other options for overlaying video. You can do an additive, multiplicative, or subtractive overlay by using the Add, Mult, and Sub options in the Add Sequence Strip menu. These overlay methods carry out the corresponding operations on the input strips.

The Glow effect adds a blur to highlights of the image with luminance levels above a particular threshold. The effect is shown in Figure 5.35. The threshold, size of the glow, and other parameters of the glow can be set in the Effect panel, and the intensity of the glow can be animated by using the Fac Ipo for the Glow strip.

FIGURE 5.35
An image without and with Glow

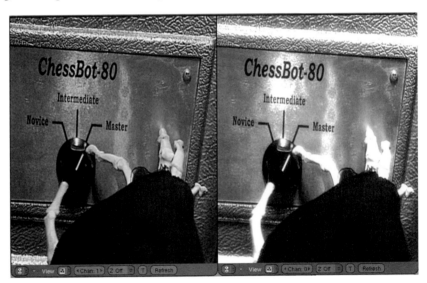

Working with Plug-ins

You can use external plug-ins to get a wider variety of effects. A repository of available VSE plug-ins can be found at www-users.cs.umn.edu/~mein/blender/plugins/sequence.html. To use these, first download the plug-in that is appropriate to your operating system. Then select the sequence or sequences you want the effect to operate on and add a Plugin strip from the Add Sequence Strip menu. A file browser will open, and you will be asked to load the plug-in from your hard disk. Find the plug-in and click Select Plugin. Read the notes for the specific plug-in to find out what parameters can be set and how they can be animated.

An example of an external plug-in is the Old Movie plug-in shown in Figure 5.36, which turns a video sequence into a grainy, scratched, black-and-white sequence.

FIGURE 5.36
The Old Movie
plug-in effect

Meta-Strips

In order to keep your editing area uncluttered, it is possible to combine multiple strips into single *meta-strips*. To do this, select the strips you want to combine and press the M key to create a meta-strip. You can unpack a meta-strip by selecting it and pressing Alt+M.

Working with Blender Scenes in the VSE

In addition to video and image sequences, you can also create sequence strips directly from Blender scenes. This makes compositing 3D animations very easy. Moreover, in addition to ordinary 3D scenes, you can use scenes composited with the node system, enabling you to bring the full power of the node system to bear directly in the VSE.

Adding Captions to a Video

A simple but useful method of adding captions or subtitles to a video is to use Blender's 3D text and the flexibility of the 3D window to place the text and to composite it over the video in the VSE. To add a caption to the video file end_zone_clip.avi on the CD in this way, follow these steps:

1. Copy the video file from the CD to your hard drive. This particular clip is encoded at a frame rate of 24fps, so be sure to set your frame rate to 24fps in the Format panel of the Render buttons area before adding the video. Add the video to the VSE editing area by pressing the spacebar and selecting Movie + Audio, as shown in Figure 5.37, and then navigating to the location of the movie on your hard drive and clicking Select Movie. Put the current frame at frame 1 and press spacebar+S to snap the strips to the first frame, as shown in Figure 5.38. In the Sequencer panel of the Sound Block buttons area, select Scrub so that you can listen to the soundtrack while scrubbing the current frame indicator forward and backward through the video. Find the first spoken line of the film, where the Death character says "Check." This will be the line you will caption.

2. Turn now to Blender's 3D viewport. Delete the default cube by pressing the X key, and press 0 on the number pad to enter Camera view. From the Scene drop-down menu in the header, select Add New, as shown in Figure 5.39. Choose Full Copy, as shown in Figure 5.40. Name the new scene **Check** to remind you of the caption.

FIGURE 5.37
Adding a Movie + Audio (HD) strip

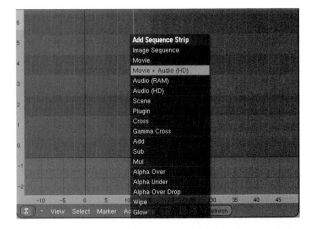

FIGURE 5.38
Snapping the strips to frame 1

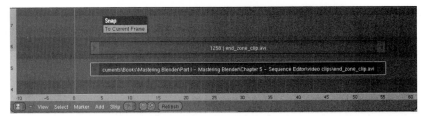

FIGURE 5.39
Adding a new scene

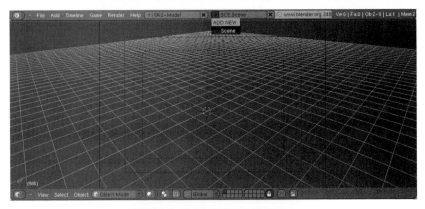

FIGURE 5.40
Selecting Full Copy

3. Be sure that you have Add New Objects: Aligned To View selected as your preference in the Edit Methods area of the Preferences window. This will ensure that added objects are correctly oriented toward the camera. Press the spacebar and choose Add ➢ Text to add a Text object, as shown in Figure 5.41. Enter Edit mode if you are not already in it and edit the text to say **Check**, as shown in Figure 5.42.

4. Add a material to the Text object in the ordinary way, by clicking New under the Material Index buttons in the Links And Materials panel of the Edit buttons area. Make the material white and shadeless, as shown in Figure 5.43.

FIGURE 5.41
Adding a
Text object

FIGURE 5.42
Editing the text

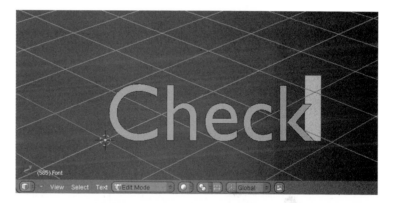

FIGURE 5.43
Shadeless white
material for
the text

5. Add a mesh plane by choosing Add ➢ Mesh ➢ Plane, as shown in Figure 5.44. Adjust the positioning of the plane so that it is just behind the Text object, by translating it in Object mode along its local Z axis, as shown in Figure 5.45. Give the plane a shadeless black material with Z transparency and an alpha value of 0.5, as shown in Figure 5.46. Position and scale the plane so that it creates a nice-fitting backdrop for the text, as shown in Figure 5.47. Finally, go to the World buttons and delete the world by clicking the X button to the right of the World name field, because no background will be needed for this scene.

FIGURE 5.44
Adding a plane

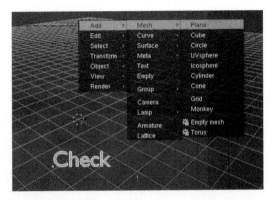

FIGURE 5.45
Positioning
the plane

FIGURE 5.46
Material for
the plane

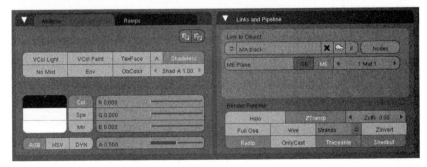

6. Go back to the VSE and add a scene by pressing the spacebar and selecting Scene from the Add Sequence Strip menu, as shown in Figure 5.48. Because more than one scene is available, you will get a choice of scenes. Choose the scene called Check, as shown in Figure 5.49. Place the Scene sequence strip in the VSE, as shown in Figure 5.50. You should be able to see the text in the Image Preview window.

FIGURE 5.47
Text and plane

FIGURE 5.48
Adding a scene

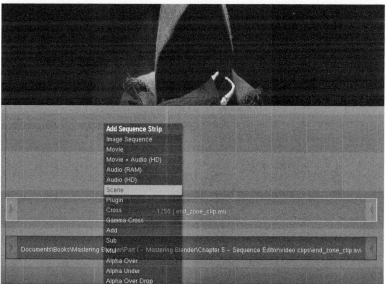

FIGURE 5.49
Selecting the
scene name

FIGURE 5.50
The text in place

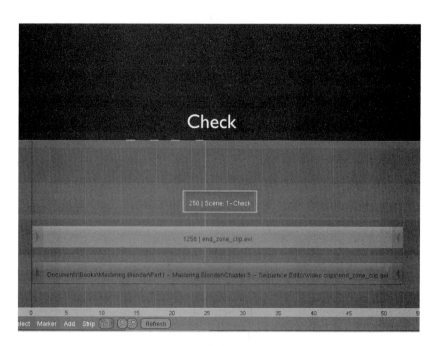

7. Select the video strip by right-clicking on the middle of the strip. Then select the Check scene strip with Shift+RMB. Press the spacebar and choose Alpha Over from the Add Sequence Strip. The text will appear over the video, just as it should. If the size or positioning is wrong, adjust it in the 3D viewport. Adjust the position of the handles of the Check scene strip so that the caption extends long enough for the viewer to read it with ease. The caption should look like the still image in Figure 5.51.

FIGURE 5.51
Alpha overlaid text

Composited Scenes

Using a scene composited with nodes as a sequence editor strip works exactly the same as using an ordinary 3D scene, except that the composited scene should have the Do Composite option set in the Anim panel of the Render buttons area. The content of the strip will be whatever is output in the Composite node of the node system.

Rendering and Output

To render a finished sequence, you must select the Do Sequence option in the Anim panel in the Render buttons area, as shown in Figure 5.52. When this is selected, the final render will come from the VSE rather than the 3D view camera.

FIGURE 5.52
Do Sequence
selected

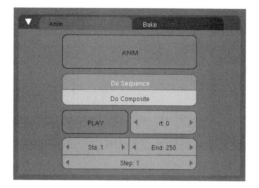

As is always the case when rendering animations, you have various choices in the format to render to. You can render to still frames or to video. You can also render to video with sound by selecting the FFMpeg option in the drop-down menu in the Format panel of the Render buttons area. When you select FFMpeg, you will be given further options for audio and video output formats. What is best for you depends on the codecs you have installed and other features specific to your operating system. I have found that selecting Xvid-encoded video and MP3-encoded audio with the Multiplex audio option does a very good job of outputting synced sound and video .avi files on both Mac and Windows. Do some experimenting to find out which combination works best for you.

You can also add text burn-ins to your video by selecting Enable Stamp and Draw Stamp in the Stamp panel, as shown in Figure 5.53. Selected information will be stamped automatically onto the upper-left corner of your video.

FIGURE 5.53
Stamp panel

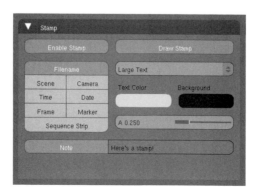

Rendering edited video with mixed sound is one of the last stages of creating movies, but there is much more to learn about Blender. In the next two parts of this book, you will learn how to automate tasks and build tools by using Python scripting, and how to create interactive content by using the Blender Game Engine (BGE).

 Real World Scenario

VISUALIZING THE FUTURE AND THE PAST

The UK studio See3D (www.see3d.co.uk) uses Blender as its primary 3D tool and makes extensive use of the VSE and composite node system to create stunning animated visualizations of a wide variety of places, products, and processes. Their clients include corporations, academic research institutes, and government organizations, and their portfolio features sectors on construction, renewable energy, urban renewal, and heritage visualization projects. Recently, their depiction of the construction of the Pontcysyllte aqueduct was featured as part of the BBC's *Hidden Histories* documentary series. The project was commissioned by the Wrexham Town Council, where the aqueduct is located, to support their bid for World Heritage Site status for the aqueduct. The video itself is a beautiful example of historical visualization re-creating the process by which Britain's longest and highest aqueduct was built more than 200 years ago. You can see the video online on the studio's website at http://see3d.co.uk/customers_heritage.htm.

The Bottom Line

Import, edit, and render video with the Blender VSE.   Blender's Video Sequence Editor (VSE) is a powerful tool for cross-platform, multiformat video editing. One of its key strengths is the ease with which it can handle a variety of different image, video, and audio formats both as input and as rendered output.

Master It   Import the video idol_clip.mov from the CD that accompanies this book. Using a Transition strip, animate the video image rotating in place. Render the resulting movie to a series of JPEG images.

Create transitions, overlays, and effects for your videos.   The VSE has a variety of built-in effects and transitions to enable you to edit video and do simple compositing quickly and easily. Alpha values of 3D scenes also work seamlessly within the VSE.

Master It   Add a caption for the robot's line "Checkmate" in the video end_zone_clip. avi. Render the output to a new .avi file with sound.

Incorporate content directly from 3D or composited scenes into your videos. You can incorporate both animated scenes from the 3D viewport and composited scenes from the node system directly into the VSE, resulting in an extraordinarily powerful and integrated compositing and editing system.

Master It Use the output of the green screen compositing exercise from Chapter 4 in the VSE. Use a wipe to transition between the composited scene strip to another video strip. Render the output to the format of your choice.

Part II

Mastering Blender Python

Chapter 6

Python for the Impatient

One of the advanced features of Blender is a fully functional, built-in interpreter for the Python scripting language. This enables you to directly access internal Blender data to automate tasks and create your own tools, as well as greatly enhance the power of several other features, from nodes to the game engine to Ipo curve drivers. However, in order to take advantage of the power that Python can give you over your Blender work, you must first get a sense of the Python language itself. This chapter provides a brief and gentle introduction to the language, suitable for people unfamiliar with Python and those who have done little or no programming at all.

In this chapter, you will learn to

- ◆ Become familiar with the basics of the Python language
- ◆ Run the Python shell and IDLE development environment
- ◆ Understand fundamental features of Python syntax

Introducing Python

The next several chapters of this book are intended to give you a thorough overview of using the Python scripting language in Blender. Because this book is aimed at Blender users and not necessarily at programmers, I am assuming little or no knowledge of programming, but of course any little bit will be helpful. If you have a background in another object-oriented programming language, you should find everything in these chapters to be smooth sailing. On the other hand, if your eyes completely glaze over at terms such as *variable*, you'll want to take it slow, but I hope that with a little patience and persistence even those of you in this category will eventually find yourselves able to accomplish what you want to with Python in Blender.

What Is Python?

Python is a widely used, general-purpose, object-oriented scripting language. It is used for everything from research to web programming and has a wide variety of third-party libraries and tools available for it. If you're reading this, you probably know by now that Python is also the language used for scripting in Blender. I'm going to assume that you don't know much more than that about Python. If you do, feel free to skip ahead to what you need.

If you're completely new to Python or to programming, the first question you might ask is, "What does *scripting* mean?" Indeed, understanding this is central to understanding how Python can be useful to you in the context of Blender, so it's worth going into a little bit of detail.

How Programs Run

There are two main paradigms for how computer programs run. Some programming languages, such as C and C++, are *compiled languages*. This means that the programmer writes the program in some plain-text format and sends that program to a piece of software called a compiler. The compiler reads the text program (also called *source code*) and outputs a *binary executable.* The binary executable is entirely encoded in ones and zeros and can't be read by human beings (at least, not without Rain Man-esque abilities of concentration). This paradigm of compiled languages is a classic model, and the insistence of open source licenses such as the GNU General Public License (GPL) on freely distributed source code is a direct corollary of this paradigm. Open source licenses such as the GPL are fundamentally intended to ensure that end users have access to software in a format that can be read and understood by humans, rather than only in binary format.

Blender is written primarily in the C language, and its development follows the compiled-languages paradigm. Most Blender users download binaries directly either in .zip files or in system-specific installers. These binaries are provided for the convenience of users, but the license doesn't require that they be freely available. What is required is that the *source* be freely available, as it is. You can download the source in an archive file from the Blender home page, and also by checking it out of the Subversion repository (this is how developers generally access the code).

The other paradigm for running computer programs is that of *interpreted languages*. With these languages, the written code is executed by a program called an interpreter, which runs simultaneously with the software that was written in the interpreted language. As an analogy, you can think of compiled languages as being like a book translation from one language to another. The compiler translates source code to machine-readable binary code, and after it has been translated, the binary code is no longer dependent on the source. In the case of interpreted languages, the analogy is (unsurprisingly) that of an interpreter of a speech who communicates simultaneously with a speaker, interpreting what is being said into another language. Both the original speaker and the interpreter need to be working simultaneously in order for the listener to understand the message.

Programs written in interpreted languages (that is, with the intention of being run via an interpreter) are often referred to as *scripts*. When Python is referred to as a *scripting language*, it is essentially just another way of saying that it is an interpreted language.

The kinds of tasks that interpreted languages are suited to are not always the same kinds of tasks that compiled languages are suited to. Scripting languages tend to excel at doing small, specific tasks quickly. They typically allow a higher level of abstraction in their syntax, making it possible to carry out complex but common tasks more simply. On the other hand, building large-scale applications is something that may be better approached using compiled languages, because in most cases, the overhead of running the interpreter slows the program's performance on large, complex tasks. The division of labor in the Blender world between the C language (application development) and Python (scripting) is a perfect example of how these two execution paradigms work together.

Scripting and Blender

In this chapter, you'll become familiar with the basics of Python and you'll be introduced to the default Python interpreter and development environment, called IDLE. For general-purpose Python use, it's important to have at least a passing familiarity with this environment. You won't spend much time on this, however, because you have another Python interpreter that will be more useful for the work you want to do. That's right, in addition to everything else, Blender itself *is* a Python interpreter.

By using Blender's built-in interpreter and application programming interface (API) to run scripts, you can access Blender assets and functionality. This can be useful for a wide variety of tasks, from automating simple but repetitive steps that would be too tedious to do by hand through the standard Blender interface, to setting up your own macros and tools, to creating sophisticated mathematical visualizations automatically with the click of a key. Furthermore, Blender's Python functionality is deeply integrated, making it possible to access Python in other ways aside from the main script interpreter. In addition to simply running scripts in Blender, you can access Python through the nodes system, use Python to drive shape keys, use Python to create constraints, trigger scripts on events during the course of an animation with script links, and incorporate full Python functionality in the game engine with Python logic bricks. In the next few chapters, you'll learn how to do all of these things and how this knowledge can open up a whole new world of Blender functionality to you.

Why Python?

In the years since Python was initially released in 1991, it has become widely used in a host of different application domains. There are several reasons for this. First, Python is relatively easy to learn. For people accustomed to other programming languages, there are syntactic features peculiar to Python that must be learned, but by and large, the functionality people expect from other languages is straightforwardly implemented in Python. For new programmers, Python implements high-level abstractions that can simplify many tasks that would require more-involved solutions in other languages, making Python comparatively easy to start programming with. Indeed, one of the biggest habits for experienced programmers to break when they begin working with Python is the tendency to want to code things in an unnecessarily complex way. Iterating through lists, for example, is done more simply in Python than in other commonly used languages.

Python's ease of use extends not just to learning the language, but also to development. Python code is known for its readability. One of Python's most notable syntactic idiosyncrasies is also a big factor in enforcing the writing of readable code. In Python, the scope of control structures such as for loops and conditionals is determined by the left-side indentation of the line. In other commonly used languages, this is usually handled by some kind of bracketing, and white space, tabs, and spaces are far less important. Python's approach helps to nearly eliminate the kinds of subtle bracketing errors that plague other languages. In Python, if the pattern of indentation in a script is not well formed, the interpreter will throw up a syntax error and the script will not be executed. If the indentation *is* well formed, on the other hand, then the scope of control structures is clearly visible at a glance. In fact, many conscientious programmers use indentations as a way of visually identifying control scopes even in languages that do not require them to. By requiring indentations, Python is able to ensure a more consistent coding style, which results in more-readable and compact code.

In addition to the high level of abstraction to simplify tasks and the advantages in readability enforced by the syntax, Python's status as a full-fledged, object-oriented programming (OOP) language takes advantage of the OOP paradigm and the benefits that come with it. OOP enables programmers to define data structures that will be used in their programs, called *classes.* Individual instances of a class are called *objects* of that class. Much of OOP involves sending and receiving queries, called *methods*, between objects. Each class has specific methods defined for it. As a simple example, imagine a class called Person and another class called Car. A specific person is an object of class Person. It is reasonable to ask what color a person's eyes are, so the question, "What color are this person's eyes?" is analogous to a method defined for Person. It doesn't make sense to ask that question about a car, so that method would not be something that is defined for the class Car. The advantage of OOP is that after you understand the basics of the programming language, interacting with libraries that have been written by others requires only that you know what classes you are dealing with and what methods you should use with those classes to get the results you want. A full reference of classes, methods, and special variables for a given framework is called its *application programming interface* (*API*). In the next few chapters, you will become familiar with Blender's API, which will be your one-stop resource for information on accessing the classes you need to script for Blender. The ease with which libraries can be created and used leads to another important advantage of Python: the vast collection of libraries available. This allows for rapid prototyping of applications, without requiring you to write a lot of code.

Another reason why Python is the scripting language of choice for Blender is that Python is open source software and can be incorporated and integrated into Blender to whatever degree is necessary without licensing issues. Python is not at all unique in this respect—many other scripting languages are also open source—but combined with the other advantages of using Python, it makes Python the obvious choice as Blender's scripting language.

Further Resources

The goal of this chapter is to give you the absolute bare minimum of Python knowledge that's necessary to follow the discussion about scripting for Blender in the next few chapters. In the upcoming chapters, Blender-specific classes and functions will get most of the attention. For details about core Python functionality, you will need to turn to other resources outside this book. Even if you plan to use Python exclusively for Blender scripting, a more thorough understanding of the tools available to you in the Python language is invaluable.

DOCUMENTATION, BOOKS, AND TUTORIALS

Official documentation for Python is available online at www.python.org, as are downloads and installation information. In addition to the online documentation, a variety of books are available on Python, which address just about any conceivable question you might have. For a clear, leisurely introduction to the Python language, I recommend *Learning Python* by Mark Lutz (O'Reilly Media, 2007). It covers many of the introductory topics included in this book in much greater depth. For more-advanced subjects such as network programming, Mark Lutz's *Programming Python* (O'Reilly Media, 2006) is the definitive Python tome. If you have programming experience with other languages and would like to get a quick but well-presented overview of the ways in which Python implementations of common features differ from those in other languages, I recommend *Dive Into Python* by Mark Pilgrim (Apress, 2004), which has the additional benefit of being freely available online in a variety of convenient formats at www. diveintopython.org. *Python Cookbook* by Alex Martelli, Anna Ravenscroft, and David Ascher (O'Reilly Media, 2005) is also a useful resource, filled with good "Pythonic" programming examples of common tasks.

The Blender-Python API

The Blender-Python API for Blender version 2.48 is located here:

```
www.blender.org/documentation/248PythonDoc/index.html
```

If you plan to do Python scripting in Blender, you will want to bookmark this or even to download a local copy. A downloadable PDF version is available here:

```
www.letworyinteractive.com/load_bpy_pdf.html
```

This is the definitive reference for the classes, methods, and variables you will need to access Blender-related data in your scripts.

For games, you will also need to be aware of the Blender GameLogic API, the most up-to-date example of which is located here:

```
www.blender.org/documentation/248PythonDoc/GE/index.html
```

A few words of warning are in order. By taking on the challenge of Python scripting in Blender, you are, in a way, stepping into the "wild, wild west" of Blender use. You are crossing over (if you haven't already) to being a power user of Blender. The Blender-Python API has so far been developed by experts for experts. Elegance, consistency, and intuitiveness have sometimes fallen by the wayside in its development as short-term necessity has taken precedence over the big picture. Make no mistake: This is not because the developers don't care or don't *like* elegance, consistency, and intuitiveness. It's because developer resources are limited, and the Blender-Python API is a corner of Blender that has not yet been subjected to the royal treatment of a complete overhaul and polishing. Plans are afoot for such an overhaul, and over the course of the next few chapters, I will give you an indication not just of where the API is at the present time, but where it is likely to go from here. Nevertheless, as a power user and a budding Blender-Python programmer yourself, you will want to refer regularly to the API and keep yourself informed about developments.

You will certainly find an eager and knowledgeable community of users and developers online to help guide you through the wild patches. You can find support in the Python forum of BlenderArtists.org, located here:

```
http://blenderartists.org/forum/forumdisplay.php?f=11
```

For Python development, there are also the #blender, #blenderpython, and #blendercoders IRC channels.

Don't be afraid to join the discussion and to point out areas where you think the API is lacking. The more people use this API and participate in its development and design, the faster improvements will come. For now, though, it has its quirks, so be patient.

Real World Scenario

THE PYTHON SOFTWARE FOUNDATION

For the first several years after Python was initially developed by Guido van Rossum, the status of the Python intellectual property went through several changes as Guido worked under the auspices of various employers. By 2001, it was clear that Python had become too widely used for this to continue and needed a stable environment to thrive. The Python Software Foundation (PSF) was founded as a nonprofit corporation in the United States, with a mission to "promote, protect, and advance the Python programming language, and to support and facilitate the growth of the international community of Python programmers." In practice, this involves maintaining and protecting trademarks and intellectual property associated with Python, and supporting Python and Python-related development in a variety of ways. The PSF provides financial assistance for conferences as well as grants for Python-related training and development projects.

The PSF was patterned after other successful open source software foundations, such as the Apache Software Foundation, which plays a similar role in promoting and supporting the widely used open source Apache HTTP server and related software. In turn, the PSF was a predecessor in some respects of the Blender Foundation.

Companies with a stake in the development of Python contribute by becoming corporate sponsor members of the PSF. Sponsor members include ActiveState, Google, Microsoft, O'Reilly Media, and Sun Microsystems, among others. Industrial Light & Magic, the Hollywood special-effects powerhouse, is among the "emeritus" sponsor members of the PSF.

Although corporate sponsorship accounts for a considerable amount of the PSF's revenue, the PSF's status as a nonprofit organization enables (and depends on) contributions by individual community members as well. If you feel inclined to help contribute to the foundation, you can make a tax-deductable donation at www.python.org/psf/donations/.

Understanding the Python Development Environment

Before moving on to the Blender-Python event, it's worthwhile to take a look at Python on its own. As previously mentioned, Python is a multipurpose language that is used for a wide variety of tasks. Even if you plan to use it exclusively for Blender, it is a good idea to familiarize yourself with the default Python development environment, because any book or tutorial you might read specifically for Python will assume familiarity with this interface.

The default installation of Python comes with the Integrated DeveLopment Environment (IDLE) graphical user interface (GUI). IDLE provides a command-line interface directly to the Python interpreter as well as a simple text editor optimized for Python coding. This section provides a basic overview of how Python code is written and executed in that environment.

AND NOW FOR SOMETHING COMPLETELY DIFFERENT . . .

You might begin to notice some sly references to a certain British television comedy troupe in discussions of Python. Indeed, the language name *Python* was originally conceived of in honor of Monty Python, rather than the constrictor snake of the same name. One of the original members of that group was Eric Idle, whose name supplies the pun for the IDLE environment.

Getting Python

If you are using Mac OS X or Linux, chances are you already have Python installed on your machine. You should check to make sure that the installed version is version 2.5. If not, you will need to install 2.5. You can download Python 2.5 from www.python.org. Follow the instructions there to install Python 2.5 on your own system.

Using the Command-Line Shell

To get started, execute IDLE. In Windows, under a default installation, you will find this program in the Start menu, under the Python 2.5 directory. On a Mac, you can find it by using the Spotlight search tool. After you run this executable, a window opens like the one shown in Figure 6.1. This is the Python Shell window.

FIGURE 6.1

The Python
Shell window

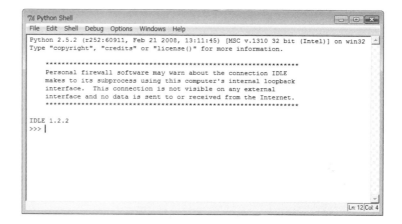

If you've used command-line interfaces such as on a Unix or Linux terminal or a DOS console, the idea of a command-line shell is already familiar. The command line enables you to write commands or requests directly (usually on a single line) and get an answer back, in this case directly from the Python interpreter. The A line that begins with three greater-than symbols (>>>) is the command-line prompt (the last line in Figure 6.1). If you type your command on this line and press Enter, the Python interpreter's reply will be printed on the next line, as shown here:

```
IDLE 1.2.2
>>> print "Hello World!"
Hello World!
>>>
```

In this example, I requested that the Python interpreter print Hello World! As you can see, that's exactly what it did.

As the command-line interface runs, the Python interpreter keeps track of the state it is in, which means that variables' values can be assigned via the command line and then retrieved later, like this:

```
>>> my_variable = "Hello World!"
>>> print my_variable
Hello World!
>>>
```

This serves as a good example, but when you're working directly in the command line, the print command is redundant. Simply entering a value in the command line will have the same effect of echoing the value. Subsequent examples of working directly on the command line of the IDLE interpreter will omit the print command; however, it is still necessary to use print when writing code in scripts, so this won't be the last you see of it.

Being able to interact with the command line also enables you to look more closely at the value of individual variables during runtime, which can be useful for debugging. For example, it might be of interest to investigate the data type of the variable assigned in the preceding code snippet. You can do this by using the type() function, which returns the data type of its argument. As you can see, the type returned is str, which is the label for the *string* data type:

```
>>> type(my_variable)
<type 'str'>
```

You'll look more closely at data types later in this chapter. For now, it is enough to know that Python defines a set of basic data types that reflect the kind of data a variable represents. The string type treats data as sequences of characters. Because the original assignment of my_variable was a sequence of characters, it was automatically classified as an object of the string type. Different types can be accessed and dealt with in different ways. In the case of the str type, another thing you can ask about it is its length, as follows:

```
>>> len(my_variable)
12
```

Direct command-line access can be useful at times for certain things (for example, a bit later in this chapter, it will provide a convenient way to observe how data types interact). However, by far the most common and important use of the Python shell is as the default output and error report interface. When you run a script, this is where the print statements will print to by default, and when the script runs into trouble, this is where the errors will appear. This is what makes the Python shell truly invaluable. In fact, when you're working primarily in the environment of the Blender-Python interpreter, you will not have command-line input access. The Blender-Python shell interface is output only. Nevertheless, it remains indispensable for identifying errors.

Using the IDLE Editor

Generally, of course, programs are not executed one line at a time in a command-line environment. The norm is to write a script in a file and to execute that script by sending it to the interpreter (or calling it from within the interpreter, which amounts to the same thing). You can create a Python script with any ordinary text editor, but because you already have IDLE open on your desktop, let's use that.

Open a new file in the IDLE editor by choosing New Window from the File menu of IDLE, as shown in Figure 6.2.

FIGURE 6.2
Opening a new
file in IDLE

After you do this, a new window opens that at first glance appears similar to the one that's already open. It's not the same, though. This is not a shell window, but a text editor in which you can write complete scripts. The IDLE editor is a powerful editor with a variety of features for Python coding. For general-purpose Python programming, this will likely be your starting point and might be the only editor you ever need. For work in Blender, however, there are more direct alternatives, so a cursory look at the IDLE editor is sufficient.

Running Scripts

Scripts you write in IDLE can be executed directly from the editor by choosing Run Module from the Run menu in the header bar of the editor, or by pressing F5. Try it now by typing `print "Hello World!"` as the first line of the file. Note that the `print` command here is necessary, because you are not working directly on the command line. You will need to save the file before executing it. Save it with .py as an extension and then run the script. The `print` command's output will be sent to the command line in the Python Shell window.

There are other ways to run scripts. You can run scripts simply by double-clicking the .py file's icon, although this may not produce the results you expect unless a script has been specifically coded as a freestanding application with a GUI of its own. It is also possible to run scripts from the command line of your operating system.

There are even more options for executing Python code in the environment of Blender. Some of the more specialized methods are described in Chapter 8, "The Many-Headed Snake: Other Uses of Python in Blender." The main way to execute scripts in Blender is analogous to the way scripts are run in IDLE. Although from time to time in the remainder of this chapter, I use the IDLE command-line interpreter to show some simple examples of how data types interact, for the most part I assume that you are doing your programming directly in Blender.

Using the Blender-Python Environment

Blender contains a built-in development environment for Python that has many of IDLE's features with the added advantage of being directly integrated into Blender. To access this environment, go to the Window Type menu in any Blender window and select the Text Editor window type, as shown in Figure 6.3. The Blender text editor appears, as shown in Figure 6.4.

FIGURE 6.3
Selecting the
Text Editor
window type

FIGURE 6.4
The Blender
text editor

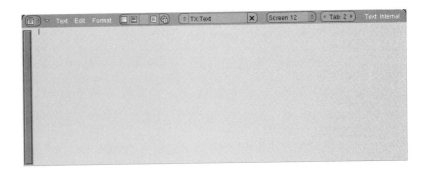

For a quick experiment, try running the same program that you previously ran in IDLE. Type the line **print** "**Hello World**" into the text editor window. Run the code by pressing Alt+P. Check the Blender console to see the output, as shown in Figure 6.5. After all this time wondering what that strange black window was for, now you know!

FIGURE 6.5
Script output in
the Blender console

THINK DIFFERENT ABOUT CONSOLE OUTPUT

The Blender console appears automatically in Windows whenever you run Blender, and it stays open for the duration of your Blender session. On a Mac, the console is more hidden. You can find the console by searching for *console* in Spotlight; however, the Mac console is not exclusively devoted to Blender output—it also reports on other system activity. For the purpose of scripting, I recommend running Blender from a terminal command line on a Mac and in Linux/Unix. When you do this, your terminal window will serve the purpose of the Blender console.

You'll use the Blender console a lot when you do Python scripting. It is where you will get most of the feedback you need for debugging, among other things.

Thus far in this chapter, you've learned enough about accessing the Python interpreter to get started with scripting. Now all you need to know is how to write Python code! The rest of this chapter is devoted to a quick overview of basic Python syntax.

Understanding Python Syntax

Python is similar to Perl and other scripting languages in that it has a procedural syntax that is augmented by object-oriented functionality. This means that Python programs execute in a step-by-step (procedural) way, using loops and conditionals, and accessing object data by using methods defined for classes. There are three fundamental things that you need to know in order to use Python: how individual units of data are represented and accessed, how the overall procedural flow of a program is determined, and how to work with classes and objects so you can understand and use an API such as the Blender-Python API.

Data Types and Structures

Python has several built-in basic data types. Each data type has its own way of interacting with operators and has specific ways in which its information can be accessed. In this section, you'll learn about the most commonly used data types, which are the following:

Integers (int) are numbers that can be represented without fractions or decimal points. Positive integers are sometimes referred to as *natural numbers* or *counting numbers,* but integers can also be negative. Integers are often used to iterate over lists or to identify unique entities.

Floating-point numbers (float) are numbers that include a decimal point. They behave as an approximation of real numbers, and are the appropriate data type to use when you need to work with real numbers.

Boolean values (bool) are true or false values. They take the value True or False.

Strings (str) are sequences of characters. When you want to work with words or text, str is the data type to use.

Lists (list) are ordered collections of entities. The entities in lists can be of any other data type, and individuals can be accessed by an integer index. They can be added to and altered easily, making them appropriate when a dynamic ordered collection is needed.

Dictionaries (dict) are unordered collections of entities, in which pairs of entities have a key-value relationship. Values can be accessed via their corresponding keys.

Tuples (tup) are similar to lists but are limited in how they can be altered. They can be processed faster than lists, which makes them appropriate when an unchanging ordered collection is needed.

Lists, dictionaries, and tuples are particularly important data types because they contain other objects and enable access to them. Procedural control in Python almost always depends on manipulating these data structures. The following examples are best viewed in the interactive IDLE command-line GUI environment.

INTEGERS AND FLOATING-POINT NUMBERS

Integers and floating-point numbers (floats) are represented in Python by sequences of digits. Floats also contain a decimal point. Python can usually handle the interactions between integers and floating-point numbers in a natural and invisible way. For example, if you try to multiply an integer with a float, the answer will be the float that you intuitively expect.

STRINGS

Sequences of characters are appropriately handled as strings in Python. Of course, in a computer program *everything* is a sequence of characters, so it is necessary to identify strings by using single quotes or double quotes. Single or double quotes may be used interchangeably for strings in Python. If you have a string that contains single quotes, you can avoid the need to escape those quotes by using double quotes as your string delimiter. Sequences of characters that are not delimited by quotes are not treated as strings in Python. If the sequence is not a special function word in Python, the Python interpreter will try to treat the sequence as a variable. If this is not what you intended, chances are this will lead to an error.

There are numerous methods that can be called on strings. You can return the length of a string or individual characters by index similarly to the way you would a list, which you will see in the next section.

LISTS AND TUPLES

Lists are represented in Python as ordered collections of entities within square brackets, where each entity is separated by a comma. An example of a list is shown here:

```
['a', 'b', 'c']
```

This list has three elements, the strings 'a', 'b', and 'c'. The len(*list*) function returns the length of the list, as shown here:

```
>>> len(['a','b','c'])
3
```

Elements of lists can be accessed by their individual indices. List indexes start with 0 in Python, so the first element in the list is at index 0, and the last element of a list of length *n* is at index *n*-1. The notation for this is the index integer placed in square brackets immediately after the list. This notation is most commonly used when the list is stored in a variable, as you will see later in this chapter, but it can also be used with the list in plain notation, as shown here:

```
>>> ['a','b','c'][0]
'a'
>>> ['a','b','c'][1]
'b'
>>> ['a','b','c'][2]
'c'
```

Index access to lists in Python is very powerful. You can return not just individual elements but also *slices* or *sublists*, by indicating the start index and the index to which you want the sublist to extend (noninclusively). In this example, the [1:4] indexes are called, which returns the sublist extending from index 0 to index 3 of the original list:

```
>>> ['a','b','c','d','e'][1:4]
['b', 'c', 'd']
>>>
```

Two important methods defined for lists are append() and extend(). Both add elements to lists. In some cases, these methods can be used interchangeably, but the way they are used is different. The first method, append(), adds a single element to a list. The append() method changes the list in place, and does not, itself, output anything. To see how the list has changed, you need to pass it to a variable as follows so you can print the value after changing it:

```
>>> mylist = ['a','b','c']
>>> mylist.append('d')
>>> mylist
['a', 'b', 'c', 'd']
```

The other common way to add elements to lists is to add the entire contents of another list to the first list, which is done using extend() as shown here:

```
>>> mylist = ['a','b','c']
>>> mylist.extend(['d','e','f'])
>>> mylist
['a', 'b', 'c', 'd', 'e', 'f']
```

In this case, the argument for extend() is itself a list, and the resulting list is the concatenation of the original list with the contents of extend(). Note that if append() is called with a list as an argument, the effect is quite different:

```
>>> mylist = ['a','b','c']
>>> mylist.append(['d','e','f'])
>>> mylist
['a', 'b', 'c', ['d', 'e', 'f']]
```

If append() is used with a list argument, the entire new list is appended *as a single element* in the original list. In this example, the new, postappend list has four elements, the last of which is itself a list.

Tuples are similar to lists in many respects. Instead of using square brackets, they are identified by round brackets. Their elements can be accessed by index similarly to the way lists can be. Tuples cannot be appended to or extended, and you cannot assign new values to individual items in tuples. For this reason, tuples are suitable only for collections that are fixed at the time of their creation.

DICTIONARIES

Whereas lists are collections of items that are ordered and accessible by an integer index, dictionaries are collections of items that are accessible via reference to other items. Dictionaries are represented by a comma-separated collection of pairs. The elements of the pairs are separated by colons, and the whole collection is within curly brackets, as in this example:

```
{'brit': 32, 'john': 25, 'mary': 29, 'tom': 74}
```

Each pair is called a *key-value pair*; the item to the left of the colon is the *key*, and the item to the right is its corresponding *value*. A value in a dictionary can be accessed by using its key, just as an element of a list is accessed by using its index:

```
>>> {'brit': 32, 'john': 25, 'mary': 29, 'tom': 74}['mary']
29
```

A list of all the keys in a dictionary can be output by using the keys() method, as shown here:

```
>>> {'brit': 32, 'john': 25, 'mary': 29, 'tom': 74}.keys()
['tom', 'john', 'mary', 'brit']
```

OPERATORS

Operators are the way a programming language determines the relationships between various data elements in a program. You've already seen an important operator, the = operator, or *assignment operator*. The purpose of this operator is to assign the value on the right of the operator to the variable on the left side of the operator. Be careful: Although this looks like an equal sign, it is not the sign used to indicate that two terms have the same value.

Python's *comparison operators* are as follows:

Operator	Value
==	Equal to
>=	Greater than or equal to
>	Greater than
<=	Less than or equal to
<	Less than
!=	Not equal to

Furthermore, logical terms can be put together using either the and or or keyword.

Python has other operators also. It is important to realize when working with operators that they often have different meanings depending on the data type they are used with. Each data type listed in the previous section has different properties. One of the ways in which these data types differ is the way they behave with regard to operators. A good example of this is the + operator. If you use this operator between integers, as in this example, the predictable result is integer addition:

```
IDLE 1.2.2
>>> 5+1
6
>>>
```

Using the + operator with floating-point numbers is similarly predictable. However, when working on strings, the meaning of the operator changes. In this case, the + operator becomes the string concatenation operator, as you can see in this example:

```
>>> "Hello " + "World!"
'Hello World!'
>>>
```

If the + operator is used with lists, as in the following code, it has yet another meaning, namely list concatenation, which is to say the same meaning as extend():

```
>>> ['a','b','c']+['d','e','f']
['a', 'b', 'c', 'd', 'e', 'f']
```

If you try to use the + operator with two data types for which it means different things, an error will arise, as in this case:

```
>>> "Hello World!" + 5
```

```
Traceback (most recent call last):
  File "<pyshell#51>", line 1, in <module>
    "Hello World!" + 5
TypeError: cannot concatenate 'str' and 'int' objects
```

Another interesting example of operator behavior is the * operator. For integers and floats, it behaves as an ordinary multiplication operator. For strings and lists, however, it can be used with an integer to output a string or list consisting of the original string or list repeated the number of times indicated by the integer argument:

```
>>> "Hello" * 3
'HelloHelloHello'
>>> ['a','b','c'] * 3
['a', 'b', 'c', 'a', 'b', 'c', 'a', 'b', 'c']
```

Python is full of high-level tricks like this, and it is impossible for this book to do more than scratch the surface. This much knowledge of operators should be enough to get you going on scripting for Blender.

VARIABLES

Python variables are represented as alphanumeric strings (without quotes, to distinguish them from actual Python strings). Unlike some languages such as Perl, in which variable names begin with specific characters to indicate their data type, variable names in Python can freely be used for any data type. In fact, the same variable can be assigned differently typed values one after another. You can check an item's type by using the type() function. In the following example, the variable my_variable is initialized with a value of 10. When the type is checked, Python reports that the variable is an int. Then a new value of "Hello" is assigned to the variable, and checked again to find that the variable is now of the string type:

```
>>> my_variable = 10
>>> type(my_variable)
<type 'int'>
>>> my_variable = "Hello!"
>>> type(my_variable)
<type 'str'>
```

Variables must be given a value before they can be accessed in any way, even in conditionals. Undefined variables in your code will result in an error in Python.

The difference between global and local variables will become clearer when the topic of defining functions is addressed. In short, variables that are initialized inside the definition of a function are *local* to that function, meaning that they cannot be accessed directly from outside the function in which they were defined. *Global* variables, on the other hand, are defined outside all functions, and can be accessed from within any function. You'll read more about this later in this chapter.

Control Flow

Control refers to the order in which a sequence of programming instructions is followed; repetition, iteration, and conditionality are all part of the control flow of a program. A core set of statements is used in Python to determine control flow. These include the `for` and `if/else` statements.

INDENTATION, NOT BRACKETS

One of the most immediately noticeable differences between Python and other common programming languages is the way it identifies control structures. Most languages do this with some kind of brackets; C, Perl, and Java, among others, use curly brackets to delimit control structures. Python, on the other hand, does not use brackets at all, but rather groups levels of embedding in control structures according to the left-side indentation of the code. This results in a visual immediacy for the code; control issues tend to pop out with Python code. However, it means that the interpreter is unforgiving with regard to white-space inconsistency. It also means that editing Python in more than one editor whose tab settings are different may result in errors. Some editors have features that enable you to visualize white space and distinguish between spaces and tabs. If you think you might be using more than one editor, be sure to check that the settings are consistent across editors.

The most common and simplest way to create a `for` loop is to iterate through a list, which is done like this:

```
>>> my_list = ['a','b','c']
>>> for item in my_list:
        print item

a
b
c
```

In this example a new variable, `item`, is initialized at the outset of the `for` loop. As the loop iterates through the list, this variable takes the value of each element of the list one by one. Note that there is no iteration on the index of the list items. In general, such explicit index iteration is not necessary. However, if you want to iterate over a numerical sequence, you can do so by using the `range()` function, which returns a list of integer values between two integer values (not inclusive of the second one), as shown here:

```
>>> for num in range(1,5):
        print num

1
2
3
4
```

An optional third integer argument to `range()` can be used to set the step length of the range. The default is 1. If you want to count off by two or three, you can adjust the step length.

Conditionals are set by using `if/elif/else` statements. In this example, Python iterates through the numbers 0 to 9 with a step length of two. For each number, the code checks to see whether the number is less than or equal to 2, greater than or equal to 8, or neither. The `elif` statement is Python's *else if* conditional. Note particularly the left indentation. The `if`, `elif`, and `else` statements must all be aligned along the left side in order to correspond to each other. If the left indentation of those lines does not match, this code will result in an error.

```
>>> for num in range(0,10,2):
        if num <= 2:
            print str(num) + " is small"
        elif num >= 8:
            print str(num) + " is big"
        else:
            print str(num) + " is medium"


0 is small
2 is small
4 is medium
6 is medium
8 is big
```

A handy statement for programming is the `pass` statement. This statement is a placeholder that does nothing, but it can stand in for other code in a control structure when having no command would result in an indentation error.

Other control flow statements are available for use in Python, such as `while` and some modifications to the standard `for` loop. However, for the purposes of the content of the next few chapters, `for` loops and `if`/`elif`/`else` constructions will be sufficient to know about. For further information, please refer to the Python resources mentioned at the beginning of the chapter.

Functions

Much of programming in Python involves defining functions of your own, which can then be called elsewhere, including from within other functions. For this example, I wrote the following short script into the IDLE editor and saved the file with the name `simplefunction.py` before running it with the F5 key:

```
def my_simple_function():
    print "Hello World!"

my_simple_function()
```

When you run this script, you will see that it outputs the words `Hello World!` just as if the `print` statement had been called directly. In fact, the `print` statement is being called from within the `my_simple_function()` function, which is defined using the `def` statement. Note also that as in the case of control structures, the content of a function definition is delimited not with brackets but by left indentation.

It is also possible to define functions that take arguments. To do this, a variable representing the argument is initialized in the function definition. When the function is called with a corresponding argument, the variable is instantiated with the argument value:

```
def my_simple_function(arg):
    print "Hello World" * arg

my_simple_function(5)
```

The output of this script is the repetition of the string Hello World five times, as shown here:

```
Hello WorldHello WorldHello WorldHello WorldHello World
```

Variables initialized inside a function are local to that function and cannot be accessed from outside that function. If you try to access a variable that has been defined inside a function outside of that function, Python will give an error.

Variables initialized outside the function are global and can be accessed from within the function:

```
my_global_variable = "Hello!"

def my_simple_function():
    print my_global_variable

my_simple_function()
```

This script will output the string Hello! However, things get a bit more complicated when you want to change the value of global variables in the context of a function. In this example, the variable my_global_variable begins with the value "Hello!" but is reassigned the value "World!" in the context of the function. This new value, however, remains local to the function. The global value of my_global_variable remains "Hello!" Therefore, if you call a print statement after the my_simple_function() function, the variable will be printed both with its original value and its local value from the function.

```
my_global_variable = "Hello!"

def my_simple_function():
    my_global_variable = "World!"
    print my_global_variable

my_simple_function()
print my_global_variable
```

To avoid this and to force changes made within the function to be applied to the global value of the variable, you need to use the global statement to declare the variable as a global variable within the function definition. If you add this, the output of both the function and the subsequent print statement will be World!.

```
my_global_variable = "Hello!"

def my_simple_function():
    global my_global_variable
    my_global_variable = "World!"
    print my_global_variable

my_simple_function()
print my_global_variable
```

Classes and OOP

Python is a fully object-oriented programming language, which means that data elements in the language are considered as instances of classes, which are defined to have attributes and methods. These instances of classes are called *objects*. *Attributes* refer to the kinds of data that the class has associated with it. For example, a class representing Person might have an attribute Eye Color. *Methods* are requests or messages defined for a specific class. A common type of method is one that returns an attribute value, so in this case a method for the class Person might answer the question, "What is this person's eye color?"

Defining your own classes is an important part of high-level programming in Python, particularly when programming complex systems. However, you can accomplish a great deal without having to define classes of your own, by using built-in classes and modules or libraries in which others have defined classes. For this reason, I will not go into depth about how to write class definitions here, but rather focus on the basic syntax of objects, methods, and attributes, so when it comes time to look at the Blender API, you will be able to translate the information you find there into working Python code. A simple class definition for the class Person might begin something like this:

```
class Person:
    eye_color = "Green"
    def get_eye_color(self):
        print self.eye_color
```

In this definition, there is only one attribute for a person, `eye_color`. There is also only one method defined, called `get_eye_color()`, which prints the value of the eye color variable.

As with built-in data types such as lists, strings, and integers, objects of defined classes can be passed to variables. Outside the class definition, it is possible to create an instance (object) of the Person class by assigning one to a variable, as shown in the following example (this should be added to the same script in which the Person class is defined):

```
p = Person()
p.get_eye_color()
p.eye_color = "Blue"
p.get_eye_color()
```

After assigning the object to the variable p, this script goes on to access information from p by calling `p.get_eye_color()`. The syntax here is important. Calling a method on its object is done by appending the method name onto the end of the object name, separated by a dot. The method name ends with round brackets containing whatever arguments are appropriate for the method. If no arguments are necessary, the brackets are empty. When this method is called for the first time, the string `Green` is printed out, because it is defined as the default value in the class definition.

Attribute values are also accessed by appending the value name to the end of the object name, separated by a dot. The next line of the script assigns the string `"Blue"` to the `eye_color` attribute for p. After this new value is assigned to the attribute and `p.get_eye_color()` is called a second time, the string `Blue` is printed.

In the API, you will find a large collection of descriptions of classes. Each class description also includes a description of the kinds of attributes and methods that are appropriate for interacting with objects of that class. After you get used to looking things up in the API, the information should become mostly self-explanatory most of the time. The next few chapters discuss some areas that might not be quite so obvious, to give you a sense of what kinds of inconsistencies to be on the lookout for. Becoming conversant with the way the API is intended to work will make it much quicker to get to the bottom of the problem on the occasions when things are not quite as they should be.

The *dir()* Command

A useful command that will save you tons of time looking things up in the API is `dir()`. By using this command with an object name as the argument, you can return a list of methods and attributes defined for the class of any object. Because in Python everything is an object, this means you can call `dir()` on any data you want to, even on methods themselves, and get a list of all the appropriate methods for that class. If you call `dir()` on the p variable representing a person from the previous section, the following list will be returned:

```
['__doc__', '__module__', 'eye_color', 'get_eye_color']
```

The first two methods are standard for all classes, and are used to include documentation notes and information about the module in which they are defined. The other two elements in the list are the attribute and method you defined previously: `eye_color` and `get_eye_color`, respectively.

Modules

One of the main benefits of working in an OOP environment is that classes created by other people can be easily used by anyone who knows the API for the classes. It should not be necessary to see the actual code of the class definition in order to work with a class; all you should need is to know what attributes the object has, what methods are defined for the class, and what the methods return. In principle, you should be able to ignore everything else about how the classes and methods are specifically implemented.

To use classes defined by other people, you need to import the module in which the class is defined. Any Python script can be a module, and any class defined in a script can be imported into another script in this way. Modules are imported by using `import modulename` at the beginning of the script in which you want to use the imported classes. When this is done, classes from the module can be used, but it is necessary to preface calls to the class with the module name, as in `modulename.classname`. To use the class name without having to always append the module name, you must import the class from the module by using `from module-name import classname`. A common shortcut that can be used when the module does not contain an unwieldy number of classes is `from modulename import *`, which imports all classes from the module.

You will use this kind of construction a lot when working in the Blender-Python environment, because most of the classes you will be working with come from Blender-related modules enumerated in the API. In the next chapter, you will get familiar with the API and learn how to use it to access the information you need about your 3D assets in the Python environment.

The Bottom Line

Become familiar with the basics of the Python language.   Python is a widely used language for scripting in many different application areas. It is known for its ease of use, readability, and speed of development.

Master It   Make sure that you have a good reference handy for Python syntax. In this chapter, I listed several good books you should consider buying. Use a Google search to find some more good online resources to quickly look up Python operators and data types.

Run the Python shell and IDLE development environment.   The simplest way to access Python directly is through the Python command-line shell, which is part of the IDLE development environment. In this shell environment, you can execute individual commands and perform introspection on variables.

> **Master It**   In this chapter, you learned that you cannot concatenate a string and an integer by using the + operator. Likewise, you cannot add a string numerically. In some cases, however, numerical data may be input (for example, in a form) as a string type. Study the references you searched for in the previous Master It exercise about type casting in Python to find out how you would convert the string "5" into an integer that can be added to another.

Understand fundamental features of Python syntax.   Python is a powerful programming language with a variety of data types, control structure options, and useful built-in functions. Its characteristic features include its reliance on indentation to represent logical structure.

> **Master It**   Create a variable my_list and assign it the list [1,2,1,3,1,4]. Call the dir() function with this list as an argument. Which of the methods returned by dir() do you think would be the correct method for removing one of the elements from the list? Experiment with the methods you think would work, and try to get rid of the number 2 from the list, so the list becomes [1,1,3,1,4]. Which method do you think will return the number of times the number 1 appears in the list?

Chapter 7

Python Scripting for Blender

In this chapter, you'll begin writing Python scripts for Blender. This requires becoming familiar with Blender's Python coding environment and the Blender-Python API. This chapter teaches you how to place objects in Blender's 3D space and manipulate their associated values in your script. You'll also learn how the Blender-Python interface construction tools work, which will enable you to create interactive scripts and tools. The goal is to show you not only how to accomplish the specific tasks in this chapter's tutorials, but also how to mine the sometimes daunting API specifications for the information you need to accomplish your own goals.

In this chapter, you will learn to

◆   Edit and run scripts in Blender

◆   Find what you need in the Blender-Python API

◆   Create an interactive script

Editing and Running Scripts in Blender

There are several tools you can use to write Python programs for Blender. In the previous chapter, you saw the default Python editor available in IDLE. To get started with Blender scripting, though, the best option is in Blender itself.

The Blender Text Editor

Like any other window type, the Blender text editor can be accessed from the Window Type menu in the left corner of any window header. The text editor window is shown in Figure 7.1.

The basic functionality in the File and Edit menus is standard and will be familiar to anyone who has used a word processor or text editor. The Format menu has various options that are of specific use for Python scripting. The Indent and Unindent options will add a tabbed indentation to (or remove one from) selected blocks of text. This can also be done from the keyboard with Tab and Shift+Tab, respectively. Because the structure of a Python program is determined by the pattern of indentation, this is obviously a handy shortcut.

The Comment menu item adds a # symbol to the beginning of each line in a selected block of text, which *comments out* that line of code. Commented-out code is ignored by the interpreter, so this is a good way to add comments to help explain the code to other programmers who might have cause to read it (or to yourself, for when you come back to your script after a long time away!) You can also use the Comment and Uncomment options to remove and replace blocks of code from your script for testing purposes, without having to delete and rewrite them. Commenting out code to help narrow down the source of a problem is a commonly used method of debugging. Finally, the Convert Whitespace option in the Format menu enables you to convert white space from spaces to tabs and vice versa, which can be useful for fixing problems that can result from using multiple editors with different tab settings.

The five buttons shown in Figure 7.2, from left to right, toggle full-screen view, line numbering, word wrap, color-coded syntax highlighting, and enabling Python text plug-ins. The two rows of icons represent the default icon set and the new (and incomplete) icon set.

FIGURE 7.1

A script displayed in the text editor

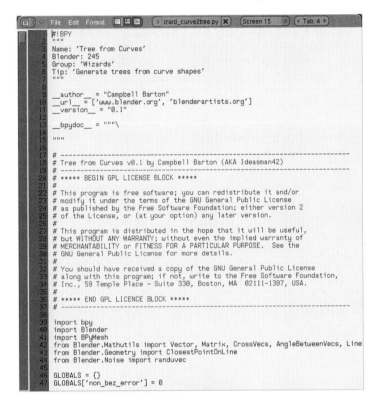

FIGURE 7.2

Toggle buttons for full-screen view, line numbering, text wrap, syntax highlighting, and Python text plug-ins

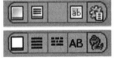

PYTHON TEXT PLUG-INS

A relatively new feature is the ability to run Python text plug-ins from the Text Plugins submenu of the Text menu. Running these will enable you to use several helpful features, such as automatic suggestion of members, classes, or types; code completion; and fast ways to navigate code. Experiment with these to create the editing environment that is most comfortable for you, and check the 2.48 online release notes for details of how to get the most out of these new features.

CUTTING AND PASTING

Whereas most applications use a common system clipboard for cutting and pasting, Blender uses its own private clipboard, which means that the traditional Ctrl+C and Ctrl+V copy and paste hot keys do not work between clipboards. Within Blender, copying and pasting text uses Ctrl+C and Ctrl+V (this is also true when you are copying and pasting between multiple instances of Blender that are open simultaneously). However, if you want to copy and paste text between the Blender text editor and some external text editor or word processor, you must also press the Alt key while cutting or pasting. In Blender, Ctrl+Alt+C will copy selected text to the system clipboard, and Ctrl+Alt+V will paste text from the system clipboard.

Script Format and Templates

Blender Python scripts follow certain conventions. You don't necessarily have to follow them if you are writing scripts for yourself, but if you plan to release your scripts for use by others, or if you want to make sure that your scripts can be fully integrated into the Blender environment and included in menus, be sure that you have them properly formatted. Several ready-made templates are already written and can be accessed via the Text menu in the text editor header as shown in Figure 7.3.

FIGURE 7.3
Loading a
script template

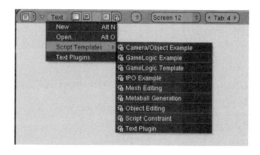

The first thing you'll see in the template files is the script header, which looks like this:
```
#!BPY

"""

Name: 'My Object Script'
Blender: 244
Group: 'Object'
Tooltip: 'Put some useful info here'

"""
```

This is a special header for Blender scripts. If a script is placed in the .blend/scripts subdirectory in your Blender installation directory when Blender is started up, that script will appear in the appropriate Scripts submenu based on its Group entry. A script with the preceding header would appear in the Object submenu, shown in Figure 7.4.

FIGURE 7.4
The Object
submenu of the
Scripts menu

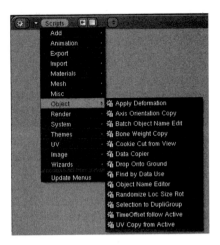

Typically, scripts that are intended to be made available for others' use should include licensing information. If you aim to have your script included in an official release of Blender, the script must be licensed with a GPL-compatible license. You can copy and paste the GPL text directly from other scripts into your own. If you choose to use another license, make sure that it accurately reflects how you want people to treat the script. Don't assume that people will read your mind and understand what they can and can't do with your script in the absence of licensing information.

The remainder of the template's content is an outline for the actual code. The rest of this chapter covers in depth the issues of defining functions and writing your script.

The Scripts Window

When scripts with interface code are executed, they run in a special Blender window type called the Scripts window, which by default replaces the text window containing the script for the duration of the script's running. You can open the Scripts window without running a script, but there won't be much in it, just a header and a blank gray area. You can call scripts from the Scripts menu in the header of this window, but in general, you will not access this window directly very often. Its purpose is to provide an environment for your script's interface, as you will see by the end of this chapter.

Introducing the Blender-Python API

The most important document for building Blender-Python scripts is the API. This contains a complete list of all the modules defined for Blender, all those modules' classes, and the attributes and methods defined for objects of those classes. If you want to do Python scripting for Blender, the API will be your best friend. The Blender 2.48 API can be found online at www.blender.org/documentation/248PythonDoc/index.html. An offline copy can be found on the CD that accompanies this book, for your convenience.

AN API FOR EVERY OCCASION

The term *Blender-Python* API as used in this book refers to the API for the Blender and bpy modules used for scripting purposes in Blender proper. Be aware that this is *not* the same API used to integrate Python into the Blender Game Engine (BGE)—although, with some restrictions, it can also be used in the game-engine context. The Blender GameLogic API and other BGE-related Python use is discussed in Chapter 11, "Python Power in the Blender Game Engine."

Appendix B, "Blender-Python API Module and Class Hierarchies," lists the modules and classes documented in the API. You'll notice that the lists are redundant. The name of the class as listed in the "Class Hierarchy" section also includes the module to which the class belongs. For example, the first entry in the Class Hierarchy list is Armature.Armature, the class that contains definitions for Armature objects. The naming scheme is simple and follows similar Python conventions: To the right of the dot is the class name proper, and to the left is the name of the module in which the class is defined. To use this class in your script, you need to import this module.

These hierarchy lists are the place to begin to solve your problem. Read the descriptions and find the class that looks most closely related to the Blender objects you want to work with. If you want to write a script that in some way manipulates armatures, for example, you would want to investigate the Armature module and the Armature.Armature class more closely.

If you click the Armature link in the Module Hierarchy in the HTML version of the API (either online or included on the CD that accompanies this book), you will see a page that gives you information about the Armature module. In most cases, the top page for a module will begin with some Python code examples. It's highly recommended to read these, because they will often contain exactly what you want, and in some cases may be the only real documentation available for some newer features. The rest of the Module API page lists the classes, functions, and any special variables defined in the module. Common module functions are Get() and New(), which are used, respectively, to retrieve a list of objects (in this case, armatures) from the current Blender session and to create a new instance (object) of the main class defined in the module. The use of special variables is highly dependent on the module and classes they are associated with. Their names should give you clues to their meaning, and in most cases you will find examples of their use among the code samples.

In the Classes list on the Armature module page, the first class listed is Armature. Clicking this link will take you to the same page that Armature.Armature on the Class Hierarchy page links to. On the Class API page, you'll see two concise lists, one of instance methods, which are methods defined for individual objects of the class, and the other of instance variables, which represent the various possible attributes of objects of the class. These attributes may be of any type. If you look at the list of attributes for Armature objects, you will see that many of the attributes take Boolean values. The bones attribute, on the other hand, returns the armature's bones, listed in a specially defined class called BonesDict, which is an extension of the built-in dictionary type. On the API page, if you scroll down, more detailed descriptions and in some case code samples are listed for each method and attribute.

Keep in mind that this book is not intended as a reference book but as a book of tutorials and explanations. Your reference book for Python scripting in Blender is the API itself, and it will be absolutely indispensable after you start wanting to do your own thing. Being able to confidently navigate the API is 90 percent of becoming a skilled Blender-Python scripter, and the best way to get to know the API is to work with it. In the next section and in Chapter 8, "The Many-Headed Snake: Other Uses of Python in Blender," you will see examples of how to access and manipulate various kinds of 3D data. More important, you will develop a feeling for how to get what you need out of the API.

Real World Scenario

STATE-OF-THE-ART VIRTUAL REALITY AT METAVR

Modeling and animating with Blender isn't all just fun and games. At MetaVR, one of the industry leaders in virtual reality software, integration with Blender has been a central part of the development of their Virtual Reality Scene Generator (VRSG) software, which has been used extensively for real-time, immersive military training by the armed forces of several countries. Blender developer Campbell Barton was contracted to author MetaVR's Blender plug-in, which enables users to create new content for use in the VRSG environment, including fully rigged, animated characters.

This work resulted in the ability to create scenes involving tens of thousands of buildings and trees, and the creation of a character library of more than 100 human characters that could be exported simultaneously to the VRSG format, with automatic level-of-detail generation and infrared texture map creation. Numerous current features of Blender were the direct result of MetaVR's investment in this project, including BVH export functionality, the array modifier, UV projection, custom transform axes, knife snapping, improved quad-to-triangle conversions, and numeric input for transforms. Under-the-hood developments from this project include ID properties, which form the basis for the data interchange system of Blender 2.50 and future versions.

The MetaVR Blender plug-in is a quintessential example of how Python scripting can extend the possibilities of Blender by enabling users to export content to, and import content from, other formats. Blender already includes a wealth of built-in Python-based import and export scripts for most standard 3D formats. With the custom-made MetaVR plug-in, Blender was able to offer functionality that would otherwise have been limited to special VR content-creation software ranging in the tens of thousands of dollars per seat.

You can learn more about MetaVR's use of Blender in the VRSG environment at their website:

`www.metavr.com/products/vrsg/vrsg-characteranimation.html`

Creating an Interactive Script

In this section, you will build an interactive sample script from the ground up. The functionality is simple. The script will enable the user to create bouncing, colored cones in 3D space by using a script interface to set various parameters for the cones such as their dimensions, color, and the speed and height of their bouncing. It's not a very practical script, but it will give you a good sense of how a Python script works with 3D assets in Blender.

Working with Meshes, Objects, and Ipos

The first thing to look at is how to create the objects you want to work with and place them in the scene. Note that the word *object* becomes ambiguous here; in Python-speak, objects are instantiations of classes (in fact, in Python, everything is an object). In Blender, *objects* are things that have positions, rotations, and centers in the 3D space, in short, anything you can select with your right mouse button in Blender's Object mode. If you do not already know the difference between, for example, a Mesh datablock in Blender and a Mesh object to which it is associated, I recommend reviewing this before continuing with this chapter. Chapter 1 of my book *Introducing Character Animation with Blender* (Sybex, 2007) goes into the difference in some detail.

In the next few chapters, I refer to the Blender conception of objects as *3D objects* in cases where there may be any confusion, and generally reserve the term *objects* on its own for the Python meaning of the term.

IMPORTING MODULES

The first step in writing a script for Blender is to import the modules that will provide the classes you need. I'll import modules as they are needed in this example. To begin with, it will be necessary to import the Blender and bpy (Blender Python) modules. In addition, it will be necessary to call some simple mathematical functions to calculate the shape of the cone mesh. These functions are defined in the math module, which is included as part of your default Python installation. All of these modules can be imported with a single `import` statement, by simply listing the modules by name, separated by commas:

```
import Blender, bpy, math
```

To use submodules from the Blender module without having to prefix their names with `Blender.` all the time, I import the submodules specifically by name from the Blender module, using the `from module_name import submodule_name` statement. Because the first thing to do is to create a Mesh object and add it to the current Blender scene, you will need to have Object, Scene, and Mesh submodules to work with, so the next line of code will be as shown here:

```
from Blender import Object, Scene, Mesh
```

Do the same thing for math, but rather than importing a huge list of specific classes, just import the entire namespace from the math module by using the same syntax with an asterisk to represent the class names:

```
from math import *
```

MODULES IN TRANSITION

If the existence of both Blender and bpy modules seems redundant to you, that's because it is. The Blender module has been around much longer, and the bpy module is, gradually, being groomed to replace it. When classes with similar functionality exist in both modules, it is best to use the more elegant options from bpy.

Setting Default Values

For several reasons, it will be helpful to store some important values in variables. Especially later, when the interface is implemented, this will help make the code easier to modify to make these values possible to set interactively. To begin with, it's enough to set them with default values. The following values will represent, respectively, the number of vertices that make up the circular base of the cone; the X and Y coordinates of the cone object's starting location, the radius of the cone; the height of the cone; the speed at which the cone bounces; the height to which the cone bounces; the red, green, and blue values of the cone's material color; and the name of the Cone Mesh object.

```
cverts = 10
varX = 0
varY = 0
varRad = 1
varHeight = 2
varSpeed = 1
varBHeight = 5
varRed = 1
varGrn = 0
varBlu = 1
varNam = "MyCone"
```

Creating the Mesh

A Mesh object (note that I'm talking here about a *Python* object of class Mesh, not a Blender 3D Mesh object, which is, as you'll see soon, a Python object of class Object) has a list-like attribute that represents its vertices. A vertex is represented by three integers indicating its X, Y, and Z coordinates. The Mesh object also has a list of faces, which is a list of three or four vertices, depending on whether the face is a triangle or a quad. The vertices in these lists are identified by their index in the object's list of vertices. The first thing to do is to collect these vertices and faces together in proper Python lists.

It's clear already where the central vertex in the base of the cone and the cone's peak will be, so you can assign those vertices to the list immediately. For faces, it's not yet clear what they will be, so I'll initialize the faces list as an empty list:

```
list_of_vertices = [[0,0,0],[0,0,varHeight]]
list_of_faces = []
```

The next step is slightly more complicated. The value of `cverts` represents the number of vertices in the circular base of the cone. Placing these vertices requires some light trigonometry. Using the `range()` function introduced in Chapter 6, "Python for the Impatient," iterate from 0 to 9 and generate coordinates on a circle for X and Y values of each vertex. The Z coordinate is zero for all of them. For each iteration of the `for` loop, the generated coordinate triple is appended to the list of vertices. For each iteration after the first one, append two triangular faces to the list: one between the last two generated vertices and the central vertex of the base, and one between the last two generated vertices and the peak of the cone. Note that the triples representing faces each start with 0 and 1, which are the indices of the base vertex and the peak vertex, as defined previously. j+1 and j+2 begin counting from the next index after these two:

```
for j in range(0,cverts):
    x = sin(j*pi*2/(cverts-1))*varRad
    y = cos(j*pi*2/(cverts-1))*varRad
    z = 0
    list_of_vertices.append([x,y,z])
    if j > 0:
        list_of_faces.extend([[0,j+1,j+2],[1,j+1,j+2]])
```

This is all that's necessary to define the geometry, but at this point there's still no Mesh object for the geometry to be part of. All you have so far are a couple of lists of numbers.

To create the Mesh object, use the method from the bpy module. Name the Mesh object coneMesh:

```
coneMesh = bpy.data.meshes.new(varNam)
```

Finally, you can pass the vertices and faces to the object by using the extend() method to concatenate the lists you just generated with the (by default empty) list of vertices and faces of the Mesh object:

```
coneMesh.verts.extend(list_of_vertices)
coneMesh.faces.extend(list_of_faces)
```

PLACING 3D OBJECTS IN THE SCENE

You can run the script by pressing Alt+P or by choosing Run Python Script from the File menu. If you run this script now, a Mesh datablock will indeed be created. It won't be exciting to look at, though, because the datablock will not be associated with any 3D object and therefore won't exist in Blender's 3D space. To put the mesh into a 3D object in the scene, you first need to retrieve the active scene. That is done by using the bpy module, like this:

```
scn = bpy.data.scenes.active
```

The variable scn now holds the currently active scene object. A new Mesh 3D object is created in the scene by passing the mesh and the name of the new 3D object to objects.new(), like this:

```
meshOb = scn.objects.new(coneMesh, varNam)
```

After the object has been created, it will be placed by default at the 0,0,0 point in the 3D space. To change this, use the setLocation() method as follows:

```
meshOb.setLocation(varX, varY, 0)
```

If you run the script now with Alt+P, you'll see a cone appear as shown in Figure 7.5. You're almost finished with the first part of the tutorial, but not quite. There's still something a bit off about this cone. When you build an object raw from vertices and faces, the direction of the normals can turn out haphazardly. In this case, you can see this either by looking at the object in Textured Draw mode as shown in Figure 7.6 (it helps to add a lamp to get the best view of this) or by entering Edit mode and selecting Draw Normals in the Mesh Tools More tab, resulting in the view shown in Figure 7.7.

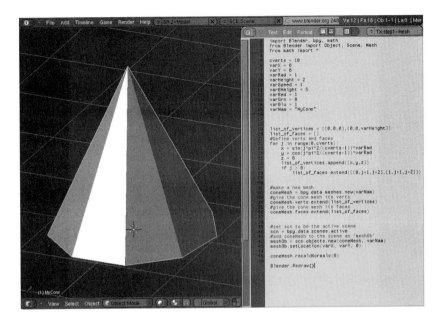

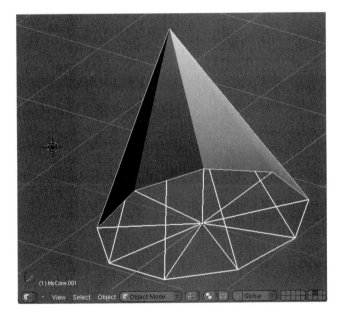

FIGURE 7.7
Draw Normals
turned on to view
Normal direction

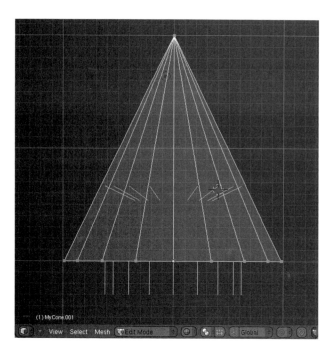

Just as you can recalculate normals to point outward with Ctrl+N when modeling, you can recalculate normals outside in Python by using the `recalcNormals()` method for Mesh objects. The argument can be 0 or 1 to make the method recalculate the normals outward or inward, respectively. In your script, the method call will look like this:

```
coneMesh.recalcNormals(0)
```

Note that this method requires that the mesh be associated with a 3D object. If you call this method on a mesh before it has been added to a scene as a 3D object, the method will result in an error and complain that it cannot find an object for the mesh. So be sure to call this method only after you have called `scn.objects.new(coneMesh, varNam)`.

If you run the script now, you will notice that nothing happens in the 3D window until you click on it, or rotate it, or in some other way cause Blender to update the window. You can remedy this by forcing Blender to redraw the 3D window after the object has been created, like this:

```
Blender.Redraw()
```

If you run the script now, you should see your cone appear immediately. If you want to check your work against my code, you can find the script so far on the CD that accompanies this book in the file **cones_tutorial.blend**. The script is located in the text **step1-mesh**, which you can access via the Text drop-down menu in the text editor header.

ADDING A MATERIAL

As a final step in creating the cone mesh, let's add a material to the mesh. The class for this is Material, which is defined in the Material module in the API. Refer to the API page for a complete list of methods and attributes for use with Material objects. To use the Material class in your script, you need to add Material to the modules you import at the beginning of the script. The code for this step can be found in the text step2-material in the .blend file.

To create a new material, use the New() class method and pass the resulting new object to a variable, like this:

```
mat = Material.New('Material')
```

You now have a Material object called mat. The next thing to do is to add this to coneMesh's collection of materials. At this point, you will run into a strange and glaring inconsistency in the implementation of the API. A mesh's materials collection *should* behave in all respects like a Python list. However, the current implementation has a few inconsistencies (not to say *bugs*), and this is one of them. In fact, you cannot simply append mat to coneMesh.materials by using the append() method. There is a grotesque but functional workaround for this: You can copy coneMesh.materials to a new variable, which in this case is called mats, append mat to mats, and then pass the value mats back to coneMesh.materials:

```
mats = coneMesh.materials
mats.append(mat)
coneMesh.materials = mats
```

Yes, it's hideous, and nobody knows that better than the developers. So rest assured that these kinds of inconsistencies will be addressed as soon as resources allow. For the time being, if you've read this far, I assume that you want to learn Python scripting for Blender and you're made of sturdy enough stuff to continue!

Passing red, green, and blue (RGB) values to the mat is straightforward. The RGB list is contained in the attribute rgbCol. You can assign a triplet list to that attribute as follows:

```
mat.rgbCol = [varRed, varGrn, varBlu]
```

The variables used here were defined earlier in your script. Red, green, and blue are 1, 0, and 1 respectively, so the resulting cone will be purple. Be sure that your Blender.Redraw() call comes after all of this, so the 3D viewport is redrawn only after you've set up your material.

ADDING IPOS

The goal of this tutorial is to make a script that adds bouncing cones to the 3D scene. As you know if you've done a minimum of animation with Blender, the way this is done is with Ipo curves. In this section, I'll show you how to work with Ipos in Python.

The first thing you need to know is which modules and classes you'll be working with. Look over the list of modules in the API and take a wild guess at which one will give you access to Ipo information and let you create Ipos. If you guessed that it's the module called Ipo, you are correct. If you guessed that it's the module just below Ipo in the list, IpoCurve, you're also correct. You'll need both, and you'll need to understand the difference between them. To use them in this script, you will need to add Ipo to the import statement at the beginning of your script.

I strongly recommend reading the class descriptions of both the Ipo class and the IpoCurve class (and indeed any class you plan to use). It's always good, and usually necessary, to refer directly to the API, and you should get into the habit now.

In short, an Ipo object represents a collection of IpoCurves belonging to a specific Ipo type for an object. The `curves` attribute of the Ipo object contains a list of the associated IpoCurve objects. There are 10 types of Ipos. For each of those types, there is a set of IpoCurve constants that represents the curves that can belong to the Ipo type. Ipo types are the following:

◆ Material

◆ Lamp

◆ World

◆ Camera

◆ Object

◆ Curve

◆ Constraint

◆ Texture

◆ Pose/Action

◆ Sequence

You should recognize these Ipo types, as they are the same types that are keyed directly in Blender. You probably also have an idea of which IpoCurves are associated with each Ipo type. A complete list can be found on the Module Ipo page in the API. By way of example, the constants for Object type IpoCurves are as follows:

◆ OB_LOCX

◆ OB_LOCY

◆ OB_LOCZ

◆ OB_DLOCX

◆ OB_DLOCY

◆ OB_DLOCZ

◆ OB_ROTX

◆ OB_ROTY

◆ OB_ROTZ

◆ OB_DROTX

◆ OB_DROTY

◆ OB_DROTZ

- ◆ OB_SCALEX

- ◆ OB_SCALEY

- ◆ OB_SCALEZ

- ◆ OB_DSCALEX

- ◆ OB_DSCALEY

- ◆ OB_DSCALEZ

- ◆ OB_LAYER

- ◆ OB_TIME

- ◆ OB_COLR

- ◆ OB_COLG

- ◆ OB_COLB

- ◆ OB_COLA

- ◆ OB_FSTRENG

- ◆ OB_FFALL

- ◆ OB_RDAMP

- ◆ OB_DAMPING

- ◆ OB_PERM

The first two characters of the constants tell you that these are Object type Ipo curves. The portion after the constant tells you what the curve animates.

In addition to these constant values, which are attributes of Ipo objects, IpoCurve objects themselves have specific name attributes that represent the kind of curves they are. The possible name values for IpoCurve objects can be found on the IpoCurve Class page in the API. There is a one-to-one correspondence between the possible names for the IpoCurve of a specific Ipo type and the Ipo constants representing those curves.

To create a new Ipo object, use the New() class method. The arguments represent its type and its name in Blender. In this case, the only thing we're going to animate is the Z location, which is an Object attribute, so the Ipo is of type "Object". The next thing to do is to call the addCurve() method on the Ipo object. As the name indicates, this adds an IpoCurve object to the Ipo's list of curves. As I mentioned previously, IpoCurves have fixed names that refer directly to the value that they animate. This curve's name is LocZ, which is passed as the argument to addCurve(). These things are done in the following two lines of code:

```
ipo = Ipo.New("Object","Ipo")
ipo.addCurve('LocZ')
```

The next thing to take care of is a value to determine the speed of the bouncing movement. As anyone who has done a minimum of working with Ipo curves in Blender is aware, the speed with which an animated value changes is a result of the steepness of the curve at that point in time. Later, the speed of the bounce is going to be made adjustable in an interface, so I want to determine the position of the second point on the Ipo curve based on that value. Previously, you defined a value varSpeed and gave it a default value of 1. You'll use that now as the denominator of a value that will control how many frames it takes the cone to reach the top of the bounce. By default, it will take 10 frames. If varSpeed goes up, the speed will increase, and if it goes down, the speed will decrease. Later, the maximum and minimum limits for this value will be set in the interface code. The speedOffset value is defined like this:

```
speedOffset = 10/varSpeed
```

Now it's time to set the control points on the IpoCurve. If you look closely at the entry for the IpoCurve object, you'll see that the first instance variable listed for it is bezierPoints, which is defined as a "a list of BezTriples." This should tip you off that there's one more class you will need to become familiar with, the BezTriple class. Surf over to the BezTriple Module and Class pages and give them a good read before continuing. You will need to add the BezTriple class to those that you import at the beginning of the script.

A BezTriple represents a single Bezier control point as three points in space: the control point itself and the two Bezier handles that extend from it. If you are not familiar with working with Bezier curves or editing Ipos, you should review these topics in order to fully understand how BezTriples work.

A BezTriple can have either three or nine coordinate values. If it has three coordinate values, the control point and both handles are assumed to share the three (X, Y, and Z) coordinates. If it has nine coordinate values, they are arranged with the handles as the first three and last three values, and the control point as the middle three values. Note that BezTriples are a general-purpose class for Bezier curve handles. Because Bezier curves exist in Blender in 3D, each control point and handle must have three coordinate values to determine its location. However, for the special case of IpoCurves, which are clearly 2D curves, there is no Z axis. This means that when working BezTriples on IpoCurves, every third coordinate value is ignored.

You will define three points. The first point is at 0. The second point represents the top of the bounce arc. The third point represents the return to the ground. Each point is a single BezTriple, defined by nine coordinates. All Z coordinates are set to 0, but they can be set to any integer or float value and it won't make a difference. The first BezTriple sets the control point of point1 at 0, and sets the handles −0.05 and 0.5 units along the X axis. Placing the handles close to the control points makes for a sharper curve. The second point, point2, is set with all Y values at varBHeight, with the X value of the control point placed at the frame represented by speedOffset. By contrast to the close handles of the first point, the handles on the middle point are set +/−5 units from speedOffset, yielding a gentler arc at the top of the bounce. The last point brings the Y values back down to 0 and places the control point at speedOffset*2. The handles are once again located 0.5 units to each side of the control point.

```
point1 = BezTriple.New(-.5,0,0,0,0,0,.5,0,0)
point2 = BezTriple.New(speedOffset-5,varBHeight,0,
    speedOffset,varBHeight,0,speedOffset+5,varBHeight,0)
point3 = BezTriple.New(speedOffset*2-0.5,0,0,
    speedOffset*2,0,0,speedOffset*2+0.5,0,0)
```

Now that the points have been defined, you can add them to the curve, which is accessed by using the constants described previously, like this:

```
ipo[Blender.Ipo.OB_LOCZ].append(point1)
ipo[Blender.Ipo.OB_LOCZ].append(point2)
ipo[Blender.Ipo.OB_LOCZ].append(point3)
```

Note that each of the points is appended one by one. Be warned: There is another inconsistency lurking here. Although `append()` is a Python list method, and another Python list method, `extend()`, would appear to be suitable for adding all three points at once, the Python list `extend()` method is not defined for this collection of points. What's more, an attribute called `extend` is defined for this object, but it means something entirely different—it determines the extend type of the curve. Extend types (and interpolation types) of IpoCurves are listed on the IpoCurve class page in the API. In this case, use the cyclic extend type, which is represented by the value 2.

```
ipo[Blender.Ipo.OB_LOCZ].extend = 2
```

Finally, attach the Ipo to the Mesh object by using `setIpo()` like so:

```
meshOb.setIpo(ipo)
```

You can now run the script with Alt+P. The cone will appear in the 3D space, and when you press Alt+A (or the Play button on the Timeline) to play the animation, the cone will bounce up and down. You can look at the Ipo curve created by the script by selecting the object and opening an Ipo Editor window with Object Ipos selected in the drop-down menu.

You've now finished the first half of this tutorial. The code covered so far can be found in the `step3-ipos` text in the drop-down of the tutorial `.blend` file. The next part of the tutorial will move on to building an interface from which you can set values and execute commands in this script.

Building the Interface

Before proceeding to build the actual interface for this script, it would be a good idea to take a look at a self-contained, bare-bones Blender-Python interface script. All Blender-Python interface scripts are essentially the same, and so understanding a stripped-down example will be helpful when constructing a more complex interface.

A MINIMAL INTERFACE SCRIPT

To make this simple interface, create a new text file in your Blender text editor by clicking Add New in the Text menu. Enter the following code in its entirety into the window. You can check your code against the `simple-interface` text in the tutorial `.blend` file for this chapter.

```
1    from Blender import Draw
2
3    def gui():
4        Draw.PushButton("Press Me!", 0, 5, 30, 100, 25, "pressButton")
5        Draw.PushButton("Quit", 1, 110, 30, 100, 25, "quit")
6
7    def event(evt, val):
8        if evt == Draw.ESCKEY:
```

```
9            Draw.Exit()
10
11   def button_event(evt):
12       if evt == 0:
13           print "Button Pressed!"
14       if evt == 1:
15           Draw.Exit()
16
17   Draw.Register(gui, event, button_event)
```

After you execute this code with Alt+P, the simple two-button interface shown in Figure 7.8 appears in the Scripts window. If you press the button labeled Press Me! the words `Button Pressed!` will appear in the Blender console, as shown in Figure 7.9. If you click the Quit button or press the Esc key, the script will end and the text editor window will return.

FIGURE 7.8
A very simple interface

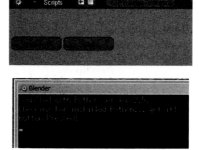

FIGURE 7.9
Responding to the button press

The lynchpin of the whole script is found in the last line, `Draw.Register(gui, event, button_event)`. This command is required in any Blender-Python GUI script. In turn, it requires that the Draw class be imported. The Draw class handles most of the work of drawing the interface elements such as buttons, sliders, and fields.

What `Draw.Register()` does is to bring together the three core functions that define an interface. Each argument represents the name of a function. The first argument will become the name of the function that sets up the GUI. The second argument will be the name of the function that handles predefined event triggers such as keyboard and mouse input. The third argument will be the name of the function that handles *button events*, that is to say events that arise from some element in the GUI being triggered. The actual names of these functions are not important, but they must match the name of the function defined to play the appropriate role.

The rest of this simple script is simply defining these three functions. Let's start with `event()`. The `event()` function takes two arguments. The first argument is the event that triggered the function call. Check the Module Draw API page for a list of all possible keyboard and mouse events. In this case, there's only one key that has any effect, the Esc key. This is indicated as an attribute of Draw in the form of `Draw.ESCKEY`. The method called in that case is `Draw.Exit()`, which closes the script. The second argument to `event()` simply distinguishes between key presses and key releases. When a key is pressed, `event()` is called with a value of 1, and when a key is released, `event()` is called with a value of 0.

The button_event() function is similar, but instead of built-in event types, it takes as its argument a button event index determined by the definition of each button in the gui() function. There are as many indexes as there are buttons, and the button index determines what the function will do. In this case, the button with the 0 button event index will trigger the words Button Pressed! to be printed to the console, and the button with 1 as its event index will quit.

Finally, the buttons and their properties are defined in the gui() function, using a line of code such as Draw.PushButton("Press Me!", 0, 5, 30, 100, 25, "pressButton"). Several types of interface elements are available. Draw.Pushbutton() is a clickable button. The arguments its constructor takes here represent the text written on the button, the button event index, the X coordinate of the upper-left corner of the button, the Y coordinate of the upper-left corner of the button, the height of the button in pixels, the width of the button, and the name of the button. The other button is set up exactly the same way, except with different values; notably, its index is different, which causes it to be associated with a different pattern of action, namely quitting.

Now that you're familiar with the basic workings of the Blender-Python interface system, it's time to move on and see how to build a more complex interface that will be suitable for the task at hand.

An Interface for Creating Bouncing Cones

Before starting on building the interface itself, let's take a look at what the final result should be. It is always a good idea to at least have some kind of mock-up of how you want your interface organized before starting to code it. In this case, there must be a space to give the cone a name, places to set the dimensions of the cone in terms of height and radius, the cone's color, the starting location, and the height and speed of the bounce. Including the various test labels for each of these areas, I have set up an arrangement in 13 vertically arranged rows, as shown in Figure 7.10.

FIGURE 7.10
The goal

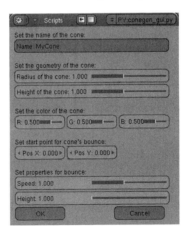

Setting Up the Interface Logic

The basic structure for this interface is the same as for the simple example you just saw, except that in this case a variety of variables will be set using the sliders and fields, and when the OK button is pressed, instead of simply printing a message to the console, the cone will be created. In order for that to happen, the cone-creation code must be placed into a function that can be called from within the button_event() logic. So it is clear from the beginning that at least four specific functions need to be defined. In fact, the creation of the camera and lamp will also be placed into functions.

To begin, let's map out an overview of the script's structure like this (for typesetting reasons, the module import list has been broken over two lines. You can copy the code directly as it is written here, or you can list all of the modules on a single line, separated by commas):

```
import Blender, math
import bpy
from Blender import Camera, Object, Ipo, IpoCurve, Scene
from Blender import Lamp, Mesh, Material, BezTriple, Draw, BGL
from math import *
def MakeCamera():
    pass
def MakeLamp():
    pass
def MakeCone():
    pass
def gui():
    pass
def button_event():
    pass
def event():
    pass
MakeCamera()
MakeLamp()
Draw.Register(gui, event, button_event)
```

There are a couple of things here to take note of. One is the use of `pass` as a placeholder. Python is sensitive to indentations, and any line that ends with a colon requires that the next line be correctly indented. Using `pass` enables you to define a function that does nothing at all for the time being without resulting in an error.

Another thing to note is that BGL is included as another class to be imported. This is Blender's OpenGL Python class and is necessary for working with the text labels in the interface. Finally, the function calls to `MakeCamera()` and `MakeLamp()` are also included. These need to be called only once, and there's no need for them to be called from within the interface logic.

SETTING VARIABLES

Several variables will be used throughout the scripts. These should be defined before the function definitions. Some of the variables used in the previous example will be set here:

```
conv = 2*math.pi/360
cverts = 10
scn = bpy.data.scenes.active
```

Also, it is often convenient to set some constants with button event values (these are just ordinary variables, but they will be treated as constants in that they are not intended to be changed). With multiple buttons, it is a good idea to assign each button event index to a variable with a meaningful name. The naming convention used here follows that of Olivier Saraja, who credits

Yves Bailly with originating it. It's simple: Each event variable begins with the prefix EV; then an underscore; then BT for buttons, SL for sliders, NB for number fields, or ST for string fields; another underscore; and finally a brief descriptive name for the specific function. Note that all of these are considered button event indices, even though sliders and number fields are distinguished from push-button style buttons. Also note that in this specific script example, only the first two will actually be used as button event indices in the button_event() function. This step is included only as an example of good practice. Certainly in cases where more than a few button events are being registered in button_event(), this kind of organization will be helpful.

```
EV_BT_OK = 1
EV_BT_CANCEL = 2
EV_SL_RADIUS = 3
EV_SL_HEIGHT = 4
EV_SL_SPEED = 5
EV_SL_BHEIGHT = 6
EV_NB_POSX = 7
EV_NB_POSY = 8
EV_SL_R = 9
EV_SL_G = 10
EV_SL_B = 11
EV_ST_NAME = 12
```

Finally, the default interface elements are created. The Draw.Create() method creates a generic interface element and sets its default value. This enables us to set these variables as global variables (which must be defined outside any function definitions) and to give them their starting values. It also prevents Python from having an error when the MakeCone() definition calls their value attributes. Later, in the gui() function definitions, these will be redefined as specific interface elements such as push-buttons, sliders, and number fields.

```
stringName = Draw.Create("MyCone")
sliderRadius = Draw.Create(0.50)
sliderHeight = Draw.Create(1.00)
numberPosX = Draw.Create(0.00)
numberPosY = Draw.Create(0.00)
sliderR = Draw.Create(0.50)
sliderG = Draw.Create(0.50)
sliderB = Draw.Create(0.50)
sliderSpeed = Draw.Create(1.00)
sliderBHeight = Draw.Create(1.00)
```

DEFINING THE FUNCTIONS

You have already mostly defined one of the most important functions here, MakeCone(). You can use the code you wrote in the previous section to build the cone. You need to indent the entire code one more indentation (you can do this by selecting the code and choosing Indent from the Format menu) and place the copied code under the def MakeCone(): line of code.

The only changes you need to make are the variable settings. Instead of the default settings you used previously, set the variables to take their values from the interface variables you defined a moment ago. Otherwise, all the code is exactly the same until the point where you assign the Ipo to the object. Don't include `Blender.Redraw()` here. That can be called outside this function:

```
def MakeCone():
    varX = numberPosX.val
    varY = numberPosY.val
    varRad = sliderRadius.val
    varHeight = sliderHeight.val
    varSpeed = sliderSpeed.val
    varBHeight = sliderBHeight.val
    varRed = sliderR.val
    varGrn = sliderG.val
    varBlu = sliderB.val
    varNam = stringName.val
```

Use the rest of the previous cone-creation code verbatim (but indented, because it is now inside a function definition), up to and including this line:

```
meshOb.setIpo(ipo)
```

The other functions are simpler but contain many of the elements you have already seen. `MakeLamp()` creates a new Lamp object, attaches it to the scene, and places it in space:

```
def MakeLamp():
    lmp = Lamp.New('Lamp','MyLamp')
    lampOb = scn.objects.new(lmp, 'Lamp')
    lampOb.setLocation(3,-10,8)
```

`MakeCamera()` does the same with the camera:

```
def MakeCamera():
    cam = Camera.New('persp','MyCamera')
    camOb = scn.objects.new(cam, 'Camera')
    scn.objects.camera = camOb
    camOb.setEuler(58*conv, -1.25*conv, 53*conv)
    camOb.setLocation(13, -10, 12)
```

THE *EVENT()* AND *BUTTON _ EVENT()* FUNCTIONS

As you saw previously in this chapter, the keyboard-event-handling function `event()` and the button-event-handling function `button_event()` are at the heart of the interface code. Again, the names of these functions are arbitrary, but they must be the second and third arguments, respectively, to `Draw.Register()` in your script.

Let's look at `button_event()` first. This is where the button indices are evaluated and, depending on which button was pressed, it is decided what functions to execute. As I mentioned, this script will use only two button indexes: `EV_BT_OK` and `EV_BT_CANCEL`. In the `gui()` function in the next section, these indices will be associated with specific buttons. As you can guess, the first will be associated with the OK button, and the second will correspond to the

Cancel button. This function determines that if the EVT_BT_OK index is received, `MakeCone()` will be executed, followed by `Blender.Redraw()` to update the view. If EV_BT_CANCEL is the received index, the `Draw.Exit()` method is called, ending the script.

```
def button_event(evt):
    if evt==EV_BT_OK:
        MakeCone()
        Blender.Redraw()
    elif evt == EV_BT_CANCEL:
        Draw.Exit()
```

There's not a lot of keyboard interactivity needed in this script, but in addition to the Esc key exit, I'll add a pop-up menu for verification. This is an object of class PupMenu. If OK is clicked here, `Draw.Exit()` is called.

```
def event(evt, val):
    if evt == Draw.ESCKEY:
        ext = Draw.PupMenu("Do you want to exit?%t|OK %x1")
        if ext == 1:
            Draw.Exit()
```

THE *GUI()* FUNCTION

The `gui()` function puts the graphical user interface together. Be sure to put *all* GUI elements directly in this function. Do not define other functions with GUI elements and try to call them from within the `gui()` function. Although this is legal from the standpoint of Python, it is not supported by the Blender-Python interface. You will probably not get explicit errors, but your GUI will not behave properly.

In the case of this script, as is often the case, there's not much happening in this function other than the methodical placement of GUI elements. The first line of the function definition declares the global variables used by the function, so when they are changed, the values of the variables will be changed globally (For typesetting reasons, the global variables are declared here in two separate lines. You can copy this code directly, or you can declare all global variables on a single line, separated by commas):

```
def gui():
    global stringName, sliderRadius, sliderHeight, sliderSpeed, sliderBHeight
    global numberPosX, numberPosY, numberPosZ, sliderR, sliderG, sliderB
```

The placement of the text labels requires two lines of code. The first line uses the BGL class's `glRasterPos2i()` method to set the X and Y positions of the starting point of the text. The interface will have a left-side margin of 10 pixels. The Y value is counted from the bottom of the Scripts window. There are a total of 13 lines in this interface, and the bottom line will begin 10 pixels above the bottom edge of the window, with each line placed 30 pixels above the one below it (interface elements will be 25 pixels high). Therefore, the topmost line should have a Y value of 370. It is a good idea to organize these values into a list ahead of time, but in this example I skipped that step.

```
BGL.glRasterPos2i(10, 370)
Draw.Text("Set the name of the cone:")
```

Working our way down the lines of the interface, the next element is the string entry field in which the user will enter the Cone object's name. Note that the variable used here is a global variable that has previously been defined as a generic interface element. Now it is defined specifically as a string entry field by using Draw.String() with arguments representing the following, in order: the string label in the field; the element's button event index; the X value of the element; the Y value of the element; the width of the element; the height of the element; the default value (this is already defined, so it takes its own previously defined value); the maximum length of the string; and the element's tooltip, which will be displayed when the mouse is moved over the element in the interface.

```
stringName = Draw.String("Name: ", EV_ST_NAME, 10, 340, 310,
    25, stringName.val, 32, "Name of the object")
```

Three more interface element types are introduced throughout the remainder of this function: Draw.Slider(), Draw.Number(), and Draw.Pushbutton(). Each of the interface element methods has its own list of required arguments. The arguments for each element are enumerated in order in comma-delineated lists as follows:

Draw.Slider()   Label, event index, X value, Y value, width, height, default value, minimum value, maximum value, real-time toggle (if nonzero, events are emitted as the value changes; if zero, an event is emitted only after the slider has been moved), tooltip

Draw.Number()   Label, event index, X value, Y value, width, height, default value, minimum value, maximum value, tooltip

Draw.Pushbutton()   Label, event index, X value, Y value, width, height, tooltip

Knowing what the arguments mean to each of these methods, you should be able to clearly see what the remainder of the script is doing. Line by line, the interface elements are positioned in the interface:

```
BGL.glRasterPos2i(10, 310)
Draw.Text("Set the geometry of the cone:")
sliderRadius = Draw.Slider("Radius of the cone: ", EV_SL_RADIUS, 10,
    280, 310, 25, sliderRadius.val, 0.25, 2.00, 1, "Set length of radius")
sliderHeight = Draw.Slider("Height of the cone: ", EV_SL_HEIGHT, 10,
    250, 310, 25, sliderHeight.val, 0.25, 2.00, 1, "Set height of cone")
BGL.glRasterPos2i(10, 220)
Draw.Text("Set the color of the cone:")
sliderR = Draw.Slider("R: ", EV_SL_R, 10, 190, 100, 25, sliderR.val,
    0.00, 1.00, 1, "Set the red component")
sliderG = Draw.Slider("G: ", EV_SL_G, 115, 190, 100, 25, sliderG.val,
    0.00, 1.00, 1, "Set the green component")
sliderB = Draw.Slider("B: ", EV_SL_B, 220, 190, 100, 25, sliderB.val,
    0.00, 1.00, 1, "Set the blue component")
BGL.glRasterPos2i(10, 160)
Draw.Text("Set start point for cone's bounce:")
numberPosX = Draw.Number("Pos X: ", EV_NB_POSX, 10, 130, 100, 25,
    numberPosX.val, -5.00, 5.00, "X coordinate")
numberPosY = Draw.Number("Pos Y: ", EV_NB_POSY, 115, 130, 100, 25,
    numberPosY.val, -5.00, 5.00, "Y coordinate")
```

```
BGL.glRasterPos2i(10, 100)
Draw.Text("Set properties for bounce:")
sliderSpeed = Draw.Slider("Speed: ", EV_SL_SPEED, 10, 70, 310, 25,
    sliderSpeed.val, 0.25, 2.00, 1, "Set bounce speed")
sliderBHeight = Draw.Slider("Height: ", EV_SL_BHEIGHT, 10, 40, 310,
    25, sliderBHeight.val, 1, 10, 1, "Set bounce height")
Draw.PushButton("OK", EV_BT_OK, 10, 10, 100, 25, "Confirm")
Draw.PushButton("Cancel", EV_BT_CANCEL, 220, 10, 100, 25, "Cancel")
```

Putting It All Together

The last lines of your script will look like this:

```
MakeCamera()
MakeLamp()
Draw.Register(gui, event, button_event)
```

When the script is run, the camera and lamp are positioned immediately, and the interface is started up. The rest of the action takes place within the functions described previously.

Something you will often see in Python scripts is to place the main function calls within a conditional that checks whether the script is being called on its own, as an independent script, or whether it is being used as an external module for its class definitions. To follow this common usage, the function calls would appear like this:

```
if __name__ == '__main__':
    MakeCamera()
    MakeLamp()
    Draw.Register(gui, event, button_event)
```

The full code for the program can be found in the conegen_gui.py text file, accessible via the drop-down menu in the text editor header in the cones_tutorial.blend file on the CD that accompanies this book.

This tutorial's approach was inspired by several excellent tutorials by others, and I'm indebted to both Jean-Michel Soler and Olivier Saraja for their informative websites. Jean-Michel's site at http://jmsoler.free.fr/didacticiel/blender/tutor/eng_index.htm includes some interesting discussions on creating 3D mathematical "potatoids" with Python scripts, and Olivier Saraja's website at http://feeblemind.tuxfamily.org/dotclear also includes a variety of useful tutorials. I recommend that you visit their sites to learn more about Python scripting and other aspects of Blender.

AVOIDING MEMORY LEAKS

In this chapter's example, calls to Draw button elements are assigned to global variables, whereas calls to Draw.Text() are made directly, without a variable. This is due to a quirk in the Draw module that can result in a memory leak error in some cases if button elements are called directly. The resulting error message will read Error Totblock. If you see this error, make sure that all of your Draw button elements are being passed to global variables.

USING THE RIGHT REDRAWS

Don't use redraw functions from other modules between the time when Draw.Register() is called and the time when Draw.Exit() is called. The Draw submodule's own Draw.Redraw() and Draw.Draw() functions should be used here instead, if necessary.

The Bottom Line

Edit and run scripts in Blender.   Blender has its own internal text editor that you can use to write scripts or commentary. The text editor features line numbering and color-coded syntax highlighting.

> **Master It**   Get accustomed to working with the Blender text editor. Open an Object script template by going to the File editor and choosing Script Templates ➤ Object Editing. Run the script with Alt+P. Find the place in the code where the number of objects in the scene is printed out. Change that line so only the number of selected objects in the scene is printed.

Become familiar with the Blender-Python API.   If you code in Blender-Python, the API will become your faithful companion. A large part of learning to script for Blender is becoming comfortable navigating the API.

> **Master It**   An important step in using the API is to read the API itself and figure out what its various modules and classes do. Look over the API now. Which class would you use if you wanted to work with a Text object in the 3D space? What method would you use to set the text string for this object?

Create an interactive script.   Blender's Python API includes tools for designing graphical user interfaces for your scripts that enable you to set parameters and execute commands interactively.

> **Master It**   Alter the cone generator example in this chapter to create a similar script that creates bouncing text objects instead of creating bouncing cones. You should be able to input the color, placement, speed, and height of bouncing just as you do with the script in this chapter, but in place of adjusting the dimensions of the cone object, add an option to input the text of the Text3d object that the script creates.

Gallery

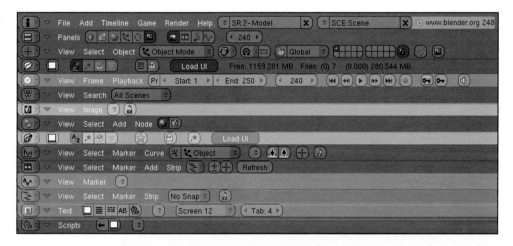

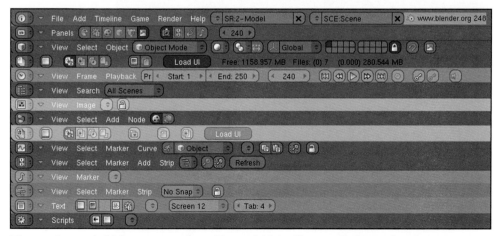

The top image (which corresponds to Figure 1.13 in Chapter 1) shows the alternate icon set included on the CD. The middle and bottom images (which correspond to Figure 1.14 in Chapter 1) show the differences between the default icon set and the alternate icon set in a collection of Blender window headers.

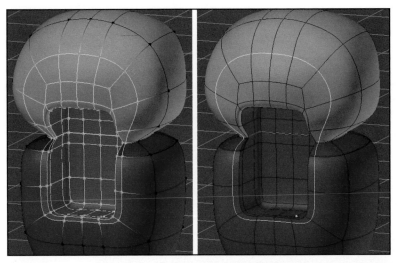

The first image (which corresponds to Figure 1.24 in Chapter 1) shows the Region To Loop selection option. The second image (which corresponds to Figure 1.25 in Chapter 1) shows loop and ring selections for Vertex selection mode. The third image (which corresponds to Figure 1.26 in Chapter 1) shows loop and ring selections in Edge selection mode.

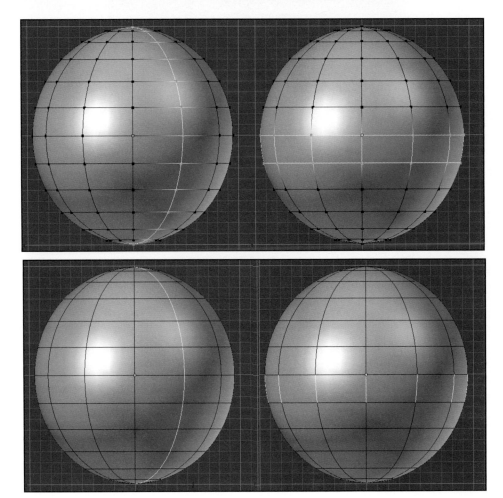

The first image (which corresponds to Figure 1.27 in Chapter 1) shows ring selection in Face selection mode. The second image (which corresponds to Figure 1.29 in Chapter 1) shows the three manipulator widgets. The third image (which corresponds to Figure 1.30 in Chapter 1) shows the widgets in mid-transformation.

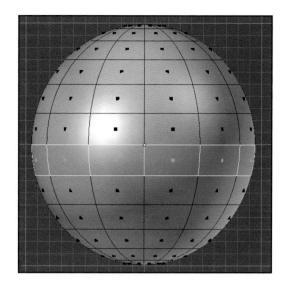

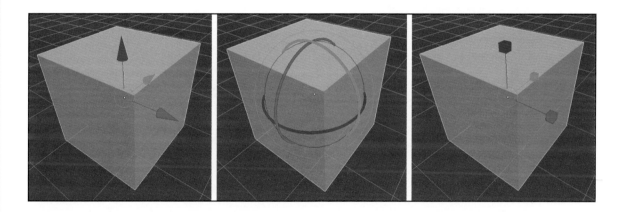

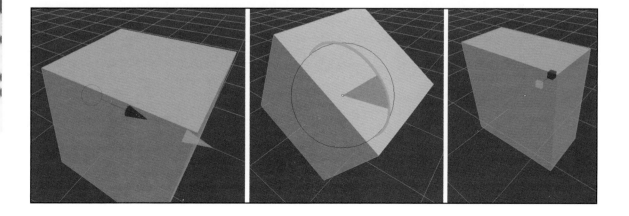

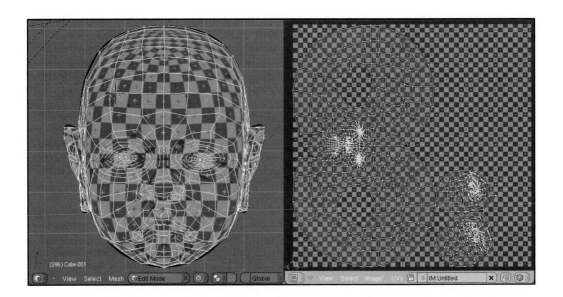

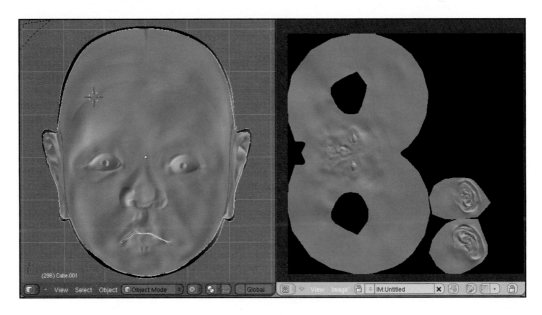

The top image (which corresponds to Figure 2.66 in Chapter 2) shows the mapping of a test pattern image on the UV-unwrapped mesh. The bottom image (which corresponds to Figure 2.68 in Chapter 2) shows the baked normal map texture.

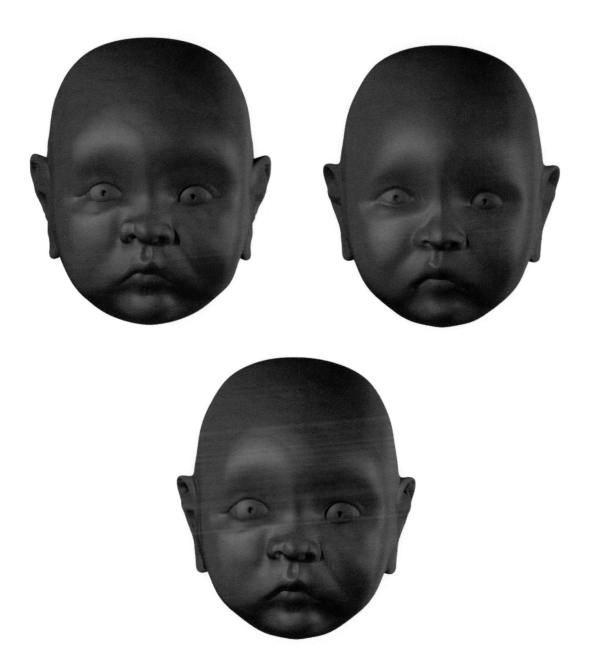

These three images (which correspond to Figure 2.71 in Chapter 2) show renders of three meshes. The top-left mesh is the original high-poly sculpted mesh. The top-right mesh is the low-poly mesh created using the retopo tool. The bottom mesh is the low-poly mesh with a baked normal map applied.

The top image (which corresponds to Figure 3.2 in Chapter 3) shows a train with UV-mapped materials. The background sky map gives reflective surfaces more realism. The bottom image was created by Colin Litster and makes use of UV textures and node-based materials (which corresponds to the image at the end of Chapter 4).

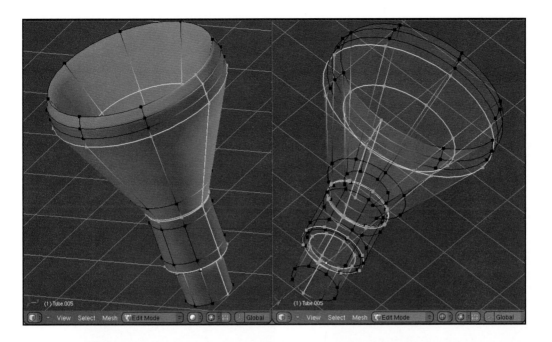

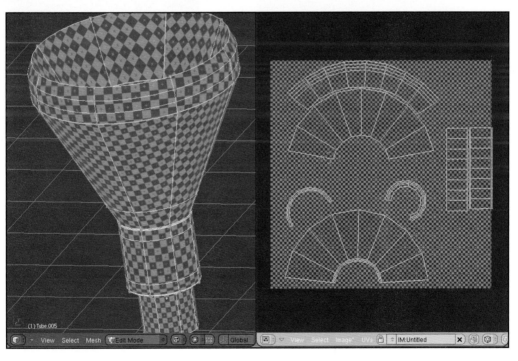

The top image (which corresponds to Figure 3.5 in Chapter 3) shows the selection of edges for marking seams in preparation for UV unwrapping. The bottom image (which corresponds to Figure 3.8 in Chapter 3) shows the resulting UV-unwrap pattern.

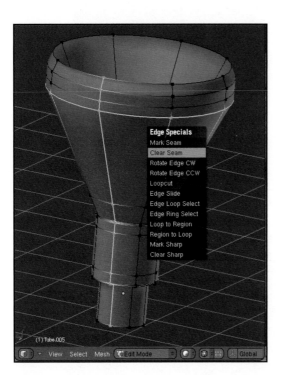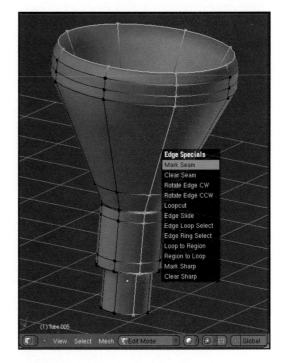

These images (which correspond to Figures 3.34 and 3.35 in Chapter 3) show the original pattern of seams being cleared and a new, different seam pattern being marked.

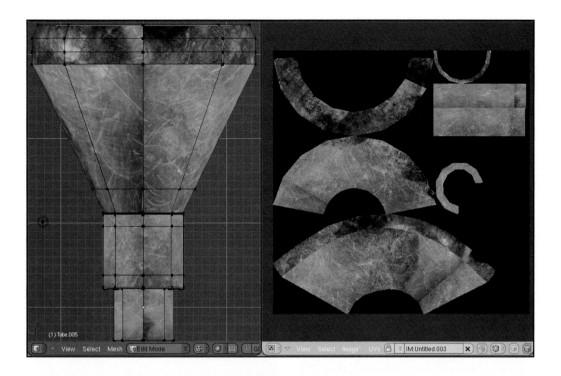

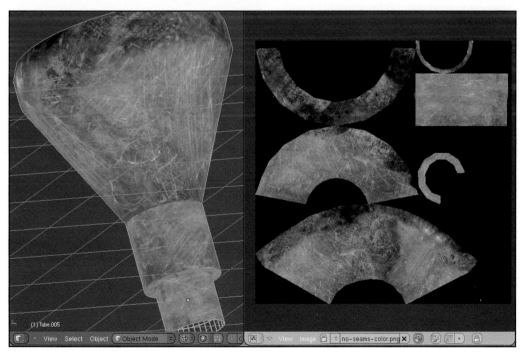

The top image (which corresponds to Figure 3.39 in Chapter 3) shows the original baked texture with seams from the first mapping. The bottom image (which corresponds to Figure 3.49 in Chapter 3) shows the texture after the seams have been eliminated in GIMP.

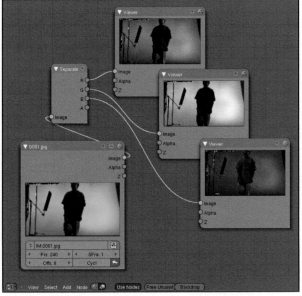

The top image (which corresponds to Figure 4.1 in Chapter 4) shows four frames from the short green-screen video sequence included on the CD. The bottom image (which corresponds to Figure 4.10 in Chapter 4) shows the node setup for separating the colors and the values for each color channel.

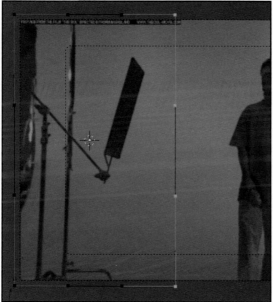

The top image (which corresponds to Figure 4.20 in
Chapter 4) shows a Bezier circle added to the 3D scene.
The bottom two images (which correspond to Figure 4.26 in
Chapter 4) show the curve before and after three subdivisions
have been made along the right edge.

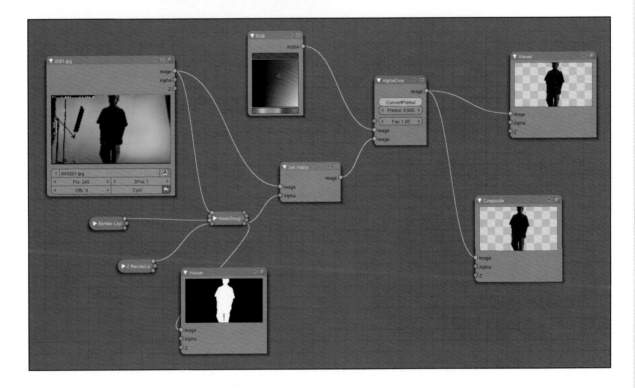

The top image (which corresponds to Figure 4.28 in Chapter 4) shows a new hook being added to a control point on the curve. The bottom image (which corresponds to Figure 4.56 in Chapter 4) shows the node setup for compositing the figure over a colored background.

These images (which correspond to Figure 4.57 in Chapter 4) show subtle artifacts that can arise if the Premul value is not set correctly. White streaks are visible in the background on the right and left of the top image, and the white gap around the figure is more pronounced.

The top image (which corresponds to Figure 4.58 in Chapter 4) shows green spill clearly around the edge of the foreground figure. The bottom image (which corresponds to Figure 4.61 in Chapter 4) shows the green channel reduced.

FOOTAGE FROM THE FILM "THE IDOL" DIRECTED BY NORMAN ENGLAND   WWW.THEIDOL-MOVIE.COM

FOOTAGE FROM THE FILM "THE IDOL" DIRECTED BY NORMAN ENGLAND   WWW.THEIDOL-MOVIE.COM

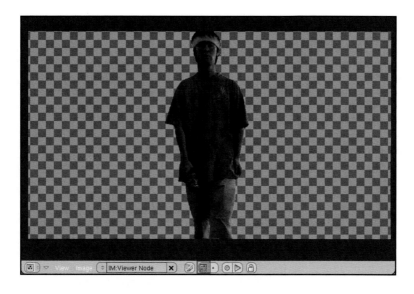

The top image (which corresponds to Figure 4.63 in Chapter 4) shows the figure with alpha zero background. The highlighted button in the header enables alpha viewing in the UV/Image editor. The bottom image (which corresponds to Figure 4.64 in Chapter 4) shows the figure composited over a new background.

The top two illustrations (which correspond to Figure 4.65 in Chapter 4) show the image before and after adding a purple tint to highlighted areas for color correction. The bottom illustration (which corresponds to Figure 5.14 in Chapter 5) shows strips after they have been cut nondestructively with Shift+K. Note the translucent colored extensions that indicate the truncated video.

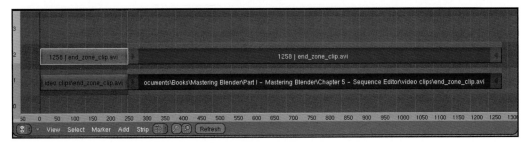

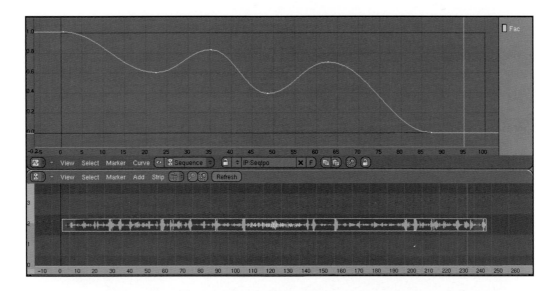

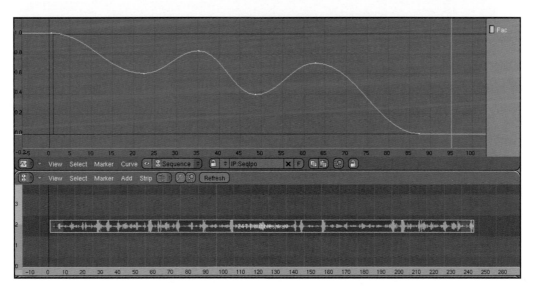

These images show the difference between the default 100-frame mapping for Ipo curves and the option to lock the Ipo's frames to the sequence frames. In the top image (which is a color reproduction of Figure 5.19 in Chapter 5), the current Ipo frame of 95 corresponds to a frame 95 percent of the way to the end of the sequence strip, in this case about frame 232. In the bottom image (which is a color reproduction of Figure 5.21 in Chapter 5), the current Ipo frame is the same frame number as the current sequence frame: 95.

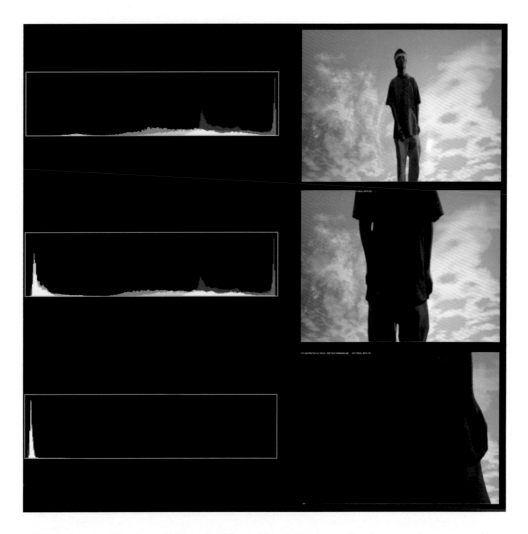

This color reproduction of Figure 5.22 from Chapter 5 shows the change in histograms for three different frames of video. Note how the darker frames correspond to higher values at the left end of the histogram.

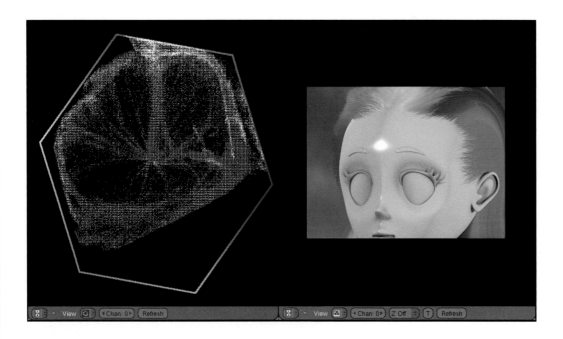

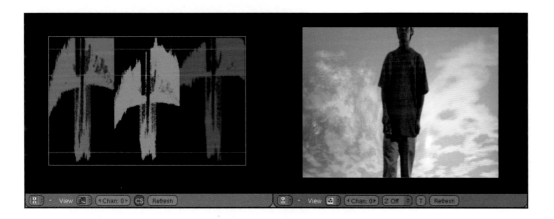

The first illustration (which corresponds to Figure 5.23 in Chapter 5) shows the VSE Chroma Vectorscope display. The points on the graph indicate the color and saturation of pixels in the video image. The second illustration (which corresponds to Figure 5.25 in Chapter 5) shows the VSE Luma Waveform display with color separation. Rows of pixels in the video image are shown as curves representing their luminance levels. Note the dip in the middle of the curves, where the light is obscured by the foreground figure in the video image.

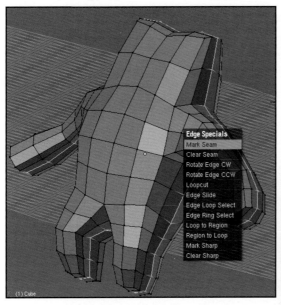

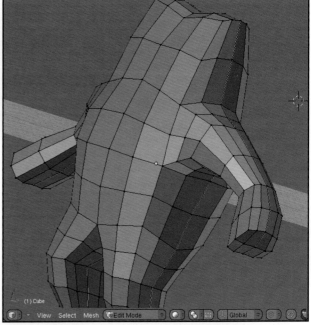

The first and second image (corresponding to Figure 9.20) show the process of marking a seam on a character mesh and the resulting marked seam, highlighted in orange. The third image (corresponding to Figure 9.46) shows selected edges on the mesh where seams will be marked to unwrap the sky box.

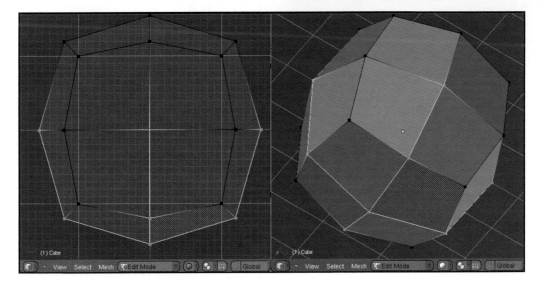

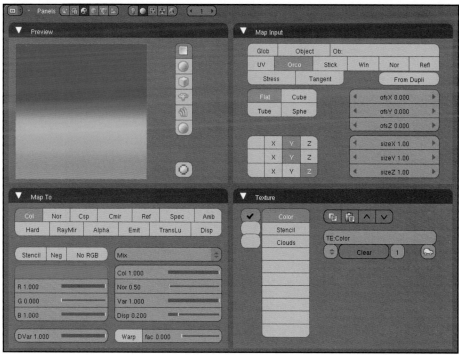

The first four panels at the top (which are color reproductions of the panels shown in Figure 9.47 in Chapter 9) illustrate texture values for a blended texture using a colorband. The second four panels at the bottom (which are color reproductions of the panels shown in Figure 9.48) illustrate mapping values for the texture on a material.

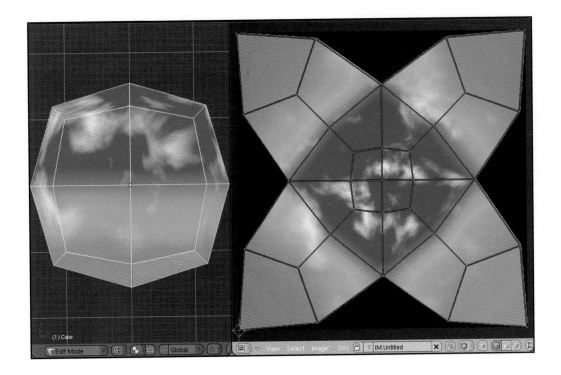

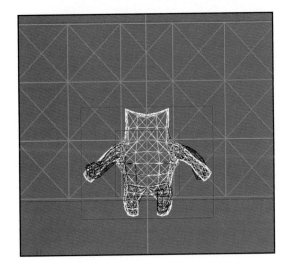

The top two windows (which are color reproductions of the Figure 9.58 images in Chapter 9) show the baked procedural texture UV-mapped onto the sky box. The bottom image (which corresponds to Figure 10.15 in Chapter 10) shows the game character in Wireframe mode with the game physics display option turned on. The collision boundary for the armature is too small, causing the character to sink into the floor.

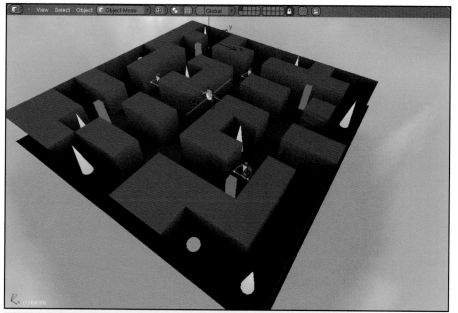

The top image (which corresponds to Figure 10.29 in Chapter 10) shows a simple game world setup with a maze, sky box, enemies, and goals. The middle image (which corresponds to Figure 11.13 in Chapter 11) shows a game environment with two colored cubes and multiple cameras. The bottom image (which corresponds to Figure 11.18 in Chapter 11) shows an in-game view of a simple multiple-viewport setup. The camera view on the left follows the blue cube, and the camera view on the right follows the red cube. The camera view inset in the middle shows a birds-eye view of the game board.

IMAGE © 2008 SOENKE MAETER

This stunning image from the book's cover is "Reaching Out" by Soenke Maeter, winner of the 2008 Blender World Cup challenge. You can read more about this image and how it was made at www.itsartmag.com/features/reachingout.

Chapter 8

The Many-Headed Snake: Other Uses of Python in Blender

Writing scripts is only one of the ways to exploit the power of Blender's Python integration. It is sometimes desirable to use Python's programming power without being subject to the restrictions that come with running external scripts. For this reason, a variety of options exist that integrate Python even more deeply into the ordinary workings of Blender. Using these options, you can embed Python code directly into Ipo drivers, constraints, and nodes, or use script links to execute code automatically at specific times during the animation process. This chapter describes these methods.

In this chapter, you will learn to

- ◆ Control Ipo curves by using PyDrivers
- ◆ Incorporate Python scripts into your scene with PyNodes and PyConstraints
- ◆ Use script links and space handlers to obtain even greater levels of interactivity

Extend Blender Functionality with Python

As you saw in Chapter 7, "Python Scripting for Blender," using Blender as a Python interpreter affords the user a great deal of power in working with 3D objects and assets. In Chapter 11, "Python Power in the Blender Game Engine," you will be introduced to even more possibilities when you take a look at incorporating Python into the Blender Game Engine.

However, even this is not the whole story of what you can do with Python in Blender. Python has been specially integrated into Blender in other ways that enable you to extend specific Blender functionality with embedded Python code.

As is often the case with scripting-related features, much of the documentation on this functionality is geared to experienced programmers. Code samples are available to refer to in the online Blender release notes, but these samples can be daunting for people whose main interest is in 3D and Blender itself, who are not accustomed to reading code and writing Python programs. In this chapter, you will see relatively simple examples of these powerful features. When you have mastered the basics of how they work, you will be able to apply what you learn elsewhere to create powerful and practical Python-enhanced functionality of your own.

Working with PyDrivers

Blender users who do character animation or other work that requires sophisticated, complex movements to be controlled in simple ways should already be aware of the power of Ipo drivers in general. If you have not worked with Ipo drivers, I recommend that you first read the chapter of my book *Introducing Character Animation with Blender* (Sybex, 2007) that deals with using Ipo drivers to set up poseable rigs. Even if you do not need this specifically for character work, you will find that any nontrivial rigging task will benefit from a knowledge of how to use Ipo drivers.

The way Ipo drivers work is to create a mapping from one value to another. For example, a bone's position within a given range might be used to control the influence of a shape key on the mesh, or its rotation might be used to drive a preanimated action. However, as powerful as Ipo drivers are, they are limited by this direct mapping between two values. If the relationship between the driver and the driven value cannot be represented by a single Ipo curve, it can't be encoded as an Ipo driver.

PyDrivers enable you to harness the power of Python to create more-complex drivers. A PyDriver drives an Ipo by using a single line of code that can incorporate whatever values you want. Unlike some of the other uses of Python described in this chapter, PyDrivers do not enable complete scripts with such things as sophisticated control structures and access to external modules. You can use only what you can fit into a single line of Python code, so the scripts are necessarily compact. Part of this compactness involves several shorthand notations specific to PyDrivers, which enable you to access common data types in a simple way. These shorthand forms are as follows:

- ob('*Name*') to access the object named *Name*

- me('*Name*') to access the mesh named *Name*

- ma('*Name*') to access the material named *Name*

For a simple example, you can create an object whose length is a measure of another object's volume. For simplicity's sake, assume that the object whose volume you are using is a cube. Because volume of a cube is a function of three separate Ipo values (the product of the X scale, Y scale, and Z scale), it is not possible to do this by using traditional Ipo drivers. You need to use a PyDriver to incorporate all the values and calculate the resulting value. To set up a PyDriver with this effect, follow these steps:

1. Start a fresh Blender session and duplicate the default cube with Shift+D. The new cube will behave as a "measuring stick" to indicate the volume of the original cube. Scale the new cube down so the two cubes are as shown in Figure 8.1. I've added a black material to the new cube to visually distinguish the two cubes more clearly. Typically, measuring indicators scale in one direction only, so enter Edit mode and shift the geometry of the black cube so that the object center is flush with the left side, as shown in Figure 8.2.

2. The black cube's X axis scale Ipo is the value that needs to be driven. With the black cube selected in Object mode, open an Ipo editor window. Left-click ScaleX on the Ipo list to the right of the window. Press the N key to bring up the Transform Properties floating window, as shown in Figure 8.3. Click Add Driver to add a driver. By default, Ipo drivers

are based on Ipos associated with objects, and so the default OB field requires an object to be added. This is not what you want, so click the script icon, as indicated in Figure 8.4. This changes the field to a PyDriver field, as shown in Figure 8.5.

FIGURE 8.1
The default cube and a smaller cube for measuring volume

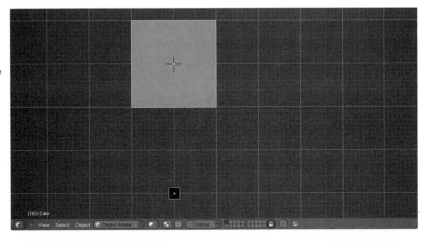

FIGURE 8.2
Shift the geometry of the measuring cube so the center is flush with the side.

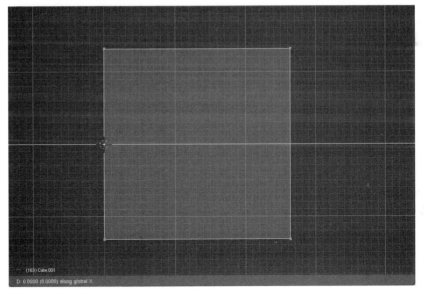

3 All that's left is to type the Python expression into the field, as shown in Figure 8.6. The exact expression in this case is as follows:

```
ob('Cube').SizeX*ob('Cube').SizeY*ob('Cube').SizeZ
```

This is the product of the Cube object's sizes on the X, Y, and Z axes.

FIGURE 8.3
Viewing Transform
Properties in the
Ipo editor

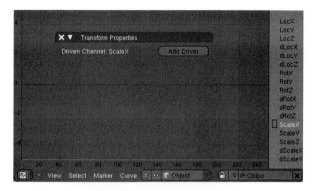

FIGURE 8.4
The driver
object field

FIGURE 8.5
The PyDriver
input field

FIGURE 8.6
The PyDriver

The result is shown in Figure 8.7. When you scale the original Cube object, the second object, your measuring stick, will grow in length according to the volume of the original cube.

This is a simple example, but I hope that it has given you a sense of the power of PyDrivers. PyDrivers can be used whenever you need to make an Ipo dependent on a function involving multiple other Ipos. You can drive an Ipo by using the distance between objects or bones, differences between degrees of rotation of multiple objects, or a variety of other factors.

In my book *Bounce, Tumble, and Splash! Simulating the Physical World with Blender 3D* (Sybex, 2008), I discuss the use of PyDrivers to control the stretching of a spring. The spring armature consists primarily of two bones, one for each end of the spring. In the example, the shape of the spring is not dependent on the position or location of any single object or bone, and therefore is not suitable to be driven by an ordinary Ipo driver. Instead, the shape must be driven by the distance between the two bones on the end, making it an ideal candidate for a PyDriver. Please see that book for a complete description of the rig and how the PyDriver is used.

FIGURE 8.7
Representing vol-
ume by length

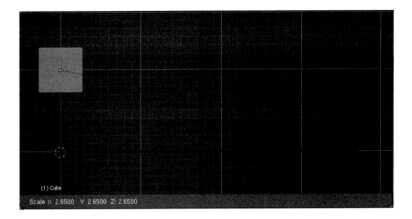

Using PyNodes

As you've already seen in previous chapters, Blender has a powerful node-based system for materials and compositing. As the name suggests, *PyNodes* (also known as *dynamic nodes*) are an extension of this system, whereby you can implement your own node functionality in Python. Unlike PyDrivers, PyNodes enable full-fledged scripts to be incorporated as nodes. The node inputs behave as arguments to the Python script, and the outputs are values that are returned by the script. Like many other advanced Python-related features, PyNodes are still somewhat experimental, and the API for working with them is subject to potentially significant changes in future versions.

The functionality of a PyNode is contained in a class definition structured like this:

```
class ClassName(Node.Scripted):
    def __init__(self,sockets):
        #socket definitions
        my_float_socket = Node.Socket('MyFloatSocket',
            val = 0.0, min = -1.0, max = 1.0)
        my_list_socket_in = Node.Socket('MyListSocketIn',
            val = [1.0, 1.0, 1.0])
        my_list_socket_out = Node.Socket('MyListSocketOut',
            val = [1.0, 1.0, 1.0])
        sockets.input = [my_float_socket, my_list_socket_in]
        sockets.output = [my_list_socket_out]
    def __call__(self)
        #node functionality
```

The first line begins the class definition. You can choose the name of your class here. The argument for the definition must be `Node.Scripted` so Blender knows that this is a scripted node. Likewise, the arguments for __init__ should be `self, sockets`. The argument for __call__ should be `self`.

The __init__ definition is where the input and output sockets on your node are set. Sockets are created by calling Node.Socket(*socket name*, *default value*). The socket's name will be used elsewhere to access its value. Input and output sockets are identical at this stage. The data type expected by the socket is automatically determined based on the default value you assign to the val parameter. In the sample code, my_float_socket is assigned a value of 0.0 for its val parameter, so it will automatically be recognized as a float data type. An optional min and max parameter determine the boundaries of this value. If you don't include these, the default minimum and maximum are 0.0 and 1.0, respectively. The variable my_list_socket_in is initialized with a list, so it will be treated accordingly. The sockets.input and sockets.output attributes are lists of input and output sockets, respectively. The socket objects in these lists will appear as input and output sockets on your node.

The __call__ method is best illustrated with a working example. In this example, I'll show you a simple setup that enables you to incorporate information from the scene into the node logic for your material in a way that would be impossible without PyNodes. Specifically, this will make the output material black or white depending on whether the total number of objects in the scene is even or odd. Once again, the specific task is simple, but it should serve as a small demonstration of the power of PyNodes. To set up the dynamic material, follow these steps:

1. Begin by creating a node material with two material node inputs. If you're not sure how to do this, you should review Chapter 3's section on basic node material creation before continuing. Make the two materials visually distinct. I set one of the materials to be completely white and the other to be completely black, as shown in Figure 8.8. I named them White and Black, respectively.

FIGURE 8.8
A basic node material setup with two material nodes

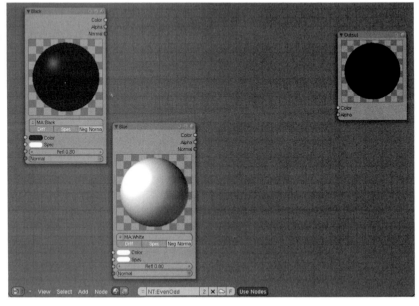

2. Leave the node editor aside for the moment and open a text editor window. Add a new text file by choosing the Add New header menu entry, and name it **EvenOdd**. Enter the following code, as shown in Figure 8.9:

```
1 import Blender
2 from Blender import Node, Scene
3
4
5 class EvenOddNode(Node,Scripted):
6    def __init__(self, sockets):
7        col1 = Node.Socket('Color1', val = 4*[1.0])
8        col2 = Node.Socket('Color2', val = 4*[1.0])
9        col3 = Node.Socket('OutColor', val = 4*[1.0])
10       sockets.input = [col1, col2]
11       sockets.output = [col3]
12   def __call__(self):
13       col1 = list(self.input.Color1)
14       col2 = list(self.input.Color2)
15       scn = Scene.GetCurrent()
16       o_e = bool(len(scn.objects)%2)
17       if (o_e):
18           self.output.OutColor = col2
19       else:
20           self.output.OutColor = col1
```

FIGURE 8.9
The PyNode code

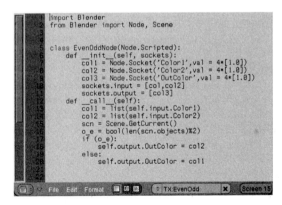

3. Now that a Dynamic node class has been defined, you can return to the node editor to add the node. Add a generic Dynamic node as shown in Figure 8.10, and then select the specific PyNode from the drop-down menu indicated. After you have done this once, you will be able to add the node by pressing the spacebar and then choosing Add ➤ Dynamic ➤ EvenOdd, as shown in Figure 8.11.

FIGURE 8.10
Adding the node

FIGURE 8.11
A generic
dynamic node

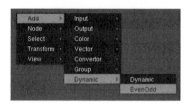

4. After you have connected the input nodes and the output node to the new PyNode as shown in Figure 8.12, the setup is complete. Make a render (I have added a black edge to the render to make things stand out a bit). Duplicate the cube with Shift+D and render again. You should find that whenever there is an odd number of cubes, the cube renders as a white material, and when there is an even number, the cube renders black, as shown in Figure 8.13.

FIGURE 8.12
The finished
node setup

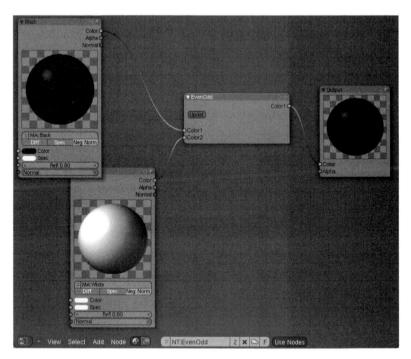

Figure 8.13
The even/odd node in effect

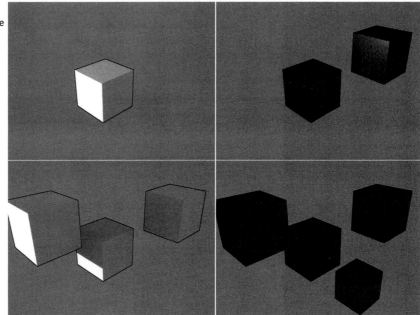

Let's look a bit closer at the code you just used. Lines 1 and 2 are familiar. It is always necessary to import Node to create a PyNode, but Scene is necessary here only because you need to access the count of scene objects, so this module call is specific to this PyNode's functionality. The first part of the class definition is essentially the same as the example presented earlier in this section. All three variables—col1, col2, and col3—are sockets that take red, green, blue, and alpha (RGBA) list values. Recall that the multiplication operator when used with a list and an integer results in copying the contents of the list as many times as the integer represents, so each of these val attributes is actually being assigned the list [1.0, 1.0, 1.0, 1.0].

In the __call__ method definition, the variable names col1 and col2 are reused. Because variables defined within a method definition are local, there is no namespace overlap here; the variables are completely different. They are related in terms of their values, though, so reusing the name makes sense. Here, they hold the list contents of the values coming into the input sockets. Their value is updated each time a change is made to the node network. An update can also be forced by clicking the Update button on the node, which should be done if the code is changed.

Retrieving the scene information in line 15 should be familiar from Chapter 7. In line 16, a Boolean object is created from the remainder of the number of objects in the scene divided by 2 (this is the meaning of the % operator in Python). If there are an odd number of objects, the result of this operation is 1, which is converted to a Boolean True value. If the number of objects is even, the result will be 0, which is converted to a Boolean False value. Finally, this Boolean value is used in an if/else control structure to determine which of the two input values is passed to the output value.

For great resources on PyNodes, check out the PyNode Cookbook at `http://wiki.blender`
`.org/index.php/Resources/PyNode_Cookbook`, and the related threads on BlenderArtists.org
and CGSociety, which can be found at `http://blenderartists.org/forum/showthread`
`.php?t=125741` and `http://forums.cgsociety.org/showthread.php?t=636058`, respectively.

Working with PyConstraints

Constraints in Blender operate on objects or bones and are used to restrict certain properties to
values determined by the constraint. Copy Location and Copy Rotation constraints, for example,
are used to restrict the constrained object's location or rotation to that of another target object.
The built-in constraints system is quite powerful and enables you to have a high degree of control over the behavior of objects. Nevertheless, it is possible to conceive of a nearly unlimited
number of possible constraints that might be useful but are not specifically coded as individual
built-in constraints. For this kind of flexibility, it becomes necessary to code your own constraints. Fortunately, the *PyConstraints* system makes this possible.

In this section, you'll see a basic PyConstraint implemented to do a simple task: The constrained object's transformation values are calculated to be the average of the transformation
values of three target objects. Each type of transformation—location, rotation, and scale—is
included in the constraint as an option, with location being set as the default. With this default
setting, the constrained object will be held to a point between the three target objects, and its
position will be adjusted when any of the target objects are moved, as though it is connected by
a bungee cord to the three objects. To set this up, follow these steps:

1. Create the objects you will be working with. The example uses a Monkey object and three
   cubes. Name the Cube objects **1**, **2**, and **3**. Position the Cube objects around the Monkey
   object as shown in Figure 8.14.

FIGURE 8.14
A Monkey object
and three cubes

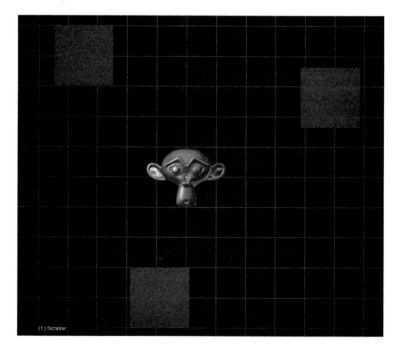

(1) Suzanne

2. With the Monkey object selected in Object mode, find the Add Constraint drop-down menu in the Constraints panel in Object buttons context. Choose Script from the Add Constraint drop-down menu, as shown in Figure 8.15. When you do this, the generic Script constraint panel shown in Figure 8.16 appears. As you can see, there is a drop-down menu for selecting the script that will define the constraint. This is not much use at this point, because no script has yet been created.

3. To write your constraint script, open a text editor window. You should recall from Chapter 7 seeing the Script Templates menu item under the File menu. There you'll find a Script Constraint template, as shown in Figure 8.17. Select that to get started with the constraint. It's always a good idea to begin with a template and to recycle code where possible, and in this case, a close look at the template itself will tell you a lot about how PyConstraints are coded. Rename the text to **average.py**.

4. The first line of any PyConstraint script, and also of the template you've just opened, must contain only the string #BPYCONSTRAINT. This indicates to Blender that the script must be accessible to the constraints system. You can add multiline comments and documentation between the triple quotes. The next few lines import the necessary modules. You can import other modules in addition to the ones listed by default, but Draw, Mathutils, and math are required for the operation of PyConstraints, so don't delete any of these lines. Finally, the default number of targets, assigned to the NUM_TARGETS variable, is 1. For the present constraint, three targets are involved, so change this value to **3**, as shown in Figure 8.18.

FIGURE 8.15
Adding a
Script constraint

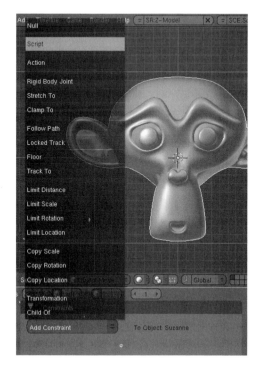

FIGURE 8.16
A Script constraint
on Suzanne

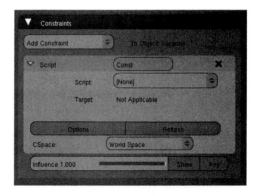

FIGURE 8.17
Opening a Script
constraint template

FIGURE 8.18
Changing the num-
ber of targets value

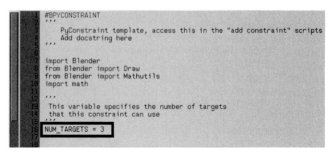

5. The next stage is where you really start to program the constraint. The `doConstraint()` function is where target object values and settings are brought together and the location, rotation, and scale of the constrained object are calculated. The arguments of the `doConstraint()` function are as follows:

`obmatrix` The constrained object's rotation matrix. This is a 4-by-4 matrix that encodes the object's rotation, location, and scale. It's not necessary for you to understand how this information is encoded in the matrix or how to manipulate the matrix directly. Instead, you will use methods to retrieve location, rotation, and scale information for X, Y, and Z axes.

`targetmatrices` This is a list of matrices corresponding to each of the targets. The length of this list is the same as the value you entered as the NUM_TARGETS value. Each of the matrices in the list can be accessed by using the same methods that you use to access the constrained object's matrix, enabling you to work with accessible translation, rotation, and scale values.

idprop   This is a dictionary containing the options for the constraint and their values as set by the user in the Options dialog box.

Before making any changes, take note of what's being done at the start of this function. The obloc, obrot, and obsca variables are given the values for the translation, rotation, and scale by using the translationPart(), *toEuler()*, and scalePart() methods, respectively, on the obmatrix object. Each of these new variables consists of a list of X, Y, and Z values representing the associated transformation. You'll want to use the same methods to retrieve the human-readable transformation information for each of the target object matrices.

Because there are three targets, you can collect the location, rotation, and scale information in lists. As you can see in Figure 8.19 in the highlighted area marked A, three lists are defined: one for the target objects' location information, one for their rotation information, and one for their scale information. After that, a for loop is used to loop through the target matrices, which have been passed into the function via the targetmatrices argument. For each of these target matrices, use the methods discussed previously to extract the needed transformations and append the transformation information to the appropriate list. Now you have easily accessible lists of the rotation, location, and scale information for each target object.

FIGURE 8.19

Editing the doConstraints() function

```
25 |'''
26 def doConstraint(obmatrix, targetmatrices, idprop):
27     # Separate out the tranformation components for easy access.
28     obloc = obmatrix.translationPart()  # Translation
29     obrot = obmatrix.toEuler()          # Rotation
30     obsca = obmatrix.scalePart()        # Scale
31
32     targloc = []
33     targrot = []
34     targsca = []
35
36     for targmats in targetmatrices:
37         targloc.append(targmats.translationPart())
38         targrot.append(targmats.toEuler())
39         targsca.append(targmats.scalePart())
40
41     # Define user-settable parameters.  # Must also be defined in getSettings().
42     if not idprop.has_key('loc_toggle'): idprop['loc_toggle'] = 1
43     if not idprop.has_key('rot_toggle'): idprop['rot_toggle'] = 0
44     if not idprop.has_key('scale_toggle'): idprop['scale_toggle'] = 0
45
46     # Do stuff here, changing obloc, obrot, and obsca.
47     if idprop['loc_toggle'] == 1:
48         for axis in range(0,3):
49             obloc[axis] = ((targloc[0][axis]+targloc[1][axis]+targloc[2][axis])/3)
50     if idprop['rot_toggle'] == 1:
51         for axis in range(0,3):
52             obrot[axis] = ((targrot[0][axis]+targrot[1][axis]+targrot[2][axis])/3)
53     if idprop['scale_toggle'] == 1:
54         for axis in range(0,3):
55             obsca[axis] = ((targsca[0][axis]+targsca[1][axis]+targsca[2][axis])/3)
56
57
58     # Convert back into a matrix for loc, scale, rotation,
59     mtxloc = Mathutils.TranslationMatrix( obloc )
60     mtxrot = obrot.toMatrix().resize4x4()
61     mtxsca = Mathutils.Matrix([obsca[0],0,0,0], [0,obsca[1],0,0], [0,0,obsca[2],0], [0,0,0,1])
62
63     # Recombine the separate elements into a transform matrix.
64     outputmatrix = mtxsca * mtxrot * mtxloc
65
66     # Return the new matrix.
67     return outputmatrix
68
```

A

B

C

The highlighted area marked B in Figure 8.19 sets the default values for the cases in which the user has not selected any options. This code uses the has_key() built-in method for dictionaries to assess whether a particular key exists in a dictionary. In this case, if the key does not exist, it is created with a default value. If the key loc_toggle (for toggling the location option) does not exist, it is set to a value of 1. The other two values, toggling rotation and scale, are set by default to 0.

The highlighted area labeled C is where the actual constraint is applied to the transformation of the constrained object. There are three if clauses, corresponding to each of the user options of constraining location, rotation, and scale. Each of the if clauses is the same but applies to a different type of transformation. The first one applies to translation. The first line—for axis in range(0,3):—iterates through the indexes of the list representing the object's position. For each of the axes, the corresponding value of the constrained object is set to be equal to the sum of the corresponding values of the target objects, divided by 3. If the user opts for it, the same is done with rotation and scale.

6. The last thing that needs to be coded is the pop-up dialog box that enables the user to select which transformations the constraint will affect. There will be three toggle variables controlling the options, as shown previously. In lines 92, 93, and 94 in Figure 8.20, the defaults are set exactly as they were in the doConstraints() function, as follows:

```
if not idprop.has_key('loc_toggle'): idprop['loc_toggle'] = 1
if not idprop.has_key('rot_toggle'): idprop['rot_toggle'] = 0
if not idprop.has_key('scale_toggle'): idprop['scale_toggle'] = 0
```

These must be defined in both functions. In lines 97 to 99, the actual widgets are created to go into the pop-up dialog button for the user to set these values. Recall the **Draw.Create()** method from Chapter 7. The same thing is being done here:

```
ltoggle = Draw.Create(idprop['loc_toggle'])
rtoggle = Draw.Create(idprop['rot_toggle'])
stoggle = Draw.Create(idprop['scale_toggle'])
```

Next, these widgets are added to a list called block, which is then used as an argument for Draw.PupBlock(), the Draw method for creating a pop-up block. The resulting value is passed to retval:

```
block = []
block.append(("Average Loc", ltoggle, "Toggle average location."))
block.append(("Average Rot", rtoggle, "Toggle average rotation."))
block.append(("Average Scale", stoggle, "Toggle average scale."))

retval = Draw.PupBlock("Constraint Template", block)
```

Finally, if retval has a value, the idprop dictionary values are updated to reflect the choices the user made:

```
if (retval):
    idprop['loc_toggle'] = ltoggle.val
    idprop['rot_toggle'] = rtoggle.val
    idprop['scale_toggle'] = stoggle.val
```

7. Now that the constraint has been coded, you can select it by name in the Scripts drop-down menu in the Script constraint panel, as shown in Figure 8.21. When you do, you'll see the fields for each of the target objects as shown in Figure 8.22. Enter the names of the Cube objects in these fields. As you can see, there are also fields for vertex groups. If you enter a vertex group defined on the object in this field, the constraint will be calculated from the median point and rotation of the vertices in the vertex group.

FIGURE 8.20
Editing the
getSettings()
function

```
def doTarget(target_object, subtarget_bone, target_matrix, id_properties_of_constraint):
    return target_matrix


'''
This function draws a pupblock that lets the user set
the values of custom settings the constraint defines.
This function is called when the user presses the settings button.
    idprop: (IDProperties) wrapped data referring to this
            constraint instance's idproperties
'''
def getSettings(idprop):
    # Define user-settable parameters.
    # Must also be defined in getSettings().
    if not idprop.has_key('loc_toggle'): idprop['loc_toggle'] = 1
    if not idprop.has_key('rot_toggle'): idprop['rot_toggle'] = 0
    if not idprop.has_key('scale_toggle'): idprop['scale_toggle'] = 0

    # create temporary vars for interface
    ltoggle = Draw.Create(idprop['loc_toggle'])
    rtoggle = Draw.Create(idprop['rot_toggle'])
    stoggle = Draw.Create(idprop['scale_toggle'])

    # define and draw pupblock
    block = []
    block.append(("Average Loc", ltoggle, "Toggle average location."))
    block.append(("Average Rot", rtoggle, "Toggle average rotation."))
    block.append(("Average Scale", stoggle, "Toggle average scale."))

    retval = Draw.PupBlock("Options", block)

    # update id-property values after user changes settings
    if (retval):
        idprop['loc_toggle']= ltoggle.val
        idprop['rot_toggle']= rtoggle.val
        idprop['scale_toggle']= stoggle.val
```

FIGURE 8.20
Editing the
getSettings()
function

FIGURE 8.21
Selecting the
constraint

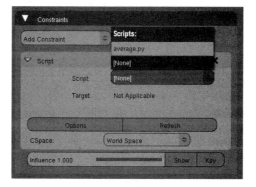

FIGURE 8.22
The constraint
panel

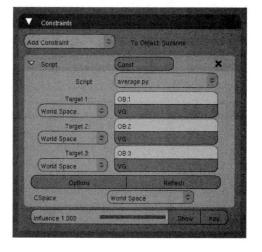

When you click the Options button, the dialog box shown in Figure 8.23 opens. Use this dialog box to select which transformation types the constraint will apply to.

8. Now that the constraint is complete, you can control the transformations on the Monkey object by translating, rotating, or scaling the cubes. The resulting behavior is illustrated in Figure 8.24 for location. Figure 8.25 shows the constraint with both location and rotation affected, and Figure 8.26 shows the constraint with location, rotation, and scale affected.

FIGURE 8.23
The Options
dialog box

FIGURE 8.24
Averaging location
values only

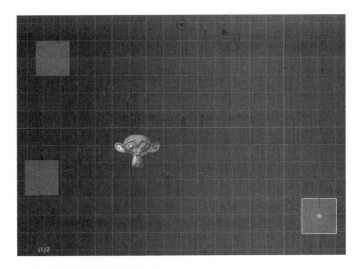

FIGURE 8.25
The constraint
with rotation and
location selected

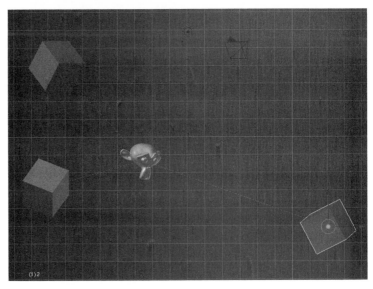

FIGURE 8.26
The constraint
with all three
options selected

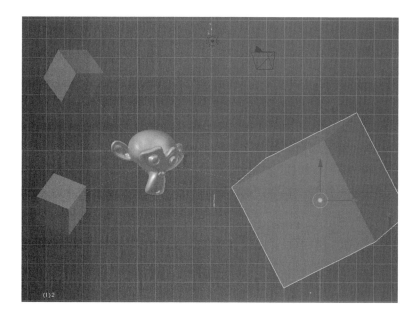

Using Script Links and Space Handlers

This chapter has discussed some approaches to integrating Python code more tightly into the Blender environment. There are several more-important ways to integrate Python into your Blender animations and workflow. *Script links* enable Python scripts to be called automatically upon certain events. *Space handlers* are special cases of script links that enable you to place interactive interface elements directly over the 3D view.

On-the-Fly Script Execution with Script Links

The ordinary way to execute scripts, as you saw in Chapter 7, is to use Alt+P in the text editor window or to call the script from the appropriate menu. However, at times you won't want to execute a script by hand. For example, you might want a script to execute every time a frame changes during an animation or when triggered by some other event. In these cases, you need to use script links.

To use script-linked scripts, you first need to enable script links, which can be done in the Scriptlinks panel in the Script buttons context, shown in Figure 8.27.

FIGURE 8.27
Enabling
script links

After this is done, you can add a script link by clicking New and selecting a text file from the menu list that appears. By default, the only text available when you first start Blender is called Text, so if you try to add a script link now, that will be the only option. When a text (presumably a script) is selected, a second menu appears, as shown in Figure 8.28, which gives a list of the events that a script-linked script can be triggered by. These events depend on whether the script links are connected to the scene (the default), to an object, to a material, or to the world. This is selected by using the three buttons below the Enable Script Links button on the Scriptlinks panel. The events that can be selected for Scene script links are as follows:

◆ OnSave

◆ OnLoad

◆ Render

◆ Redraw

◆ FrameChanged

The following are events that can be selected for Object, Material, and World script links:

◆ ObDataUpdate

◆ ObjectUpdate

◆ Render

◆ Redraw

◆ FrameChanged

FIGURE 8.28
Scriptlinks
events menu

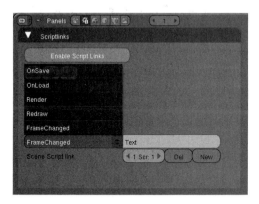

These names should be self-explanatory. When the selected event happens, the script is run. For example, if FrameChanged is selected, the script is run each time the frame advances in an animation.

USING THE REGISTRY TO WORK WITH PERSISTENT DATA

When a script is enabled as a script link, it is called repeatedly each time the triggering event happens. Each time the script is called, it executes and ends. This means that the script's variable namespace is cleared each time. There is no way, within the scripts alone, to pass variable values from one execution of the script to the next. This presents a big problem, because it is often necessary to refer to persistent values when running scripts. Fortunately, there is a Blender module that enables you to store data to be accessed by any script run within a single Blender session. As you will see shortly, this is useful not only for persisting data values over multiple executions of the same script, but also for passing values between separate scripts that run simultaneously, as in the case of space handlers.

A SIMPLE SCRIPT-LINKED EXAMPLE

In this example, you'll use a script-linked Python script to gradually shift the color of a material. The red, green, and blue values will be incremented slightly with each animation frame, using different increment values so they go out of sync and create new color combinations. When any color value reaches 1, a toggle is flipped, and the value is decremented. When the color value reaches 0, the toggle is flipped again and the value is again incremented. Because the direction of the increment cannot be known from only the current values on the material, it is necessary to store the increment toggle variables' value (one for each color) as a persistent variable using the registry. To prepare to run this script, open a fresh Blender session. Make sure that a material is assigned to the default cube. Create a text file called **color.py** and enable script links with color.py selected as the text file and FrameChanged selected as the triggering event.

The color.py script itself begins in a familiar way. It imports Blender and the Scene and Registry modules, and then retrieves the current scene and passes it to a variable:

```
import Blender
from Blender import Scene, Registry

scn = Scene.GetCurrent()
```

The next step is to define a function for updating the registry. The registry stores a dictionary (actually, it stores multiple dictionaries, and each dictionary represents a single script namespace). When you update the registry, you need to be sure that the contents of the dictionary are the correct values that should be persisted. In this case, the values that are being persisted are the r_inc, g_inc, and b_inc values, which represent the increment toggles for red, green, and blue. The values will be 1 for incrementing and 0 for decrementing. What update_Registry() does here is to create a dictionary and then pass it the values of the arguments that the function was called with. Don't confuse the dictionary's keys, which are strings (you can tell by the quotes), with the variables that represent their values. After this dictionary is constructed, it is sent to the registry by using the Registry.SetKey() method. The first argument of this method is the name of the dictionary that represents this script's namespace. I called it *Colors* to reflect the name of the script. The second argument of the method is the dictionary that holds the persistent values. Finally, a Boolean argument determines whether this information will also be cached to an external file.

```
def update_Registry(r_inc, g_inc, b_inc):
    d = {}
    d['r_inc'] = r_inc
    d['g_inc'] = g_inc
    d['b_inc'] = b_inc
    Blender.Registry.SetKey('Colors', d, False)
```

After defining the means by which the registry will be updated, you can now progress to accessing the registry information. This is done by using the Registry.GetKey() method and passing the returned value to a dictionary. However, before accessing the contents of the dictionary by key, you need to make sure that they exist (they won't exist, of course, until after the first time they are set). Python does not take kindly to attempts to access nonexistent keys or variables, and trying to do this will cause an error in Python, rather than simply returning a 0 or False value, as is the case in some other languages. Because of this, Python has a special structure for evaluating the existence of variables and dictionary keys: the try/except structure. In this case, the script progresses by first evaluating whether the dictionary contains data (it has been declared in the previous line, so it is not necessary to use the try/except structure to ascertain its existence). If the dictionary contains no data, the increment variables are set to 1. If the dictionary does have data, Python *tries* to set the variables based on values from the dictionary. If these values have not yet been set, the except statement calls update_Registry() and sets the increment toggle values to 1:

```
rdict = Registry.GetKey('Colors')
if rdict:
    try:
        r_inc = rdict['r_inc']
        g_inc = rdict['g_inc']
        b_inc = rdict['b_inc']
    except: update_Registry(1, 1, 1)
else:
    r_inc = 1
    g_inc = 1
    b_inc = 1
```

The remainder of the script should all be familiar from Chapter 7. The active object and its Mesh datablock are retrieved, and then the red, green, and blue material color values are modified. If the increment value is 1, the value is incremented. If not, the value is decremented. If the value reaches 1 or 0, the toggle is reversed:

```
ob = scn.getActiveObject()
mesh = ob.getData(mesh=True)

if r_inc == 1:
    r = mesh.materials[0].rgbCol[0] + 0.1
    if r >= 1:
        r = .99
        r_inc = 0
else:
    r = mesh.materials[0].rgbCol[0] - 0.1
    if r <= 0:
        r = .01
        r_inc = 1

if g_inc == 1:
    g = mesh.materials[0].rgbCol[1] + 0.08
    if g >= 1:
```

```
            g = .99
            g_inc = 0
    else:
        g = mesh.materials[0].rgbCol[1] - 0.08
        if g <= 0:
            g = .01
            g_inc = 1

    if b_inc == 1:
        b = mesh.materials[0].rgbCol[2] + 0.09
        if b >= 1:
            b = .99
            b_inc = 0
    else:
        b = mesh.materials[0].rgbCol[2] - 0.09
        if b <= 0:
            b = .01
            b_inc = 1
```

Finally, the material is assigned the new RGB values, and the registry is updated with the new increment toggle values:

```
mesh.materials[0].rgbCol = [r,g,b]
update_Registry(r_inc, g_inc, b_inc)
```

Make sure that the cube is selected as the active object, and then run the animation by using Alt+A over the 3D viewport or pressing the Play button on the Timeline. The cube's material will cycle through an endless variety of color combinations.

Viewport Interactivity with Space Handlers

You can create interface elements that appear directly laid over the 3D viewport with space handlers. Space-handler scripts are written as two separate script components, each in a separate file. Both files must be loaded into the Blender text editor in order for the space-handler script to be fully functional.

The first component is the Draw component, which handles placing the interface elements over the 3D viewport. The second component is the Event component, which handles user interaction with the space handler. These two components are in fact completely independent. If they are run separately, you may have a nice-looking but unresponsive interface, or an invisible interface that responds correctly to user interaction. Because these two components are independent of each other, once again it is important to give the scripts away to share information. This can be done by using the Blender registry as described in the previous example. Another way to do it is to use IDProperties. IDProperties are a powerful and convenient way to associate arbitrary values to arbitrary Blender datablocks in the form of properties. The associated properties are saved along with the .blend file and are accessible anytime. For example, you can associate a Python list to a Cube Mesh object, or a dictionary to a Scene datablock. In short, you can attach any Python data structure to any Blender object or datablock and store this relationship as a persistent part of a .blend file.

KEEPING UP WITH DEVELOPMENT

Space handlers are an experimental feature in Blender, and, like many things, should be expected to change and improve as development progresses in this area. Serious Blender users should always study the release notes for new releases and keep abreast with the latest wiki documentation and API updates. The examples I give here represent the best ways I know of to approach the tasks at hand in the current version of Blender. Understanding these methods, and understanding their limitations and weaknesses, will help you to understand the reasoning behind future developments as well. Furthermore, the more you know about how things are done now, the better position you will be in to influence future development by reporting bugs and becoming involved in feature discussions and planning.

In the following example, a graphical button is placed over the center of the 3D viewport. As shown in Figure 8.29, when the mouse is over the button, the button's appearance changes and the 3D view switches from Orthographic to Perspective View mode. When the mouse is moved off the button, the view returns to Orthographic mode and the button returns to its original appearance. You will find the complete space-handler setup in SpaceHandlerIDprop.blend.

FIGURE 8.29
Graphical button without mouse-over and with mouse-over

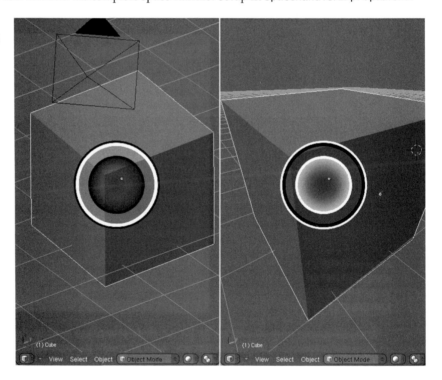

Before creating the script, copy the graphics from the CD that accompanies this book. The files are called spot.png and rspot.png. The images are PNG files with gradated alpha channels as illustrated in Figure 8.30, which shows the images laid over a UV test grid pattern so you can see their transparency clearly. Place those files somewhere accessible on your hard disk.

FIGURE 8.30
The two
button images

THE DRAW COMPONENT

Create a new text in the text editor and name it. I named this one spacehandler_draw.py to make it clear that it is the Draw component of the space handler (there are no special rules about how to name these scripts). The Draw component of a space handler is identified to Blender in the first line of the script, which must be this line:

```
# SPACEHANDLER.VIEW3D.DRAW
```

The next two lines are familiar import commands:

```
import Blender, bpy
from Blender import Image, Draw, Window, BGL, Registry
```

The next two lines are calls to the BGL Blender OpenGL module. These lines enable alpha blending between overlay images and the background. The PNG overlay images I'm using need to be alpha-blended, so these lines are necessary:

```
BGL.glEnable( BGL.GL_BLEND )
BGL.glBlendFunc(BGL.GL_SRC_ALPHA, BGL.GL_ONE_MINUS_SRC_ALPHA)
```

The next few lines set up the IDProperties that will be used in this script. First, you need to choose a Blender datablock to associate the properties with. This is an arbitrary decision, but the scene itself is an appealing choice. The first line here retrieves the active scene by using the bpy module. The next few lines define a function called update_props(), which is analogous to the update_Registry() function you saw in the previous example. However, instead of updating values in the Blender registry, it updates values in the properties dictionary that is associated with scn, the active scene. When this function is called later in the script, these values will be associated with the scene. It's that simple! The next few lines simply check to see whether there are already values associated with the scene IDProperty keys. If so, then radius, mouseover, and orth are assigned those values. If not, they are assigned the default value of 0.

```
scn = bpy.data.scenes.active

def update_props():
    scn.properties['radius'] = radius
```

```
            scn.properties['mouseover'] = mouseover
            scn.properties['orth'] = orth

        try:
            radius = scn.properties['radius']
            mouseover = scn.properties['mouseover']
            orth = scn.properties['orth']
        except:
            orth = radius = mouseover = 0
```

Depending on the value of mouseover, the main button or the reversed button image will be loaded by using the *Image.Load()* method of the Image module. The sys.expandpath() method is used to create a full path value for use in *Image.Load()* from a relative path. The // string stands for the directory that the script is in.

```
        spot = Blender.sys.expandpath("//spot.png")
        rspot = Blender.sys.expandpath("//rspot.png")
        if mouseover == 0:
            image = Image.Load(spot)
        elif mouseover == 1:
            image = Image.Load(rspot)
```

To place the button in the center of the viewport, you must retrieve the image's size by using getSize() and retrieve the window's area with Window.GetAreaSize(). The next few lines of code should be self-explanatory. The zoom variable represents the zoom factor by which I'm adjusting the original image's size. Finally, the value of radius is set, which will be sent to the event component the next time the IDProperties are updated, two lines later. First, the image is drawn on the screen by using the Draw.Image() method, whose arguments are the X location in the viewport, the Y location in the viewport, and the zoom factors for width and height.

```
        iwidth, iheight = image.getSize()
        w,h = Window.GetAreaSize()
        wH = w/2
        hH = h/2
        zoom = 0.3
        iwH = (iwidth*zoom)/2
        ihH = (iheight*zoom)/2
        radius = ihH

        Draw.Image(image, (wH-iwH), (hH-ihH), zoom, zoom)
        update_props()
```

That's all there is to the Draw component. This takes care of the interface's appearance. The next step is to make it work by writing the Event component.

THE EVENT COMPONENT

The Event component of the space handler begins similarly to the Draw component, except that the first line identifies it as an event script rather than a draw script, and the Image and BGL modules do not need to be imported. Otherwise, things are the same. Once again, you need to define update_props():

```
# SPACEHANDLER.VIEW3D.EVENT

import Blender
from Blender import Draw, Window, Registry
scn = bpy.data.scenes.active

def update_props():
    scn.properties['radius'] = radius
    scn.properties['mouseover'] = mouseover
    scn.properties['orth'] = orth

try:
    radius = scn.properties['radius']
    mouseover = scn.properties['mouseover']
    orth = scn.properties['orth']
except:
    orth = radius = mouseover = 0
```

At this point, the main if structure of the Event component begins. Blender checks each event, and if the mouse is moved (Draw.MOUSEX or Draw.MOUSEY events, as listed in the Draw module of the API), the code in the if structure is executed:

```
if Blender.event == Draw.MOUSEX or Blender.event == Draw.MOUSEY:
```

Once again, the window area size is calculated. This time, the mouse coordinates are also retrieved by using Window.GetMouseCoords():

```
w,h = Window.GetAreaSize()
wH = w/2
hH = h/2
x,y = Window.GetMouseCoords()
```

The following lines retrieve a list of currently existent windows, pass the list to winData, retrieve the ID of the specific window in which the space handler is running, and pass it to winID. The for loop that follows sets the range of X and Y values to represent only the window that the space handler is running in, so mouse movements over other windows will have no effect.

```
winData = Window.GetScreenInfo()
winId = Window.GetAreaID()
for win in winData:
    if win["id"] == winId:
        xmin,ymin,xmax,ymax = win["vertices"]
```

If the mouse is over the correct view window, the location of the mouse is calculated with respect to the center of the scene, where the button is located:

```
if xmin < x < xmax and ymin < y < ymax:
    # Correct the mouse position for this 3d view
```

```
        y -= ymin
        x -= xmin
        # Calculate mouse position from the center point
        # of the view
        y -= hH
        x -= wH
```

The Pythagorean theorem is used to calculate whether the mouse location is within the distance of the radius from the center. In Python, the operator ** means *to the power of.* In the code, the main conditional structure determines whether the mouse is over the button. After this is determined, the mouseover value is set appropriately and the registry is updated immediately to make the information available to the Draw component, so the image can be changed. Next, the orth toggle is checked. If it is already True and the mouse is over the button, nothing happens. If it is not yet toggled on, Window.QAdd(winId,Draw.PAD5,1) is called. This adds a command to the command queue of the window. The arguments represent the window ID in which the command will be added, the event that will be triggered, and a value representing whether the command should be interpreted as a button press (1) or a button release (0). The second argument, the command itself, is a Draw event. The list of these events can be found in the API in the Draw module. *Draw.PAD5* represents the number pad 5 key, which toggles Orthographic and Perspective views in Blender. In this way, moving the mouse onto and off the button becomes equivalent to pressing the number pad 5 key. The next line—Window.QHandle(winId)—executes the queued commands (there is only one) and flushes the queue.

Finally, the orth value is toggled, the window is redrawn, and the registry is updated:

```
    if y**2 + x**2 < radius**2:
        mouseover = 1
        update_props()
        if orth == 1:
            pass
        else:
            Window.QAdd(winId,Draw.PAD5,1)
            Window.QHandle(winId)
            orth = 1
            Window.Redraw()
            update_props()
    else:
        mouseover = 0
        update_props()
        if orth == 0:
            pass
        else:
            Window.QAdd(winId,Draw.PAD5,1)
            Window.QHandle(winId)
            orth = 0
            Window.Redraw()
            update_props()
```

EXECUTING THE SPACE HANDLER

To run the space-handler script, you need to have both components loaded in the Blender text editor. When the scripts are present in the text editor and are correctly identified as space-handler components in their first lines, they will be accessible via the View menu in the 3D viewport header, as shown in Figure 8.31. Using this menu, you can toggle each of the components on and off independently. This "independence" may be useful for debugging, but in general, the two components should both be toggled on for the space handler to work properly.

FIGURE 8.31
Accessing space-handler scripts via the View menu

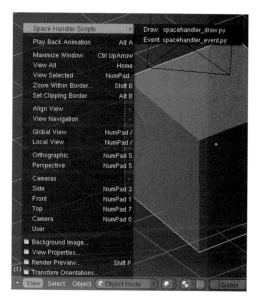

Real World Scenario

IMPROVED ERGONOMICS AND SPEED WITH A PEN TABLET AND SPACE-HANDLER ICONS

A vivid practical example of using space handlers is Michael Williamson's extension of Dolf Veenvliet's tablet icon overlay script, shown here. Michael is a professional CG artist whose studio, Cowtools Media, offers concept art, art direction, and creative consultancy to film and video game developers. After years of working with various 3D applications in senior roles within companies such as Sony Computer Entertainment, Electronic Arts, and Criterion Games—most notably as art director on the Criterion Games *Burnout* franchise—Michael switched to Blender as his primary 3D tool when he struck out on his own with his fledgling studio. However, when he began using a tablet PC, he found Blender's built-in support for pen-tablet workflow lacking. During a bout of bad wrist strain in the middle of a major contract job, Michael decided to do something about it. A simple icon overlay script for pen-tablet manipulations had already been made available by Blender developer Dolf Veenvliet, so Michael started with that as a basis and added icons not only for rotating, panning, and zooming the 3D space, but also for a wide variety of hot keys and menus that don't have easy button access. With Michael's overlay script, you can carry out all major 3D manipulation and modeling operations with one hand, without ever touching the keyboard.

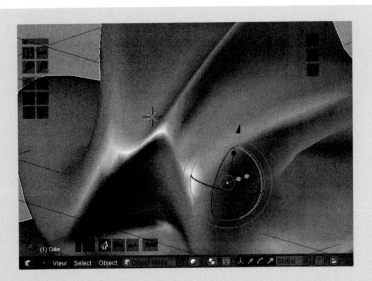

In addition to creating new ergonomic options, the script also enhances the usefulness of alternate input devices such as the 3Dconnexion SpaceNavigator. Although Blender has had basic SpaceNavigator support for some time, the Blender reliance on keyboard shortcuts renders the SpaceNavigator much less useful than it could be, because the user's hand must continually jump from the SpaceNavigator to the keyboard. With the tablet icon overlay script, the SpaceNavigator can be used to its fullest alongside the pen-tablet, resulting in fast and intuitive 3D interactivity. You need the keyboard only when entering text or numeric values.

You can find the full tablet icon overlay script on the CD that accompanies this book in the file TabletOverlay.zip. To use it, unzip the directory and place the entire TabletOverlay directory in your .blender/scripts subdirectory. Start Blender, and load the scripts by selecting Load Tablet Overlay from the Help menu. After you've done this, you can run the Draw and Event space-handler scripts from the 3D window's View menu, as you learned how to do in the previous section.

The Bottom Line

Control Ipo curves by using PyDrivers.   PyDrivers enable you to drive Ipo curves based on a Python expression. Because such expressions can incorporate multiple input values and can calculate complex functions, PyDrivers are much more powerful and flexible than traditional Ipo drivers.

Master It   Write a PyDriver that drives the red value of a material color based on the spatial distance between two bones in an armature. If the bones are less than 1 BU apart from each other in space, the material should be black. If the bones are more than 3 BUs apart from each other in space, the material should be red. To do this, you will need to study the API entry on the Pose module, and also the entry for the Vector class of the Mathutils module. You will need to retrieve the pose from the Armature object, and then retrieve the bones (specifically the bones' head coordinates) from the pose to get the locations of the bones. You'll then subtract one bone's position from the other, find the length of the resulting vector, and map the result by using simple arithmetic.

Incorporate Python scripts as nodes and constraints with PyNodes and PyConstraints.
PyNodes and PyConstraints enable further integration of Python into your Blender environment by giving you the means to create your own nodes and constraints with the full power of Python scripts.

Master It   Create a PyConstraint that takes three target objects and locks the constrained object to the imaginary line between the first target object and the second target object. Use the third target object as a control object to determine where along the line the constrained object is placed, so the four objects form a T-shape, with the constrained object at the intersection. If the control object is moved beyond the end of the imaginary line, the constrained object should remain fixed to the location of the object at the nearest end of the imaginary line. The solution of this exercise requires some light trigonometry. You will also want to read the Vector class documentation of the Mathutils module in the Blender Python API.

Use script links and space handlers to obtain even greater levels of interactivity.   Script links and space handlers can be used to execute Python scripts based on Blender events such as animation frame changes and to integrate script interface elements directly into the 3D view.

Master It   Adapt the space-handler script in the example to work with a square image rather than a circular image. The mouse-over behavior should be correct for the image shape. Also, instead of switching between Orthographic and Perspective View modes, make it switch between Solid and Wire Draw modes.

Part III

Mastering the Blender Game Engine

Chapter 9

Creating Assets for the Blender Game Engine

One of Blender's most distinctive features as a 3D tool is its built-in game engine for the creation of interactive content. In addition to games, the Blender Game Engine (BGE) can be used to create architectural walk-throughs, interactive data visualizations, educational tools, and a wide variety of other types of content. This chapter gives a complete overview of the BGE's core functionality.

In this chapter, you will learn to

◆ Model, rig, and texture a 3D character for use in the Blender Game Engine

◆ Create a simple game environment of a maze and skybox by using texture baking

◆ Place objects in the game environment, and set options for materials and lighting in the game engine

Creating Content for the Game Engine

The Blender Game Engine (BGE) has long been a distinctive feature of Blender among 3D content-creation applications. The BGE enables quick and simple creation of highly interactive 3D environments coupled with a state-of-the-art built-in physics engine in the Bullet physics library. With the recent release of Yo, Frankie! (the result of the Blender Foundation's Apricot project to create an open game prototype), the BGE has garnered more attention than ever before.

The biggest strength of the BGE is its ease of use and the relative speed with which creators can create their work. The BGE lacks some of the functionality of high-powered professional game-creation tools (although the Apricot project did much to narrow the gap), but it excels in creating fast, high-quality prototypes, visualizations, and walk-throughs. Unless you are creating a high-budget commercial video game, the BGE likely will enable you to do whatever you want.

In the next few chapters, you will learn the basics of using the game engine, and some things that aren't so basic. One thing that this chapter doesn't discuss in depth is how to fully exploit the Bullet physics engine to make the most of the extraordinary real-time rigid body simulation possibilities in the BGE. Physics simulation with the BGE is covered in detail in my book *Bounce, Tumble, and Splash! Simulating the Physical World with Blender 3D* (Sybex, 2008), so if you're interested in going further with physics in your games and interactive content, please refer to that book.

If you have read that book, you already know about setting up basic logic blocks, so the example in this chapter deals with something a little bit more sophisticated: a rigged character model. Don't worry—this chapter starts at the very beginning, so even if you've never touched the game engine in your life, it will get you up to speed and teach you how to create the assets you will be working with. In Chapter 10, "Making Things Happen in the Game Engine," you will set up the interactive logic that will enable the user to participate in the game experience.

Modeling a Simple Low-Poly Character

Before you can do anything interesting with the game engine itself, you need something for the game engine logic to act on. In this section, you'll create a character from scratch that will eventually become the protagonist in a simple game example.

There are several ways in which this character, as simple as it is, will represent the goals of modeling for the game engine. For one thing, the character will be created with a minimum of polygons and vertices. The character's face and distinguishing characteristics will be accomplished with UV textures, rather than highly detailed mesh models. This is a fundamental requirement for 3D assets that are intended for use in real time. No matter how much power and speed you have available, there are always better ways to use resources than to add unnecessary detail to the mesh geometry. On the other hand, the Subsurf modifier is not available in the game engine, which means that the mesh's smoothness in the game environment depends on the real geometry of the mesh. A balance must be struck in which your model has enough polygons to look nice from the necessary angles, but does not have an excess of vertices to weigh it down in real time. To build the simple character mesh, follow these steps:

1. Begin with the default cube. Press the 1 key on the number pad to get into Front view. Enter Edit mode by pressing the Tab key, and make sure that the entire mesh is selected (if it's not already) by pressing the A key. Press the W key to bring up the Specials menu and select Subdivide Smooth, as shown in Figure 9.1. The result will be a 24-sided polygon.

FIGURE 9.1
Subdivide Smooth
on the default cube

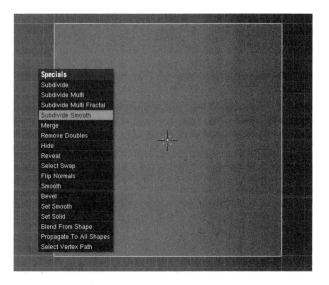

2. When the view is opaque, only the visible vertices are selected by the B key Box select tool. For the next step, you want to ensure that front and back vertices are all selected, so make sure your view is in Wireframe or Transparent Draw mode. You can toggle between solid and wireframe by using the Z key. In Wireframe view, press the B key and box-select the lower-right faces. Press the E key and select Region to extrude the faces together, as shown in Figure 9.2. Move the extruded face downward slightly, and then scale down with the S key to result in something like what is shown in Figure 9.3. After confirming this scaling with the left mouse button, scale again by pressing the S key. This time, however, constrain the scaling to the Z axis by pressing the Z key, and then type

in the numerical value **0** to scale the selection to 0 on the Z axis, flattening it as shown in Figure 9.4. Finally, complete the basic leg shape by extruding once more and scaling and translating the extruded face as shown in Figure 9.5.

FIGURE 9.2
Extruding the lower-right faces

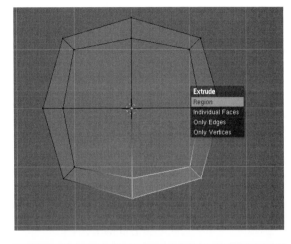

FIGURE 9.3
Adjusting the extruded face by scaling down

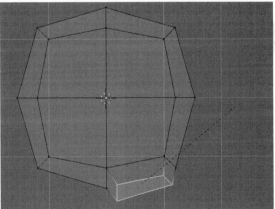

FIGURE 9.4
Scaling to zero along the Z axis

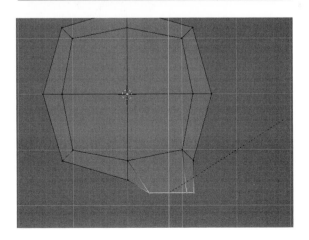

FIGURE 9.5
Completing
the leg with one
more extrusion

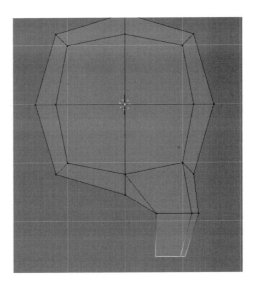

3. From here, the modeling will be done using the Mirror modifier. Select the vertices on the left half of the model and delete them with the X key, as shown in Figure 9.6. Again, be sure you get both front and back vertices. Apply a Mirror modifier by selecting it from the Add Modifier drop-down menu in the Modifiers tab, shown in Figure 9.7. Activate Do Clipping and set the Merge Limit value to 0.01, as shown in Figure 9.8.

FIGURE 9.6
Selecting and
deleting the other
half of the subdi-
vided cube

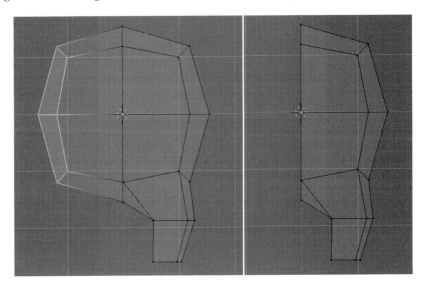

FIGURE 9.7
Mirror modifier

FIGURE 9.8
Mirror modifier
settings

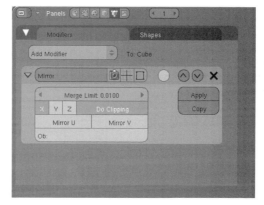

4. Select the upper-right vertical faces, where the shoulders will be, and extrude them several times, as shown in Figure 9.9. With each extrusion, rotate, scale, and translate the extruded face to form the shape of arms. After the second time extruding, scale to zero along the X axis to flatten the face. You can select edge loops along the arms to do further tweaking by holding down the Alt key (or the Option key on a Mac) while right-clicking one of the edges of the loop, as shown in Figure 9.10.

FIGURE 9.9
Extruding arms

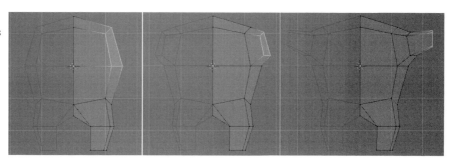

FIGURE 9.10
Tweaking an
edge loop

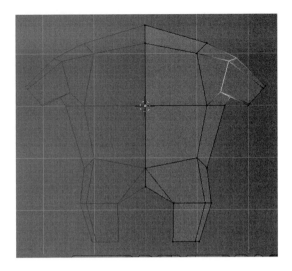

5. Press 3 on the number pad to change the angle to Side view. Select all vertices with the A key and scale slightly along the Y axis to slim the character as shown in Figure 9.11. Go back into Front view by pressing 1 on the number pad, and finish extruding the arms as shown in Figure 9.12. Extrude the top faces of the character to create the head as shown in Figure 9.13. Scale down slightly and rotate to create some simple, vaguely catlike ear shapes, as shown in Figure 9.14.

FIGURE 9.11
Slimming the
character along
the Y axis

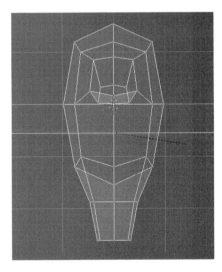

FIGURE 9.12
Completing
the arms

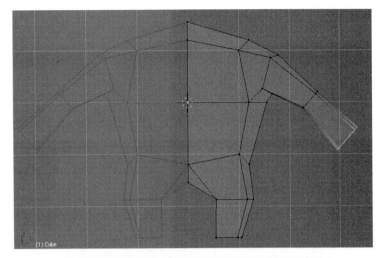

FIGURE 9.13
Extruding the head

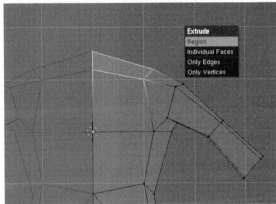

FIGURE 9.14
Scaling and rotat-
ing to create the
character's ears

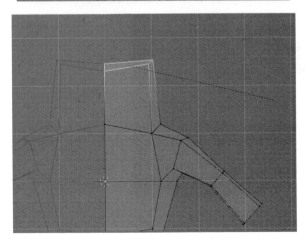

6. In the Side view, select the knee loops and translate them forward slightly along the Y axis as shown in Figure 9.15. Then select the elbow loops and translate them backward slightly to create the bends at the joints as shown in Figure 9.16.

7. The mirror modeling part is over, so make the Mirror modifier real by clicking Apply on the Mirror Modifier panel.

FIGURE 9.15
Adding a bend to
the knees

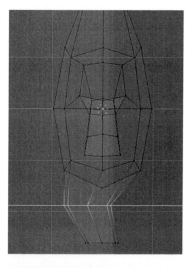

FIGURE 9.16
Adding a bend to
the elbows

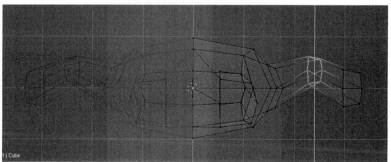

8. The shape of the character is essentially finished. However, two things should still be addressed. One is the geometry; this mesh character is really a little bit too simple to deform well, so a little extra geometry would help when working with armatures. The other thing to note is that the character is very blocky looking. Normally, you might consider using a Subsurf modifier to deal with this, but Subsurf modifiers are not handled by the game engine. Instead, select the entire mesh, press the W key, and select Subdivide Smooth, as shown in Figure 9.17. This adds geometry while smoothing and rounding the shape, as shown in Figure 9.18. The model is still quite low poly, so this will not weigh down the game play.

FIGURE 9.17
Subdivide Smooth

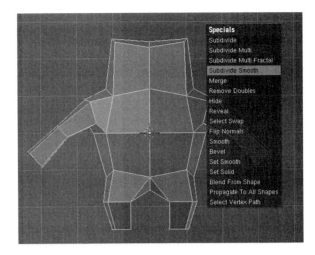

FIGURE 9.18
The finished mesh

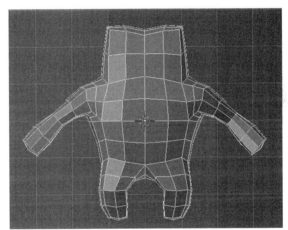

Texture Painting

For this character, a simple UV-mapped skin texture will be sufficient. In recent versions of Blender, a new Texture Paint mode has been developed that enables you to do 2D texturing directly in Blender and bypasses the need for exporting UV maps for use in other software. For this character, Texture Paint will be more than adequate for doing the texturing. To set up and use the Texture Paint feature on the character, follow these steps:

1. To unwrap the surface coordinates of the character, you need to create seams. For a simple character like this one, it is enough to create a single seam to separate the front from the back. Do this by holding down the Alt key and right-clicking one of the edges in the loop to select the edge loop as shown in Figure 9.19, and then press Ctrl+E and select Mark Seam to create a seam along that loop, as shown in Figure 9.20. If this is difficult to see in grayscale, refer to the duplicate image printed in the full-color insert of this book.

FIGURE 9.19
Select the entire
edge around the
character

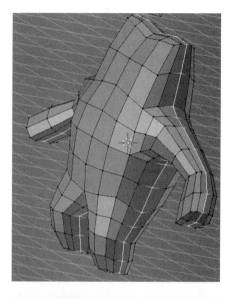

FIGURE 9.20
Marking the seam
with Ctrl+E

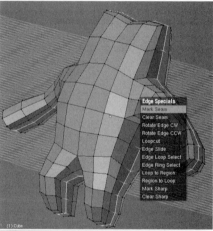

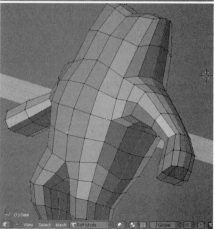

2. Split your work area and open a UV/Image editor, as shown in Figure 9.21. In the 3D viewport, select all vertices of the character by pressing the A key, and then select New from the Image menu in the UV/Image editor header, as shown in Figure 9.22. Set the Width and Height values for the image at 1024 and select the UV Test Grid option in the dialog box that appears, as shown in Figure 9.23. Add a UV texture to the mesh in the Mesh panel of the Edit buttons context.

FIGURE 9.21
Opening a UV/Image editor

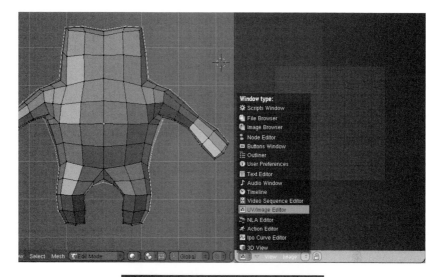

FIGURE 9.22
Creating a new image

FIGURE 9.23
Options for the new image

3. The new image will automatically be concealed beneath the UV mapping of the character mesh. By default, UV mapping maps an image onto each individual polygon in a mesh, which is represented by a stack of square (or triangle) polygons over the image. This is the blue square you're seeing in the UV/Image editor. Press the U key to unwrap the mesh so that the image can be properly mapped to the full mesh. The Unwrap dialog box appears, as shown in Figure 9.24. When you're finished unwrapping the mesh, the mapping will be as shown in Figure 9.25. Note that when displayed with the Textured draw type in the 3D viewport header, the UV test grid image can be seen mapped onto the character.

FIGURE 9.24
UV-unwrapping
the mesh with
the U key

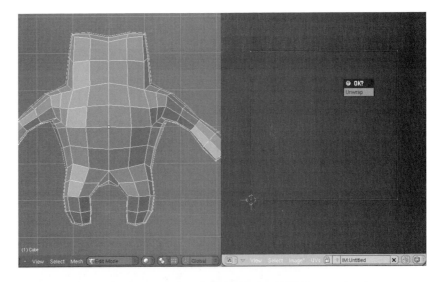

FIGURE 9.25
The unwrapped
mesh

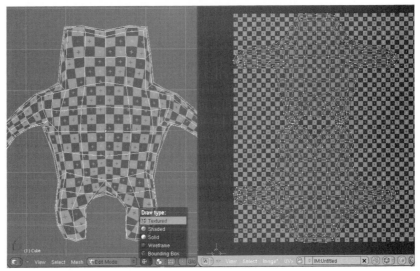

4. In the 3D viewport header, select Texture Paint from the Mode drop-down menu. When you do this, the Paint tab becomes available in the Edit buttons area. You can control the color, size, opacity, falloff, spacing, blend method (mix, lighten, darken, add, multiply, burn, and so on), and other parameters of your brush on this panel, and use your mouse to paint directly onto the model. A good texture painting setup involves a 3D viewport, the Paint buttons panel, and a UV/Image editor to see the actual painted image, as shown in Figure 9.26. (You can paint directly onto this image also by selecting the paint-brush icon button in the UV/Image editor header.) If you want to retain a set of brush parameters for use later, simply add a new brush by selecting New from the BR drop-down menu. The previous brush will remain as it was defined. In this way, you can create your character's surface texture something along the lines of Figure 9.27.

FIGURE 9.26
Texture Paint mode

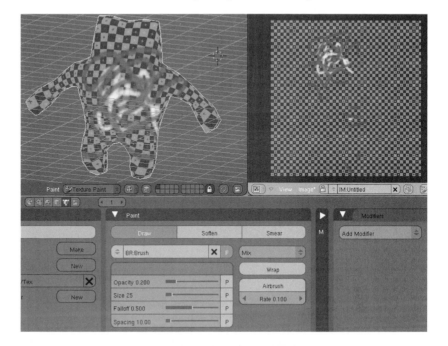

FIGURE 9.27
The fully painted character

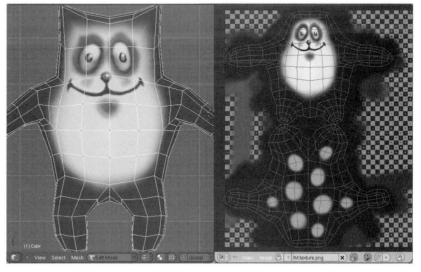

Rigging and Animating the Character

Now that the character is modeled and textured, it is time to rig the character with an armature and to create a simple animated walk action for it. To rig the character, follow these steps:

1. In Object mode, select the character mesh. Press Shift+S and select Cursor To Selection to ensure that the cursor is snapped to the center of the character (this should also be the center of the 3D space). Press the spacebar and choose Add ➢ Armature. Go to the Armature tab in the Edit Buttons area and make sure that X-Axis Mirror and X-Ray are selected, as shown in Figure 9.28.

FIGURE 9.28
Armature settings

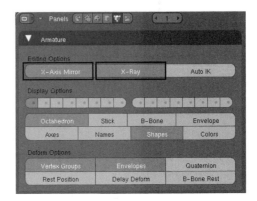

2. Extrude the shoulder bones by using Shift+E, as shown in Figure 9.29. Shift+E is necessary only the first time you extrude mirrored pairs of bones. After that, you can use the E key alone to extrude from a mirrored bone, and the extrusion will automatically be mirrored as in Figure 9.30. Select the head (the thicker end of the octagon) of the original bone by right-clicking the tip, and then extrude the legs, once again using Shift+E for the original mirrored extrusion (see Figure 9.31) and the E key for the legs themselves (see Figure 9.32).

3. Tab into Object mode. Select the character mesh first, and then hold the Shift key down and right-click to select the armature as well. Press Ctrl+P to create a parent relationship between the mesh and the armature, and select Armature, as shown in Figure 9.33. A dialog box pops up for you to select whether and how you want Blender to skin the mesh to the armature. Select Create From Bone Heat, as shown in Figure 9.34. This is a cutting-edge skinning feature that does an excellent job of automatically associating vertices to the correct bones. For many simple rigs such as this one, it is the only step you need to completely skin your rig! No weight painting, no tweaking vertex weights. You can now go ahead and experiment with posing your character, as shown in Figure 9.35. To return your character to rest pose, simply select the posed bones (the A key selects all bones) and press Alt+R to remove rotation.

FIGURE 9.29
Mirror-extruding
with Shift+E

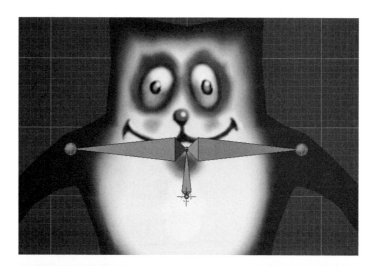

FIGURE 9.30
Extruding with
the E key

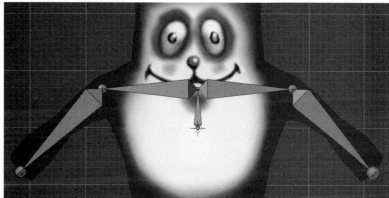

FIGURE 9.31
Mirror-extruding
the legs with
Shift+E

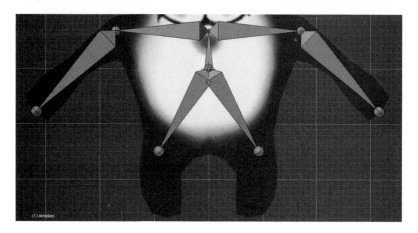

FIGURE 9.32
Extruding the legs
with the E key

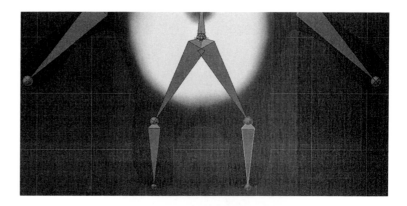

FIGURE 9.33
Making the arma-
ture parent

FIGURE 9.34
Creating vertex
groups from
bone heat

Now that the character is rigged, you can create a simple walk cycle action for use in the game engine. The focus of this exercise is just to create a basic walk action that will be integrated into the game logic in Chapter 10. As you probably know, a two-key walk cycle such as the one described here is not nearly an adequate demonstration of Blender's character-animation capabilities. For a much more in-depth look at rigging for character animation and creating armature animations such as walk and run cycles, refer to my book *Introducing Character Animation with Blender* (Sybex, 2007). As the Yo, Frankie! game prototype demonstrated, the game engine is capable of handling quite complex levels of character animation, including inverse kinematic (IK) constraints. For the present purposes, however, a simple walk cycle is sufficient. To create it, follow these steps:

FIGURE 9.35
Skinned and ready
to roll

1. Make sure that you are on frame 1 on the Timeline and in Pose mode with the armature selected. Select the left leg and rotate it forward by pressing the R key followed by the X key to constrain its rotation around the global X axis, as shown in Figure 9.36. Go into Side view by pressing the 3 key on the number pad, select the other leg, and rotate it backward as shown in Figure 9.37. Rotate the left arm backward in the same way, using the X key to constrain the rotation to the axis as shown in Figure 9.38, and rotate the right arm forward in Side view as shown in Figure 9.39. Shift-select both arms and both legs, and press the I key to key location and rotation as shown in Figure 9.40.

FIGURE 9.36
Left leg
rotated forward

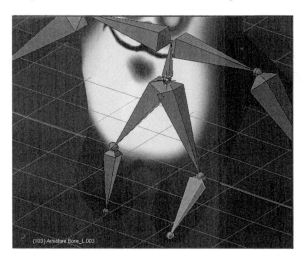

FIGURE 9.37
Right leg
rotated back

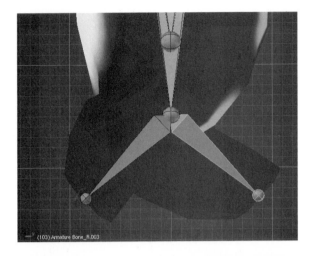

FIGURE 9.38
Left arm
rotated back

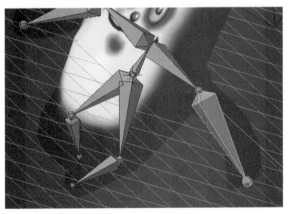

FIGURE 9.39
Right arm
rotated forward

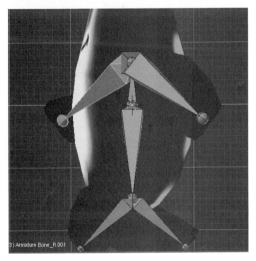

FIGURE 9.40
Keying all
posed bones

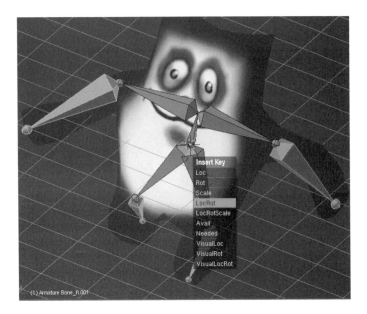

2. Split your workspace and open an Action editor window, as shown in Figure 9.41. The four keys you just made should be visible on frame 1. Advance 10 frames forward by pressing the up arrow key on your keyboard. At this frame (frame 11), you will want to key the mirror of the previous pose. To do this, use the clipboard buttons in the 3D viewport header. The clipboard buttons for both the classic and new icon set are shown in Figure 9.42. The leftmost button copies the current pose to the clipboard. The middle button applies the clipboarded pose to the armature, and the rightmost button applies the mirror of the clipboarded pose to the armature. First, with the four keyed bones selected, press the leftmost button to copy this pose to the clipboard. Then press the rightmost button to apply the mirror of the pose to the armature. The character should switch poses immediately, with the keyed bones selected. Press the I key to keyframe the new bone positions a shown in Figure 9.43. Last, select the four keys on frame 1 by using the B key to box-select. Copy those keys with Shift+D and move them 20 frames to the right, holding down the Ctrl key as you move them to constrain them to whole frames, as shown in Figure 9.44.

FIGURE 9.41
Keys in the
Action editor

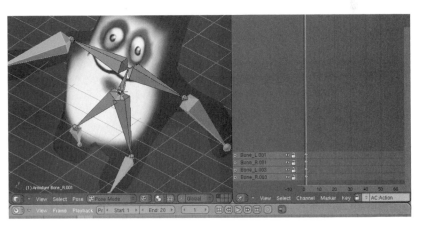

FIGURE 9.42
Clipboard buttons
in two icon sets

FIGURE 9.43
Keying the mir-
rored pose from
the clipboard

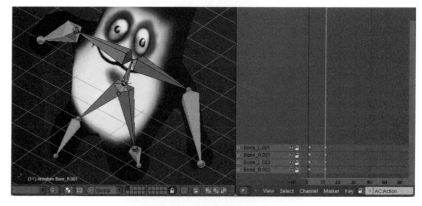

FIGURE 9.44
Copying keys with
Shift+D and sliding
20 frames

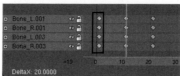

  Real World Scenario

ADVANCING THE GAME ENGINE BY FLYING LEAPS WITH YO, FRANKIE!

The most significant recent developments in the Blender Game Engine were the result of the Apricot project, the third major open content production project of the Blender Foundation after two short films, and the first to focus on game creation. The Apricot project was a six-month effort produced by a team of game creators and developers from around the world using Blender and the BGE in conjunction with the Crystal Space open source game-creation platform. This resulted in the game prototype Yo, Frankie!, which is available on DVD at the Blender e-shop. The core team for the Apricot project consisted of Campbell Barton (Blender developer and Game Logic devel-oper), Christopher Plush (art director and BGE lead game designer), Dariusz Dawidowski (Crystal Space lead game designer), Frank Richter (Crystal Space developer), Pablo Martin (B2CS developer), and Pablo Vazquez (lead artist) supported by Brecht van Lommel, Margreet Riphagen, and Ton Roosendaal of the Blender Institute.

The team got a jump on the process of game design by committing early on to reusing assets that had been created previously for the Blender Foundation's open short film *Big Buck Bunny*. Frankie, the sadistic flying squirrel from *Big Buck Bunny*, was selected as the protagonist of the game, and the Frankie rig was adapted for game engine use as shown here.

Basing the game world and characters on work that had been previously accomplished for the film enabled the team to focus on game play and developing the Blender game-creation tool chain. One of the goals of the Apricot project was to explore the potential of integrating Blender and Crystal Space together into a state-of-the-art game-creation pipeline. Finalizing such a pipeline proved to be beyond the scope of the project, but in the process an enormous amount of development went into the Blender game engine itself, making an even more powerful tool for visualization and prototyping. Improvements in view navigation, handling of UV textures, and asset management are among the big developments out of Apricot. Details about specific features developed for the project can be found under the Development link on the official Yo, Frankie! website at www.yofrankie.org.

3. The action is now finished. If you set the start and end frames in the Timeline to 1 and 20, respectively, and click the Play button (or press Alt+A while the cursor is hovered over the 3D viewport), the action will repeat continuously. In the name field in the Action editor header, give this action the name **Walk**, as shown in Figure 9.45.

FIGURE 9.45
Renaming the action

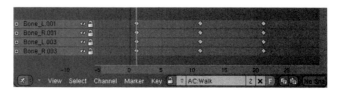

Setting Up the World

Now that you've created a character for your game, it's time to create the game environment. This will consist of a background sky and a maze through which the character will move.

Baking Procedural Textures for a Simple Skybox

In *Bounce, Tumble, and Splash! Simulating the Physical World with Blender 3D*, I describe how to use world texture mapping to create skies for animations. This method does not apply to the game engine environment, however. Instead, for games it is necessary to use a *skybox*, which is an actual Mesh object on which the sky texture is mapped directly. You can use any sky texture you wish for your skybox; it could be a hand-painted sky, a photograph, or an image created in a sky and terrain simulation program. This depends on the look and atmosphere you want in your game.

The following example shows you what might be the simplest way to get a passable sky background by using procedural textures in conjunction with Blender's powerful texture-baking functionality. To set up your skybox, follow these steps:

1. Open a fresh Blender session. Just as you did when you created the character in the previous section, enter Edit mode, select all vertices of the default cube, press the W key, and select Subdivide Smooth to create a 24-sided polygon. Select the nine vertices that make up the edges shown in Figure 9.46, forming a cross shape across the bottom of the mesh. If the edges are hard to see, check this book's full-color insert for a color print of this image. Press Ctrl+E to bring up the Edge Specials menu, and select Mark Seam from that menu.

FIGURE 9.46
Selecting edges for seams on a subdivide-smoothed cube

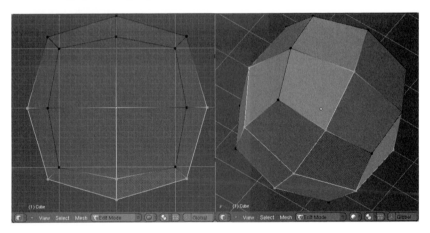

2. The next step is to create the combination of textures that will later be baked to an image. To do this, add a material to the cube. Make sure the material is shadeless by selecting the Shadeless option on the Material tab in the Material buttons area. The material needs three textures. First, create the texture shown in Figure 9.47 for the color of the sky. The texture is a linear blend texture with a colorband representing the colors in the sky from horizon (on the left) to zenith (on the right).

The mapping of this texture on the material is as shown in Figure 9.48. (Full-color prints of these images can be found in the color insert of the book.) The mapping type is Orco; and the X, Y, Z mapping is altered so that the blend pattern goes up and down rather than left to right. The Map To value is to Col, because this texture will represent the color of the sky. This texture is the top texture channel in the stack on the Texture panel. The third texture down is the Cloud texture. The Cloud texture itself is shown in Figure 9.49, and its mapping properties are shown in Figure 9.50. Finally, in the middle channel is a Stencil texture. This texture does not influence the color of the sky directly, but simply stencils out the clouds so that they fade toward the horizon. The texture here is shown in Figure 9.51, and its mapping is shown in Figure 9.52.

FIGURE 9.47
The sky Color texture

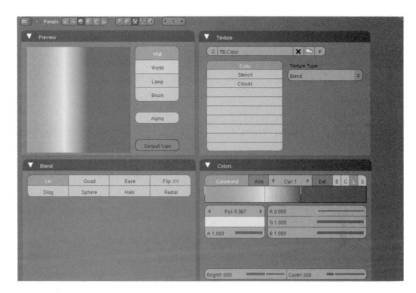

FIGURE 9.48
Mapping for the sky Color texture

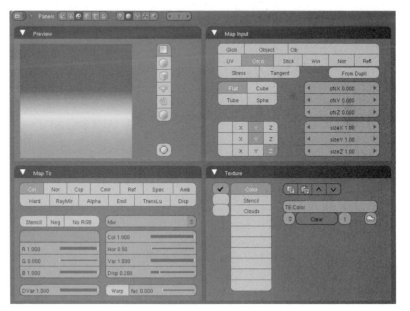

FIGURE 9.49
The Clouds texture

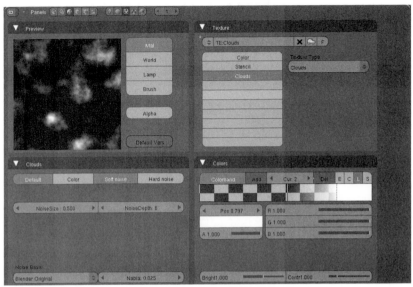

FIGURE 9.50
Mapping for the
Clouds texture

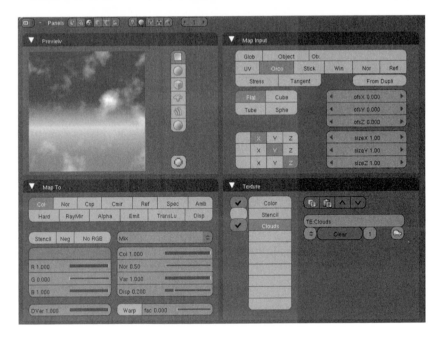

FIGURE 9.51
The sky
Stencil texture

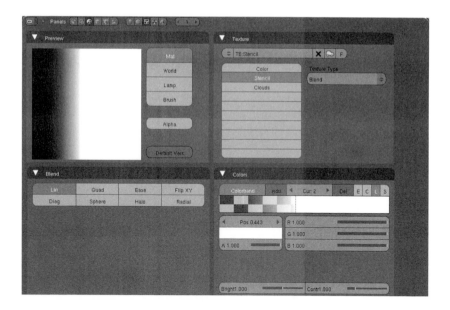

FIGURE 9.52
Mapping for the
sky Stencil texture

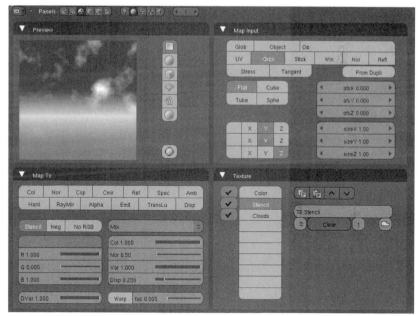

If you preview the box by using the Shift+P preview in the 3D viewport, you should see something like the image in Figure 9.53.

FIGURE 9.53
Previewing
the skybox

3. The procedural textures for the sky are now in place. The next step is to bake these textures to a UV-mapped image. To do this, split your workspace and open the UV/Image editor. Make sure the Skybox object is in Edit mode and all faces are selected with the A key, and then open a new image in the UV/Image editor by choosing New from the Image menu in the header, as shown in Figure 9.54. Set Width and Height to 1024 and select UV Test Grid in the New Image settings. Just as in the previous example with the character, the UV/Image editor will be covered by a blue square representing the stacked quad polygons of the mesh. Once again, add a UV texture in the Mesh panel of the Edit buttons context, and then press the E key to unwrap the mesh. Because you have already made seams, the mesh should unwrap as shown in Figure 9.55. You'll also notice that when the Textured draw type is selected from the drop-down menu of the 3D viewport, the UV test grid texture can be seen on the Skybox object, as shown in Figure 9.56.

FIGURE 9.54
Opening a new
image in the UV/
Image editor

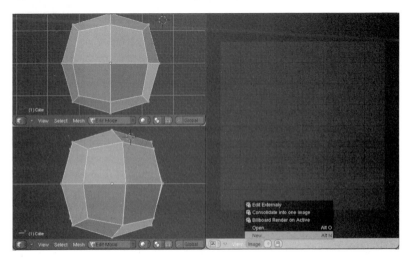

FIGURE 9.55
The unwrapped
skybox

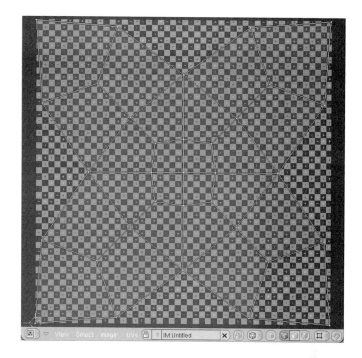

FIGURE 9.56
The object in Tex-
tured Draw mode

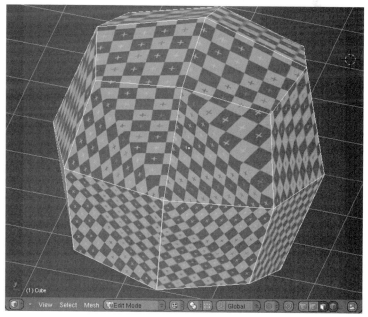

There are now two factors affecting the appearance of the skybox. The first is the original material you created with the sky Color and Clouds texture. The second is the UV texture from the image you just created. The draw type determines which of these is shown in the 3D viewport. If you render the image at this point, only the actual material will be visible. If you enter the game engine, the visibility will depend on the game settings you choose (as discussed in the next section of this chapter), but in any case the procedural textures on the material will not be visible.

4. Next, you need to bake the material appearance to the UV-mapped texture itself. To do this, go to the Bake tab in the Render buttons, shown in Figure 9.57. Select Textures, and click Bake. The process of baking textures is essentially the same as rendering, except that rather than being used to create an image from the camera's perspective, the render result is projected onto the UV-mapped image texture, as shown in Figure 9.58, which can also be seen in the color insert of the book.

FIGURE 9.57
The render baking tab

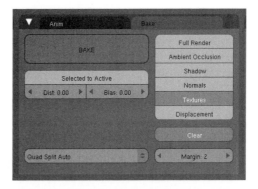

FIGURE 9.58
The baked sky texture

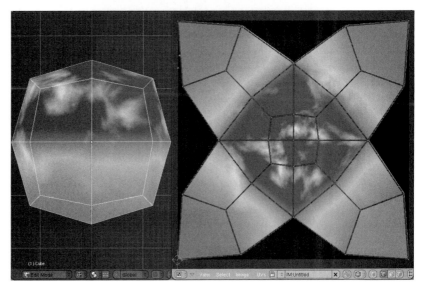

5. Pack the image into the `.blend` file by choosing Pack Image or Pack Image As PNG from the Image menu in the UV/Image editor, or by saving the image specifically to an image file by choosing Image ➤ Save As and then packing all data from the Blender File menu. If you do not do this, the baked texture will not persist the next time you close and open Blender.

6. By default, polygons are visible only from the side of their normals in the game engine. In the case of a skybox, the mesh needs to be visible from the inside, rather than the outside, which is the reverse of the default direction of the normals. To view the normals, set normals to draw in the Mesh Tools More tab with the Skybox object selected in Edit mode, as shown in Figure 9.59. To flip the normals, press the W key and select Flip Normals. The result can be seen in Figure 9.60.

FIGURE 9.59
Setting normals to draw

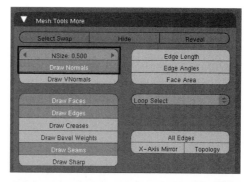

FIGURE 9.60
Before and after flipping the normals

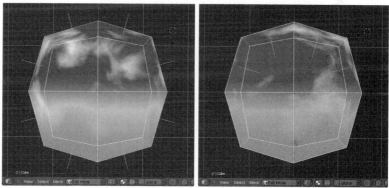

7. The skybox is now complete, and the sky is now mapped onto the mesh as a textured face. The actual material is no longer necessary. If you wanted to, you could even completely delete the material from the mesh, and the skybox would still appear correctly in the game engine. The final section of this chapter describes the relationship between materials, textured faces, and the game engine in more detail. Finally, change the Object name from Cube to **Skybox** by entering the new name into the OB field in the Links And Materials tab in the Edit buttons area.

Creating a Simple Maze

For the mock game example in the next chapter, your character will make its way through a maze. Creating the maze is simple. Follow these instructions to model the maze:

1. In a fresh Blender session, delete the default cube and add a Plane object. If the plane is rotated, go into Object mode and clear the rotation with Alt+R. In Edit mode, select all with the A key and scale upward by a factor of 50. Press W and select Subdivide Multi, as shown in Figure 9.61, and enter **10** as the Number Of Cuts, resulting in a divided plane. Enter Face Select mode by clicking the Select Mode button that is furthest to the right (shown in both classic and new icon sets in Figure 9.62). The plane in Face Select mode will appear as shown in Figure 9.63.

FIGURE 9.61
Subdividing the scaled-up plane

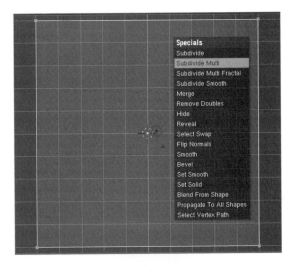

FIGURE 9.62
Face Select mode in new and classic icon sets

FIGURE 9.63
The subdivided plane in Face Select mode

2. Hold down the Shift key and right-click to select faces one by one in the maze pattern shown in Figure 9.64. Rotate the space so you are not looking straight down at the plane, and extrude the maze pattern downward by pressing E and then Z to constrain the extrusion to the Z axis, as shown in Figure 9.65. Viewed in Orthogonal Side view, the extrusion should look something like Figure 9.66.

3. Again holding down Shift and right-clicking, select all upward-facing faces, both at the upper and lower level of the extruded maze, as shown in Figure 9.67. All faces except the walls of the maze should be selected. Press P and choose Separate Selected, as shown in Figure 9.68. This will create a new, separate object from the selected portion of the mesh, as shown in Figure 9.69. Figure 9.70 shows the walls portion on its own. You can view objects isolated by selecting the object and pressing the forward slash (/) key on the number pad.

FIGURE 9.64
Selecting the maze pattern

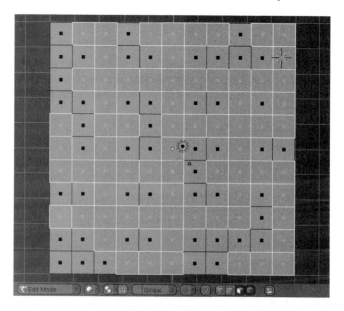

FIGURE 9.65
Extruding the maze pattern

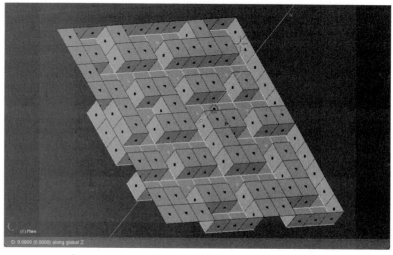

FIGURE 9.66
Orthogonal Side
View of the maze

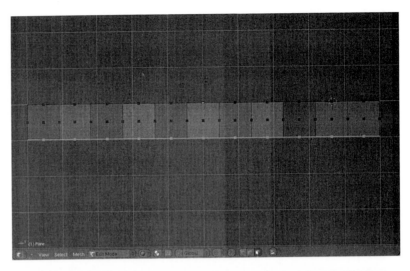

FIGURE 9.67
Selected faces
shown at an angle

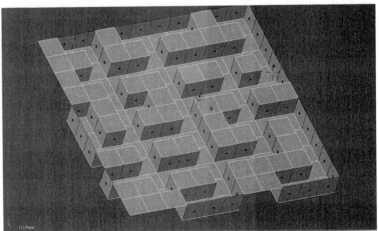

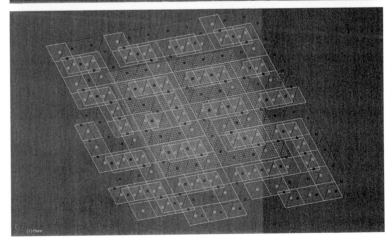

FIGURE 9.68
Separate selected
with the P key

FIGURE 9.69
The mesh
separated into
two objects

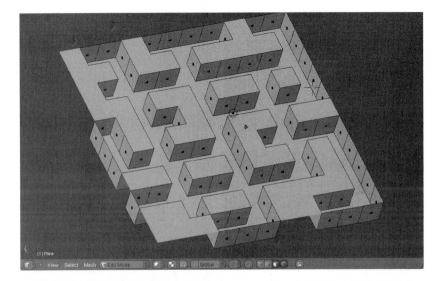

FIGURE 9.70
Using the slash
key to display
the Walls object
on its own

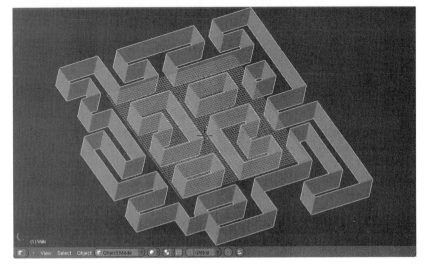

4. To keep things organized, give the two objects descriptive object names, such as Floor and Walls, and create a new Group to place them in. In the Object And Links tab with Floor selected, choose Add New from the Add To Group menu, as shown in Figure 9.71. Name the new group **Maze**. Then select the Walls object and add it to the Maze group, as shown in Figure 9.72.

FIGURE 9.71
Creating a
new group

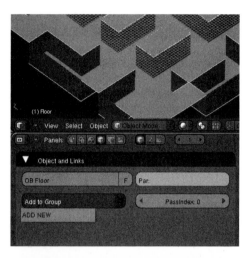

FIGURE 9.72
Adding the
Walls object to
the Maze group

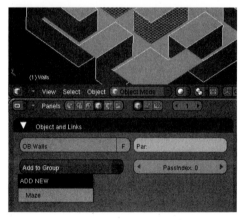

The maze is now completely modeled. In the next section, you'll learn more details about how materials, textures, and lights work in the game engine. Combined with what you've learned in this chapter already, this will give you all the information you need to texture the walls and floor of the maze as you like, which will be left as an exercise to do on your own.

Getting More Familiar with the BGE Environment

The BGE environment is fairly straightforward to use. As is the case with ordinary rendered animations, layers in the 3D viewport are used to determine what is rendered (in fact, layers have a bit of extra meaning in the game engine context, which you'll learn more about in the following chapter). Pressing P in Object mode activates the game engine and begins game play. Pressing Esc ends the game play and returns to Blender proper. Many new Blender users unfamiliar with the game engine have given themselves a shock by pressing P and watching Blender appear to freeze before their eyes. Simple as it is, there are a few things you need to be aware of in order to set up a game-based environment based on assets created in other files, and a few points about how things work in the game engine environment are worth being aware of before you go further.

Placing Your Objects in the Game World

The first thing you will want to do is to add the objects you have created for your game into a new Blender file representing the game itself. This is done by using the Append function. In this example, you'll begin by appending the skybox and the maze to a new file. Adding the character and armature will be left as an exercise to do on your own.

To add the skybox and maze to your game environment, follow these steps:

1. Start a new session of Blender and delete the default cube with the X key. From the File menu, select Append Or Link, as shown in Figure 9.73. A file browser window opens. Navigate to the location of the `sky.blend` file you created previously. The Blender file browser treats `.blend` files as file systems themselves, so you can navigate into that file as though it were a directory. Drill down into the `Object` directory and select the object called Skybox, as shown in Figure 9.74. Click Load Library, and the skybox appears in your 3D space.

FIGURE 9.73

Append Or Link

FIGURE 9.74

Finding the Skybox object on your hard disk

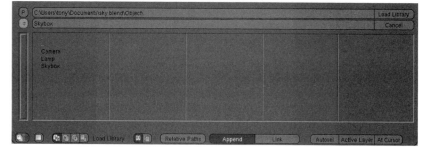

2. Repeat step 1 to navigate into the file containing your maze objects. This time, however, don't enter the `Object` directory in the `.blend` file, but rather enter the `Group` directory. Recall that you placed the Walls object and the Floor object together into a group called Maze. Select that group as shown in Figure 9.75, and click Load Library to load the entire group of objects into the 3D space.

3. When the maze and skybox are together in the 3D window, it will become immediately apparent that something is wrong, as you can see in Figure 9.76. The skybox is no bigger than a basketball in relation to the maze! Clearly the sky needs to be much bigger. Scale the sky up by about a factor of 50, and press Ctrl+A to apply the scale.

SCALING AND THE GAME ENGINE

Scaling in the game engine can be a source of trouble if not done carefully, particularly when rigid body physics and collision detection come into the picture. In general, everything in the game engine should be at scale 1. To ensure this, either scale your Mesh objects by selecting all vertices in Edit mode and scaling the mesh, or scale them in Object mode and apply the scale with Ctrl+A immediately after scaling. It is especially important that physics properties (the Actor button) should be applied only to meshes of scale 1. If you change the scale after activating physics on a mesh, the collision boundaries will be wrong.

Armatures should be scaled in Object mode and then have their scale applied with Ctrl+A. In some cases, this can cause animated actions to alter from how they were intended. I have found that in these cases, entering Edit mode, selecting all bones, and recalculating bone roll angles with Ctrl+N generally will fix animation problems caused by scaling the armature.

Setting Material Options

There are several ways to influence how things look in the BGE. The simplest way to texture things for the BGE is shown in the examples in this chapter. As you may have noticed, no mention has been made of materials. If you're used to working with Blender for rendering or animation, you probably have noticed that the UV textures in these examples were applied directly to the mesh, without any intermediary material. This is referred to *Textured-Face* or *TexFace* in Blender, and this used to be the only way the game engine would handle surfaces. The situation has gotten a bit more complex since the early days of the TexFace-only game engine, but people familiar with the basics of Blender materials will find the current possibilities more intuitive, because you can now use actual Blender materials and powerful shaders that enable near-photorealistic scenes and surfaces to be rendered in real time.

TexFace materials remain useful. If you truly want only the texture as is, and the surface should not interact with lamps or shadows (for example, in the case of a skybox), TexFace texturing remains ideal. You can use it as discussed in this chapter of course, without any material assigned to the object at all, and you can also use an actual material with the TexFace option selected, as shown in Figure 9.77. In either case—if a UV texture is present on the mesh and there is no material, or if the material is set to be a TexFace material—a Texture Face tab will be available in the Edit buttons area when the mesh is in Edit mode, as shown in Figure 9.78.

FIGURE 9.75
Appending the
Maze group

FIGURE 9.76
Mismatched scale

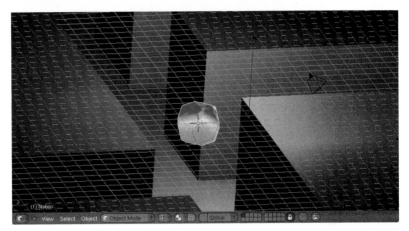

The Texture Face tab has several useful options for game engine use. The Twoside option enables textured faces to be seen from both the front and back, rather than the default of being seen from the front only. The Alpha option enables the face to take the Z transparency of the image texture.

If you want your objects to be subject to lighting conditions in the game engine, you should have them use Blender materials. The character example earlier in this chapter is a good example. TexFace mode is excellent for doing texture painting because it enables you to see the surface texture directly in the 3D viewport and act on it in real time. For that reason, the tutorial used TexFace mode. However, in the actual game engine, it might be better to use a material, with the texture UV-mapped to the color channel of the material, just as you would for an ordinary still render or rendered animation.

FIGURE 9.77
A TexFace material

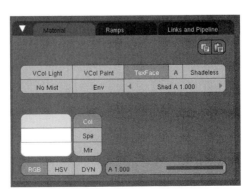

FIGURE 9.78
Texture Face
options

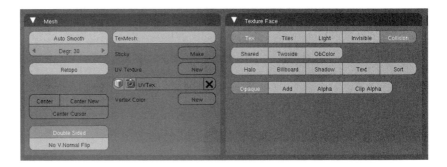

Using Lighting in the Game Engine

As mentioned previously, lights in the game engine do not affect TexFace objects. Blender materials, however, can be illuminated in the game engine in real time by lamps. All five Blender lamp types—omnidirectional lamps, spotlights, area lights, sun lamps, and hemi lamps—work in the game engine and can be animated or controlled in the same way as other objects.

Illuminating many objects in real time can slow things down. Furthermore, the quality of the illumination depends on the density of the mesh being illuminated, as shown in Figure 9.79. The only difference between these setups is the number of times the mesh is subdivided. High numbers of vertices, of course, become a liability for speed of game play.

FIGURE 9.79
Greater mesh density produces better illumination patterns.

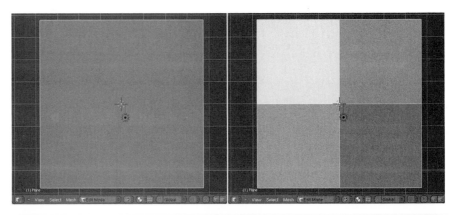

FIGURE 9.79
Continued

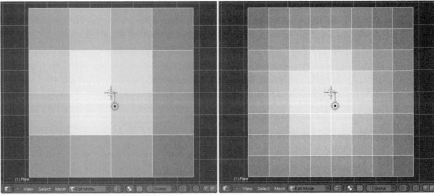

FIGURE 9.79
Continued

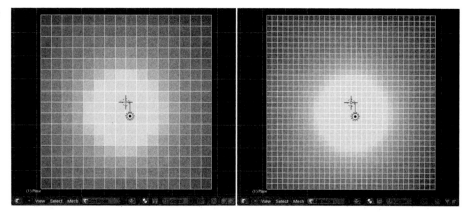

Vertex Painting for Light Effects

You can "paint" lighting-like effects directly onto meshes by using vertex painting, available in the Mode menu of the 3D viewport header, as shown in Figure 9.80. Vertex painting works directly on the mesh: Each individual vertex can be assigned a vertex color, but the colors applied using vertex painting are visible even if there is a UV texture or a material applied. Because vertex-painted colors interact with the color of the material or the textured faces, vertex paint can be a good way to simulate the effect of lighting in a game environment. If the lighting does not change on an object, using vertex painting to fake its illumination can be a good way to speed things up. If the lights move or the object moves with respect to lights, real-time lighting will yield more-convincing results.

FIGURE 9.80
Vertex Paint mode

The Bottom Line

Model, rig, and texture a 3D character for use in the Blender Game Engine.   A simple, low-poly rigged character is ideal for experimenting with the game engine. Modeling, rigging, and animating in the Action editor can all be done quickly and easily in Blender.

Master It   The example described in the tutorial uses TexFace texturing and therefore cannot be illuminated in real time with lights in the game engine. Fix this by creating a Blender material with the same UV-mapped texture so the character can be illuminated with lights in the game engine.

Create a simple game environment of a maze and a skybox by using texture mapping.
Simple modeling, combined with some clever texturing tricks, is enough to create an interesting in-game environment. Baking textures to images is a great way to adapt Blender procedural effects to use in the game engine.

Master It Texture the walls and floor of your maze in an interesting way.

Place objects in the game environment and set options for materials and lighting in the game engine. Appending objects and groups to a .blend file is a crucial skill for managing 3D assets on any kind of nontrivial Blender project. Understanding how materials and lighting interact in the game engine will enable you to get exactly the look and atmosphere you're after for your game or interactive environment.

Master It In this chapter, you appended the skybox and maze to the game, and then resized them both to make them suitable to each other. Next, append the character to the scene as well. Use grouping to append the armature and mesh simultaneously. Resize the character appropriately, and remember to apply the new scale. Test your animated action with the new scale. If there are problems, recalculate the bone roll angles in Edit mode.

Chapter 10

Making Things Happen in the Game Engine

Now that you've created a character and a simple environment for use in the game engine, the next thing you need to know is how to add user interactivity. The Blender Game Engine (BGE) has several ways in which interactivity can be programmed into a game environment. In this chapter, you will learn about Blender's built-in game design tools: logic blocks.

Logic blocks have the advantage of using Blender's built-in graphical user interface to implement interactive functionality. For nonprogrammers, this affords an easy way to get started with game creation without needing to know any programming. For greater scalability and versatility, Python can also be used, which is the topic of Chapter 11, "Python Power in the Blender Game Engine." Using Python in the game engine also relies on logic blocks to a certain extent, so regardless of how you ultimately want to program your Blender games, you will need to be familiar with the logic block system.

In this chapter, you will learn to

♦ Control characters and scenes by using logic blocks

♦ Use properties, messages, and states to create complex interactions

♦ Work with textures to create dynamic text and in-game 2D animations

♦ Incorporate sound effects into your game environment

Working with Logic Blocks

Logic blocks are the BGE's way of controlling how user input controls in-game events and how those events in turn control other events. Using logic blocks, you can make a character respond to your keyboard input, trigger a level change when a certain number of points are collected, and even set up some basic artificial intelligence (AI) behavior for your character's enemies.

In my book *Bounce, Tumble, and Splash! Simulating the Physical World with Blender 3D* (Sybex, 2008), I introduce some basics of logic blocks for the purpose of using the BGE's rigid body simulation functionality for animation. In this book, I go into much more detail about working with armatures, using properties, and other functionality more specific to interactive content and game creation. Only the very basics of working with rigid bodies and game physics are touched on here. If you are interested in setting up more-sophisticated rigid body interactions or in using BGE rigid body behaviors in your Blender animations, I recommend that you refer to *Bounce, Tumble, and Splash!* for more information on those topics.

The idea behind logic blocks is simple. Logic blocks enable you to associate cause-and-effect relationships and action-reaction behaviors with objects in the game environment. In this chapter, you'll learn how to work with logical relationships that are built into the BGE logic blocks system. In the next chapter, you'll learn how to expand the logic to include Python scripts, leading to countless new possibilities for game design.

Understanding Logic Block Basics

As mentioned previously, the logic block system enables units of logic to be associated with 3D objects. Every logic block is associated with a single 3D object. Logic blocks may affect more than one object's behavior, however, and they may "communicate" with each other (as you will see later in the "Using Properties, Messages, and States" section). For this reason, there is not always a fixed, "correct" way to set up game logic. When you get a sense of how logic blocks work, you will develop intuitions about which objects should have which logic blocks associated with them.

After you have placed your character in the scene, you need to add user controls to enable the player to move the character around that scene. Because both the motion of the character and the defined actions can be controlled through the armature, the sensible way to set up these logic blocks is to associate them with the character's Armature object.

To get started with logic blocks, enter the Logic buttons context in the Buttons area by pressing F4 or by clicking the leftmost context button on the Buttons area header (the one with a Pac-Man-like icon image on it). Then select the Armature object in your scene (in Object mode), and you will see the panels shown in Figure 10.1.

FIGURE 10.1
The GameLogic buttons

The leftmost quarter of this panel is where rigid body physics is controlled. Objects that need to be affected by physical forces will need to be activated as Actors, which will be discussed later in this chapter. This part of the window is also where collision boundaries (Bounds) are controlled, and where object Properties are set.

The remaining three-fourths of the Logic buttons area is devoted to the logic blocks proper. Logic blocks fall into three distinct types, which are organized in columns from left to right. The logic block types are as follows:

Sensors   The logic blocks in the leftmost column are sensors. Sensor logic blocks handle the cause side of the game logic. Sensors are defined to look for specific triggers for events.

Actuators   The logic blocks on the right are actuators. Actuators are the logic blocks that make things happen as a result of the sensors connected with them.

Controllers   The middle column is where the controllers reside. Controllers connect sensors to actuators. Although in the simplest cases they may initially seem superfluous, controllers are the heart of the BGE game logic. They behave as Boolean logic gates with multiple sensor inputs. In cases where Python scripts are used in the BGE, the scripts themselves take on the role of controllers.

Making the Character Walk

To set up the basic walking motion of the character, you'll use all three of these logic block types. To do this, follow these steps:

1. In the Sensor column, add a new sensor to the Armature object by clicking Add beside the Armature tag. This tag appears in the area only if the Armature object is selected in the 3D window. When you do this, you will see the logic block appear as shown in Figure 10.2. The default sensor type is Always, which means that this sensor will act as a constant trigger for events that are connected to it. This isn't what you need here, though. Because the character will be controlled using keyboard buttons, select Keyboard from the drop-down menu shown in Figure 10.3. The text field to the right of the drop-down menu is where you can give the logic block a name. This can be helpful to keep things orderly, but the name is optional and arbitrary.

FIGURE 10.2
Adding a sensor to the Armature object

FIGURE 10.3
A Keyboard sensor

2. Click the light gray button next to the word Key so that it displays the message Press A Key. The next key you press will be entered in this Keyboard sensor. Press the up arrow on your keyboard, and Uparrow appears, as shown in Figure 10.4.

FIGURE 10.4
Uparrow
selected in the Key-
board sensor

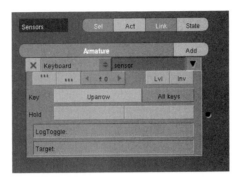

3. In the Controller column, add a controller in the same way you added a sensor previously, by clicking Add. A logic block like the one shown in Figure 10.5 appears. The default controller type is And, which means that if multiple sensors are connected to the left side of the controller, the actuator on the right will be triggered only when all of the sensor criteria are met. Also, you will notice a grid of 30 squares similar to the way layers are represented in the 3D viewport header. These represent states. By default, new controllers are placed on state 1, as shown. Activating and deactivating different states enables you to have control over when different logic blocks are applied, as you will see in more detail later in this chapter. Connect the sensor to the controller by holding the left mouse and drawing the mouse from the small circle on the right of the sensor to the circular connector icon to the left of the controller so that a line appears between them.

FIGURE 10.5
Adding a controller

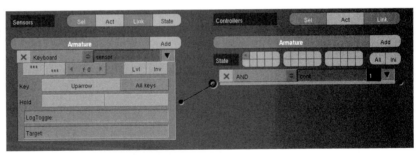

4. To complete this logical circuit, add an actuator to the Actuator column. The default actuator is a Motion actuator. As you can see from this drop-down menu in Figure 10.6, there are many options for the kinds of events you can call with an actuator. In this case, you'll start by making the armature walk according to the walk cycle set up in the last chapter, so select Action from the drop-down menu as shown. Recall that the walk cycle action you created in Chapter 9, "Creating Assets for the Blender Game Engine," was called Walk, and it cycled from frame 1 to frame 20. Enter the name of the action in the AC field, and the start and end frame numbers in the Sta and End fields, respectively.

FIGURE 10.6
Adding an
Action actuator

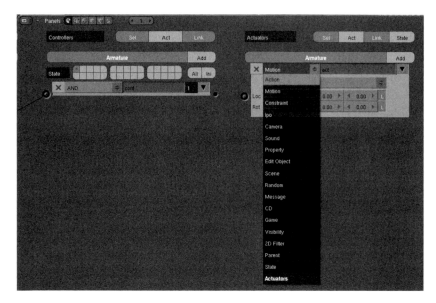

5. Select Loop Stop from the play mode drop-down menu next to the AC field. This deter-mines how the action will be played when the actuator is triggered. The play mode will play the action once. Loop End will loop the action as long as the actuator remains trig-gered, and when the actuator is released, the action will continue to play until its end frame. Loop Stop will discontinue the action midway through as soon as the actuator is released. This is the most natural setting for a walk cycle in this situation. The settings for the Action actuator are shown in Figure 10.7.

FIGURE 10.7
Settings for
the Walk Action
actuator

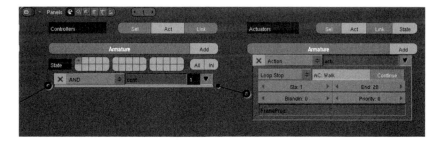

6. Connect the actuator to the controller in the same way you connected the sensor to the controller. If you enter the BGE game-play mode now with the P key, you will find that pressing the up arrow key on your keyboard will activate the walk cycle. This is the first step to getting your character to be fully controllable.

7. At present, the character is going through the motions of walking, but it's not moving anywhere. To make the character move, you need to add a Motion actuator as shown in Figure 10.8. If your armature's axes are the same as mine, the forward movement for the armature is in the negative Y direction. On the Motion actuator, the three columns of values represent X, Y, and Z axes in that order, so to make the object move along the Y axis negatively, put a negative value in the middle Loc field. A value of –0.05 will yield an appropriate speed. The L button you see to the right of those values ensures that the local coordinates are used, so it should be selected.

FIGURE 10.8

A Motion actuator

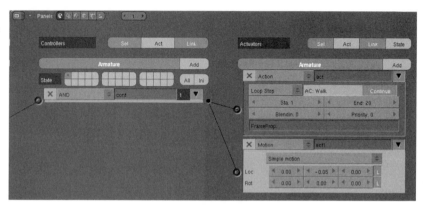

8. To give the character the ability to turn right, add a sensor for the right arrow on the keyboard and connect it via a new controller to another Action actuator identical to the previous one, and a Motion actuator with a negative Rot value around the local Z axis, as shown in Figure 10.9. Do the same to make the character turn left with the left arrow key and walk backward with the down arrow key.

FIGURE 10.9

Logic blocks for turning right

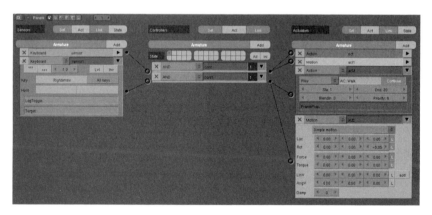

If you press P now, you should find that your character now is able to walk around the scene. However, the vertical placement of the character does not change, so it may seem that your character is walking on air, and furthermore walls and obstacles do not put up any resistance. To remedy this, you must enable some dynamic properties on your character.

ADDING DYNAMICS TO THE CHARACTER

When you add an object to a scene, it is automatically created with certain basic physical properties, because the Physics button is pressed by default. This mimics the behavior of earlier Blender versions that did not have the capability to completely disable all physics effects. In this default state, an object will not move or be influenced by forces such as gravity; however, the object *will* act as an obstacle for other physical objects. With the Physics button deselected, there will be no interaction between the object and other objects; physical objects will pass through this object as though it is not there.

When Physics is selected, you then have the option to make the object an Actor, which means that forces and interaction will be calculated with respect to this object and its surroundings. If Actor is selected, you can choose to make the object Dynamic, enabling it to move in response to forces on it, and also to make the object a Ghost object, which will prevent it from being an obstacle and enable objects to pass through it without resistance. These options are not mutually exclusive. The Ghost option is different from having no physics applied at all because it allows for the possibility that the Ghost object could also be dynamic, whereas no dynamic behavior is possible if Physics is fully disabled.

If the object is set to be dynamic, then other parameters related to its mass and collision boundaries also can be set. Finally, if the object is dynamic, it becomes possible to set the object as a rigid body object. This means that not only will it move in space in response to directional forces, but it will also have a full complement of angular rigid-body forces calculated, resulting in a much more realistic tumbling and bouncing motion. In the case of rigid body simulation, the type of collision boundary selected also will have a considerable impact on the behavior of the object. All of these options are discussed at great length in my book *Bounce, Tumble, and Splash!*, which I recommend if you are interested in learning more about rigid body physics.

In the present case, rigid body dynamics are not necessary for the character. The character should settle on the floor and treat walls as obstacles, but for the present game the character doesn't need to be able to tumble and roll around (which would make it difficult to control with the simple walking motion you've set up so far). For this reason, it is enough to make the character dynamic only, without rigid body physics. To set this up, follow these steps:

1. Because the character's mesh is parented to the armature, it is enough to ensure that the armature behaves dynamically. Select the Armature object in Object mode and make it an actor by clicking the Actor button in the Logic buttons panel. Also click Dynamic, as shown in Figure 10.10. You can leave the other values as they are for the moment. This is all that's needed to make the armature dynamic. With the mesh armature-parented to the armature, the mesh's own Physics settings will be disregarded in the game engine environment. To keep things uncluttered, you can disable these settings entirely, as shown in Figure 10.11.

2. If you press P now and enter Play mode, you should see the character drop down onto the floor. However, as you can see in Figure 10.12, the character is presently dropping down too far into the floor. The reason for this is that the armature's collision boundary is too small. If you look at the character in Wireframe view in Object mode, you will see the collision boundary radius shown as a dotted line, as in Figure 10.13. Armatures have only one option for collision boundary shapes; they are always spherical, and the bounds are set by the Radius parameter. Another way to see what's happening here is to use the Show Physics Visualization option available in the Game drop-down menu, as shown in Figure 10.14. With this activated, you will see all physical boundaries explicitly drawn in the game-play

environment, as shown in Figure 10.15. A color reproduction of this image is included in the color insert of this book. As you can see more clearly there, the physical bounding box of the armature is colliding properly with the floor, but it is too small for the character.

FIGURE 10.10
Making the armature dynamic

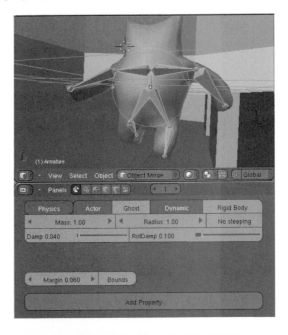

FIGURE 10.11
Disabling Physics on the mesh

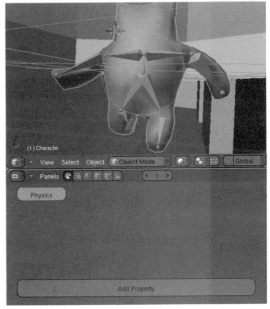

FIGURE 10.12
The character sinks
into the floor.

FIGURE 10.13
The collision
radius on the
armature

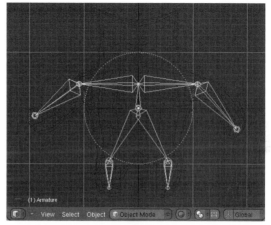

FIGURE 10.14
Showing physics
visualization

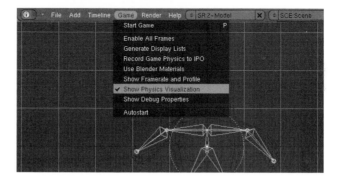

3. To fix the bounding-box problem, adjust the radius of the armature's collision boundary so that the dotted line encompasses the full character, as shown in Figure 10.16. In this case, the appropriate setting for the Radius value is 1.6.

FIGURE 10.15
Game-play mode in Wireframe view with physics visualization

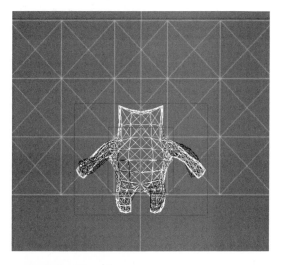

FIGURE 10.16
Adjusting the radius

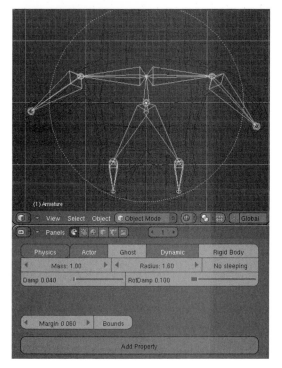

Setting Up the Camera

If you press P while you are in Camera mode, or if you create a free-standing executable game using the game engine, the game will be displayed from the point of view of the active camera in the scene. There are several ways to ensure that the camera stays focused on your character. The simplest way is to simply parent the camera to the armature with the camera pointing at the armature. If you do this, the camera's motion will be controlled directly by every movement of the armature. This is okay for some purposes, but the resulting camera movement is very stiff and the effect can be unnatural. For some 3D games, it is good to have a camera that can follow the character loosely and respond in a more natural way to the character's movement, generally staying at a set distance but responding in a more flexible way to the character's movements than if it were parented. This is what the Camera actuator is for.

The Camera actuator is a logic brick that can be set on a Camera object, as shown in Figure 10.17. In this example, I use an Always sensor so that the Camera actuator is always active. The Camera actuator itself has a field for the name of the object the camera should be pointing toward, in this case Armature, and also fields for the height it should try to maintain, the minimal distance from the object it should be allowed to come, and the maximum distance from the object it should be allowed to get. Setting these values as shown in the figure will result in smoother and more natural looking camera behavior than you would get by simply parenting the objects.

FIGURE 10.17
The Camera actuator targeted on the Armature object

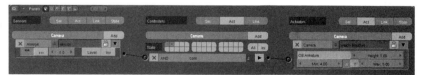

Using Properties, Messages, and States

In addition to sensors, controllers, and actuators, other features help make the Blender logic block system a powerful programming language all in itself. These include properties, messages, and the newly-developed state system, a result of the Yo, Frankie! open game project. *Properties* enable you to store and change values in the game engine environment. They serve a purpose directly analogous to variables in an ordinary programming language. *Messages* provide another way for logic blocks to communicate with other logic blocks, even when they are not directly connected. They can be useful for synchronization or cases when a logic block should have an effect that is broadly recognized by other logic blocks. *States* enable a kind of meta-level of control over sets of logic blocks and can be used to enable or disable whole collections of logic blocks at once.

Setting Up Bad Guys

The game you're putting together in this chapter is a simple maze game in which the goal is to collect Cone objects while avoiding evil wizard enemies. This section describes a simple setup for the bad guys that will provide a challenge to navigate without being too confusing to set up.

It is loosely based on a much more complex tutorial example provided by BlenderArtists. org user Mmph! His example uses a large number of logic blocks to create a rudimentary but convincing form of AI (artificial intelligence) and is very much worth checking out at http:// blenderartists.org/forum/showthread.php?t=100512. The method described in that thread is quite clever; however, it pushes the boundaries of what is advisable to do with logic blocks. For effects as sophisticated as AI, Python scripting is probably the least cluttered and easiest way to work. Nevertheless, the simplified bad-guy movement logic presented here should give you a clear idea of how properties work and how they can be used to control characters' behavior.

For the following tutorial, you can either append the BadGuy object to your own scene or use the badguy_nologic.blend file itself to follow the tutorial. The end result of the following steps can be found in the file badguy_logic.blend. The initial setup looks as shown in Figure 10.18.

The *path nodes* are simply cubes that have been resized to be about the height of the bad-guy character. As usual in the game engine, do your resizing in Edit mode and leave the object scale at 1. In the Mesh buttons, I've applied an empty UV texture to make the cones shadeless in the game engine, and I've colored them red using vertex painting. I suggest you create one first and add the logic described in the next section, and then copy it three times. Logic blocks are copied along with objects, so this approach will save you having to set up the logic for each path node individually.

Path Node Logic Blocks

The path nodes will be used to guide the bad guys' movements around the board. At any given time, the bad-guy character will be set to track to a single node and move in the direction of that node. When the bad guy runs into a node, it will then switch to tracking toward the next node in the path. When the bad guy hits the last node, it will track back to the first node, completing a cycle around the course.

You need to set up some physical characteristics. Specifically, the path nodes should be set as Ghost actors, as shown in Figure 10.19. This will enable them to be passed through by other objects, but also ensure that their collision boundaries are calculated when necessary.

As shown in the figure, the path node uses two properties. You can add these by clicking Add Property. Set the property type by using the drop-down menu for the property. Fill in the name and start value of the property in the appropriate fields. The D button to the right of each property will toggle, displaying on and off. If the D button is pressed, the property's value will be displayed in-game if the Show Debug Properties option is chosen from the Game menu on the User Preferences header.

FIGURE 10.18
A bad guy and
four path nodes

FIGURE 10.19
Physics and
properties for
path nodes

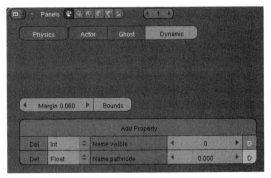

The top property shown is named visible. It is an integer; therefore, Int is selected from the property type drop-down menu. Its start value is 0. This property will be used to toggle the visibility of the path nodes in-game, in case this is necessary for troubleshooting. The second property is called pathnode. This property is used only to identify that the object is a path node. The property's value will never be checked, only whether the object has this property. For this reason, it is okay to leave the type as the default float type, and the default value of 0.000.

The logic to toggle the visibility of the path nodes is shown in Figure 10.20. The first sensor is a Keyboard sensor that responds to the I key. When the I key is pressed, it triggers a Property actuator. Property actuators come in three flavors: Assign, Add, and Copy. Assign is used to assign an arbitrary value to a property, Add is used to increment or decrement a property value, and Copy is used to copy a value from another property to a target property. In this case, you'll use the Add option with a value of +1. This means that when the I key is pressed, the value of visible will be incremented by one.

FIGURE 10.20
Visibility toggle

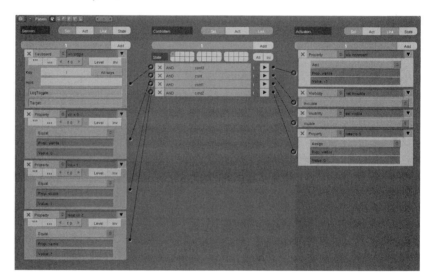

The remaining sensors are all Property sensors, meaning that they trigger events whenever the relevant property has a specific value. The first one represents the case when the visible value is 0. It connects to a Visibility actuator set to Invisible. So by default, the path nodes will be invisible, because the start value of visible is 0. The next sensor down represents the case in which the value of visible is 1. This triggers a Visibility actuator set to Visible. Finally, the Property sensor for the case when the value is 2 triggers another Property actuator, this time an Assign actuator, which assigns a 0 value to the property, thus resetting the toggle.

After you've set up the logic on the first path node, copy the object three times and place it around the maze as shown in the figure. Name the objects **1**, **2**, **3**, and **4** so that they are positioned in numerical order.

BAD-GUY LOGIC BLOCKS

To keep things reasonably uncluttered, I'll describe the bad-guy logic in several steps. The first thing to do is to set up the necessary physics and properties as shown in Figure 10.21. Like the main character, the bad guy will be a dynamic actor, but without rigid body physics. It will have two integer properties. The targ integer property represents the target node that the bad guy is presently moving toward. The inc property will eventually be used to determine whether the bad guy is traversing the path nodes in incrementing order or in decrementing order, thus moving clockwise or counterclockwise around the path. The wizard property will enable other game objects, particularly the main character, to identify the object as a bad-guy wizard. Finally, the bump property will be used to determine when a collision should make the bad guy reverse its direction.

FIGURE 10.21
Bad-guy
wizard physics
and properties

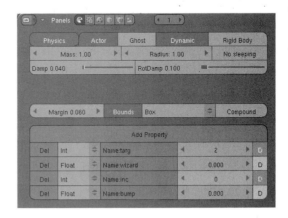

The basic move logic for the bad guy in the forward (incrementing) direction is shown in Figures 10.22, 10.23, 10.24, and 10.25. These four figures all show the same logic, but with different blocks open for viewing. In Figure 10.22, you can see the Always sensor, which is connected to the Motion actuator. This ensures that the bad-guy wizards continue moving forward at all times. In Figure 10.23, the sensor is activated if the targ property's value is 1, and triggers an Edit Object actuator with the Track To option selected. The target object in the OB field is 1. This means that while the value of targ is 1, the bad guy will continue to aim (and move) in the direction of the object called 1. Analogous logic blocks must be added, as shown, to correspond with cases when the targ value is equal to 2, 3, and 4.

Figure 10.24 shows the means by which the targ value itself is incremented. A Ray sensor is used to determine whether the BadGuy object has struck a node. If so, a Property actuator of type Add increments the targ value by one (+1). When the targ value reaches 5, a Property logic block of the Assign type is used to assign the value of 1 to the targ property, resetting it.

FIGURE 10.22
Bad-guy
motion logic

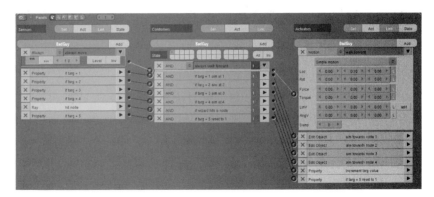

FIGURE 10.23
Bad-guy
tracking logic

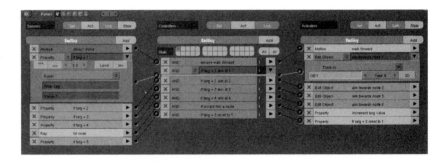

FIGURE 10.24
Bad-guy incre-
menting logic

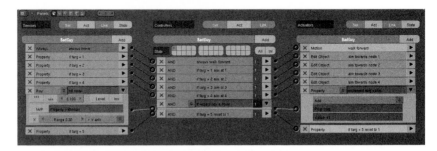

FIGURE 10.25
Bad-guy node-
reset logic

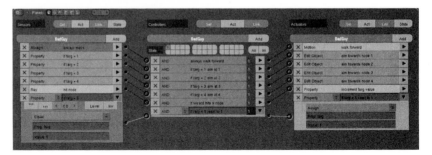

The final bad-guy logic will toggle the clockwise/counterclockwise direction of the bad guys by incrementing the inc value. This will happen whenever the bad guy runs into an object with a bump property (this of course includes other bad-guy objects). Because they are dynamic objects, the bad guys could bump against each other and be thrown off course, or could be pushed into a position where they cannot reach the next path node. In this case, it is desirable to add a random switch so that from time to time they change directions arbitrarily. In this way, they are much more likely to free themselves if they become jammed somewhere, and it also leads to less-predictable patterns of movement.

To do this, you add logic to the Empty object as shown in Figure 10.26. This logic has a Random sensor timed to emit once every 100 frames on average. It triggers a Message actuator with the subject line switch. In turn, the sensor shown in Figure 10.27 will fire when this message is emitted. In the final bad-guy motion logic, this random message triggers an increment or decrement in the targ value, depending on whether the bad guy is already moving in an incrementing or decrementing direction.

FIGURE 10.26
Random switch
message on the
Empty object

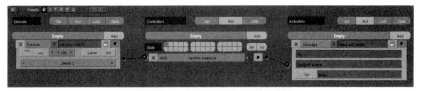

FIGURE 10.27
Bad-guy
Message sensor

The full bad-guy motion logic is shown in Figure 10.28. It is very much like the logic explained previously, except that logic is added for the cases in which the bad guys are traveling in the reverse (decrementing) direction around the path. There are too many logic blocks here to show them all unfolded, and furthermore, as you can see, the logic blocks here are already pushing the limits of what logical connections can be easily understood at a glance. I recommend that you take a close look at the file game.blend on the CD that accompanies this book if you need further insight into how this logic works.

Note that if you watch the bad guys in action from the top view, the weaknesses of the very rudimentary path-finding algorithm used here quickly become apparent. The bad guys occasionally get stuck, and their movement becomes predictable. Nevertheless, the basic techniques described in this section will enable you to implement much more robust and sophisticated path-finding algorithms of your own.

FIGURE 10.28
Full bad-guy
motion logic

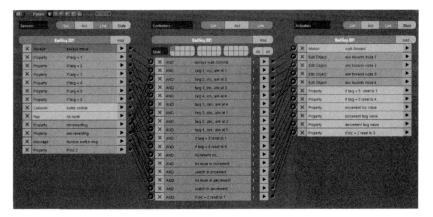

Collecting Treasure and Racking Up Points

If you open the game.blend file on the CD that accompanies this book, you'll see the final game setup along the lines of Figure 10.29. (The color insert in this book shows these figures in color.) I've placed three BadGuy objects on the path, one of them going the opposite direction from the other two (that is to say, one of them has an initial inc property value of 1, whereas the others have a value of 0). You'll also see eight yellow cones and three green balls.

The object of the game is to collect the cones without hitting a wizard. When you collect all eight cones, you'll see a congratulatory message, and the game will end. If you hit a wizard, the game will end and the message won't be so congratulatory. The green balls make you bounce up and down, enabling you to get a view of the layout of the maze and the locations of the cones, and also protect you from the wizards. Of course, the effect of the green balls is temporary.

FIGURE 10.29
The final
game setup

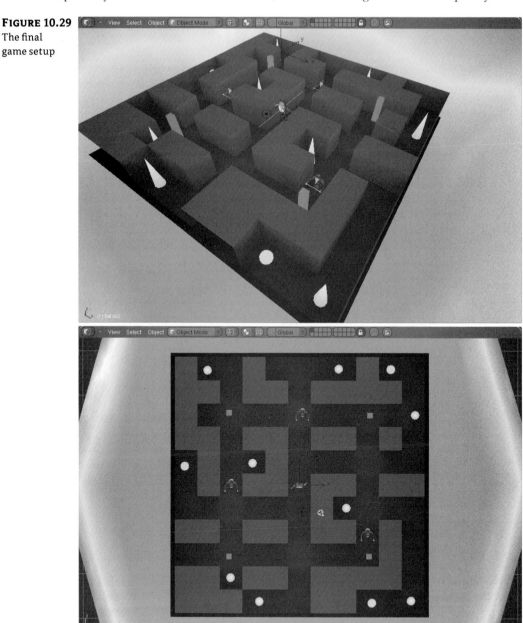

To set up these game-play features, you need to add logic to the cones and balls, and add a bit more logic to the Empty object. The temporary protection you get from picking up the green balls will require the use of states in the character logic.

USING CONE, BALL, AND EMPTY LOGIC

The logic associated with the Cone object is simple, as you can see in Figure 10.30. A Near sensor is used, with a distance of 0.25 to determine when the character is close enough to touch the cone. The character is recognized by the char property. When the conditions on the sensor are met, two actuators are activated. The first is an Edit Object actuator set to End Object, which removes the Cone object from the scene. The second actuator is a Message actuator, which broadcasts a message with cone_touch as its subject. This message will be received by the Empty object, and will result in incrementing the point counter on the Empty object, as shown in Figure 10.31.

FIGURE 10.30
Cone logic

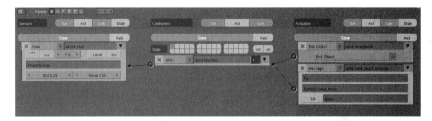

FIGURE 10.31
Empty logic

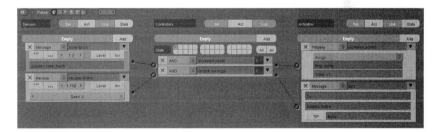

The logic on the ball is almost the same as the logic on the cone, as you can see in Figure 10.32. The only difference is the subject of the message that gets sent. In this case, the subject is ball_touch. This will be received by the armature, and will initiate the special protected state as described in the next section.

FIGURE 10.32
Ball logic

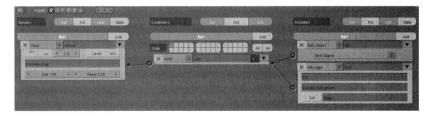

USING STATES

You've already seen the States panel in the Controllers column of the logic buttons, but so far you haven't made any use of it. *States* determine which controllers are active at any given time. Each controller and its connected sensors and actuators are associated with one state. Any combination of the 30 possible states can be active at any given time. States can be activated or deactivated by using a State actuator.

In Figure 10.33, you can see the States panel. Each of the 30 light-gray squares represents a state. Darkened states such as the upper-left state in the figure are selected, meaning that their logic is currently visible. States can be selected or deselected analogously to layers in the 3D window, using Shift+LMB to select multiple states. States with a dot in them are states that have associated logic blocks. In the figure, the leftmost three states in the upper row all have logic blocks associated with them. The black dots represent states that are part of the initial state mask. That is, these are the states that will be active when the game begins. You can select the current initial states by clicking the Ini button to the right of the states, and you can select all states by clicking the All button. On the left, the State button is actually a drop-down menu. You can set the currently selected mask to be the default state mask by selecting Store Init State.

FIGURE 10.33
The States panel

To get the temporary protection effect from the green balls, three states will be used. The first state will contain the main logic described previously for the character. It will also contain the logic for what to do when a green ball is touched. The first state will be active at initialization. When the green ball is touched, the second state is deactivated (subtracted) and the third state is activated (added), as shown in Figure 10.34.

FIGURE 10.34
Character logic for state 1

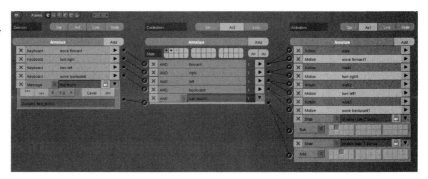

The second state, shown in Figure 10.35, will contain the logic for ending the game when the character hits a wizard. This state will also be active on initialization, because this is the default behavior. When this state is deactivated, the character can collide with the wizards without ending the game.

The third state will contain an Always sensor connected to a Motion actuator that makes the character bounce up and down for as long as the state is active. It also contains a Delay sensor set to 1,000 frames that will connect to two State actuators: one that reactivates the second state and one that deactivates its own state, state 3. The state 3 logic is shown in Figure 10.36.

By selecting all three states, you can view all the logic for all three states. This can also be done by deselecting the State visualization filter at the top of each logic block column. With all the states visible, the logic for the character looks like what's shown in Figure 10.37.

FIGURE 10.35
Character logic for state 2

FIGURE 10.36
Character logic for state 3

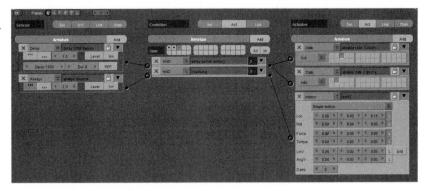

FIGURE 10.37
Complete character logic

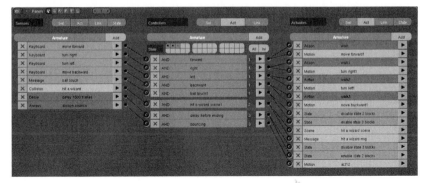

Creating Special Effects with Textures

There are several useful techniques for creating special effects with textures that are not at all obvious to a casual user of Blender. This section describes two of the main ones: the use of textures to create dynamic text, and animated textures.

Creating Dynamic Text

You can use 3D text in the Blender game engine, but you have to convert it to a mesh in advance with Alt+C in Object mode. If you do this, be sure that the normals are pointing in the correct direction. Otherwise, your text, like any mesh face, will not be visible in the game engine by default. This may be a reasonable way to add text to your game. However, if you need your text to be dynamic, that is, if you want to be able to assign string values to the text on the fly as the game is played, mesh text will not work. For this, you need to use a texture.

To use texture-based text, you must have the font you want to use in a correctly formatted image texture. You can use the file `arialbd.tga` from the CD that accompanies this book. Alternately, you can use any TrueType font to create your own texture file via the FTBlender application that can also be found on the CD.

Preparing the Font

Preparing the font is simple when using FTBlender on Windows. Simply unzip the file `FTBlender.zip` from the CD. The directory you create will contain a file called `ftblender.exe` and another file called `ftpblender.blend`. Place the TrueType font file in the same directory as these two files, as shown in Figure 10.38. Open the `ftpblender.blend`. file by double-clicking, and execute the Python script in that file with Alt+P. The `ftblender.exe` program will automatically be called and will create the appropriate layout for the font image file. Press F2 to save the image file as a Targa file, as shown in Figure 10.39.

FIGURE 10.38
A directory with a TrueType font and FTBlender

FIGURE 10.39
The rasterized font Targa file

USING A TEXTURED FACE FOR DYNAMIC TEXT

To use a textured face for dynamic text, follow these steps:

1. Add a plane to your scene. This works best if you go into Camera view with the 0 key on the number pad, and add the object with the Add New Objects: Aligned To View option selected in the Edit Methods section of the User Preferences area. You should wind up with something along the lines of what you see in Figure 10.40. Don't scale the object.

FIGURE 10.40
Adding a plane to the Text scene

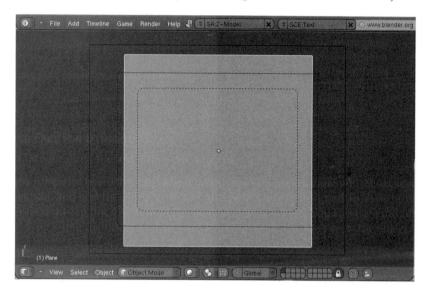

2. Split your work area window and open a UV/Image Editor window. In the 3D viewport, tab into Edit mode on the plane. In the UV/Image editor, select Open from the Image menu and open the font Targa file you want to use. Select Textured view in the 3D viewport (you can do this by pressing Alt+Z). You should see something like what is shown in Figure 10.41, with the image mapped onto the plane.

FIGURE 10.41
Texturing the plane with the font file

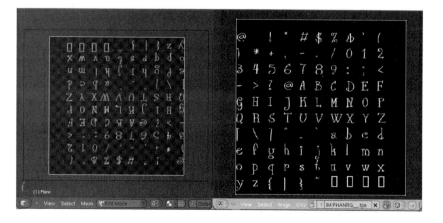

3. In Edit mode, scale the plane so that the @ symbol shows on the plane. Make the fit as snug as possible on all sides of the symbol, and rotate the mapping if necessary to make the symbol appear right side up, as shown in Figure 10.42. It is important that you do this in Edit mode, and that you have not altered the shape of the plane in Object mode.

FIGURE 10.42
Mapping the plane
to the @ symbol

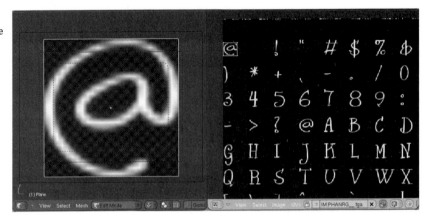

4. Make sure that the plane's face is active by entering Face Select mode and right-clicking the face. A face can be selected without being active, and it must be active for this step, so double-check. An active face is indicated by a grid of small, white dots. When the face is active, you will be able to access the Texture Face buttons in the Edit buttons area. The values in the Texture Face buttons should be set as shown in Figure 10.43. In particular, Text and Alpha should be selected.

FIGURE 10.43
Texture Face
settings

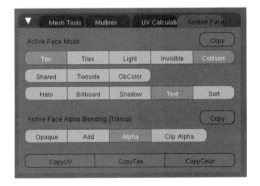

5. In Object mode, enter the Logic buttons and add a property to the Plane object. Name the property **Text** and select String as the property type. In the value field, enter the string you want as the text in your game. In the example in Figure 10.44, the string is MyText. In the 3D viewport, this is displayed as shown in Figure 10.45. Don't worry about the superfluous @ symbol on the plane—this will disappear in the game environment.

FIGURE 10.44
The Text property

FIGURE 10.45
Resulting
dynamic text

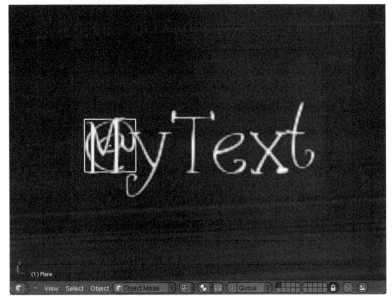

Creating Animated Textures

The wizard bad guys in the game have a particular quality, as you can see by looking at Figure 10.46 or by running the game from the CD included with this book. Between their hands is an animated arc of electricity. This is accomplished by using an animated texture on a single face.

You've already seen how to create UV-mapped textures for the game engine and other purposes. It is important to realize that the same model can have more than one UV map associated with different portions of its mesh. When you do UV unwrapping with the E key in the UV/Image editor, only selected faces are unwrapped and included in the mapping. In Figure 10.47, the bad-guy body mesh is selected in Edit mode. The entire mesh except for the polygon face between the wizard's hands is selected. The resulting UV unwrapping, along with its texture, is shown in Figure 10.48.

FIGURE 10.46
Electric Wizard
bad guy

FIGURE 10.47
Body mesh
selected

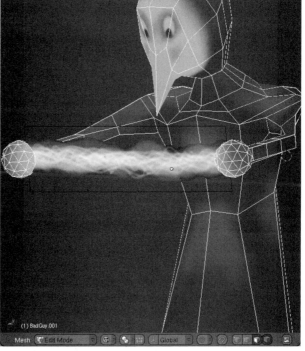

FIGURE 10.48
Body UV map

An animated texture in the Blender game engine works by encoding several individual frames of animation in the same image. In the current example, the frames are positioned side by side in the texture-mapped image. The final animated texture consists of 10 frames. A single frame of the "electricity" animation is shown in Figure 10.49. Nine other similar images were created in GIMP and saved as PNG files with alpha values (the checkerboard background represents transparency). The images are each 420 pixels wide.

To animate these in the game engine, you need to create a new image file in which all 10 of the frame images are positioned side by side. They must be positioned exactly, down to a single pixel width, and so the final animated texture file will be 4200 pixels wide. In Figure 10.50, the model is shown with the single face selected and active. In the UV/Image editor, a new image is added with the animated texture file, as shown in Figure 10.51. Note that only the first "frame" of the animation, that is to say the leftmost 420 pixels worth of the image, is mapped directly to the plane. You can position the vertices in the UV/Image editor directly by selecting Image Properties from the View menu, selecting a single vertex, and inputting its X and Y coordinates directly. The leftmost vertices should be at X coordinate 0, and the rightmost vertices should be at X coordinate 420.

FIGURE 10.49
Original electricity image

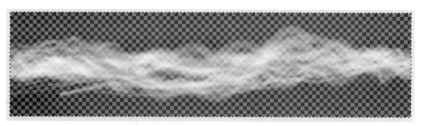

FIGURE 10.50
Electricity face selected and active

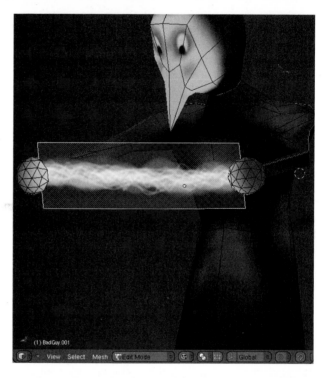

FIGURE 10.51
Electricity UV map

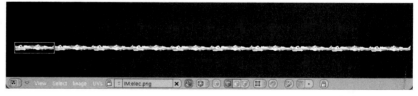

Finally, open the Real-Time Properties dialog box, also found under the View menu. Set the real-time properties as shown in Figure 10.52. Both Anim and Tiles should be selected. Anim Start and End values should be 1 and 10, respectively, because the animation is 10 frames long. Enter **12** as the speed (12 frames per second is sufficiently fast for this kind of animation). Tiles should have an X value of 10, indicating that the image is repeated 10 times horizontally. Finally, set the Texture Face values as shown in Figure 10.53. Select Tiles, Alpha, and Twoside to ensure that the texture is visible from both the front and the back of the face.

After you have all this set up, your animated texture will come to life when you press P to start the game engine.

Real World Scenario

BORO-TORO: AN AWARD-WINNING, WII-CONTROLLED, PHYSICAL-PUZZLE GAME IN BGE

One of the 2008 winners of Dare to Be Digital (the United Kingdom's premier student game-design competition), was Boro-Toro—a beautifully designed and original horizontal-scrolling puzzle game that uses Blender's built-in Bullet physics with an optional Wii controller to provide terrific game-play effect. The game was created by DarkMatter Designs, a team composed of students from Wolverhampton University. Each member of the team was responsible for specific areas of the design and production of the game to complete the complex, multilevel game within the competition's 10-week timeframe. The team consisted of Adam Westwood (project lead/designer/texture & UI artist), Graham Ranson (programmer), Matthew Booton (programmer/composer), Owen Schwehr (artist/animator), and Yves Wheeler (programmer)—none of whom had had any experience working with Blender when the project began. They kept a video blog of their progress, which can be viewed on YouTube at the following URL:

    www.youtube.com/darkmatterdesigns

A report on the project, including a video trailer and a link to the game itself can be found here:

    www.blendernation.com/2008/09/17/boro-toro-blender-game-a-winner-in-british-
    dare-to-be-digital-contest/

As one of the three top winners of the competition, Boro-Toro is now up for a British Academy of Film and Television Arts (BAFTA) award for video game design, to be announced in March 2009.

FIGURE 10.52
Real-time
properties

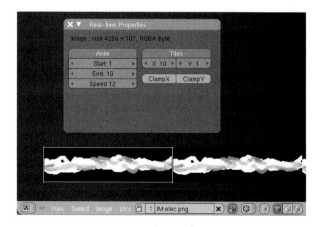

FIGURE 10.53
Texture Face
settings

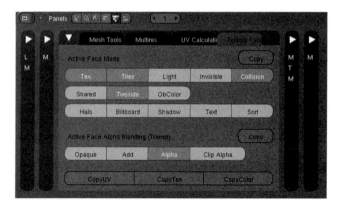

Working with Sound in the BGE

No game-creation tool would be complete without some way to incorporate interactive sound effects. Blender offers powerful options for working with sound. In this section, you will learn the basics of how to add a 3D sound effect.

To set up a simple 3D sound effect, follow these steps:

1. Fire up a new Blender session, leaving the default cube in place. Before you can work with sounds in the BGE, you must open the sound files in Blender. Do this by splitting the main workspace and opening an Audio window from the Window Type drop-down menu, as shown in Figure 10.54.

FIGURE 10.54
Opening an
Audio window

2. From the Audio window header drop-down menu, select Open New. Use the file browser to find the file bubbles.wav on your hard disk. You can find this file on the CD that accompanies this book. After you open the file, it will appear in the Audio window, as shown in Figure 10.55.

4. Select the Cube object in the 3D space and add the necessary logic to play the sound. The logic consists of an Always sensor, an And controller, and a Sound actuator, with the name of the sound from the Audio window entered in the SO field. Set the playback mode to Loop Ping Pong in the drop-down menu, as shown in Figure 10.56. This will

play the sound repeatedly, but every other individual playback will be reversed, creating a seamless, continuous sound. Press P to enter the game-play mode, and you should hear the sound of bubbles rising.

FIGURE 10.55
A .wav file in the Audio window

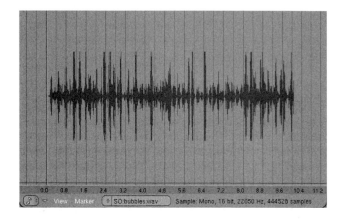

5. To demonstrate the effect of 3D sound, add some simple motion logic to control the movement of the cube. Set up Keyboard sensors for the up, right, left, and down arrows, and connect them with Motion actuators moving the cube positively and negatively along the X and Y axes, as shown in Figure 10.57. This will enable you to "drive" the cube around in a rudimentary way.

6. Finally, go to the Sound panel in the Render buttons context, as shown in Figure 10.58. (This can also be done by pressing F10 four times.) You will see the sound block information for the .wav file you just added. Click the 3D button to make the sound a 3D sound.

FIGURE 10.56
Logic for the sound loop

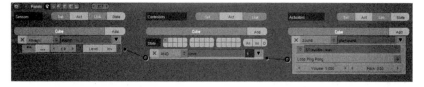

FIGURE 10.57
Motion logic for the cube

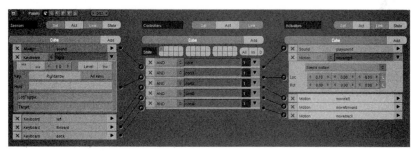

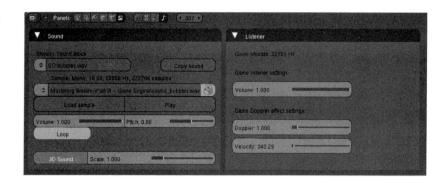

You're all finished setting up the 3D sound. When you run the BGE now, you will find that the sound's volume is dependent on the proximity of the Cube object to the camera. Be sure that you are in the Camera view (press 0 on the number pad) when you enter the game-play mode.

You now know the basics of working with sound. Experimenting with the options available on the Sound actuator will deepen your knowledge. In Chapter 11, you will learn about accessing sound via the Python GameLogic API.

The Bottom Line

Control characters and scenes by using logic blocks.   Interactive control in the Blender game engine is made possible by using the powerful logic block system. With this system, you can use sensors, controllers, and actuators to trigger game events on a variety of types of input.

>   **Master It**   In the chapter, you saw how to make the character walk forward and turn right. Set up a similar character that can turn left and walk backward as well.

Use properties, messages, and states to create complex interactions.   Like a full-powered programming language, the BGE logic block system enables you to store and modify values in the form of properties, to set up communications between different logic blocks using messages, and to control which logic blocks are active at what times by using states. In this way, complex interactions are made possible, limited only by the graphical nature of the logic blocks.

>   **Master It**   Set up logic so that the wizards change directions whenever they hit the character, as well as when they hit each other.

Work with textures to create dynamic text and in-game 2D animations.   Textures in the BGE can be used for a variety of interesting effects. Dynamic text whose content can be updated by logic blocks and in-game animations can be created by using specifically mapped textures with certain parameter settings.

>   **Master It**   Use the method described in this chapter to create a 2D walk cycle animation. Use orthogonal renders of the character walk cycle you created in Chapter 9, and then put those renders together in a single image, using a 2D image-editing program such as Photoshop or GIMP. Map the image onto a plane in the game engine to create a walking 2D cutout character.

Incorporate sound effects into your game environment. Sounds can be controlled by Sound Actuators similarly to other effects in the BGE. Special features exist to automatically control the sound on the basis of its distance from the camera.

Master It Browse the free sound files website www.freesounds.org and find some other interesting sound effects. Follow the steps in this chapter to add a new 3D sound to a moving object in the 3D space.

Chapter 11

Python Power in the Blender Game Engine

As you saw in Chapter 10, "Making Things Happen in the Game Engine," the Blender Game Engine (BGE) is a powerful tool for 3D interactive content creation and visualization. The logic block system enables artists to quickly set up interactive logic without the need for programming knowledge. Nevertheless, the logic block system has its limitations. When the logic becomes moderately complex, the stacks of connected blocks can become difficult to read and debug. External data cannot be accessed by logic blocks, and many commands do not have logic block equivalents. Fortunately, Python can also be incorporated into your game engine creations, greatly expanding the possibilities of what you can do.

In this chapter, you will learn to

◆ Replace multiple logic block setups with a few lines of Python code

◆ Use Python to create effects in the BGE that would not be possible using logic blocks alone

◆ Create unique game environments with sound effects and multiple viewports

From Logic Blocks to Python

Blender's logic blocks are a great way to define game logic in many cases. Among the advantages of working with logic blocks are that they are highly accessible for nonprogrammers, they contain numerous built-in functions that make logic blocks fast to work with even for programmers, and they are an entirely self-contained system in the BGE. However, many cases require a more powerful approach to creating game logic. Already you have seen that when the logic becomes moderately complex, logic blocks quickly become unwieldy and difficult to read. There are many functions that do not exist in logic blocks and need to be written specially. Finally, the self-contained nature of logic blocks also represents a limitation. If you want to work with certain kinds of external resources in your game, you have to turn to Python.

The BGE's Python interpreter enables you to create game logic by programming directly in Python. Although a simple way to think of Python scripting in the BGE is as a replacement for logic blocks, it is more true to say that it is an enhancement of the logic block system. You still must use logic blocks, but with Python you can use far fewer of them and stretch their functionality much further.

Controlling a Character with Python

A Python script in the BGE plays the role of the controller from the standpoint of logic blocks. However, rather than simple Boolean logical operations such as AND, OR, and XOR, a script controller can take an arbitrary number of sensor inputs and arrive at the appropriate actuators to trigger based on instructions in the Python code. For this reason, all of the sensors that must be accessed by the script connect to the same controller, and likewise with actuators.

In an example in Chapter 10, four sensors were used to control a character's movement: a Keyboard sensor for each of the four arrow keys, up, down, right, and left. The rigged character on its own can be found in the file `character.blend` on the CD that accompanies this book. You can follow along with this section using that file. The result, with logic blocks and script, is in the file `character_python.blend`.

To duplicate the controls from Chapter 10 by using a Python script, the same four sensors are needed. Some actuators are also needed. Previously, you had separate Motion actuators for each motion: moving forward, turning right, turning left, and moving backward. With a Python script, you can set the specific values of an actuator within the script, so you won't need four separate Motion actuators. Nevertheless, you will need one Motion actuator, which will be used to handle all four cases. You will also need an Action actuator for the Walk action, although, again, the specific values for the actuator can be set within the script.

The resulting logic block setup is shown in Figure 11.1. As you can see in the left column, the situation with sensors is more or less identical to how it would be in a pure logic blocks setup. Only the first sensor is shown unfolded, so you can see that Uparrow is selected in the Key field. The other three sensors likewise have the appropriate key selected in the Key field. In the rightmost column of actuators, you see a Motion actuator and an Action actuator. However, you'll notice that neither of these operators has any settings changed from the default, aside from their names.

FIGURE 11.1
The goal

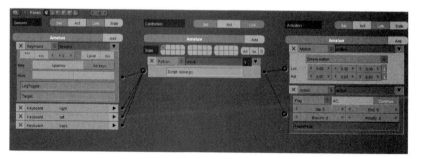

NAMING YOUR LOGIC BLOCKS

It is worth noticing that both the sensors and actuators have descriptive names. These names, as usual, are arbitrary, and the only thing that really matters is that each name be unique (this is enforced by Blender regardless). However, these names are how the Python script will access the logic blocks, so it is important to give them meaningful names that will make your code readable later.

The center column is where things are most different from the pure logic block approach. Rather than a long stack of controllers, there is only one controller, with Python selected from the Controller Type drop-down menu and the name of the corresponding script, in this case `move.py`. If you try to enter the name of this script now, however, you will find that Blender will unceremoniously delete your entry from the field. You must enter the name of an existing text file in the text editor. So open a text editor window and select Add New from the header menu. Name the new text **move.py**. Now go back and enter this name in the Script field on the Python controller.

After these preliminary steps have been completed and the necessary sensors and actuators have been plugged into the script controller, it is time to turn to the code itself.

THE GAMELOGIC MODULE

The module that distinguishes Blender's in-game Python functionality is the GameLogic module. When a Python script is executed from within the BGE, GameLogic is automatically imported. Most of the game-engine-specific functionality you will need to use will be accessed via methods defined in this module. The GameLogic module is distinct from the main Python Blender API. The GameLogic module's own API can be found here:

```
www.blender.org/documentation/248PythonDoc/GE/
```

It is also convenient to take advantage of the OOP paradigm and rely on Python's built in dir() command to find out what functions are available for each object, as this section describes.

"CATCHY" CLASS NAMES

As you browse the BGE Python API, you'll no doubt notice that the classes' names are all prefixed by the letters *KX* and an underscore. This is a remnant of the history of the BGE. When it was first implemented, it was given a catchy name—literally. The name given to the game engine at that time by its original creator, Erwin Coumans, was Ketsji, pronounced *catchy*. Erwin used the *KX* in the class names as a way to indicate that the classes belonged to the Ketsji game engine. The name Ketsji has since fallen out of use, but the KX prefix remains on the class names.

To set up the character controls, the first thing to do in the controller script is to abbreviate the GameLogic module name by assigning it to a shorthand variable called GL. This is not so important in simple cases like this one, but it's good practice for longer, more-complicated scripts, because GameLogic gets called a lot. So the script begins with this line:

```
GL = GameLogic
```

The next step is to access the logic block that the script is being called from and assign it to a variable. This is done with the getCurrentController() method. This line is always required in BGE scripts that use sensors or actuators. The logic block returned by this method is passed to the variable cont in the line shown here:

```
cont = GL.getCurrentController()
```

Every code block has an owner, which is the object to which it is associated. The object that is active when you create a new code block will be that block's owner. In this case, because the armature is the object that is affected by the logic, the code blocks must be associated with the armature, as you saw previously in Figure 11.1. So, how do you return the owner of a controller in the Python code? There are two ways to find the answer to the question. One is to look it up in the API. Another way is with the dir() command mentioned previously. To do this, temporarily add the following line to your script:

```
print dir(cont)
```

You now have a three-line script called move.py associated with a Python controller, which is in turn connected to the Keyboard sensors and actuators shown previously in Figure 11.1. Place your Blender window in such a way that the terminal is visible, and enter game-play mode by pressing P. In game-play mode, press one of the four arrow keys, up, down, right, or left. When you do so, you will trigger the script to run, and the controller's dir() value will be printed to the terminal as follows (without the line breaks):

```
['getActuator', 'getActuators', 'getExecutePriority',
 'getName', 'getOwner', 'getScript', 'getSensor',
'getSensors', 'getState', 'isA', 'setExecutePriority',
 'setScript']
```

This is a list of all the methods defined for controller objects. As you can see, just reading this list will give you a few ideas of what kinds of things you can request from controllers. Because you're interested in accessing the Armature object that is the owner of the controller in this example, it is intuitively clear that the getOwner() method is the one you want. The line of code to retrieve the owner is as follows:

```
own = cont.getOwner()
```

SENSORS AND ACTUATORS

You now have access to the controller and to the object that owns it. The next thing to do is to retrieve the necessary sensors. Again, the output from the dir() command will tell you how to do this. You can either output all the sensors as a list with getSensors() or you can output specific individual sensors by name with getSensor(). In this case, do the latter in order to keep the sensors distinct and assign them to meaningfully named variables, as shown in the following code:

```
#Sensors
forward = cont.getSensor("forward")
right = cont.getSensor("right")
left = cont.getSensor("left")
back = cont.getSensor("back")
```

The retrieval of the actuators works in exactly the same way:

```
#Actuators
motion = cont.getActuator("motion")
action = cont.getActuator("action")
```

GAME LOGIC IN PYTHON

Now all the necessary logic block components are accessible within the script, and the code for the movement itself can begin. Start by setting some variable values. Set values for the variables speed and rspeed with the values you want to use for forward-walking speed and rotation speed for when the character turns. The default values for walk and turn are set to 0, because the character should not be moving when the script is first executed:

```
speed = .07
rspeed = 0.02
walk = 0
turn = 0
```

As you saw, the Motion and Action actuators in the logic blocks did not have any of their fields filled in. These values can be provided in the script itself, and this is the point where that is done for the Action actuator. Review the discussion of the Action actuator in Chapter 10 if you need a reminder of what the individual fields mean, and print the output of dir(action) to find out what other methods are available for accessing an Action actuator.

The Action actuator should use the Walk action created in Chapter 9, "Creating Assets for the Blender Game Engine." The start frame should be 1, and the end frame of the action loop should be 20. Finally, the Loop Stop play mode should be selected, which is done using the setType() method. The play modes are represented by integers: 0 represents the Play play mode, 1 represents the Property play mode, 2 represents the Flipper play mode, 3 represents the Loop Stop play mode, and 4 represents the Loop End play mode.

The code for setting these various Action actuator parameters is as follows:

```
action.setAction("Walk")
action.setStart(1)
action.setEnd(20)
action.setType(3)
```

The actual "logic" part of the code is simple. Once again, use the dir() command to print out a list of methods appropriate for sensors. The isPositive() method is used to return whether the sensor is currently being activated. For example, in this code, forward.isPositive() will return a True value if the up arrow is being pressed. The variables defined previously are used here to assign the appropriate values to walk and turn, according to the input from the sensors.

```
if forward.isPositive():
    walk = speed
if back.isPositive():
    walk = -speed
if left.isPositive():
    turn = rspeed
if right.isPositive():
    turn = -rspeed
```

Another if conditional is needed to set the Action activator as active when the character is moving and inactive if the character is not moving. The GameLogic method addActiveActuator(*name*,*active*) is important when working with actuators in Python. Anytime an actuator's parameters are changed, this method must be called in order for the new parameters to be realized in the game. When the second argument is 0, the actuator is rendered inactive. So in order to have the character walk when the movement sensors are positive, the following conditional is used (note that the backslash is used to break the line for formatting purposes for this book. You can leave the backslash out and put the entire conditional on one line):

```
if forward.isPositive() or back.isPositive()\
or left.isPositive() or right.isPositive():
    GL.addActiveActuator(action,1)
else:
    GL.addActiveActuator(action,0)
```

The addActiveActuator() method needs to be called again to activate the Motion activator with the correct parameters for making the character move. Once again, dir() will tell you what the possible methods are that can be called on a Motion actuator. In this case, you use setDLoc() and setDRot() to set the location and rotation speed. The order of the arguments represents the order of the fields on the Motion actuator logic block, and the final 1 argument makes the coordinates local, just like the button on the logic block (a 0 value here would make the coordinates global). The code for setting these parameters and adding the active animator is as follows:

```
motion.setDLoc(0,0,walk,1)
motion.setDRot(0,turn,0,1)
GL.addActiveActuator(motion,1)
```

And with that, the movement controls for the character are finished. Run your game by pressing P and test it out. Watch the console for errors or warnings from Python.

Python Power for the BGE

Now that you know the basics of how to control a character with Python, you should be on track to understanding how to mimic much of the core functionality of logic blocks with Python. The API and the dir() command will be your friends as you explore this further. This section describes various ways you can use Python to get effects that are difficult or impossible to achieve with only logic blocks.

Creating a Teleportation Machine with Python

Using Python, it is simple to place an object anywhere in the 3D space. The next example shows you how to teleport objects from one place to another when a sensor is triggered. The setup here is as shown in Figure 11.2, and you can find the .blend files on the CD that accompanies this book. The completed file is called portals.blend, and the starting file with no logic, physics, or script attached is called portals_nologic.blend.

OBJECTS AND LOGIC BLOCKS

In the scene, there are five Torus primitive objects and one Icosphere object. They are placed on the Y origin plane at Z,X coordinates (beginning with the sphere) [-10,10], [-10,0], [0,10], [0,0], [10,10], and [10,0]. The Sphere is directly above a ring, and the other two pairs of rings are aligned vertically. The objects' names are Sphere, Torus1, Torus2, Torus3, Torus4, and Torus5, and they are arranged as shown in Figure 11.3.

FIGURE 11.2
Rings and a ball for "teleportation"

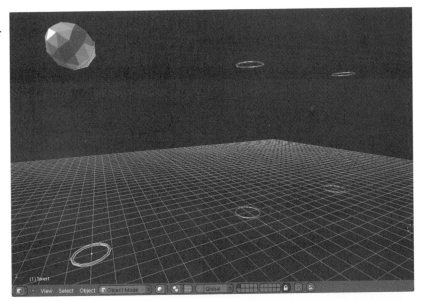

FIGURE 11.3
The position and object names of the rings

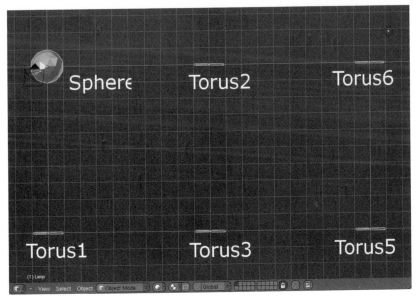

The effect that will be created in this example will have the sphere fall as a rigid body, affected by gravity, and when it "passes through" the ring below it, it will be "teleported" to the top ring in the column to the right. It will fall to the ring below that one and again be teleported to the top ring in the next column. It will be caught in the last ring.

The first thing to do is to set the Sphere to be a rigid body object, by selecting Rigid Body in the Physics type drop-down menu in the Logic Buttons area, as shown in Figure 11.4. You can leave all the other values at their defaults.

FIGURE 11.4
Setting the
sphere to be a
Rigid Body object

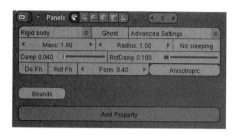

If you press the P key now, the Sphere will drop and be caught by the first ring, Torus1. This collision is what should trigger the script to handle the teleportation functionality, so the next step is to set that up.

The teleportation script will be called via a controller and sensor on the Sphere object. When the sphere senses that it has collided with a ring, it will run the script. As you saw in Chapter 10, the way for an object to be recognized by other objects is to use properties. For this reason, it is necessary to create properties for each of the rings. Add an int type property called port to each ring, as shown in Figure 11.5. Give the properties integer values that correspond with the object names. Torus1 should have a prop value of 1; Torus2 should have a prop value of 2; Torus3 should have a prop value of 3; and so on.

FIGURE 11.5
Adding a port
property to Torus1

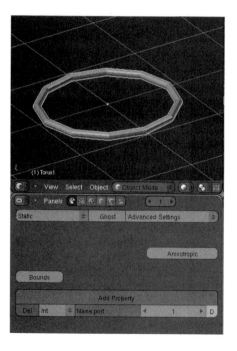

Open a text editor and add a new text called portal.py. To the Sphere object, add a Collision sensor and a Python controller as shown in Figure 11.6. The Collision sensor is called hitportal, and it is activated on collision with objects with property port. The Python controller calls the portal.py script.

FIGURE 11.6
Logic for the
sphere

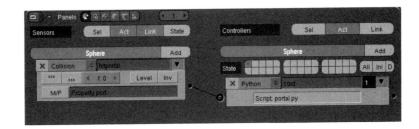

CODE FOR THE TELEPORTATION MACHINE

Now that the objects and logic blocks are in place, you can turn your attention to the code. The code begins by assigning the GameLogic module to a shorthand variable, as in the previous case. Then, the controller and owner are retrieved and assigned to variables as shown here:

```
GL = GameLogic
cont = GL.getCurrentController()
own = cont.getOwner()
```

Aside from the owner object, which is the Sphere, it is also necessary to retrieve the other objects from the scene. The *GameLogic.getCurrentScene()* method will return the current scene. The scene, in turn, uses the getObjectList() method to return a collection of objects. I use the term *collection* here because, in spite of the name of this method, the object that is returned is *not* a Python list, but rather a specifically designed class that can be accessed by name in a way analogous to a Python dictionary. This sort of arbitrariness occurs from time to time in the Python API, and it is one of the reasons why it is so helpful to use dir() often to find out exactly what methods are available for the class you're working with, and to refer to the API to find out other ways it can be accessed.

The collection returned by the getObjectList() method can be accessed by the 3D object names as keys. Note that the object names in the BGE are slightly different from the ordinary Blender 3D object names; they have the string OB appended to the beginning of the name. The following code assigns the actual 3D Torus objects to appropriately named variables:

```
torus1 = GL.getCurrentScene().getObjectList()["OBTorus1"]
torus2 = GL.getCurrentScene().getObjectList()["OBTorus2"]
torus3 = GL.getCurrentScene().getObjectList()["OBTorus3"]
torus4 = GL.getCurrentScene().getObjectList()["OBTorus4"]
```

OBJECT NAMES IN THE GAMELOGIC API

When you access objects with Python from within the BGE using the GameLogic module, it is necessary to append OB to the beginning of the names of 3D objects. This is due to an inconsistency in the way the BGE handles object names internally. This is unfortunately not the only inconsistency. In certain cases it is also necessary to append ME to the beginning of the names of meshes. These quirks are good to keep in mind, because they may be helpful for troubleshooting in cases when the BGE is not treating your object or mesh names as you expect.

The next lines of the code retrieve the Collision sensor from the controller, and then query the Collision sensor for the object that was hit. As always, the dir() command can be relied on to find out the name of the appropriate methods. Calling dir() on a Collision sensor object will display a list of methods that includes the method getHitObject(). This is the method to use to retrieve the object that was collided with. In the following code, the object is passed to a variable called hit:

```
col = cont.getSensor("hitportal")
hit = col.getHitObject()
```

To make sure that the property calls are well defined in the subsequent code, you add an if clause to ensure that hit has an actual value. What happens next depends on the port property value of the hit object. If the port value is 1, the object's location is set to a location just below the second upper ring. If the port value is 3, the location is set to just below the rightmost upper ring. Note that in both of these clauses, place[2] refers to the Z axis coordinate of the position dealt with. Subtracting 0.8 has the effect of placing the ball just below the upper rings.

```
if hit:
    if hit.port == 1:
        place = torus2.getPosition()
        place[2] = place[2] - 0.8
        own.setPosition(place)
    if hit.port == 3:
        place = torus4.getPosition()
        place[2] = place[2] - 0.8
        own.setPosition(place)
```

If you run the BGE now, the results might not be as you expect. With the settings described so far, the ball will not fall straight through the series of rings but rather will collide with the first ring it strikes, and the forces from that collision will affect its trajectory as it emerges from the next ring in the series. To remedy this, set the ring dynamics to Ghost in the Logic buttons area.

Creating a Login Screen

In this section, you'll walk through an implementation of a simple login screen with name and password fields. Python is necessary here to process the name and password to ensure that they match, and also to handle other functions of the login screen. In the example, the name and password data is stored in a simple dictionary within the script itself, but you could also load the data from an external database (to learn how to do this, you will need to refer to general Python documentation for accessing the database of your choice).

The starting setup for this section, without the Python code or logic, can be found on the CD that accompanies this book, in the file login_nologic.blend. The finished login screen is in the file login.blend.

OBJECTS AND LOGIC BLOCKS

To get started, I placed a number of objects in the 3D space to create a login screen as shown in Figure 11.7. The login screen is made up of three vertex-painted planes that compose the text fields themselves. Above the fields are textured planes for dynamic text exactly like the ones described in Chapter 10. Two small circles are placed over the left side of each text field, which will be used to indicate which text field is active to type into. A separate scene called Welcome was also created, as shown in Figure 11.8. This scene contains only a single dynamic text plane, as described in Chapter 10.

FIGURE 11.7
The initial setup for the login screen

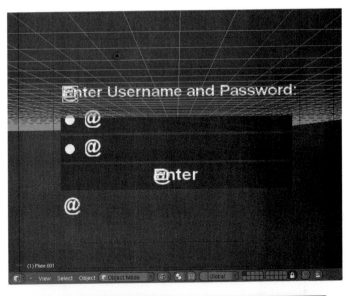

FIGURE 11.8
A separate scene for the welcome screen

The username and password dynamic text objects need to have several properties set up for them, as shown in Figure 11.9. Each needs a `text` property to contain the text itself, which in both cases should be initialized with empty values. The username object also has a property called `username`, and the password object has a property called `password`. The other dynamic text objects in the scene need only `text` properties with the desired text strings as values.

FIGURE 11.9
Properties for
name and pass-
word dynamic
text objects

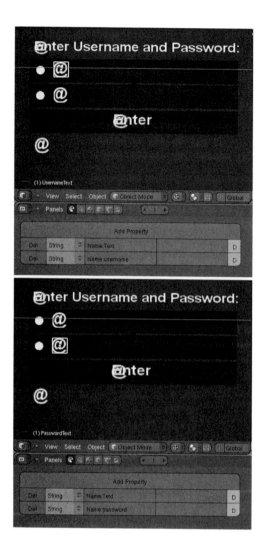

The main logic for processing the input will be attached to the camera. This is a completely arbitrary decision. It would be just as easy to associate this logic with another object in the scene, or to create a new object such as an empty specifically to associate the logic with. The camera seems as intuitive a place as any to associate this logic, so that's what I chose. Because the camera will take the logic for processing the input, it will be necessary to create some properties on the camera relating to the input, shown in Figure 11.10. Specifically, there needs to be a property called `input` of type string, which will be used to receive text strings typed in from the keyboard. The other property necessary is a Boolean property I called `keystrokelog` that will be used to tell the Keyboard sensor to interpret input as a string. It should be set to the value True.

FIGURE 11.10
Properties on
the camera

The full logic for the password-processing functionality is shown in Figure 11.11. It includes the required five sensors, a script controller that calls a script named `Control.py`, and a Scene actuator that will set the scene to the Welcome scene when the password matches the username.

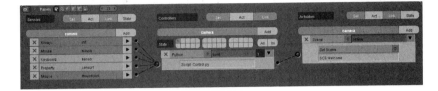

FIGURE 11.11
Logic blocks on the camera

Before moving on to the code of `Control.py`, take a closer look at those five sensors connected to the script controller. You can see all five sensors in their unfolded state in Figure 11.12. The first sensor is an Always sensor that ensures that the script runs constantly. This sensor is called `init` because one of its purposes is to ensure that the initialization code is executed immediately, but this sensor is not accessed directly in the code, so it does not really matter what its name is. The next sensor is a Mouse sensor of type Mouse Over Any, and its name is `mouse`. As you might guess, this sensor will register as positive if the mouse is moved over any object from the perspective of the camera in the game-play environment. The next sensor is a Keyboard sensor. Instead of choosing a specific key, the All keys option is selected. Furthermore, the value `keystrokelog` is entered into the LogToggle field. As you recall, the `keystrokelog` property is a Boolean type property with a value of True. Setting LogToggle to True enables keyboard input to be interpreted as a string. The Target field determines which property the string is passed to. The value `input` is entered into this field so that the string will be passed to the `input` property.

To print the input to the screen letter by letter, you need to add a sensor that fires each time a letter is entered. This is done using a Property sensor of type Changed with a Prop value of `input`. This means that the sensor will fire every time the `input` property changes, which happens every time a letter is pressed, thanks to the Keyboard sensor.

Finally, another Mouse sensor registers when the mouse is left-clicked. The name of this sensor is `mouseclick`.

ACCESSING KEYBOARD INFORMATION DIRECTLY IN PYTHON

The example here uses the sensor logic block to set the keyboard key for the Keyboard sensor. It is also possible to work with keyboard information directly in Python by using the GameKeys module. This is one of the three modules that make up the BGE API, the other two being GameLogic and Rasterizer, which is discussed later in this chapter. In the BGE API, you will find a list of the key codes for accessing individual keys with GameKeys. One possible usage of GameKeys is to set the key that a keyboard sensor takes with the setKey() method. For example, setting a Keyboard sensor called sensor to fire when the F1 key is pressed would use this line of code:

```
sensor.setKey(GameKeys.F1KEY)
```

FIGURE 11.12
A closer look at
the sensors

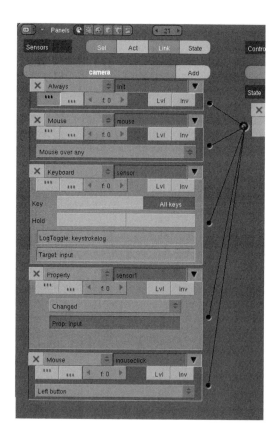

PYTHON CODE FOR A LOGIN SCREEN

As in the previous examples, the code begins by creating a shorthand for the GameLogic name. After that, the Python hassatr() function is called to assess whether GameLogic has an attribute called init. GameLogic attributes are how values can be persisted and accessed throughout a game-play session. Upon the first iteration of this script, GameLogic does not have any such attribute, so the code in the if clause will be executed. This results in several initialization steps.

First, the showMouse() method of the Rasterizer module is imported and set to 1, which causes the mouse pointer to be visible within the game-play environment. Next, the GL.password and GL.name attributes are created and given empty string values. These attributes will now persist throughout the game-play session. Finally, GL.init is created and given a value of None. This will prevent this code from being executed again, because the hassatr() function will result in a True value the next time it is called.

```
GL = GameLogic
if not hasattr(GL, "init"):
    from Rasterizer import showMouse
    showMouse(1)
    GL.password = ""
    GL.name = ""
    GL.init = None
```

ONCE-OFF EXECUTION AND PERSISTENT VARIABLES IN THE BGE

BGE Python scripts are executed when the associated sensors are activated. Scripts associated to Always sensors are executed over and over again in rapid succession. Of course, variable values do not generally persist beyond a single execution of a normal Python script, which means that when scripting for the BGE, it is necessary to have another way to ensure that values can be made to persist throughout an entire game session. The solution to this problem is also the solution to the problem of how to execute a given piece of code only once, at the start of a game-play session. The way to do this is to assign *attributes* to the GameLogic object itself. You can create arbitrarily named attributes for GameLogic and assign them values, which will be accessible by any script run at any time during a single game-play session. The syntax for this is GameLogic.attributename = value. To execute a particular section of code once only, use Python's hassattr() function to determine whether the GameLogic object has a particular attribute associated with it. If hassattr() returns 0 (False), execute the once-off code, and then define the attribute for GameLogic, so that the hassattr() function will not return 0 the next time it is called. An example of this technique is the use of the init attribute in the login screen script in this chapter.

As in the previous examples, the current controller, its owner, and its associated sensors and actuators are retrieved and sent to aptly named variables, which is done with the following code:

```
cont = GL.getCurrentController()
own = cont.getOwner()
mouse = cont.getSensor("mouse")
mouseclick = cont.getSensor("mouseclick")
scene = cont.getActuator('scene')
```

Once again, the collection of objects (not strictly a Python list) is retrieved by using getObjectList() on the current scene:

```
object_list = GL.getCurrentScene().getObjectList()
```

The next block of code is a function definition. This definition must precede calls to the function. The function to define here is validate_pass(*name*, *password*) which, as the name suggests, will return a True value if the name/password combination checks out.

The first line of the validate_pass function creates a dictionary called passwords, which has key-value pairs of usernames and passwords. For the present purposes, I've created a toy example by defining the dictionary directly. If you want to retrieve username/password pairs from a database or other external resource, you can write a function to do this. It's beyond the scope of this book to cover how to access a database from a Python script, but such information is widely available in general-purpose Python documentation.

The remainder of the function is a try/except structure in which Python attempts the try clause and, if this fails, executes the except clause. The try clause tests the name and passwd values to see if they correspond to a key-value pair in the passwords dictionary. If so, the current scene is set to the Welcome scene by using the setScene() method. The GL.addActiveActuator(scene,True) line is necessary, as you've seen previously, to activate the scene actuator. The except clause here simply clears the values of the password and name properties and blanks the two text fields:

```
def validate_pass(name, passwd):
    passwords = {"myname":"mypass",
                "bob":"bobspass"}
    try:
        if passwords[name] == passwd:
            scene.setScene('Welcome')
            GL.addActiveActuator(scene,True)
    except:
        GL.password = ""
        GL.name = ""
        password_input.Text = ""
        username_input.Text = ""
```

The main body of the code follows. The code is divided into two conditions. The first condition is if the current scene is the default scene called Scene. The second condition, toward the end of the script, deals with the case in which the scene has changed to the Welcome screen scene.

If the current scene is the main scene, the first thing that is done is that its objects are retrieved and assigned to variables. In addition, an empty string is assigned to a variable called mask:

```
if GL.getCurrentScene().getName() == "Scene":
    field1 = object_list["OBfield1"]
    field2 = object_list["OBfield2"]
    button = object_list["OBbutton"]
    circle1 = object_list["OBCircle1"]
    circle2 = object_list["OBCircle2"]
    username_input = object_list["OBUsernameText"]
    password_input = object_list["OBPasswordText"]
    cam = object_list["OBcamera"]
    mask = ""
```

Next, the case in which the mouse is moved over an object is considered, with the if mouse.isPositive() conditional clause. This block of code will be executed anytime the mouse is over any object. The getHitObject() method is called on the Mouse sensor to retrieve the specific object that the mouse is over. This object is passed to the hit_object variable:

```
if mouse.isPositive():
    hit_object = mouse.getHitObject()
```

The idea here is for the field that has the mouse over it to be active. This should be indicated by the appropriate white circle becoming visible and it should result in the text input going to the appropriate variable. If the username field has the mouse over it, the white circle on that field should be visible and any text the user types should be interpreted as username input. Likewise, if the password field is active, typed text should be interpreted as password input. There is one more thing that these clauses do; if the mouse has been moved from another place, the input is cleared. This has the effect of clearing fields when the mouse has been moved away and then returned to the field, which may not be ideal behavior. This can be changed, but for the sake of keeping it simple for this example, I will accept this minor idiosyncrasy. Note a difference between the case of field1, the username field field2, and the password field. In the first case, the cam.input value is passed to both GL.name (the GameLogic property storing the username) and username_input.Text (the dynamic text object representing the username text field). In the password case, the value is passed from cam.input to GL.password, but not directly to the dynamic text object. Rather, a variable called mask is introduced, and a string of asterisks the same length as the password value is passed to this variable. This string is passed to the dynamic text object, so the password is concealed:

```
if hit_object == field1:
    if field1.active == 0:
        cam.input = ""
    circle1.setVisible(1)
    circle2.setVisible(0)
    field1.active = 1
    field2.active = 0
    username_input.Text = GL.name = cam.input
elif hit_object == field2:
    if field2.active == 0:
        cam.input = ""
    circle1.setVisible(0)
    circle2.setVisible(1)
    field1.active = 0
    field2.active = 1
    GL.password = cam.input
    for x in range(len(GL.password)):
        mask = mask + "*"
    password_input.Text = mask
```

The else portion of the clause deals with the case in which the mouse is not over any object. This sets both circles to be invisible and both fields to be inactive:

```
else:
    circle1.setVisible(0)
    circle2.setVisible(0)
    field1.active = 0
    field2.active = 0
```

Another, much shorter conditional clause checks to see whether the mouse-click event is positive. If so, the script checks whether the object under the mouse is the button object. If so, the previously defined validate_pass() function is called to validate whether the username text input matches the input password:

```
if mouseclick.isPositive():
    if hit_object == button:
        validate_pass(username_input.Text, GL.password)
```

The top-level if clause checked whether the current scene was the login screen scene. If the scene has been changed to the Welcome scene, the only thing that needs to be done is to access the OBWelcome text and pass the GL.name value to the text, so that the user is welcomed by name:

```
elif GL.getCurrentScene().getName() == "Welcome":
    list = GL.getCurrentScene().getObjectList()
    list["OBWelcome"].Text = "Welcome, "+GL.name+"!"
```

Working with Viewports

In addition to GameLogic and GameKeys, the third module that makes up the BGE API is Rasterizer. This module deals with how the visible pixels of the game are arranged on the screen. Using this module, it is possible to enable the display of multiple viewports.

You can see a simple example of this by setting up an imaginary two-player game. In the file viewports_nopython.blend, you'll find the initial setup for this game, with the complete game logic. In Figure 11.13, you can see the setup illustrated. This figure is reproduced in color in the color insert of the book. There is a red cube and a blue cube, named RedCube and BlueCube, respectively. Each cube has a camera associated with it, likewise named RedCamera and BlueCamera. You can add cameras to a scene in the same way you add other objects, by pressing the spacebar and choosing Add ≻ Camera from the menu.

FIGURE 11.13
Two cubes and corresponding cameras

The game logic is simple, along the same lines of the motion control logic you read about in Chapter 10. Each cube can go forward, and turn right and left. The keys to control the blue cube are E, S, and D, and the keys to control the red cube are O, K, and L. Each camera has a Camera actuator associated with it, targeted on the appropriate cube. You can see the logic for the red cube and its camera summarized in Figure 11.14.

FIGURE 11.14
Logic blocks for RedCube and Red-Camera

Finally, there is one more camera, OverheadCamera, placed above the entire scene, as shown in the upper-left corner of Figure 11.15. The birds-eye view of the game board from

OverheadCamera is shown in Figure 11.16. To look through this camera, hold down the Ctrl key while you press 0 on the number pad to make it the active camera. After you do that, pressing the 0 key on the number pad will always shift the view to this camera.

FIGURE 11.15
OverheadCamera placed above the board

FIGURE 11.16
The view from OverheadCamera

Finally, a new Text object called `viewports.py` is created, and a script controller is connected to an Always sensor on the game board Plane object, as shown in Figure 11.17. Again, the choice of the object to attach this logic to is arbitrary. The plane is as sensible a place as any.

FIGURE 11.17
The `viewports.py`
script controller

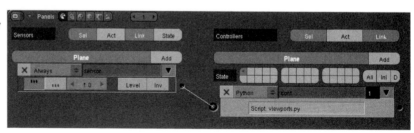

The content of the `viewports.py` is of course where the real action is in this example. The first thing you need to do is to import the module that handles putting the game imagery on the screen. That module is Rasterizer. Import the module just as you would with any other module, as shown here:

```
import Rasterizer
```

To divide the game view area between viewports, you first need to retrieve the height and width of the total view area. The Rasterizer module enables you to access this information as follows:

```
height = Rasterizer.getWindowHeight()
width = Rasterizer.getWindowWidth()
```

The next few lines of code should be familiar from previous examples in this chapter, in which the scene and the objects in the scene are retrieved and assigned to variables:

```
scene = GameLogic.getCurrentScene()
obList = scene.getObjectList()
redcam = obList["OBRedCamera"]
bluecam = obList["OBBlueCamera"]
overview = obList["OBOverviewCamera"]
```

To set viewports dimensions, use the `setViewport()` method on the appropriate Camera object. The method takes four arguments. They represent, in order, the following parameters: the position of the left side of the viewport, counting left to right from zero to the width of the full view area; the position of the bottom edge of the viewport, counting bottom to top from zero to the height of the full view area; the right side of the viewport, counting left to right from zero to the width of the viewing area (if this number is smaller than the first argument, the viewport will not be visible); and finally, the top edge of the viewport, counting bottom to top from zero to the height of the full view area (if this number is smaller than the second argument, the viewport will not be visible). The overview camera is set to be visible over the other two viewports by using the setOnTop() method. Finally, you need to enable each of the viewports by calling enableViewport(True) on each camera object individually:

```
bluecam.setViewport(0,0,width/2,height)
redcam.setViewport(width/2,0,width,height)
overview.setViewport(width/4,0,width*3/4,height*1/3)
overview.setOnTop()

bluecam.enableViewport(True)
redcam.enableViewport(True)
overview.enableViewport(True)
```

When you run the game-play mode now, you will see a split-screen view with an overlaid viewport, as shown in Figure 11.18. This figure is reproduced in color in the color insert of the book.

FIGURE 11.18
Playing the game with multiple views

Accessing Sound with Python

In Chapter 10, you saw how to work with basic BGE sound controls, including the 3D sound option. In this section, you'll see how to access this data with Python and gain a greater level of control over it.

Begin with a logic block setup associated with the Blender default cube, as shown in Figure 11.19. This logic setup has a Sound actuator identical to the one shown in Chapter 10. The actuator is attached to a Python script controller for a script called volume.py (as always, this must be created in the text editor first). Three sensors lead into the controller. The first sensor is an Always sensor. The second sensor is a Keyboard sensor triggered on the U key, which will raise the volume. The third sensor is a Keyboard sensor triggered on the D key, which will decrease the volume.

FIGURE 11.19
Sensors and actua-
tors connected
to the volume.py
controller

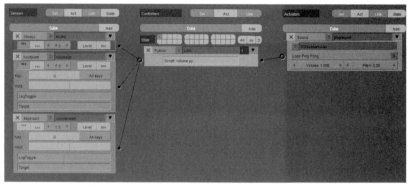

Unlike the example in Chapter 10, the 3D button in the Sound panel of the Render buttons area shown in Figure 11.20 should *not* be selected.

FIGURE 11.20
3D sound
is deactivated

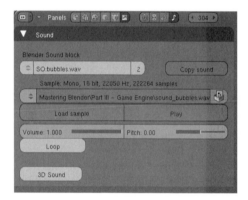

The code of volume.py is as follows. To keep the volume consistent over repeated calls of the script, you need to store the value in a GameLogic attribute. The way to do this, as you saw previously in this chapter, is to assign a value GL.vol in the context of an initialization loop using hassatr(). Possible volume values range from 0 to 10, so set GL.vol to mid-volume, at 0.5.

```
GL = GameLogic
if not hasattr(GL, "init"):
    GL.vol = 0.5
    GL.init = None
```

As always, the controller, owner, actuators, and sensors must be retrieved, as you see here:

```
cont = GL.getCurrentController()
own = cont.getOwner()
play = cont.getActuator("playsound")
volumeup = cont.getSensor("volumeup")
volumedown = cont.getSensor("volumedown")
```

Just as in the previous cases of working with sensors in Python, the isPositive() method is called to assess whether the sensor is being triggered. The code here simply sets up two if conditionals: one for the case of increasing the volume and one for the case of decreasing the volume:

```
if volumeup.isPositive():
    if GL.vol < 1.0:
        GL.vol = GL.vol + 0.01
if volumedown.isPositive():
    if GL.vol > 0.0:
        GL.vol = GL.vol - 0.01
```

The new volume value is set to the Sound actuator by using the setGain() method. Finally, as in all cases in which an actuator must be refreshed, the GL.addActiveActuator() method is called with the play actuator as its first argument and True as its second argument:

```
play.setGain(GL.vol)
GL.addActiveActuator(play, True)
```

When you press P and enter the game-play environment, you will be able to control the sound of the bubbles by using the U and D keys. The finished example can be found in the file soundcube_volume.blend on the CD that accompanies this book.

 Real World Scenario

VISUALIZING FISH POPULATION DATA WITH THE BGE

An extraordinary example of the practical usefulness of Python and the BGE can be seen in the collaborative fish population visualization project carried out by the University of British Columbia (UBC) Fisheries Centre and students in the UBC Masters of Digital Media program. The ambitious project focused on taking large amounts of complex statistical data describing projected populations of marine life and the results of fishing policies on the populations. Although the collected data was compelling, the researchers of the Fisheries Centre needed a way to make it accessible to nonbiologists and nonstatisticians.

The result of the collaboration is a dynamic 3D underwater environment with animated marine life in densities reflecting actual projections of the data. The user can select marine species and set parameters for fishing policy in real time, and the projected effect on the fish population will become immediately visible. The team at UBC hopes that this unique marriage of game technology and intuitive data visualization can help to influence how fishing policy is made in the future.

You can read more about the project at the following BlenderNation.com site:

```
www.blendernation.com/2008/04/09/"sh-population-data-visualisation-internships-
at-great-northern-way-campus-vancouver/
```

The UBC team has also created a video describing their project, and an excellent video tutorial on some of the specific techniques they used to make the visualization:

```
http://mdm.gnwc.ca/?q=blog/20080329/is-not-movie
```

```
http://mdm.gnwc.ca/?q=blog/20080219/blender-tutorial
```

Further Resources

If you've followed this entire book to the end, you should now have a solid grounding in many of the most advanced areas of Blender functionality. But even a quick glance at the Python Blender API or the GameLogic API is enough to know that there is a great deal out there still to learn. Blender's functionality is almost endless and expanding all the time. Even the relatively limited corner of functionality discussed in this chapter, using Python in the BGE, is impossible to do justice to in such a small amount of space. For this reason, you will want to turn to other resources to deepen your knowledge.

The first place you should turn is to the Blender Foundation's e-shop, where you can satisfy your thirst for Blender knowledge and support your favorite open source software application at the same time. You'll find the second edition of *The Official Blender GameKit* by Carsten Wartmann, which covers all the latest features of the BGE in depth and will help you explore some of the nooks and crannies that you have not yet been introduced to. You'll also find the DVD of Yo, Frankie! the Blender Foundation's own open game project. This is without a doubt the most sophisticated game created so far by anyone using the BGE as the primary game engine, and the added bonus of having all original files and resources at your disposal, not to mention extensive tutorials, makes this an absolute must-own.

The forum at BlenderArtists.org remains one of the most important resources available to any Blender user. In the Game Engine section of the forum, you'll find gurus who will answer the most obscure questions and give you tips for creating almost any effect.

If you're interested in creating a first-person shooter (FPS), look no further than Social's FPS template:

    http://blenderartists.org/forum/showthread.php?t=85219

If you want to create a network game or online interactive 3D environment, check out the BZoo project, which offers a framework for networking designed specifically for the BGE. You can read about BZoo and download it from the following website:

    http://bzooworld.org/

A collection of tutorials on how to set up particle-like effects, including flames, in the BGE can be found here:

    http://gameblender.wikia.com/wiki/Special_Effects_Tutorials

Finally, a variety of excellent general BGE tutorials can be found at the following excellent users' websites:

    www.blendenzo.com/indexTuts.html

    http://bgetutorials.wordpress.com/tutorials/

There are many others. Keep an eye on BlenderNation.com for the latest developments and tutorials to be made available. At the same time, if you create a useful tool, an interesting visualization, a helpful tutorial, or a killer game, don't be shy about letting the community know about it, either through the forums at BlenderArtists.org or by submitting a news item at BlenderNation.com. The Blender community is always supportive and always eager to hear about the interesting uses to which people are putting this extraordinary software. In the meantime, with what you've learned from this book, you should be able to confidently forge ahead on your own advanced Blender projects.

Happy Blendering!

The Bottom Line

Replace multiple logic block setups with a few lines of Python code.   By using a Python script controller to coordinate your sensors and actuators, you can accomplish the same things as with logic blocks, but much more efficiently and with much less clutter. For larger, complex projects, using Python makes it vastly easier to keep your logic organized.

Master It   Add some more movements to the walking character from this chapter. Create a new action and implement it in the BGE with Python so that pressing the W key will make him wave.

Use Python to create effects in the BGE that would not be possible using logic blocks alone.   Not every possible game engine behavior is encoded in logic block form. Setting an object's location is a simple example of something that requires Python to do. More-complex operations requiring variables or data structures also require the power of a fully functional programming language like Python.

Master It   Implement a Python script that makes the default cube follow the mouse around the viewport.

Create unique game environments with sound effects and multiple viewports.   Effects like real-time control of sound volume and split-screen views can help to make your interactive 3D environment more engaging and immersive. With Python, these effects are easy to achieve.

Master It   Create an environment with one stationary object and another object that can be moved around similarly to the cube in the viewports example. Have the stationary object emit a sound such that the volume of the sound increases to one when the objects are at their closest together, and decreases to zero as the objects get farther apart.

Appendix A

Solutions

Chapter 1: Controlling Your Environment

Set the options available to you in the User Preferences window. A wide variety of often-overlooked options are available in the User Preferences window, including settings for View & Controls, Edit Methods, and Themes, among others.

> **Master It** Create your own preferred default starting state and save it so that it will be active every time you start Blender.

> **Solution** When the desired options have been set and the desired starting window configuration is in place, press Ctrl+U to save the settings to a .Blend.blend file. Place this file in your .blender directory and open Blender with your new options in place. (A sample .Blend.blend file is included on the disk that accompanies this book.)

Use lesser-known methods for selecting, grouping, and organizing 3D elements to speed up your workflow. There are numerous ways to select and group objects and 3D elements that can considerably increase your speed and efficiency when working.

> **Master It** Use the selection methods described in this chapter to make the face selections as shown in the following graphic.

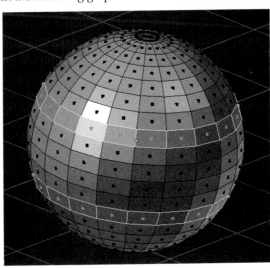

You should be able to make this selection using a single (modified) mouse click followed by a single hot key combination. There are several ways to do this.

Solution   Press Alt+RMB on one of the perpendicular edges in the top face loop. Press Shift+G and select Perimeter.

Prepare for changes in the evolving Blender interface by understanding the principles behind its unique design.   Blender is constantly evolving. It is in your interest to stay informed about developments, in particular at a time when the 2.5 release is promising big developments in usability.

Master It   Inform yourself about the status of the 2.5 event recode and GUI update.

Solution   Information about this can be found at the Blender website at www.blender.org and http://wiki.blender.org/index.php/BlenderDev/Blender2.5, and news items are posted regularly at www.blendernation.com. The developer discussions on the subject can be found in the developer mailing list archives at http://lists.blender.org/pipermail/bf-committers/, and any early builds that may be available for download can be found at www.graphicall.org. William Reynish's full paper on the UI can be found at http://download.blender.org/documentation/bc2008/evolution_of_blenders_ui.pdf.

Chapter 2: Sculpting and Retopo Workflow

Get the most out of Blender's sculpting functionality.   Blender's multires modeling and sculpting features provide a powerful and versatile set of tools for 3D sculpting.

Master It   Nothing is more important than practice for improving your skills at sculpting. Following the guidelines in this chapter, create at least three more sculptures of human heads. Try sculpting old people, women, and men. Try working from orthogonal references as described in this chapter and also try freehand from informal photographs. When you're comfortable with heads, experiment with working on full-body sculptures. Note your impressions on the differences between the various subject matters and how they are sculpted.

Solution   Your model will be unique. Study the file baby.blend and compare how the shapes of the face are modeled to get an idea of how your model is progressing. When you've finished, try showing your work on a thread in www.blenderartists.org/forum in the Focused Critique forum to get suggestions on how you can improve it.

Use retopo to convert a sculpted form into a polygon model with correct edge loop geometry.   Blender's retopo feature enables you to create a new model whose shape is identical to another object, making it possible to recast a very high polygon sculpted object into a lower-polygon model with elegant edge loop geometry that can be easily deformed, animated, and rendered.

Master It   Select the model you are most happy with from the previous exercise and use retopo to create a lower-poly model of the same shape. Pay attention to edge loop geometry and keep the density of the mesh as low as you can while representing the underlying shape as accurately as possible.

Solution   Your model will be unique. Study the structure of the retopo model in the baby_retopo.blend file to get a sense of how your model is progressing. When you've finished, try showing your work on a thread in www.blenderartists.org/forum in the Focused Critique forum to get suggestions on how you can improve it.

Use normal map baking to capture finely sculpted detail for use on a low-poly model.   In order to represent the detail of a very high poly sculpted object, Blender enables you to bake the surface normal information of the sculpted object onto a 2D texture called a normal map, which is then used as a UV texture on the lower-poly model, yielding the illusion of a highly detailed surface.

Master It   Follow the steps described in this chapter to bake a normal map from your sculpted object to the retopoed model you created in the previous exercise.

Solution   A successful normal map should make your rendered retopo mesh look as similar as possible to the original sculpted mesh. The image of the three baby heads in this chapter will give you a rough idea of the kind of similarity you should see. When you've finished, try showing your work on a thread in www.blenderartists.org/forum in the Focused Critique forum to get suggestions on how you can improve it.

Chapter 3: Creating Realistic Images with UV Textures and Node-Based Materials

Use Blender's texture-mapping functionality effectively.   Blender has a powerful set of UV-mapping tools that rank among the best in the industry. Using these tools enables you to place 2D textures exactly as you want them on the surface of a 3D model.

Master It   Find the file engine.blend on the CD that accompanies this book. Create seams, unwrap the mesh, and export a UV face-layout file for use in GIMP. Apply a UV test grid image to the mesh.

Solution   An unwrapping can be found in the file engine_unwrap.blend on the CD.

Mix textures to create almost any surface effect.   By using Blender's UV texture and texture-baking features, particularly in combination with a powerful image-manipulation application such as GIMP, you can create a wide variety of seamless texture effects.

Master It   Using the metal_texture.jpg file included on the CD, or other textures that you find online or create yourself, use the methods described in this chapter to create seamless color and bump map textures for the engine.blend model.

Solution   One solution can be found in the file engine_tex.blend on the CD.

Make the most of the Blender material system to create complex materials and shaders. Creating textures is only the first part of making convincing materials. Mapping them correctly to the material and setting their parameters correctly are crucial to getting realistic material effects.

Master It   Combine the two textures you created in the previous exercise in a single material with both color and bump qualities. Set the shader properties in a way that creates a convincing metallic look.

Solution   One solution can be found in the file engine_mat.blend on the CD.

Chapter 4: Video Compositing with Nodes

Blender's composite node system is a flexible and powerful way to combine multiple original-image and video sources to achieve a wide variety of effects. One of the many things that the system enables is the creation of green screen mattes, which can be used to separate a fore-ground figure from its background in order to composite it into other scenes.

Use the Blender composite node system to pull a green screen matte.   When you know in advance that you will be compositing a character or object into a scene, a common technique is to shoot the original video of the foreground figure against a colored background screen. This makes it possible to eliminate the background quickly and easily by using color chan-nels in the node compositor.

Master It   Using a nodes setup based on the example in this chapter, add a background image from an image file to create a fully composited image such as the one shown in Figure 4.64. You can use the sky_map.jpg file included on the CD.

Solution   See the file greenscreen_final.blend for a possible solution to this exercise.

Use curves and hooks to do simple rotoscoped garbage matting.   Background clutter in the original footage can cause imperfections in the matte. To block these out, garbage matting is used. In cases when the garbage matte must interact with the silhouette of the foreground figure, some hand-keying or rotoscoping may be necessary.

Master It   Using a 3D curve animated with hooks, add a second garbage matte to the video example used in this chapter to cover the debris in the background of the right side of the frame.

Solution   See the file greenscreen_final.blend for a possible solution to this exercise.

Manipulate the video's color channels to reduce color spill.   Anytime you composite foot-age shot under one set of lighting conditions with footage shot under another set of lighting conditions, color mismatches can occur. This is particularly the case when a green screen is used, which can cause a green cast or spill in the original footage. To eliminate this, it is pos-sible to work directly with the color channels to adjust the mix of red, green, and blue energy in the image to better match the background.

Master It   In the composited image you made in the first "Master It" exercise of this chapter, create a slightly purple screen that affects only the most brightly lit highlights of the foreground figure to attain results similar to those in Figure 4.65.

Solution   See the file greenscreen_final.blend for a possible solution to this exercise.

Chapter 5: Working with the Video Sequence Editor

Import, edit, and render video with the Blender VSE.   Blender's Video Sequence Editor (VSE) is a powerful tool for cross-platform, multiformat video editing. One of its key strengths is the ease with which it can handle a variety of different image, video, and audio formats both as input and as rendered output.

Master It   Import the video idol_clip.mov from the CD that accompanies this book. Using a Transition strip, animate the video image rotating in place. Render the resulting movie to a series of JPEG images.

Solution   Select the video strip and add a Transition strip. In the Effect panel, set rot Start as 0.0 and rot End as 360. Animate a Sequence Fac Ipo for the strip from value 0 to value 1. Select Jpeg from the drop-down menu in the Format panel in the Render buttons area, set Do Sequence, and then click Anim.

Create transitions, overlays, and effects for your videos.   The VSE has a variety of built-in effects and transitions to enable you to edit video and do simple compositing quickly and easily. Alpha values of 3D scenes also work seamlessly within the VSE.

Master It   Add a caption for the robot's line "Checkmate" in the video end_zone_clip. avi. Render the output to a new .avi file with sound.

Solution   Make a full copy of the Check scene you created in this chapter, and name the new scene Checkmate. Edit the text and adjust the shape of the background plane appropriately. Add the new scene strip exactly as you did the Check strip, and position the strip in the appropriate place. Add the Alpha Over strip in the same way you did in the example in the chapter. Select FFMpeg from the drop-down menu in the Format panel, and select Xvid as the video codec, MP3 as the audio, and the Multiplex Audio option.

Incorporate content directly from 3D or composited scenes into your videos.   You can incorporate both animated scenes from the 3D viewport and composited scenes from the node system directly into the VSE, resulting in an extraordinarily powerful and integrated compositing and editing system.

Master It   Use the output of the green screen compositing exercise from Chapter 4 in the VSE. Use a wipe to transition between the composited scene strip to another video strip. Render the output to the format of your choice.

Solution   You can append the composited scene into a new .blend file by using the Append or Link option in the File menu, in the same way as you would any other datablock. Add the scene as a strip in the VSE as described in this chapter, by pressing the spacebar and selecting Scene. Add a separate video sequence, either one from the CD or one of your own, by pressing the spacebar and selecting Movie, Image Sequence, or Movie + Audio, depending on the video. Select the first and the second strip in order by using Shift+RMB, and then add a strip by pressing the spacebar and selecting Wipe. When you are ready to render, be sure to activate the Do Sequence option in the Render buttons area, and then select your preferred output format and press Anim to render the video. An example of a movie created in this way is in the comp_seq.mov file on the CD that accompanies this book.

Chapter 6: Python for the Impatient

Become familiar with the basics of the Python language.   Python is a widely used language for scripting in many different application areas. It is known for its ease of use, readability, and speed of development.

Master It   Make sure that you have a good reference handy for Python syntax. In this chapter, I listed several good books you should consider buying. Use a Google search to find some more good online resources to quickly look up Python operators and data types.

Solution   *Dive Into Python* by Mark Pilgrim (Apress, 2004) has the additional benefit of being freely available online in a variety of convenient formats at www.diveintopython.org. The official documentation pages at www.python.org are also excellent references, containing almost everything you will need to know about the Python language and its syntax.

Run the Python shell and IDLE development environment.   The simplest way to access Python directly is through the Python command-line shell, which is part of the IDLE development environment. In this shell environment, you can execute individual commands and perform introspection on variables.

Master It   In this chapter, you learned that you cannot concatenate a string and an integer by using the + operator. Likewise, you cannot add a string numerically. In some cases, however, numerical data may be input (for example, in a form) as a string type. Study the references you searched for in the previous Master It exercise about type casting in Python to find out how you would convert the string "5" into an integer that can be added to another.

Solution   As you learned in the chapter, data types can be converted to strings with the str() function. Likewise, they can be converted to integers with the int() function. You can convert a string to add it to an integer by using this function as follows:

```
>>print 2 + int("5")
>>7
```

Understand fundamental features of Python syntax.   Python is a powerful programming language with a variety of data types, control structure options, and useful built-in functions. Its characteristic features include its reliance on indentation to represent logical structure.

Master It   Create a variable my_list and assign it the list [1,2,1,3,1,4]. Call the dir() function with this list as an argument. Which of the methods returned by dir() do you think would be the correct method for removing one of the elements from the list? Experiment with the methods you think would work, and try to get rid of the number 2 from the list, so the list becomes [1,1,3,1,4]. Which method do you think will return the number of times the number 1 appears in the list?

Solution   The methods remove() and count() are among the methods returned by dir() for a list. As their names suggest, these are the methods you want to use to remove an element or count the number of occurrences of an element in a list. You can remove the 2 from the list described in the exercise, and count the number of occurrences of the number 1 as follows:

```
>>my_list = [1,2,1,3,1,4]
>>my_list.remove(2)
>>print my_list
>>[1,1,3,1,4]
>>my_list.count(1)
>>3
```

Chapter 7: Python Scripting for Blender

Edit and run scripts in Blender.   Blender has its own internal text editor that you can use to write scripts or commentary. The text editor features line numbering and color-coded syntax highlighting.

Master It   Get accustomed to working with the Blender text editor. Open an Object script template by going to the File editor and choosing Script Templates ➤ Object Editing. Run the script with Alt+P. Find the place in the code where the number of objects in the scene is printed out. Change that line so only the number of selected objects in the scene is printed.

Solution   The change should be made in line 18. To find out what methods and attributes are available for the `scn.objects` object, you can print out a `dir()` call on that object. You will see that the attribute you need for this is `selected`. Thus the line should be changed to the following:

```
print 'Scene selected object count', len(sce.objects.selected)
```

Become familiar with the Blender-Python API.   If you code in Blender-Python, the API will become your faithful companion. A large part of learning to script for Blender is becoming comfortable navigating the API.

Master It   An important step in using the API is to read the API itself and figure out what its various modules and classes do. Look over the API now. Which class would you use if you wanted to work with a Text object in the 3D space? What method would you use to set the text string for this object?

Solution   The module you want for this is the Text3d module (not the Text module!). The class you would use, likewise, is the Text3d class. The method for setting the text string on a Text3d object is `setText()`.

Create an interactive script.   Blender's Python API includes tools for designing graphical user interfaces for your scripts that enable you to set parameters and execute commands interactively.

Master It   Alter the cone generator example in this chapter to create a similar script that creates bouncing text objects instead of creating bouncing cones. You should be able to input the color, placement, speed, and height of bouncing just as you do with the script in this chapter, but in place of adjusting the dimensions of the cone object, add an option to input the text of the Text3d object that the script creates.

Solution   See the file `text_exercise.blend` on the CD that accompanies this book for the solution to this exercise.

Chapter 8: The Many-Headed Snake: Other Uses of Python in Blender

Control Ipo curves by using PyDrivers.   PyDrivers enable you to drive Ipo curves based on a Python expression. Because such expressions can incorporate multiple input values and can calculate complex functions, PyDrivers are much more powerful and flexible than traditional Ipo drivers.

Master It Write a PyDriver that drives the red value of a material color based on the spatial distance between two bones in an armature. If the bones are less than 1 BU apart from each other in space, the material should be black. If the bones are more than 3 BUs apart from each other in space, the material should be red. To do this, you will need to study the API entry on the Pose module, and also the entry for the Vector class of the Mathutils module. You will need to retrieve the pose from the Armature object, and then retrieve the bones (specifically the bones' head coordinates) from the pose to get the locations of the bones. You'll then subtract one bone's position from the other, find the length of the resulting vector, and map the result by using simple arithmetic.

Solution The PyDriver on the Material Ipo for *R* should be as follows (demonstrated in the file PyDriverSolution.blend). Note that for typesetting reasons the code has been wrapped here. In fact, the entire code must be entered in the PyDriver field as a single unbroken line.:

```
((ob('Armature').getPose().bones['Bone.001'].head-
ob('Armature').getPose().bones['Bone'].head).length-1)/2
```

Incorporate Python scripts as nodes and constraints with PyNodes and PyConstraints. PyNodes and PyConstraints enable further integration of Python into your Blender environment by giving you the means to create your own nodes and constraints with the full power of Python scripts.

Master It Create a PyConstraint that takes three target objects and locks the constrained object to the imaginary line between the first target object and the second target object. Use the third target object as a control object to determine where along the line the constrained object is placed, so the four objects form a T-shape, with the constrained object at the intersection. If the control object is moved beyond the end of the imaginary line, the constrained object should remain fixed to the location of the object at the nearest end of the imaginary line. The solution of this exercise requires some light trigonometry. You will also want to read the Vector class documentation of the Mathutils module in the Blender Python API.

Solution The solution can be found in the file *PyConstraintSolution.blend* on the CD.

Use script links and space handlers to obtain even greater levels of interactivity. Script links and space handlers can be used to execute Python scripts based on Blender events such as animation frame changes and to integrate script interface elements directly into the 3D view.

Master It Adapt the space-handler script in the example to work with a square image rather than a circular image. The mouse-over behavior should be correct for the image shape. Also, instead of switching between Orthographic and Perspective View modes, make it switch between Solid and Wire Draw modes.

Solution The solution can be found in SquareSpaceHandler.blend on the CD.

Chapter 9: Creating Assets for the Blender Game Engine

Model, rig, and texture a 3D character for use in the Blender Game Engine. A simple, low-poly rigged character is ideal for experimenting with the game engine. Modeling, rigging, and animating in the Action editor can all be done quickly and easily in Blender.

Master It The example described in the tutorial uses TexFace texturing and therefore cannot be illuminated in real time with lights in the game engine. Fix this by creating a Blender material with the same UV-mapped texture so the character can be illuminated with lights in the game engine.

Solution See the file `character_mat.blend` on the accompanying CD.

Create a simple game environment of a maze and a skybox by using texture mapping. Simple modeling, combined with some clever texturing tricks, is enough to create an interesting in-game environment. Baking textures to images is a great way to adapt Blender procedural effects to use in the game engine.

Master It Texture the walls and floor of your maze in an interesting way.

Solution See the `game_objects.blend` file on the CD for hints.

Place objects in the game environment and set options for materials and lighting in the game engine. Appending objects and groups to a `.blend` file is a crucial skill for managing 3D assets on any kind of nontrivial Blender project. Understanding how materials and lighting interact in the game engine will enable you to get exactly the look and atmosphere you're after for your game or interactive environment.

Master It In this chapter, you appended the skybox and maze to the game, and then resized them both to make them suitable to each other. Next, append the character to the scene as well. Use grouping to append the armature and mesh simultaneously. Resize the character appropriately, and remember to apply the new scale. Test your animated action with the new scale. If there are problems, recalculate the bone roll angles in Edit mode.

Solution See the `game_objects.blend` file on the CD.

Chapter 10: Making Things Happen in the Game Engine

Control characters and scenes by using logic blocks. Interactive control in the Blender game engine is made possible by using the powerful logic block system. With this system, you can use sensors, controllers, and actuators to trigger game events on a variety of types of input.

Master It In the chapter, you saw how to make the character walk forward and turn right. Set up a similar character that can turn left and walk backward as well.

Solution See the file `game.blend` on the CD accompanying this book for the full logic on the main character armature, including turning left and walking backward.

Use properties, messages, and states to create complex interactions. Like a full-powered programming language, the BGE logic block system enables you to store and modify values in the form of properties, to set up communications between different logic blocks using messages, and to control which logic blocks are active at what times by using states. In this way, complex interactions are made possible, limited only by the graphical nature of the logic blocks.

Master It Set up logic so that the wizards change directions whenever they hit the character, as well as when they hit each other.

Solution The simplest way to do this is to simply add a property called bump on the character armature. The wizards already are set to change direction when they strike an object with this property, so adding it to the character will have this effect. Of course, its effect will appear only when the character is in the green-ball protected state, because the game will end on the collision otherwise.

Work with textures to create dynamic text and in-game 2D animations. Textures in the BGE can be used for a variety of interesting effects. Dynamic text whose content can be updated by logic blocks and in-game animations can be created by using specifically mapped textures with certain parameter settings.

Master It Use the method described in this chapter to create a 2D walk cycle animation. Use orthogonal renders of the character walk cycle you created in Chapter 9, and then put those renders together in a single image, using a 2D image-editing program such as Photoshop or GIMP. Map the image onto a plane in the game engine to create a walking 2D cutout character.

Solution See the image file and the .blend file in the texture walk directory on the CD that accompanies this book for a solution to this assignment.

Incorporate sound effects into your game environment. Sounds can be controlled by Sound Actuators similarly to other effects in the BGE. Special features exist to automatically control the sound on the basis of its distance from the camera.

Master It Browse the free sound files website www.freesounds.org and find some other interesting sound effects. Follow the steps in this chapter to add a new 3D sound to a moving object in the 3D space.

Solution See the file soundcube.blend for the completed results of the tutorial.

Chapter 11: Python Power in the Blender Game Engine

Replace multiple logic block setups with a few lines of Python code. By using a Python script controller to coordinate your sensors and actuators, you can accomplish the same things as with logic blocks, but much more efficiently and with much less clutter. For larger, complex projects, using Python makes it vastly easier to keep your logic organized.

Master It Add some more movements to the walking character from this chapter. Create a new action and implement it in the BGE with Python so that pressing the W key will make him wave.

Solution See the file character_wave.blend on the CD that accompanies this book for a solution.

Use Python to create effects in the BGE that would not be possible using logic blocks alone. Not every possible game engine behavior is encoded in logic block form. Setting an object's location is a simple example of something that requires Python to do. More-complex operations requiring variables or data structures also require the power of a fully functional programming language like Python.

Master It Implement a Python script that makes the default cube follow the mouse around the viewport.

Solution See the file `mouse_cube.blend` on the CD that accompanies this book for a solution.

Create unique game environments with sound effects and multiple viewports. Effects like real-time control of sound volume and split-screen views can help to make your interactive 3D environment more engaging and immersive. With Python, these effects are easy to achieve.

Master It Create an environment with one stationary object and another object that can be moved around similarly to the cube in the viewports example. Have the stationary object emit a sound such that the volume of the sound increases to one when the objects are at their closest together, and decreases to zero as the objects get farther apart.

Solution See the file `volume_objects.blend` on the CD that accompanies this book for a solution.

Appendix B

Blender-Python API Module and Class Hierarchies

In this appendix, you will find complete lists of the modules, submodules, and classes of the Blender-Python API along with brief descriptions of their functions. Details of the properties and methods associated with them can be found in the full API description in the file 248PythonDoc.tar.bz2 that accompanies this book, or online at www.blender.org/documentation/248PythonDoc/.

Module Hierarchy

The following is a list of modules and submodules in the Blender-Python API. In some cases, the names that the modules or submodules are listed under in the API documentation are different from the names of the modules themselves. This list maintains the same naming used in the current version of the API documentation.

API_intro   An overview of the contents of the API

API_related   Blender-Python–related features

Armature   The Blender.Armature submodule

BGL   The Blender.BGL submodule (the OpenGL wrapper)

BezTriple   The Blender.BezTriple submodule

Blender   The main Blender module

Bpy   The bpy module

Bpy_config   The bpy.config module

Bpy_data   The bpy.data module

Camera   The Blender.Camera submodule

Constraint   The Blender.Constraint submodule

Curve   The Blender.Curve submodule

Draw   The Blender.Draw submodule

Effect   The Blender.Effect submodule

Font   The Blender.Text3d.Font sub-submodule

Geometry   The Blender.Geometry submodule

Group   The `Blender.Group` submodule

IDProp   The `IDProp` module

Image   The `Blender.Image` submodule

Ipo   The `Blender.Ipo` submodule

IpoCurve   The `Blender.IpoCurve` submodule

Key   The `Blender.Key` submodule

Lamp   The `Blender.Lamp` submodule

Lattice   The `Blender.Lattice` submodule

LibData   The `bpy.libraries` submodule

Library   The `Blender.Library` submodule

Material   The `Blender.Material` submodule

Mathutils   The `Blender.Mathutils` submodule

Mesh   The `Blender.Mesh` submodule

MeshPrimitives   The `Blender.Mesh.Primitives` submodule

Metaball   The `Blender.Metaball` submodule

Modifier   The `Blender.Modifier` submodule

NLA   The `Blender.Armature.NLA` submodule

NMesh   The `Blender.NMesh` submodule (deprecated—use `Mesh`)

Noise   The `Blender.Noise` submodule

Object   The `Blender.Object` submodule

Pose   The `Blender.Object.Pose` submodule

Radio   The `Blender.Scene.Radio` submodule

Registry   The `Blender.Registry` submodule

Render   The `Blender.Scene.Render` submodule

Scene   The `Blender.Scene` submodule

Sound   The `Blender.Sound` submodule

Sys   The `Blender.Sys` submodule

Text   The `Blender.Text` submodule

Text3d   The `Blender.Text3d` submodule

Texture   The `Blender.Texture` submodule

Theme   The `Blender.Window.Theme` submodule

TimeLine   The `Blender.Scene.TimeLine` submodule

Types   A dictionary of Blender-Python types, for type checking

Window   The `Blender.Window` submodule

World   The `Blender.World` submodule

Class Hierarchy

The following is a list of classes in the Blender-Python API. The class names are composed of two parts. To the left of the period is the name of the module or submodule in which the class is defined. To the right of the period is the name of the individual class. See the full API for information on the properties and methods associated with each class.

Armature.Armature   This object gives access to armature-specific data in Blender.

Armature.Bone   This object gives access to bone-specific data in Blender.

Armature.BonesDict   This object gives dictionary-like access to the bones in an armature.

Armature.Editbone   This object is a wrapper for `editbone` data and is used only in the manipulation of the armature in Edit mode.

BGL.Buffer   This object is simply a block of memory that is delineated and initialized by the user.

BezTriple.BezTriple   This object gives access to generic data from all BezTriple objects in Blender.

Bpy_data.libBlockSeq   This provides a unified way to access and manipulate data types (that is, `bpy.data` objects) in Blender (these include scene, object, mesh, curve, metaball, material, texture, image, lattice, lamp, camera, ipo, world, font, text, sound, groups, armatures, and action datablocks).

Camera.Camera   This object gives access to camera-specific data in Blender.

Constraint.Constraint   This object provides access to a constraint for a particular object accessed from constraints.

Constraint.Constraints   This object provides access to a sequence of constraints for a particular object.

Curve.CurNurb   This object provides access to the control points of the curves that make up Blender Curve ObData.

Curve.Curve   This object gives access to Curve and Surface data linked from Blender objects.

Curve.SurfNurb   This object provides access to the control points of the surfaces that make up a Blender curve.

Draw.Button   This object represents a button in Blender's GUI.

Effect.Effect   This object gives access to particle-effect data in Blender.

Font.Font   This object gives access to Blender's Font objects.

Group.Group   This object gives access to groups in Blender.

IDProp.IDArray   This type enables array-style access to ID properties.

IDProp.IDGroup   This type supports both iteration and the [] operator to get child ID properties.

Image.Image   This object gives access to images in Blender.

Ipo.Ipo   This object gives access to Ipo data from all objects in Blender.

IpoCurve.IpoCurve This object gives access to generic data from all Ipo curve objects in Blender.

Key.Key An object with keyframes (Lattice, NMesh, or Curve) will contain a Key object representing the keyframe data.

Key.KeyBlock Each Key object has a list of KeyBlocks attached, with each KeyBlock representing a keyframe.

Lamp.Lamp This object gives access to Lamp-specific data in Blender.

Lattice.Lattice This object gives access to lattices in Blender.

LibData.LibData This class provides access to a specific type of library data.

LibData.Libraries This class provides a unified way to access and manipulate library types in Blender.

Material.Material This object gives access to materials in Blender.

Mathutils.Euler This object gives access to Euler rotation information in Blender.

Mathutils.Matrix This object gives access to matrices in Blender.

Mathutils.Quaternion This object gives access to quaternions in Blender.

Mathutils.Vector This object gives access to vectors in Blender.

Mesh.MCol This object consists of four integers representing an RGBA color.

Mesh.MEdge This object holds mesh edge data.

Mesh.MEdgeSeq This object provides sequence and iterator access to the mesh's edges.

Mesh.MFace This object holds mesh face data.

Mesh.MFaceSeq This object provides sequence and iterator access to the mesh's faces.

Mesh.MVert This object holds mesh vertex data.

Mesh.MVertSeq This object provides sequence and iterator access to the mesh's vertices.

Mesh.Mesh This object gives access to mesh data in Blender.

Metaball.MetaElemSeq This object provides sequence and iterator access to the metaball elements.

Metaball.Metaball This metaball gives access to generic data from all metaballs in Blender.

Metaball.Metaelem This gives direct access to meta-element data within a metaball.

Modifier.ModSeq This object provides access to a list of modifiers for a particular object.

Modifier.Modifier This object provides access to a modifier for a particular object accessed from ModSeq.

NLA.Action This object gives access to action-specific data in Blender.

NLA.ActionStrip This object gives access to a particular action strip.

NLA.ActionStrips This object gives access to a sequence of ActionStrip objects for a particular object.

NMesh.NMCol This object is a list of ints—[r, g, b, a]—representing an RGBA color.

NMesh.NMEdge   This object holds mesh edge data.

NMesh.NMFace   This object holds mesh face data.

NMesh.NMVert   This object holds mesh vertex data.

NMesh.NMesh   This object gives access to mesh data in Blender.

Object.Object   This object gives access to generic data from all objects in Blender.

Object.Property   This property gives access to object property data in Blender, used by the game engine.

Pose.Pose   This object gives access to pose-specific data in Blender.

Pose.PoseBone   This object gives access to PoseBone-specific data in Blender.

Pose.PoseBonesDict   This object gives dictionary-like access to the PoseBones in a pose.

Radio.Radio   This object wraps the current scene's radiosity context in Blender.

Render.RenderData   This object gives access to scene-rendering contexts in Blender.

Scene.Scene   This object gives access to scene data in Blender.

Scene.SceneObjects   This object gives access to the objects in a scene in Blender.

Sound.Sound   This object gives access to sounds in Blender.

Text.Text   This object gives access to texts in Blender.

Text3d.Text3d   This object gives access to Blender's Font objects.

Texture.MTex   This object links a material to a texture.

Texture.Texture   This object gives access to texture-specific data in Blender.

Theme.Theme   This object gives access to themes in Blender.

Theme.ThemeSpace   There is a subtheme for each space in Blender (except for the Scripts window, but it will be added soon).

Theme.ThemeUI   This can be accessed with `theme.get(t)`, where *t* can be ui or –1.

TimeLine.TimeLine   This object wraps the current scene's Timeline context in Blender.

World.World   This object gives access to generic data from all worlds in Blender.

The Evolution of Blender's User Interface

This appendix contains the full text of William Reynish's paper on the evolution of Blender's interface, delivered as a presentation at the 2008 Blender Conference, and made available for download in November 2008 from the official www.blender.org website. The document was written in preparation for the 2.5 event system recode, which is expected to result in many changes to the interface. This paper represents a significant step toward establishing what direction the changes should take.

As an experienced Blender animator and lead artist on the *Big Buck Bunny* open movie project, William has an unsurpassed level of familiarity with Blender's strengths and weaknesses in a professional, high-end production environment. Small frustrations for a casual user become significant impediments for somebody working long hours daily to meet rigid deadlines. For this reason, William's observations on where Blender's interface excels and where it lacks provide an excellent place to begin thinking about ways to improve it.

This document is included so that you can get a better feel for where Blender is headed in the near future and why. This is *not* documentation for Blender 2.5, and the suggestions made in this paper should not be taken as ironclad predictions of how things will work in that release. Rather, you should think of the document as a peek behind the scenes at the kinds of discussions and considerations that will lead to the changes in that version.

The original PDF version of the paper is available to download here:

http://download.blender.org/documentation/bc2008/evolution_of_blenders_ui.pdf

I'd like to extend special thanks to William for his work on the document itself and for his cooperation in sharing the original source files with me.

The Evolution of Blender's Interface

This paper takes a look at Blender's past, present, and future evolution. Blender's nonoverlapping, single-window design has won many over and inspired other applications, such as Apple's Motion and Luxology's Modo. However, over the years several inconsistencies and problems have arisen. The upcoming release of Blender 2.5 is a perfect time to make a clean cut and to implement a more modern, flexible, yet easy-to-use interface, keeping key advantages of the current UI.

Such a change will increase its attractiveness in professional environments and make it easier to integrate into more workflows. This paper discusses the challenges ahead and also provides concrete proposals for solutions going forward.

Analysis

Before we start making changes to the user interface of Blender, it's important to thoroughly understand the current usage model and how Blender's UI evolved into what it is today. Originally, Blender was designed and built as an in-house tool for artists in a small animation studio in the Netherlands. This influenced the UI design greatly, because the application developers were also the users, and the application was designed to fit the needs and workflow of a small studio working tightly together. As mentioned on www.blender.org, these key decisions were part of the original Blender design:

◆ It should be as *nonmodal* as possible and let the user access any part of the application instantly—optimal for solo artists and small studios who need to multitask.

◆ It should employ *nonoverlapping windows* in a *subdivision-based* structure, to free the artists from moving windows around on the screen and covering up content.

◆ It should be fast and efficient, using *consistent hotkeys and conventions* that don't change depending on context.

◆ It is designed to be an *integrated tool*, with all aspects of production being handled solely by Blender, thus allowing for optimized workflow that does not require jumping back and forth between several apps.

In other words, right from the start Blender's UI strove to deliver nonmodality, flexibility, and speed, as well as a sense of thinking differently about user interfaces. Since it was an in-house tool, trying new ideas was cheap, and since they themselves were the entire user base, they were able to test for efficiency immediately.

While other applications have chosen to split up the workflow into different modes (see Softimage XSI rooms, Cinema 4D plug-ins) or even separate applications (see LightWave, with its Modeler and Layout modules), Blender was designed to be deeply integrated in both its data structure and its user interface, because it lets the user visualize and edit any part of the content data at any time. This principle is what makes Blender fast, because interapplication communication (importing, exporting, and readjusting to different apps) is a slow process. Once you get everything tightly integrated together, artists can work faster and more efficiently (Figure C.1).

FIGURE C.1

Blender 2.48 multitasking example with animation and rendering happening simultaneously

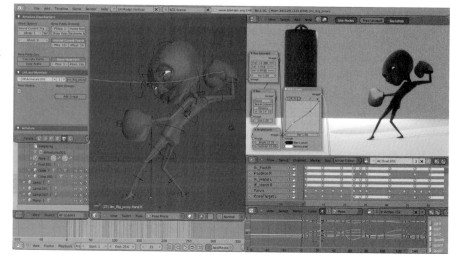

The Good

Before moving on to specific proposals for change, let's first acknowledge the main aspects of Blender's UI that really work well and needn't be altered.

First is the use of nonoverlapping windows. In complex applications like 3D content creation, having multiple views on your data is necessary. Managing that many separate windows would be highly inefficient, because the more time the artist has to spend managing the UI, the less time she has to actually work in the content (Figure C.2).

FIGURE C.2
Showing the convoluted nature of many floating windows compared to the simplicity of a nonoverlapping UI

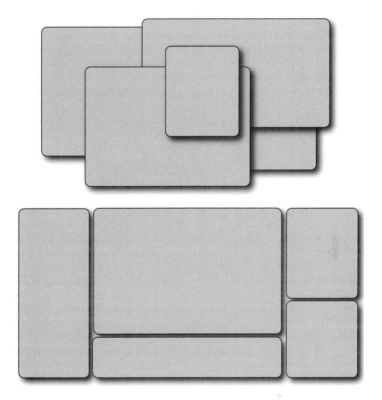

Next is nonmodality. Modality in user interfaces is bad for a number of reasons. Jef Raskin, creator of the original Macintosh user interface and author of *The Humane Interface,* effectively explains why:

> *We cannot routinely pay attention to both system state (or mode) and our task at the same time, which leads to performing a gesture appropriate to one mode (for example, in one application) while we are actually in another mode (say, at the desktop). To eliminate this difficulty, we must abandon the inherently modal desktop-and-applications style interface that is now prevalent.*
>
> *[...]*
>
> *A human-machine interface is modal with respect to a given gesture when (1) the current state of the interface is not the user's locus of attention and (2) the interface will execute one among several different possible responses to the gesture, depending on the system's current state.*

In other words, a modal interface forces the user to concentrate on what state the application is in, before she can perform an action. It moves the user's *locus of attention* away from the content she wishes to create, and to the tool itself.

Modality can refer not only to the obvious use of modes within Blender, such as Object, Edit, and Pose mode, but also to how the user interacts with the system at a deeper level. In some 3D applications, changing a material property might force the user to open a separate window that blocks the user's view, change some settings, and drop them back into the main application at the end. The changes take effect only after she is finished changing them and presses OK. This is a modal workflow, because it takes the user out of the current context and puts her into a different, temporal one, and it is obvious why workflows like this are highly inefficient, because you have to keep switching context, and your locus of attention lies on the program, not the content, and there is significant overhead in the context switching itself.

Right from the start, the Blender user interface was designed to overcome this type of modal interaction. Instead of entering another context or mode to change material properties, you simply go to the Material properties in the buttons window, make your changes, and that's it. Changes take effect immediately. There is no need to switch context and no need to click OK either (Figure C.3).

FIGURE C.3
The diagram on the left shows what Blender doesn't do. On the right you can see how changing material settings happen on the same level as changing other parts of the content.

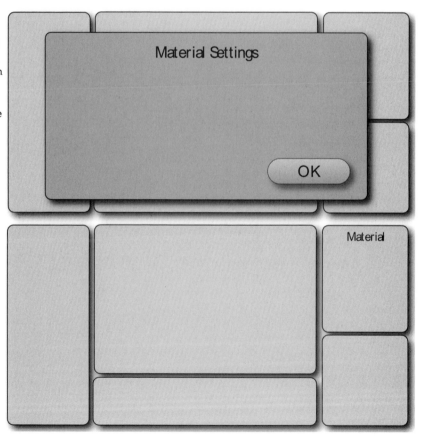

Because of Blender's modeless approach, it is possible to be doing all of these things at once, without switching applications or jumping in and out of contexts:

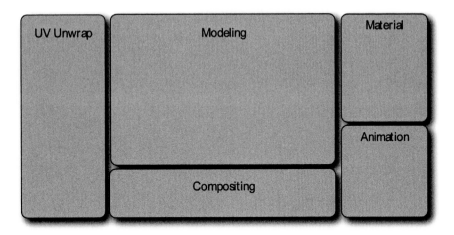

Third is consistency. Blender is designed with consistency in mind, which is important because it takes advantage of the basic human ability to develop habits, and user interfaces can exploit that. So once you get into the habit of using one area of the application, you can gracefully move onto another part with minimal hassle, because the user can reuse the knowledge and habits she has already acquired. One example of consistency in Blender is the hotkeys: In the 3D view, you use G and S on the keyboard to grab and scale, respectively, and this convention is prevalent throughout Blender—in the UV editor, the IPO editor, the Sequence editor, even the Node editor. This reuse of conventions is all over the place in Blender and makes it easier to learn, but also faster to use, because the user isn't switching context, and doesn't have to readapt every time a new editor is used.

The last strong aspect of Blender's UI that is worth mentioning is its cross-platform nature. The UI is coded using the OpenGL graphics APIs, normally reserved for 3D graphics. Since OpenGL is implemented in the system architecture of all the major platforms, it means that Blender's look and feel is exactly the same whether you are using a Mac, Linux, Windows, or even Sun's Solaris. This makes Blender the single most portable 3D application, being available on more operating systems than any other.

The benefit for the user is that even if she works in a multiplatform environment, she can count on Blender to always behave the same way. So if the user owns a Linux workstation, a Windows desktop and a Mac laptop, switching between the three will be seamless, again minimizing the need to concentrate on context—in this case, operating systems (Figure C.4).

FIGURE C.4
Blender running on multiple operating systems, yet looking exactly the same

Linux   Mac OS X   Windows

All of these qualities that have just been covered are ones that make Blender stand out among the crowd and what makes it a great tool for artists. These are the main qualities that must be kept going forward.

The Bad

The list of design features we've just covered shows that at the very basic level, the user interface of Blender is very well crafted and highly efficient. But as we move on to look at the *implementation* of these basics at a higher level in the UI, we start to see some problems. I'm going to use the Edit buttons panel as an example (Figure C.5).

FIGURE C.5
The Mesh tab in the buttons window

The design and layout of buttons and fields here is absolutely terrible—nothing less can describe it. First of all, it is illogical. It is not at all communicated that the Corner Cut drop-down menu (Innervert is currently selected in the screenshot) applies only to Fractal and Subdivide, neither is it communicated that the Limit number field relates to Rem Doubles, nor is it clear that Threshold applies to none of the tools visible in this panel (it applies to the Select Similar command found elsewhere).

Apart from being illogical, it is also inconsistent: Some of the mesh editing tools are found only in this panel; others are found in the mesh editing menu in the 3D window, yet some of these are found both places, and some of them not. Some features accessible from the Mesh *menu* have settings for it in the Mesh *panel*.

This illogical inconsistency is bad for productivity, because the user cannot count on related features being available in one place. She has to spend time searching around in the interface, finding the tools needed.

The next problem visible in this panel is that it includes a variety of very disconnected entities. First, there are some *settings* that let you alter a list of properties on the selected mesh (Auto Smooth, Double Sided, and so forth). Then there is a collection of *tools* that let you modify the mesh itself, and last there are some *tool settings* that let the user change the way tools work (Figure C.6).

FIGURE C.6
The Mesh tab includes very disconnected items.

Settings ⟶

Tools ⟶

Tool Settings ⟶

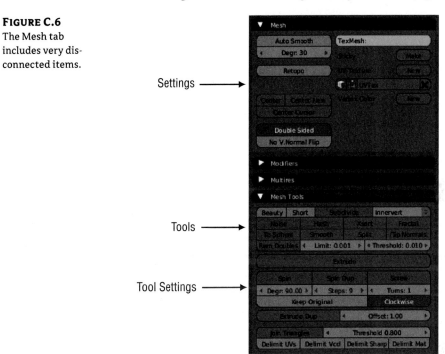

Having these different types of items cluttered together is both counterintuitive and counterproductive, because it makes the buttons window exactly what the name says: a collection of buttons, fields, and sliders that are arbitrarily collected and dumped in one place. Inconsistent design like this kills productivity, as Jef Raskin nicely explains:

> When we set about learning any interface feature that is new to us, we proceed in two phases, the first of which gradually grades into the second. In the first, or learning, phase we are actively aware of the new feature, and seek to understand and master it. If that feature is well designed, and if we use it repeatedly, we eventually enter the desirable second, or automatic, phase, in which we have formed a habit, and use the feature habitually, without thought or conscious effort.

Interface features are created to help you accomplish some task. If a feature forces you to stop thinking about your task and begin paying attention to the feature (an egregious case is where the software crashes, but even a momentary difficulty can derail your train of thought), then it is said to interfere with the task, and you have not entered the automatic phase with respect to that feature. Creating interfaces that allow users to develop automaticity across all tasks should be a primary goal of interaction designers. Such interfaces will be easier to learn and use, more productive, and far more pleasant than what we have today.

It should be our goal to create a clean system in which the user can predict where to find features, so that he can develop automaticity.

The last aspect I wish to cover is an example of something that is unnecessarily complicated: editing multiple objects. I'll give an example. Let's say the user decides she would like to view all her objects with a wireframe overlay.

With one object it is simple: The user presses the Wire button under Draw Extra in the Object tab. But with multiple objects, it becomes a complicated process. Either the user must select each object in sequence and make the desired changes each time, which is fine if you have three monkeys in your scene, but not practical if you have 300. The other way is that you can copy a set of attributes from the active object to all other selected objects, using Ctrl+C, but the problem with that is that only some settings are available for copying, and also that it is an extra step, taking the *locus of attention* away from changing settings, and instead concentrating on getting the program to copy settings you have already made to other objects (Figure C.7).

FIGURE C.7
Working with multiple objects—a nightmare if you have too many

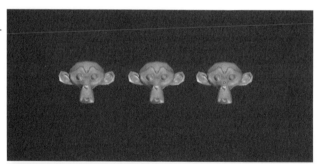

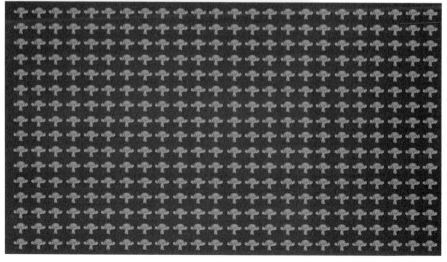

It is actually also inconsistent with Blender itself: It happens that *actions* already allow you to work in multiple objects at a time. Deleting, duplicating, transforming, and so forth, already apply to as many objects as you would like.

The aforementioned items are examples of some of the weakest spots in Blender's user interface. The buttons window is often unorganized, inconsistent, and illogical, and there are plenty of other improvable areas, such as multi-object editing, and other workflow improvements.

Design Goals

Before moving on to discuss specific improvements, I'll list a set of user interface ideals on which to base the changes. Blender's user interface should aspire to be

Nonmodal, ensuring minimal context switching and a smooth workflow.

Nonlinear, so users can perform actions in any order they choose.

Logical, exploiting human nature to eliminate searching around in the user interface.

Fast, allowing direct manipulation for speedy workflow without jumping through hoops to accomplish tasks.

Flexible, because it's always better to offer a few flexible tools that do many things than a host of complicated tools to only do one thing.

Innovative, providing solutions out of the ordinary, and not be encumbered by history.

Simple, because the Keep It Simple Stupid mantra very much applies to user interfaces.

With that in mind, Blender 2.5 is the perfect time to lay a strong foundation for the future—one that won't need to change anytime soon, one that can adjust to changes and additions of features. We must also make a clear separation between *tools, tool settings,* and *properties,* add much *clearer visual feedback,* so that the user always knows what is going on—especially when she must wait. There also has to be a focus on *ease of use.* Jef Raskin writes:

> *In spite of a commonly believed myth to the contrary, we are not novices or experts with regard to whole systems or applications, but go through the learning and automatic phases more or less independently with regard to each feature or set of similar features. If learning one of a set of features makes you automatic on the entire set, or greatly decreases the time it takes to become automatic on the rest of the set, we say that the set of features exhibits consistency.*

Through added consistency and a more logical design, we can improve ease of use at the same time as increasing speed. There has been a notion though, that ease of use is applicable to only so-called *noobs,* but as Raskin mentions, that definition is flawed. Also, ease of use is at least as important to professional users as it is to hobbyists. In fact, pros have even less time for searching around for features, and cannot waste time with inconsistent quirks that move their locus of attention away from their work.

Last, I'd like to address another misconception, this time about customizability. There has been a notion that the solution to most of the UI problems can be solved with added customizability. The notion goes that if the UI is inefficient, the user can simply customize it herself to suit her needs. This claim is wrong for several reasons:

◆ It is impossible to customize something you have not fully comprehended yet, so it in no way helps the learning process.

◆ It makes an application less predictable, because the user cannot rely on the application to always act the same.

◆ It takes focus away from the user's content, and over to managing the application itself, which is what we wanted to avoid in the first place.

◆ It undermines the portability of Blender, because you cannot rely on Blender functioning the same way across different systems.

◆ Customizability does not equate to flexibility.

◆ 99 percent of Blender users will use the default setup anyway.

This is not to say that customizability is always bad—having the ability to change the hotkeys from the defaults to match another 3D application such as Maya or Softimage XSI can make it easier for users of those applications to adapt to Blender. But, with any customizability, it is absolutely essential that the *defaults are sane*. Customizability can be good but does not solve any fundamental problems.

From here on I will discuss concrete proposals for improvement in the Blender user interface.

Properties

The main focus in this document's criticizing of Blender's UI has focused on shortcomings of the buttons window, and that is why the primary proposal revolves around it. Let's revisit the Mesh tab we used as an example earlier:

All of the inconsistent, illogical, and counterintuitive aspects of the design in this panel exist because of two things:

◆ A lack of focus and attention on UI design among developers

◆ All panels must adhere to this rule:

The panels have to be square.

The reason why all panels have had to employ equal dimensions is that they can then be stacked either horizontally or vertically (Figure C.8).

FIGURE C.8
Panels can be stacked either horizontally or vertically.

On the surface it seems like this is nice, but the problem is as follows: Panels are based on groups of controls and related features, and so not all panels require an equal amount of content. That means that some panels are very sparse while others are very dense, with lots of tiny buttons crammed together because of space constraints (Figure C.9).

FIGURE C.9
Not all panels have equal numbers of controls.

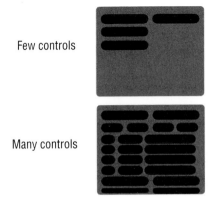

Few controls

Many controls

This is what has led to the catastrophe that is the current buttons window, because developers are no longer thinking about what context to put a button in, but rather *where there is physical space*. And, once buttons are places in the UI, not because of logical reasoning but because of physical ramifications, we get the confusing, inconsistent, and illogical layout in panels we have today.

This not only makes it hard for the user to find what he is seeking, but it undermines the entire point of having panels at all. Matt Ebb, main author of the user interface changes in Blender 2.3 writes:

> *...buttons are so spread out over the entire window that doing what should be a straightforward task such as setting up a render takes a round trip backwards and forwards all over the buttons window. Not only does this require an excessive amount of mouse-hunting and scan-reading, searching around the screen, but it makes it difficult to hide things that are not interesting. Closing a panel to hide away some buttons that a user's not interested in would also hide away completely unrelated buttons, which a user may have wanted to keep open.*

The solution to all these problems is *variable height*. By varying the height of panels, they can properly accommodate the content they include, which allows for much more logical, consistent (and therefore fast and efficient) layouts of controls. Variable height also makes Blender more future-proof in that it allows developers to easily expand panels to accommodate growing feature sets (Figure C.10).

FIGURE C.10
Fixed panels on the left vs. variable height on the right

There is one caveat to having variable height, though: It is incompatible with horizontal layouts. There is no good way to put panels of varied height side by side, without either wasting space or spilling content out of the screen space, and in fact you will see that some panels already employ this variable height paradigm in Blender. Content that is dynamic, such as constraints and modifiers, is especially applicable to using variable height, and so already does (Figure C.11 and Figure C.12).

FIGURE C.11
Panels with
variable height
incompatible with
horizontal layouts

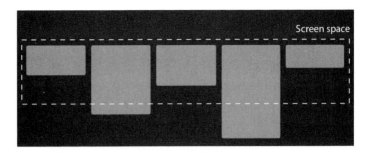

FIGURE C.12
Examples of panels
already employing
variable height

In effect it means that horizontal button layouts are already deprecated from the user stand-point—it already is nearly impossible to work with constraints, modifiers, or lists of bones by using horizontal buttons.

The main problem with moving away from horizontal buttons is that some users may have developed automaticity with this layout (they use it habitually), and change means relearning, but in Blender 2.5 so much is changing anyway. Once horizontal button layout is sacrificed, it will allow a cleaner, more consistent and logical design that can carry Blender into the future.

It also happens that stacking lists of items vertically is actually easier to skim through for the user, because you can skim down a list of left-aligned text with ease. Matt Ebb, having studied typography, explains below:

> Words in most European languages are generally shaped rectangularly [=====], which means that the most condensed layout is stacking them one on top of the other. In this situation, the eye can just track down a consistent line on the left, quickly identifying the shapes of the start of words. If these words are next to each other horizontally, the distances between them are inequal, and the eye must skip over each word, reading them all left to right in order to find the next one. It's much faster to skim, especially when you consider word recognition by identifying the word's shape rather than the next stage of deconstructing it into characters. This is pretty fundamental typography/layout theory.

This is also the reason why columns in newspapers are vertical. It is far quicker to scan through and easier to read.

Last, vertical panels are more fitting to the growing number of widescreen monitors. With a vertical panel layout on the side of the screen, the rest of the view still has a workable aspect ratio, whereas using horizontal panels on widescreen monitors results in the rest of the view becoming super-widescreen, wasting space (Figure C.13).

FIGURE C.13
A modern wide-screen display, with properties on the side

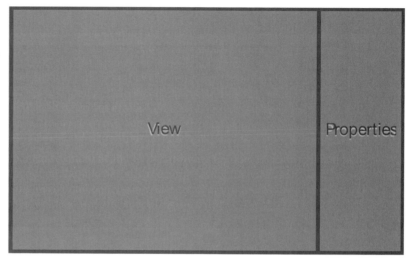

Next, we'll look at the *content* of the buttons window. Currently it includes four groups of functionality:

Tools
A tool is defined as a feature that needs additional user input, one that does not perform a task by itself, but can be used by the user to do so. As such, a tool may be *active* for a period of time, until the user is finished using that tool.

(Examples: Transform, Extrude, Subdivide, Spin, Bulge, Draw, Bevel, Mirror)

Tool settings
These options relate to the tool currently in use, and let the user set the axis of operation or the steps in a subdivide, and so forth.

(Examples: Degree, Steps)

Actions
Actions are commands that take effect immediately and are never *active*.

(Examples: Delete, Set Smooth)

Properties
Properties represent the bulk of the buttons window, and are values (radio buttons, check boxes, number fields, and lists) that are stored in datablocks for linking and reuse. In Blender 2.5, all properties will become animatable, so each value has a unique IPO curve.

(Examples: Materials, Particles, Constraints, Bones, Modifiers)

Although these groups are very disconnected in their use, they are all dumped in the buttons window, and to chaotic effect. By separating out these different entities, we can achieve a much more transparent and clean user interface, again allowing for faster usage and easier learning.

This means that the buttons window as we know it will cease to exist. Instead, it can be replaced by a Properties editor (Figure C.14).

FIGURE C.14

The Properties editor, showing Object properties

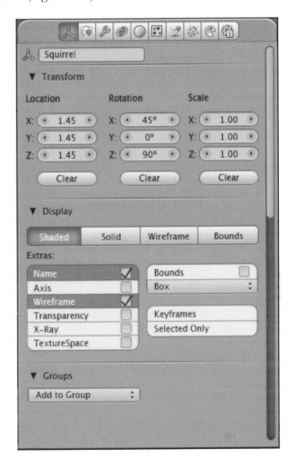

This new window type will allow users to edit any value in the scene, and include settings for

◆ Object transformations and display (stored in the Object datablock)

◆ Constraints (stored in the Object datablock)

◆ Modifiers (stored in the Object datablock)

◆ Mesh settings and UV layers (stored in the Mesh datablock)

◆   Materials (stored in the Material datablock)

◆   Textures (stored in the Texture datablock)

◆   Physics (stored in the Object datablock)

◆   Particles (stored in the Particles datablock)

◆   Script links (stored in the Object datablock)

◆   World (stored in the World datablock)

◆   Render (stored in the Scene datablock)

In order to remove as much clicking as possible, none of these categories should be made a subcontext of another. This means the tabs can stay fixed in their position, which is optimal for exploitation of human muscle memory, because the user will always know where to click, *even without looking.*

The exact layout of the buttons should also stay as fixed as possible, without moving around on the screen. Microsoft Word is a example of how moving menu items that disappear randomly can cause terrible headaches. In order to take advantage of muscle memory, and to ensure a reliable user interface, the panels should never move around or change order (except if the user explicitly wants to do this), and the buttons within them should never pop up or disappear. Instead, they can be grouped logically, with disclosure triangles, so the user can remove panels she is not focusing on.

For information about good practices regarding button layout *within* the panels, I'll refer to the Buttons Information Architecture analysis, available here:

```
http://wiki.blender.org/index.php/ButtonsIAGuidelines
```

```
http://wiki.blender.org/index.php/BlenderDev/UIAlignRulesGuides
```

```
http://wiki.blender.org/index.php/BlenderDev/DependGuide
```

Tools

Tools are defined as features that are active for a period of time, requiring additional user input, and this is why they need special thought regarding their placement in the UI. The main problem with the tools currently available in Blender today is that they are highly modal. For example, when using the Loop Cut tool, the user is unable to interact with any other part of the application before she has finished using that tool. This creates an inflexible, linear workflow where the user can do only one thing at a time (Figure C.15).

FIGURE C.15

Examples of tools available in Blender

Object	Sculpt	Mesh	Curve
Create	Draw	Translate	Translate
Translate	Bulge	Subdivide	Subdivide
Mirror	Inflate	Extrude	Extrude
etc...	etc...	etc...	Tilt
			etc...

The situation is even worse for some tools that require the user to change the tool settings *before* using the tool. One example is the Spin tool, as well as adding new objects. The workflow goes like this:

Object ➤ Setting ➤ Action

The user selects an object, sets the tool settings, and initiates the tool. This creates a very slow and cumbersome workflow, because the user must decide in advance how many vertices a sphere will include, *before* adding it. This makes it impossible to experiment, but even worse, it forces the user to keep undoing the action, and trying again, until the desired effect is achieved, ultimately wasting lots of time (Figure C.16).

FIGURE C.16

Examples of tools that enforce an Object ➤ Setting ➤ Action workflow

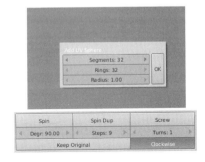

In order to fix this problem, the tools inside Blender must always obey a workflow like this:

Object ➤ Action ➤ Setting

Once the user is able to change the tool settings after initiating the tool, she no longer has to go back and adjust settings, and reinitiate the tool. She can simply select the tool and make adjustments afterward, with immediate visual feedback. Additionally, it means that there is no longer a need to press OK or to accept changes, because the tool is completely interactive (Figure C.17).

In these examples, I've mostly used mesh editing tools as examples, but the same system should apply to modeling, object manipulation, sculpting, weight painting, and so forth.

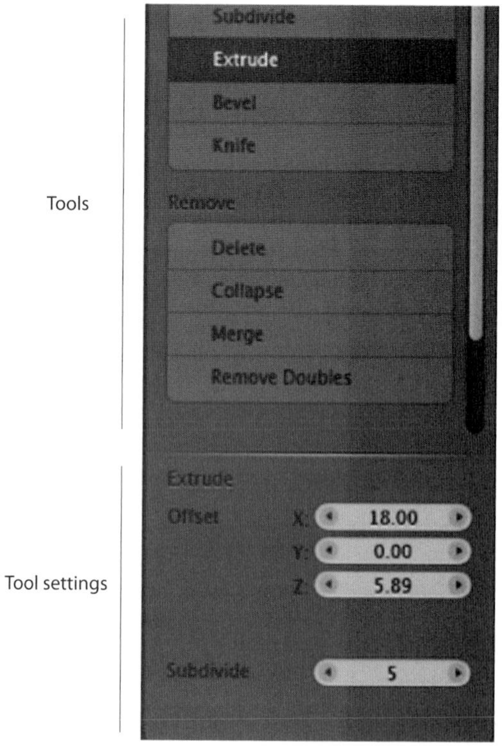

FIGURE C.17
Tools, with inter-
active tool settings
below

Tools

Tool settings

Context Sensitivity

Although modality and changing contexts are seen as counterproductive measures, it is very important to optimize for those changes of context when they do occur. Examples of these changes of context are switching from Object, Edit, and Weight Paint mode, and selecting different entities in the Outliner, or object types in the 3D view.

Currently there is a very low degree of context sensitivity: When a mesh is selected, the tab for manipulating lamp properties is still active (clicking it does nothing). This not only adds confusion, but it wastes space and adds unnecessary clutter to the UI.

The Outliner can very effectively be used as a context-sensitive selection mechanism, because it includes not only objects, but also mesh datablocks, materials, modifiers, and other groups of data. By having the Properties editor show only the items that are in a hierarchy below the selected datablock in the Outliner, it becomes easy to operate context sensitively on the data. Clicking on an object in the 3D view or the Outliner can show all datablocks (Mesh, Materials, Modifiers, and so forth) tied to that object in the Properties editor. Selecting the mesh datablock within the object using the Outliner will display that data, as well as materials, because they are a tied to meshes. Clicking on the Scene item in the Outliner will likewise take the user to the Scene Properties (Figure C.18).

Added context sensitivity ensures the user sees only what he needs. When sculpting, the Tools window would jump to sculpting tools, and when in in Edit mode, the Tools window changes to mesh tools.

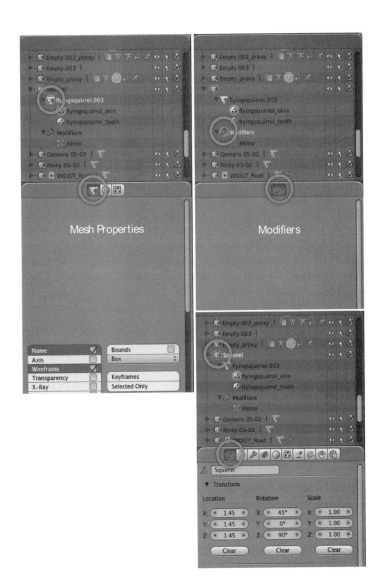

FIGURE C.18
Context-sensitive
properties

Multiple Objects

As described earlier, editing multiple objects is unnecessarily complicated, and needs to be simplified and made faster. Where you currently see only the properties of the *active* object, it could be possible to show the properties of all selected objects. If they share any value, that value is displayed normally. If not, a dash can communicate that there is a difference. Assigning a new value to multiple objects is a simple as typing it in (Figure C.19).

FIGURE C.19

A properties panel with multiple objects selected. The buttons with stripes or dashes mean there is a difference across the selection. Radio buttons can even show which options are set among the selected objects.

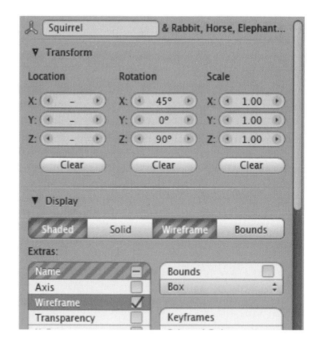

Feedback

The purpose of a graphical user interface, at the most basic level, is to communicate to the user what an application is doing. It serves as the communicator between the user and the features it includes. This is why feedback, or user communication, is important, and unfortunately Blender often isn't very good at this. Feedback is most important whenever the user has to wait—during rendering, baking, physics calculations, mesh binding—and most of these actions fail to tell the user what is going on, how long the user must wait, and how far it has progressed (Figure C.20).

FIGURE C.20

A simple progress bar, which is clear and easy to identify from across the room, when the user has gone to make coffee

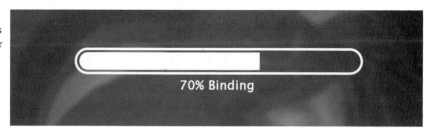

A standard application-wide progress bar that communicates how long the user must wait, and also what the user is waiting for, will make the periods of waiting less severe and obtrusive. It will also calm the user because she knows the app isn't hanging or about to crash.

Another example of an area in need of better feedback is prehighlighting. Currently in Blender, buttons highlight when the mouse cursor hovers above them. This is good because it adds predictability and a sense of assurance that clicking will indeed engage that button. Taking the same idea and applying it to objects, vertices, edges, and faces in the 3D view will similarly improve predictability—especially in very dense areas of geometry where the user may not be sure what she is selecting.

Drag-and-Drop

The great thing about drag-and-drop is that you take advantage of the physical metaphor of actually dragging something. The advent of mice and cursors in the '80s made it possible to select something on the screen, not by typing the name, not by picking it from a list, but by clicking on it directly. This type of direct manipulation is far faster than list selection and assignation because you don't need to memorize an object's name, and also because there is less interface needed. You don't need a list to look up in, for example.

While Blender uses direct mouse clicking for selecting, it does not use this for assigning materials, properties, textures, constraints, and modifiers. It makes sense to use the Outliner, but also the 3D view and Properties editor, so that you can either drag a material from the Outliner to an object in the 3D view, or drag values from the Properties editor to items in the Outliner, and so forth. This would make these sorts of assignations far faster.

Drag-and-drop can also be a great way to establish parent-child relationships: Simply drag an object onto another in the Outliner to make it a child of that object.

Graphic Design

Although the graphical representation of elements on the screen is less important than their behavior, there are definite improvements to be made. First, many of the button types look completely identical; and as you can see below, it's all but impossible to distinguish between action buttons and radio buttons, even though they are very different in their behavior. This slows down workflow, because users must do more button hunting and more squinting to find what they are looking for (Figure C.21).

More-distinct designs not only make the UI faster to use, but can make it easier to learn as well, because items can communicate their usage more effectively. We can make an action button *look* more like something that just performs an action, and radio buttons *look* like only one item can be selected (Figure C.22).

FIGURE C.21
It's hard to tell, but these are radio buttons on the left, action buttons on the right.

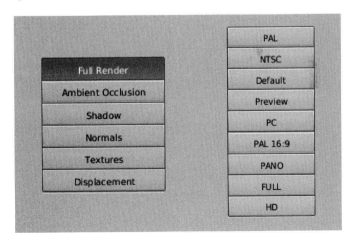

FIGURE C.22
These widgets are clearly distinguishable and also communicate their use better than before; you can visually see that the number field can be increased and decreased using the arrows; the action button looks like it has depth and can be clicked; the radio buttons look like they are connected and only one item can be selected.

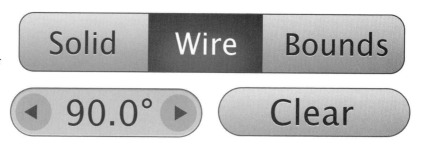

Earlier in this document it is discussed how widgets should never disappear (optimizing for muscle memory and spatial memory), but what if a button is not applicable? This state is very important to communicate, so that the user can see that a button is inactive, but most important, it makes the hierarchical relationship between buttons clearer, so that you *see* buttons changing from active to inactive when you deselect their enabling, parent widget. A lowered opacity, essentially graying out, is appropriate here, because it visually makes the widget more faint.

Blender 2.5 also means that everything will be animatable. By default, any value exposed to the user will be animatable; even radio buttons and check boxes. This means there needs to be a way to insert keyframes, and also visually tell if a button is *automated* (that is, animated—values cannot be set because the button has an IPO on it), and when it has a keyframe. Colors can be used for this, for example (Figure C.23).

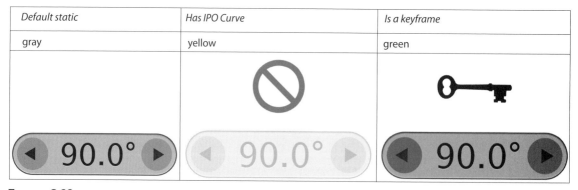

Default static	Has IPO Curve	Is a keyframe
gray	yellow	green

FIGURE C.23
Variations on widgets depending on their state. The field in the middle is inactive/not applicable, while the field on the right has a keyframe assigned to it on the current frame.

Last, there is one element that is underused in Blender: scroll bars. Although they make no sense in the 3D view where there are too many axes of movement, they are very useful whenever you have a long list of information. Whereas the original Blender UI had fixed buttons that almost never moved beyond the screen, Blender now has so many panels and dynamic content, such as constraints and modifiers, that managing long lists needs to be made easier. Apart from letting the user move up and down a list, scroll bars are also useful as a visual indication of what part of a list you are currently viewing, and how much more is off the screen. To maximize space efficiency and minimize clutter, scroll bars can be very thin and minimalist (Figure C.24).

FIGURE C.24
Scroll bars in use

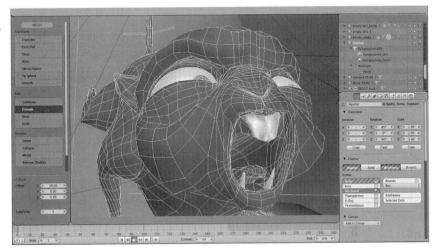

Wrap-up

Blender 2.5 represents the biggest opportunity yet for Blender's user interface. After applying improvements discussed in this paper, Blender can become much faster, easier, and more flexible at the same time.

I'll quickly recap the main changes this document proposes below:

◆ There needs to be a clear separation of properties, tools, and tool settings, which can lead to each type of entity acting more cleverly and predictably.

◆ The Object ➤ Setting ➤ Action tool workflow must be changed to Object ➤ Action ➤ Setting for improved workflow.

◆ The Outliner can be used for clever context sensitivity.

◆ Multi-object editing can make complex projects manageable again.

◆ Additional visual feedback can be added to increase usability.

◆ An application-wide drag-and-drop system can improve speed and ease of use.

◆ Strong graphic design will ease learning, and also at-a-glance-clicking, for added efficiency.

Appendix D

About the Companion CD

Topics in this appendix include:

- ◆ What You'll Find on the CD
- ◆ System Requirements
- ◆ Using the CD
- ◆ Troubleshooting

What You'll Find on the CD

If you need help installing the items provided on the CD, refer to the installation instructions in the "Using the CD" section of this appendix.

Chapter Files

All the files provided in this book for completing the tutorials and understanding concepts are located in the Chapter Files directory, and further divided into directories corresponding to each chapter. In order to open .blend files you will need to have an up-to-date installation of Blender on your computer. For the purposes of this book, you should use Blender version 2.48, which you can install from this CD or download at www.blender.org.

Blender 2.48 Software

Executable installation files for Blender 2.48 are provided for Windows and Mac OS X, both Intel and PPC architectures. The source code is provided in an archive for users of Linux and other Unix-like systems. Users of these systems who would like an executable build specific to their system and architecture can find many available in the downloads section at www.blender.org.

GIMP Software

Executable installation files for GIMP are provided for Windows and Mac OS X, both Intel and PPC architectures. A source code archive is included for users of Linux and other systems.

System Requirements

Make sure that your computer meets the minimum system requirements shown in the following list. If your computer doesn't match up to most of these requirements, you may have problems using the software and files on the companion CD. For the latest and greatest information, please refer to the ReadMe file located at the root of the CD-ROM.

- ◆ A PC running Microsoft Windows 98, Windows 2000, Windows NT4 (with SP4 or later), Windows Me, Windows XP, or Windows Vista.

- ◆ A Macintosh running Apple OS X or later.

- ◆ A PC running a version of Linux with kernel 2.4 or greater.

- ◆ An Internet connection

- ◆ A CD-ROM drive

For the latest information on system requirements for Blender, go to www.blender.org.

Using the CD

To install the items from the CD to your hard drive, follow these steps.

1. Insert the CD into your computer's CD-ROM drive. The license agreement appears.

NOTE

Windows users: The interface won't launch if autorun is disabled. In that case, click Start ➢ Run (for Windows Vista, Start ➢ All Programs ➢ Accessories ➢ Run). In the dialog box that appears, type **D:\Start.exe**. (Replace D with the proper letter if your CD drive uses a different letter. If you don't know the letter, see how your CD drive is listed under My Computer.) Click OK.

NOTE

Mac users: The CD icon will appear on your desktop; double-click the icon to open the CD and double-click the Start icon.

---

2. Read through the license agreement, and then click the Accept button if you want to use the CD.

The CD interface appears. The interface allows you to access the content with just one or two clicks.

Troubleshooting

Wiley has attempted to provide programs that work on most computers with the minimum system requirements. Alas, your computer may differ, and some programs may not work properly for some reason.

The two likeliest problems are that you don't have enough memory (RAM) for the programs you want to use or you have other programs running that are affecting installation or running of a program. If you get an error message such as "Not enough memory" or "Setup cannot continue," try one or more of the following suggestions, and then try using the software again:

Turn off any antivirus software running on your computer. Installation programs sometimes mimic virus activity and may make your computer incorrectly believe that it's being infected by a virus.

Close all running programs. The more programs you have running, the less memory is available to other programs. Installation programs typically update files and programs, so if you keep other programs running, installation may not work properly.

Have your local computer store add more RAM to your computer. This is, admittedly, a drastic and somewhat expensive step. However, adding more memory can really help the speed of your computer and allow more programs to run at the same time.

Customer Care

If you have trouble with the book's companion CD-ROM, please call the Wiley Product Technical Support phone number at (800) 762-2974. Outside the United States, call +1(317) 572-3994. You can also contact Wiley Product Technical Support at http://sybex.custhelp.com. John Wiley & Sons will provide technical support only for installation and other general quality control items. For technical support on the applications themselves, consult the program's vendor or author.

To place additional orders or to request information about other Wiley products, please call (877) 762-2974.

Index

Note to the Reader: Throughout this index **boldfaced** page numbers indicate primary discussions of a topic. *Italicized* page numbers indicate illustrations.

WILEY PUBLISHING, INC. END-USER LICENSE AGREEMENT

READ THIS. You should carefully read these terms and conditions before opening the software packet(s) included with this book "Book". This is a license agreement "Agreement" between you and Wiley Publishing, Inc. "WPI". By opening the accompanying software packet(s), you acknowledge that you have read and accept the following terms and conditions. If you do not agree and do not want to be bound by such terms and conditions, promptly return the Book and the unopened software packet(s) to the place you obtained them for a full refund.

1. License Grant. WPI grants to you (either an individual or entity) a nonexclusive license to use one copy of the enclosed software program(s) (collectively, the "Software," solely for your own personal or business purposes on a single computer (whether a standard computer or a workstation component of a multi-user network). The Software is in use on a computer when it is loaded into temporary memory (RAM) or installed into permanent memory (hard disk, CD-ROM, or other storage device). WPI reserves all rights not expressly granted herein.

2. Ownership. WPI is the owner of all right, title, and interest, including copyright, in and to the compilation of the Software recorded on the physical packet included with this Book "Software Media". Copyright to the individual programs recorded on the Software Media is owned by the author or other authorized copyright owner of each program. Ownership of the Software and all proprietary rights relating thereto remain with WPI and its licensers.

3. Restrictions On Use and Transfer.

(a) You may only (i) make one copy of the Software for backup or archival purposes, or (ii) transfer the Software to a single hard disk, provided that you keep the original for backup or archival purposes. You may not (i) rent or lease the Software, (ii) copy or reproduce the Software through a LAN or other network system or through any computer subscriber system or bulletin-board system, or (iii) modify, adapt, or create derivative works based on the Software.

(b) You may not reverse engineer, decompile, or disassemble the Software. You may transfer the Software and user documentation on a permanent basis, provided that the transferee agrees to accept the terms and conditions of this Agreement and you retain no copies. If the Software is an update or has been updated, any transfer must include the most recent update and all prior versions.

4. Restrictions on Use of Individual Programs. You must follow the individual requirements and restrictions detailed for each individual program in the About the CD-ROM appendix of this Book or on the Software Media. These limitations are also contained in the individual license agreements recorded on the Software Media. These limitations may include a requirement that after using the program for a specified period of time, the user must pay a registration fee or discontinue use. By opening the Software packet(s), you will be agreeing to abide by the licenses and restrictions for these individual programs that are detailed in the About the CD-ROM appendix and/or on the Software Media. None of the material on this Software Media or listed in this Book may ever be redistributed, in original or modified form, for commercial purposes.

5. Limited Warranty.

(a) WPI warrants that the Software and Software Media are free from defects in materials and workmanship under normal use for a period of sixty (60) days from the date of purchase of this Book. If WPI receives notification within the warranty period of defects in materials or workmanship, WPI will replace the defective Software Media.

(b) WPI AND THE AUTHOR(S) OF THE BOOK DISCLAIM ALL OTHER WARRANTIES, EXPRESS OR IMPLIED, INCLUDING WITHOUT LIMITATION IMPLIED WARRANTIES OF MERCHANTABILITY AND FITNESS FOR A PARTICULAR PURPOSE, WITH RESPECT TO THE SOFTWARE, THE PROGRAMS, THE SOURCE CODE CONTAINED THEREIN, AND/OR THE TECHNIQUES DESCRIBED IN THIS BOOK. WPI DOES NOT WARRANT THAT THE FUNCTIONS CONTAINED IN THE SOFTWARE WILL MEET YOUR REQUIREMENTS OR THAT THE OPERATION OF THE SOFTWARE WILL BE ERROR FREE.

(c) This limited warranty gives you specific legal rights, and you may have other rights that vary from jurisdiction to jurisdiction.

6. Remedies.

(a) WPI's entire liability and your exclusive remedy for defects in materials and workmanship shall be limited to replacement of the Software Media, which may be returned to WPI with a copy of your receipt at the following address: Software Media Fulfillment Department, Attn.: *Mastering Blender*, Wiley Publishing, Inc., 10475 Crosspoint Blvd., Indianapolis, IN 46256, or call 1-800-762-2974. Please allow four to six weeks for delivery. This Limited Warranty is void if failure of the Software Media has resulted from accident, abuse, or misapplication. Any replacement Software Media will be warranted for the remainder of the original warranty period or thirty (30) days, whichever is longer.

(b) In no event shall WPI or the author be liable for any damages whatsoever (including without limitation damages for loss of business profits, business interruption, loss of business information, or any other pecuniary loss) arising from the use of or inability to use the Book or the Software, even if WPI has been advised of the possibility of such damages.

(c) Because some jurisdictions do not allow the exclusion or limitation of liability for consequential or incidental damages, the above limitation or exclusion may not apply to you.

7. U.S. Government Restricted Rights. Use, duplication, or disclosure of the Software for or on behalf of the United States of America, its agencies and/or instrumentalities "U.S. Government" is subject to restrictions as stated in paragraph (c) (1)(ii) of the Rights in Technical Data and Computer Software clause of DFARS 252.227-7013, or subparagraphs (c) (1) and (2) of the Commercial Computer Software - Restricted Rights clause at FAR 52.227-19, and in similar clauses in the NASA FAR supplement, as applicable.

8. General. This Agreement constitutes the entire understanding of the parties and revokes and supersedes all prior agreements, oral or written, between them and may not be modified or amended except in a writing signed by both parties hereto that specifically refers to this Agreement. This Agreement shall take precedence over any other documents that may be in conflict herewith. If any one or more provisions contained in this Agreement are held by any court or tribunal to be invalid, illegal, or otherwise unenforceable, each and every other provision shall remain in full force and effect.